OBJECTS
of
HOPE

RELATIONAL PERSPECTIVES BOOK SERIES

Volume 18

RELATIONAL PERSPECTIVES BOOK SERIES

STEPHEN A. MITCHELL AND LEWIS ARON
Series Editors

Volume 1
Rita Wiley McCleary
*Conversing with Uncertainty:
Practicing Psychotherapy in a
Hospital Setting*

Volume 2
Charles Spezzano
*Affect in Psychoanalysis:
A Clinical Synthesis*

Volume 3
Neil Altman
*The Analyst in the Inner City:
Race, Class, and Culture
Through a Psychoanalytic Lens*

Volume 4
Lewis Aron
*A Meeting of Minds:
Mutuality in Psychoanalysis*

Volume 5
Joyce A. Slochower
*Holding and Psychoanalysis:
A Relational Perspective*

Volume 6
Barbara Gerson, editor
*The Therapist as a Person:
Life Crises, Life Choices,
Life Experiences, and
Their Effects on Treatment*

Volume 7
Charles Spezzano and
Gerald J. Gargiulo, editors
*Soul on the Couch: Spirituality,
Religion, and Morality in
Contemporary Psychoanalysis*

Volume 8
Donnel B. Stern
*Unformulated Experience:
From Dissociation to
Imagination in Psychoanalysis*

Volume 9
Stephen A. Mitchell
Influence and Autonomy in Psychoanalysis

Volume 10
Neil J. Skolnick and
David E. Scharff, editors
Fairbairn, Then and Now

Volume 11
Stuart A. Pizer
*Building Bridges: Negotiation of
Paradox in Psychoanalysis*

Volume 12
Lewis Aron and
Frances Sommer Anderson, editors
Relational Perspectives on the Body

Volume 13
Karen Maroda
*Seduction, Surrender, and
Transformation:
Emotional Engagement in the
Analytic Process*

Volume 14
Stephen A. Mitchell and Lewis Aron,
editors
*Relational Psychoanalysis:
The Emergence of a Tradition*

Volume 15
Rochelle G. K. Kainer
*The Collapse of the Self and
Its Therapeutic Restoration*

Volume 16
Kenneth A. Frank
*Psychoanalytic Participation:
Action, Interaction, and Integration*

Volume 17
Sue Grand
*The Reproduction of Evil:
A Clinical and Cultural Perspective*

Volume 18
Steven H. Cooper
*Objects of Hope: Exploring Possibility
and Limit in Psychoanalysis*

Volume 19
James S. Grotstein
*Who Is the Dreamer Who
Dreams the Dream?
A Study of Psychic Presences*

Volume 20
Stephen A. Mitchell
*Relationality: From Attachment
to Intersubjectivity*

OBJECTS *of* HOPE

Exploring Possibility and Limit
in Psychoanalysis

STEVEN H. COOPER

THE ANALYTIC PRESS
2000   Hillsdale, NJ   London

Published by
The Analytic Press, Inc., Publishers
Editorial Offices:
101 West Street
Hillsdale, New Jersey 07642

www.analyticpress.com

Index by Leonard S. Rosenbaum

Design & typography by Martin Cook Associates, Ltd.

Library of Congress Cataloging-in-Publication Data

Cooper, Steven H., 1951-
Objects of hope : exploring possibility and limit in psychoanalysis /
Steven H. Cooper.
cm. — (Relational perspectives book series ; v.18)
Includes bibliographical references and index.
ISBN 0-88163-271-6
1. Psychoanalytic counseling. 2. Psychoanalysis. I. Title. II. Series

BF 175.4.C68 C66 2000
150.19'5—dc21

00-026949

Printed in the United States of America

10 9 8 7 6 5 4 3 2 1

For Ben and Daniel

This is the thrust of psychoanalysis, of the endeavor to transform unconscious or automatic repetitions—memorial processes in which we do not encounter ourselves and others—into aware and recreative action in which we know who we are and others are, understand how we got to be that way, and envisage what we might do with ourselves as we are. In such memorial activity which weaves past, present and future into a context of heightened meaning, each of us is on the path to becoming a self. For most of us, such self-aware organization and conduct of life with others and ourselves remains a potential rather than an actuality, except for brief moments or periods. Understanding this potentiality, however, can help us to strive toward a more human life.

—Hans Loewald, "Perspectives on Memory"

If psychoanalysis could be a way of life, then such treatment might be said to have done what it was supposed to do. But psychoanalysis is no way of life. We all hope that our patients will finish with us and forget us, and that they will find living itself to be the therapy that makes sense.

—D. W. Winnicott, "The Use of an Object
and Relating Through Identifications"

The Well Dressed Man with a Beard

After the final no there comes a yes
And on that yes the future world depends.
No was the night. Yes is the present sun.
If the rejected things, the things denied,
Slid over the western cataract, yet one,
One only, one thing that was firm, even
No greater than a cricket's horn, no more
Than a thought to be rehearsed all day, a speech
Of the self that must sustain itself on speech,
One thing remaining, infallible, would be
Enough. Ah! douce campagna of that thing!
Ah! douce campagna, honey in the heart,
Green in the body, out of a petty phrase,
Out of a thing believed, a thing affirmed:
The form on the pillow humming while one sleeps,
The aureole above the humming house
. . . .
It can never be satisfied, the mind, never.

—Wallace Stevens, *The Collected Poems*

CONTENTS

Preface   ix

Acknowledgments   xxvii

Chapter 1   OBJECTS OF HOPE   1

PART I

INTIMACY AND SOLITUDE   35

Some Points of Comparison Between American and British
Relational Models

Chapter 2   INTIMACY AND SOLITUDE   41

Chapter 3   OLD AND NEW OBJECTS IN FAIRBAIRNIAN   75
             AND AMERICAN RELATIONAL THEORY

Chapter 4   MUTUAL CONTAINMENT   99
             IN THE ANALYTIC SITUATION

PART II

THE SHIFTING SURFACE   119

A Comparative View of Sources of Influence in American
Relational Theory and Ego Psychology

Chapter 5   REGRESSION AND THE OLD-NEW OBJECT   125
             CONTINUUM: Molly and the Problem
             of "Antiregression" and Progression

Chapter 6   IN LOEWALD'S SHADOW: 151
             Interpretation and the Psychic Future

Chapter 7   COUNTERTRANSFERENCE EXPRESSIVENESS   173
             AND AMERICAN EGO PSYCHOLOGY:
             A Clinical Comparative Perspective

Chapter 8   THE ANALYST'S CONSTRUCTION   197
             OF PSYCHIC POSSIBILITY

ᗠ

PART III
THE CONSPIRATORIAL TIMELESS UNCONSCIOUS   217

ᗠ

Chapter 9   THE CONSPIRATORIAL TIMELESS   219
             UNCONSCIOUS: A Comparative Approach
             to the Problem of Limits in the
             Psychoanalytic Process

Chapter 10   CONCLUDING REMARKS ON THE LOGIC   261
             OF HOPE: The Analyst's Concealed and
             Revealed Hopes in Psychoanalytic Theory

ᗠ

References   291
Index   309

PREFACE

[I]t isn't as if possibility
falls along the line of human wish, if and
when the big wish is discernible: actually,
human wishes build out into filigrees of
branching, resembling, in fact, the realms of
possibility.
> — A. R. Ammons, "Embedded Storms"

D

URING MY PSYCHOLOGY INTERNSHIP in Chicago in 1977, I was
generously invited to join a study group with clinicians far
more experienced than I; the group was led by Merton Gill.
Our approach was to listen to tape-recorded sessions of our therapy sessions with patients. I went to this group with trepidation about
whether I would have anything to contribute and even more trepidation about presenting my own work. I was immediately stunned by the
candor and brilliance of Merton Gill as he listened to our work and
presented his own. My uneasiness peaked the first time I presented a
session with a very likeable, withdrawn, and somewhat schizoid young
man with whom I was trying to find a way to talk. Clearly, we liked
each other a great deal, but one of his major conflicts revolved around
whether he would be able to peek out from his rather self-sufficient
world of fantasy to explore his feeling life and particularly whether he
could speak of what he might need from me and others in his life.

As we listened to the process and began to dissect the session, several times I used an expression that, as far as I know, was not characteristic of me. A few times, in reference to something that was going
on between us and with absolutely no awareness of using the phrase, I
said, "That would be a whole new ballgame." As we listened to more
of the hour, I was again commenting on some part of the process and

was about to say this phrase again, when Merton interrupted and said, "A whole new ballgame." We all laughed and began to talk about the affection that I felt for my patient and what was clearly a level of his affection for me that was becoming dangerous for him as he approached a crisis in his treatment. This affection contained erotic elements but seemed even more based in the newness of letting another person know him more intimately on almost any level. The crisis related to whether he would develop what Bromberg (1998), using an expression from Henry James (1875), has referred to as a different kind of "urgent errand." Could he allow himself to experience how much his "urgent errand," or in less literary terms, his psychic agenda, was already reflecting a developing process of engagement with me in contrast to his previous urgent errand involving his private world of internal objects and fantasy.

I don't know if it was on this night of excitement and anxiety or at one of the earlier weekly meetings with Gill that I decided to become a psychoanalyst. I just knew that my clinical experiences and the opportunity to talk about them in this way were compelling and completely engaging. At the same time, I began to enjoy reading about psychoanalytic process and theory. I was drawn to all kinds of theory and soon learned that I would always be a kind of theory junkie, finding value and interest in most psychoanalytic theories yet never feeling entirely satisfied with any single theory. For me, psychoanalytic theories, like the branching of human wishes, provide meaningful and varied ways of understanding "embedded storms" and "the realms of possibility."

So it is ironic that in my first book I may appear, at first glance, to have become the global-village reductionist regarding sources of influence in our psychoanalytic conceptualizations. I have come to the conclusion that the concept of hope is among the most important— "obvious but unseen" (Bion, 1967)—elements of all our sources of influence across psychoanalytic theory. In fact, I refer to the body of psychoanalytic theory as our logic of hope. I invite you, as the reader to consider whether this assertion is mere banality or whether it adds complexity and texture to the psychoanalytic dialogue between patient and analyst and also among analysts from various theoretical persuasions.

Just as I wish not to be the global-village psychoanalytic reductionist, I also hope that I am not the long lost brother of Pollyanna or Mary

Poppins. An examination of hope within the analytic dyad is not primarily an exploration of the "bright side of things" or even of the supportive elements of psychoanalytic therapy, although, indeed, these are probably still underemphasized influences in our theories of therapeutic action (Wallerstein, 1986). Nor do I wish to emphasize the benevolence of human nature or minimize the patient's complex unconscious psychology or the analyst's diverse intentions and motives in conducting analytic work. On the contrary, some of the most hopeful aspects of human growth involve the acceptance of the destructive elements of our inner lives, integrating disillusionment, envy, revenge, and grieving significant loss. I believe that psychoanalysts are in a profoundly privileged position from which to elaborate further the complexity of hopes and aims for change in the psychic future of our patients. In a letter to Freud, urging him to join him in forming a group of intellectuals to oppose war, Einstein (1931) spoke of this unique position: "You have shown with impelling lucidity how inseparably the combative and destructive instincts are bound up in the human psyche with those of love and life. But at the same time there shines through the cogent logic of your arguments a deep longing for the great goal of internal and external liberation of mankind from war" (p. 53).

Psychoanalysts, for better and worse, do bring a vision and logic of hope and liberation to the work. Yet psychoanalysis has taught us that we are indoctrinating our patients while we are trying to help. Indoctrination goes both ways in the analytic encounter. The analyst attempts to learn the patient's idiom, often through elucidating the patient's hopes. These hopes comprise wishes that span development both prior to and including the immediacy of the analytic experience. In fact, these accumulated yet always shifting hopes are probably a part of what integrates self-experience and a sense of continuity. Freud (1908) captured this notion when he said that "past, present, and future are strung together, as it were, on the thread of the wish that runs through them" (p. 148).

Balint (1968) stated that the language of psychoanalysis is "mad," and perhaps maddening, since our patients also have to learn our language and idiom in order to be understood by us. George Buchner's (1972) play *Woyzeck* dramatizes the effect of doctors on their patients, particularly with regard to indoctrination, destruction, and mind control. Buchner's play not only anticipated the art of the Weimar

Republic but also predicted the coming of Nazi medical experiments. The play is instructive for anyone who is in a position of social and personal authority. Mary Wollstonecraft Shelley's novel *Frankenstein*, along with a number of popular films dealing with the most terrifying implications of artificial intelligence (e.g., *Bladerunner*, the *Terminator* series, and *The Matrix*), depicts our unconscious fantasies about how humanity can be transformed and controlled by the objects of our creations and fantasies. Objects of hope are, by definition, potentially, or even inevitably, in a powerful position to exert change for better and worse. This power derives both from the ways that patients endow us with hope and from the hope that analysts have toward their patients. Furthermore, because of this potential for aroused wish and need, objects of hope are also often objects of disappointment, destruction, danger, competition, and envy. Our patients, like our children, become the repository for our hopes, and this process is a part of what fuels development, just as this imparting of our hopes and even induction can be highly problematic. Through the processes of identification and repudiation, through idealizing and seeing the limitations of the analyst and trusting these perceptions and experiences of what we can and cannot offer, the patient has to find his own unique way of hoping and wishing. The analyst has to find a way to genuinely observe and participate in this process.

In this book I try to elaborate my idiosyncratic blend and synthesis of American relational theory, British object relations theory, and Freudian theory with this theme as a primary focus. Despite my earlier caveat about becoming the psychoanalytic global-village reductionist, the analyst's "irreducible subjectivity" (Renik, 1995) is a stock that in my view can benefit from a bit more reduction or focus on the dimensions of hope and transference influence. What is it that allows us to endure seemingly endless participation in sadomasochistic relational patterns in analysis, often to some benefit? What is it that enables us to see unconscious conflict and relational patterns in a person who nihilistically stops himself from feeling and communicating? What is it that allows us to endure levels of frustration, enticement, sadness, hopelessness, and excitement? Why do we sometimes see and feel in our patients hope that we cannot always anticipate or plan for?

Hope is but a strand that runs throughout the psychoanalytic dialogue, but I believe that we have vastly underemphasized its influence on us, how it motivates our technical decisions, our adoption of particular theories, and most important, our view of the therapeutic action of analytic work. Hope is the reason I have never been quite convinced that theorizing is as abstract an exercise as some might think. There is an obvious wisdom in admonitions from some of our greatest intellects about the potential detachment that theory can invite or express. Goethe (1954), in *Faust*, stated: "Grey, dear friend is all theory, and green, life's golden tree" (p. 131). Einstein (1931) warned that "we should take care not to make the intellect our god; it has, of course, powerful muscles, but no personality" (p. 23). Yet in psychoanalysis our theories always express deep conviction and hope about what will happen or has happened. Indeed theory has personality. I am particularly interested in how an aspect of therapeutic action involves the dynamic tension between internal regressive experience and the way that interpretation implicitly evokes psychic futurity. I believe that an underemphasized aspect of the social contract between patient and analyst is predicated on the notion that interpretation probes, even pushes the relevance of past experience to increased capacity for observation or other forms of change.

Although the notion of hope will be a point of emphasis within this book, an appreciation of the tensions between intimacy and solitude, conscious and unconscious experience, expressiveness and privacy can help us to understand the importance of hope in all theories of therapeutic action. We adopt a particular psychoanalytic theory for many reasons, but one is that it must provide us with hope for ourselves and others. Indeed, what is a theory of therapeutic action if it is not a theory of hope? Some analysts have found that insight and knowledge about unconscious influence, as expressed through classical psychoanalytic ideals, is what is most helpful. To some extent all of psychoanalysis, at least during much of its early development, was caught up in the Cartesian quest for certainty. Like many analysts, I have turned to an interest in the subjectivity of both participants because I believe it lies at the heart of every decision in every moment of clinical work.

As I develop the themes of this book, I do so with the knowledge that, while I am interested in the broad and comparative picture of psychoanalysis, this book presents a highly personal version of psychoanalysis. I am a comparative theorist, but there is no doubt that comparative psychoanalysis entails certain hazards, particularly overgeneralization and overly schematic thinking. I am utilizing Schafer's (1983) guideline for comparative psychoanalysis—to be equally unfair to each model. Yet the value of comparative thinking is that it can provide us with an overview and the opportunity to observe with clarity the ways in which different analysts from different traditions deal with similar clinical problems. Technique cannot be dictated, though it is important for analysts who write and teach to be as clear and disciplined as possible about describing what they do. The use of oneself through interpretation or any other kind of intervention is highly personal because psychoanalysis is a process of mutual discovery for the patient and the analyst. I hope that my own journey—the small portion documented on these pages—will be of use to other analysts engaging difficult questions about how to help develop and foster meaning and growth for their patients. I view this book partly as an attempt to explore the analyst's subjectivity, filtered through the hopes of both patient and analyst, as a source of influence in all explanations of the analytic process.

A potential problem with considering the concept of hope as it relates to the patient's and analyst's experience and as it influences the analytic situation is that it can sound a bit mystifying. Yet I view this concept as organizing and elucidating in the examination of aspects of therapeutic action. For example, one of the most interesting debates related to the use of the analyst's subjectivity involves Renik's and Hoffman's differences about the degree to which a patient's idealizations (and hopes) directed toward the analyst can or should be analyzed. Hoffman (1994a, 1996) maintains that the patient's idealizations partly borrow from a repository of hopes and admiration for earlier figures of authority and that these feelings and fantasies fuel and mobilize elements of influence and change within the analytic process. Renik (1995, 1996) argues that elements of idealization of the analyst are or can be deleterious to the outcome and have not been sufficiently attended to by practitioners. I believe that both positions have elements of truth. We have probably not paid sufficient attention to analyzing the aspects of idealization that the patient uses to avoid taking responsibility for himself. Yet there is also what I call a kind of *"return of the repressed positivistic"* in the belief that we could ever analyze away these feelings. I am aware of my own "return of the repressed positivistic" in each analysis that I do. It is akin to Bion's notion of the overvalued idea—a kind of overworked formulation or idea that is both organizing and delimiting.

The *return of the repressed positivistic* appears in various psychoanalytic theories. It relates to how analysts often feel the pressure or mandate to explain, sometimes beyond our capacity to do so. Freud's startlingly brilliant elucidation of psychic determinism exerts a pressure on all analysts to explain elements of the past, present, and future. One of the major themes to emerge from this book involves an exploration of our unconscious and enacted grandiosity regarding our wishes to explain that I believe is a part of our future work in developing psychoanalytic theory. As much as anything, this enormous ambition regarding our theory and our theory of technique expresses and enacts the analyst's hopes. The implications for this enactment in our work are far reaching as it relates to unconscious and conscious growth and change fantasies that patients and analysts hold in the process of problematic and even the most successful analyses. *I believe that one of the most problematic aspects of clinical analysis is the way that we conflate analytic technique with our profound interest in the unconscious.* Confusion of these two sectors can lead to a stiffness in technique and a minimization of the spontaneity in interaction that can illuminate unconscious process. Our psychoanalytic writing tends to exaggerate this problem because, generally speaking, those who write about the process are laying stress on a particular technical stance more than is probably true of their more actual conduct in doing analysis.

The analyst in a particular treatment situation needs to maintain attention to the tensions between the patient's idealizations and hopes that obfuscate further movement and change in his life, and the universal need and value of holding on to the notion of hope. This progressive and defensive use of hope holds true for the analytic situation and in the way that we collectively debate and try to move forward in our dialogue with one another as analysts. Indeed, one of the developmental functions of the younger generation for the older is to hold on to hope, by carrying on and preserving omnipotent wishes and fantasies about continuing to live. Part of the developmental function of the older generation is to temper those hopes by past experience and even by longing—at times, envy—for the romantic and hopeful ideals expressed by the young. These generational dynamics may apply to theory development as well as to the particulars of any treatment situation.

A caveat before I describe the structure of this book. I have found a great deal of value in what has broadly been described as American relational theory. Yet I resist assigning and categorizing my ideas and technical approaches to analysis within one school of psychoanalytic theory. I believe that relational theories in the United Kingdom, Europe, and the United States have broadened Freud's classical vision of psychoanalysis to include the psychology not only of the individual but also of the analytic dyad in ways that are extremely elucidating. I am drawn to relational models in the United States in particular because I believe they have made an effort to integrate the representational world of the patient and analyst and unconscious experience in general, as they are reflected in aspects of interaction between the members of the dyad. I believe that the relational models in the United States have usefully questioned some of the basic assumptions about the developmental models of classical theory and Kleinian theory, which focus more exclusively on the mother-infant relationship. This model of early interaction presents too isomorphic a relationship between the early mother-infant bond and the patient-analyst relationship. Furthermore, this model of development stresses the mother as object of instinctual tensions while minimizing her subjectivity as a generative source of influence on the child's development. I am also critical of any developmental or psychoanalytic theory that limits itself to dyadic reality. Too much of our developmental thinking and application, by focusing on the early infant-mother dyad, deemphasize the ways in which the father exerts a formative influence from the onset of development, both representationally and interactively (Herzog, in press).

My hope is that, in the particular ways in which my work integrates aspects of ego psychology, British object relations theory, and American relational theory, I have been able to address the value of unconscious meaning, the importance of the representational world, and the extraordinary value that is provided in approaching interaction and perceptions about interaction as a way of understanding reciprocally influencing representational psychologies of both patient and analyst. I view interaction as the cumulative expression of unconscious conflict within the transference-countertransference engagement. In this sense, interaction is a conceptual linchpin to any understanding and aspect of change. This definition of interaction is quite different from the problematic ways in which the analyst can use more superficial aspects of interacting to avoid meaning and affect. The freedom to be "interactional," in the analytic sense of this word, involves a deep commitment to exploring meaning. The more we understand about the degree of mutual influence between patient and analyst, the more we also need to understand the limitations and illusions that inevitably develop in that dyad. It is this fact of psychoanalytic life that justifies the integration of theories and what I believe will continue to be a productive area of focus for psychoanalysts in the coming years.

THE STRUCTURE OF THIS BOOK

The book is divided into four sections. The introductory chapter, "Objects of Hope," deals with tensions between psychic possibility and limitation engendered by the analytic process. Part I, "Intimacy and Solitude," includes three chapters that address issues related to intimacy and solitude, containment and mutual containment of affect, and the balance between old and new experience in analytic work. Part II, entitled "The Shifting Surface," examines the differing and overlapping ways in which various models explore the nature of regression, defense analysis, and the use and expression of countertransference.

Chapter 1, "Objects of Hope," begins by exploring some of the tensions that psychoanalytic theory maintains regarding psychic possibility and limitation. I try to redress what I regard as an imbalance between the way we understand the past and the future in psychoanalytic theory and practice. I believe that in analysis we are reconstructing both the past and, paradoxically, the future as it is psychically represented and expressed in current interaction. Psychoanalysis has moved from attempting to be a science of the retrospective (how wishes and compromise formations were forged in development and mediate experience) to being a way of understanding and making meaning of how wish and hope are influenced in the present. Reconstructing the future relates to how analysts wish to influence their patients, even as they consciously try to interpret past and present psychic phenomena. This chapter also examines how the analytic attitude has lacked a way of talking about its "attitude" about wanting to influence (see Mitchell, 1997, for a similar effort). In other words, I examine the various elements of "attitude" in our analytic attitude. This attitude relates not to exhortation, but to our attempt to take or avoid responsibility for our sense of purpose about broadening psychic horizons. I refer to the relationship between analyst and patient that includes the ways in which we represent psychic possibility for each other as "objects of hope." Naturally, I expend a great deal of effort in this and other chapters on how patient and analyst are also subjects of hope.

Objects of hope denote a portion of the way in which analyst and patient relate to each other within the contemporary context of the analytic situation. This way of looking at the analytic situation refers to a number of dimensions or axes within the analytic situation. For example, Strachey (1934), Loewald (1960) and Greenberg (1986) have referred to the importance of the analyst as a new object working in conjunction with the patient's experience of the analyst as an old object. The historical transference (Cooper, 1987) overlaps with the patient's experience of the analyst as an old object and refers to the patient's experience of the analyst as in some ways congruent with important experiences with earlier caretakers. As objects and subjects of hope, we relate to each other on multiple levels of reality and selfhood. In this chapter I explore some of the relationships between social authority, hope, and transference influence.

I use the term hoped-for objects to explore the way in which theoreticians denote multiple levels of longing and hope within patients' development. We have many different ideas about what patients are looking for and what they have done to protect, preserve, or perpetuate their longings. I focus on the classical theory of Fairbairn, Winnicott, Kohut, S. Stern, Mitchell, and Hoffman, among others, to explore the ways in which hoped-for objects are conceptualized in various theoretical orientations.

Often the two levels of discourse that I am emphasizing here—the analyst and patient as objects of hope and the patient's hoped-for objects—are seen as identical. I believe this a problem both for the theory of psychoanalysis and for psychoanalytic technique.

Part I is entitled "Intimacy and Solitude." In many ways, relational theory in the United States has built on the contributions of various schools of British object relations theory. Each approach uses the countertransference as an important source of information about the patient's representational world. Each model makes use of the notion of the analyst's containment of the patient's affects and unconscious conflicts. There are also important differences. These differences include the ways in which the mind and the representational world are conceptualized, as well as technical differences in approach to the types of analyst interventions, chiefly in the area of countertransference expressiveness. In particular, the analyst's containment of affect is essential in both models but is conceptualized in differing ways in terms of technique and therapeutic action.

For example, in work with schizoidal patients, the British models have usually focused on the analyst's ability to survive the patient's "destruction" (Winnicott, 1969). This destruction refers to the patient's dread of external objects to the extent that they threaten the relinquishment and safety of a defensively insular internal object world. The analyst pays close attention to the vicissitudes of the patient's retreats from various aspects of external analytic events, which symbolize for the patient the threat of an external reality outside the patient's internal world (Steiner, 1993). The American relational approach sometimes makes a more directly expressive attempt to analyze this form of resistance, albeit honoring and respecting the patient's defensive insulation and self-sufficiency, while gradually trying to create with the patient an analytic reality that lies outside the patient's internalized world.

The analyst's stance in these approaches implicitly differs in terms of the role of containment of affects. While both models emphasize the need to contain affects that are anathema to the patient, the American relational model suggests more latitude on the analyst's part for various kinds of countertransference expressiveness. The purpose of these interventions is to analyze disavowed affects of the patient. The analyst in Fairbairn's psychology is essentially a new object to the extent that he is able to contain painful affects from the patient. Old object experiences are held by the patient to preserve a sense of safety and familiarity. New objects threaten these attachments. In contrast, in the American relational models, this containment is usually conceptualized as going only so far to promote change. Within this model, at particular points in well-developed treatments, the analyst more actively contrasts the old object transference with forms of resistance to taking in or experiencing new aspects of the analyst's presence.

These threads are explored clinically and theoretically in the following three chapters, "Intimacy and Solitude" (chapter 2), "Old and New Objects in Fairbairnian and American Relational Theory" (chapter 3), and "Mutual Containment in the Analytic Situation" (chapter 4).

Chapter 2, titled "Intimacy and Solitude," introduces some of the complementarity and difference between British and American relational theories. These approaches arose out of quite different historical contexts and are embedded in unique philosophical traditions. This book attempts to explore some of those issues related to how we listen, participate, understand, and interpret within these two traditions. Intimacy and solitude are some of the primary affective currents within the analytic situation, within the essential tensions in any person, and in any relationship. It is far too simplistic to say that issues of solitude are more emphasized in British relational theory and issues of intimacy in American relational theory, though there is a complex grain of truth contained in this statement, which I explore.

The contrast and complementarity of intimacy and solitude are among the many forms of tension within the psychoanalytic process and have formed the basis of various theoretical debates about the process. These traditions roughly parallel what Strenger (1989) referred to as the romantic and the classic traditions. Often the classic tradition is associated with a tragic view of man, a perspective that illuminates and privileges the power of psychic determinism, conflict, repetition, and solitude. Relational perspectives are sometimes associated with a more romantic view, emphasizing the potential for intimacy, communication, newness, and spontaneity. Within the classic/tragic view is a greater focus on an encapsulated, monadic unconscious. Within the romantic view is a greater emphasis on mutuality and the ubiquity of reciprocal unconscious influence. There are also differences within these two views regarding the expressiveness-containment continuum (Mitchell, 1995, 1997). My own personal synthesis of these traditions finds each approach indispensable in particular ways I explore.

Chapter 3, "Old and New Objects in Fairbairnian and American Relational Theory," explores some points of emphasis in both Fairbairnian and American relational theory related to conceptualizations of the new and old object and the implications for working in the analytic situation. Underlying much of this discussion is the belief that there are useful tensions between, on the one hand, Fairbairn's emphasis on our attachment to bad, old objects and refractory clinging to these bad objects in the face of receiving something new; and, on the

other, a construal of a push or willingness toward integrating externality and newness of objects (Winnicott, 1969; Benjamin, 1988). American relational models, which explore the complexities of interaction,
augment an understanding of Fairbairn's formulations of why we hold
on to old objects. Fairbairn's theory also offers ways of understanding
aspects of repetition, even and sometimes especially in trying to provide new experience.

In chapter 4, "Mutual Containment in the Analytic Situation," I examine how the analyst provides containment for the patient and how
the patient helps contain particular affects of the analyst. Since the containing function of the analyst's interpretation is essential in so many
aspects of analytic work, it has received a great deal of careful and
thoughtful attention. Analysts such as Strachey, Bion, Winnicott, Guntrip, Balint, Loewald, Ogden, Modell, and Mitchell, among others,
have described some of the primary features of the analyst's containment of affect for the patient. But the question of how patients help
analysts to contain various kinds of affects within the analytic process
has received considerably less attention. These elements of containment
involve working with the knowledge of the limits of the other, and
learning about the ways patients consciously and unconsciously acknowledge the quotidian aspects of the analyst's personality, particularly his limitations in relation to the patient's conflicts. Mutual aspects
of containment are extremely important in the expression and titration
of hope and the negotiation of psychic possibility within the analytic
dyad.

In Part II, "The Shifting Surface," I illustrate through various clinical examples some of the ways in which American relational theory and
ego psychology differ and overlap in their approaches to regression, defense analysis, transference analysis, and the use of the countertransference. In the four chapters in this section, I examine, through my
clinical work, the potential usefulness of trying to integrate the contributions from each of these perspectives. I am largely in agreement with
those theorists (e.g., Greenberg and Mitchell, 1983; Hoffman, 1983)
who have described ways in which these perspectives provide fundamentally different views of both mind and various aspects of analytic
stance. These differences relate to how the mind is viewed as monadic
or subject to mutual influence, whether defense is conceptualized
within a one- or a two-person model, and how countertransference is

used in analytic work. Yet there are also interesting points of overlap. For example, in recent years I have become interested in how classical models and relational models are both more free than are some developmental models to utilize clinical moments in which the analyst notes affective experiences and views of psychic reality different from or complementary to those of their patients. To be sure, within these models analysts use these moments in distinctive ways. Each model also focuses on different phases of clinical work that highlight some of the profound differences within the models.

Some interesting questions coalesce around whether differences in the types of clinical situations chosen for illustration in clinical papers also in some ways obfuscate aspects of overlap in clinical work. For example, I think that our relational literature has focused more on points of impasse, whereas ego psychology has tried to illustrate more modal moments of analytic work. This observation raises questions about how ego psychologists work with points of impasse and how the relational analysts work with situations involving less threat of stalemate or impasse. Through discussion and clinical illustrations of such issues as regression, interpretive influence, and countertransference disclosure, we will be able to explore some of the ways in which each model provides differing and overlapping perspectives.

Specifically, chapter 5, "Regression and the Old-New Object Continuum: Molly and the Problem of 'Antiregression' and Progression," explores some of the different views of regression and the nature of the developmental atmosphere that is a part of analytic work. There are tensions between the value and inevitability of regressive phenomena engendered by the asymmetrical arrangements of the analytic situation and the analyst's constructions and assumptions about old versus new object experiences. Davies's (1998) work on the postoedipal phase is explored as it relates to the variety of transferences to the analyst as well as the analyst's broad range of countertransference. In some ways, the classical model may overemphasize the patient as a naive participant, whereas more relationally oriented analysts may overemphasize the maturity or pseudomaturity of the patient (Slochower, 1997). At the very least, these are the stereotypes that emerge from our body of comparative literature that I try to disentangle in more detail. It is in the area of regression that both approaches are indispensable in using and understanding affect and process in clinical analysis. I try to explore how, as analysts, we usually each have our strengths and weaknesses in dealing with particular affects such as love, sadness, anger, or excitement. We are more or less able or comfortable interpreting patients' reluctance to experience these affects or, of course, the ways they use various kinds of experience selectively to avoid experiencing others.

American relational theory in particular has usefully challenged some of the most concrete interpretations of the developmental metaphor in analytic work, particularly within the "developmental tilt" (Mitchell, 1988) models of Winnicott and Kohut, and to some extent, Loewald. Yet I agree with Slochower (1996a) and Bromberg (1979), along with many others, that despite the many complexities of working with regression, we need a perspective that includes the inevitability and utility of regression in doing analytic work. This complexity includes both the value of the patient-as-baby metaphor emphasized in the developmental tilt models as well as the more subtle notion of defensive regression emphasized by many ego psychologists (Gray, 1990; Busch, 1995; Schlesinger, 1997). However, we also need what is emphasized in American relational models—an awareness that old and new experiences often occur in complex patterning and that we can easily take the patient-as-baby metaphor far too literally and concretely. There is no getting around the need for us to examine our constructions and assumptions about regressive phenomena.

Through a case example I discuss some of the analyst's blind spots with regard to minimizing new experiences that emerge in the context of productive regressive transferences. These examples help us to see how regressive transference phenomena can sometimes serve as resistance as much as can more obvious fears of regression, or what Sandler and Sandler (1994) refer to as "antiregressive" phenomena. In particular, I examine a case of erotic transference and countertransference in which there is a confluence of unfolding regressive phenomena and new forms of transference affects and forms of interaction.

Chapter 6, titled "In Loewald's Shadow: Interpretation and the Psychic Future," examines how the analyst's view of the patient's future can be usefully deconstructed over time. These clinical illustrations emphasize how analysts can become aware of their views of patients' future that they may have been unaware of during earlier stages of work. Relatively routine aspects of interpretation of defense and transference inevitably express the analyst's ideas and feelings about change. To the extent that we can uncover our implicit expectations about the psychic future of our patients, our awareness can augment our usual ways of understanding the transference and utilizing countertransference experience. Through clinical examples in chapters 7 and 8, I explore the more active, prospective, and expressive use of the countertransference, particularly as it is expressed to patients in the course of analytic work. In each of these chapters I examine how ego-psychological approaches might differ in the conceptualization of defense and the use of countertransference, more specifically some of the dimensions of the analyst's subjectivity and how these relate to our participation in broadening patients' opportunities for psychic possibility.

In chapter 7, "Countertransference Expressiveness and American Ego Psychology: A Clinical Comparative Perspective," I present a comparative approach to a relatively routine clinical moment and interaction. In this interaction, I use countertransference expressiveness, a particular kind of analyst disclosure, to explicate the back-and- forth attention to intrapsychic and to interpersonal processes. I advance some of my thinking about disclosure from a constructivist or perspectivist orientation and how this can be understood in relation to the points emphasized within an ego psychology model. I hope to illustrate many elements of defense interpretation in countertransference expressiveness and the many unacknowledged elements of expressiveness within the American ego psychology model.

In chapter 8, "The Analyst's Construction of Psychic Possibility," I emphasize a particular function of analyst disclosure that not only relates to how the analyst is an icon of psychic possibility, but also expresses this possibility, at times more explicitly, through various kinds of interpretations and disclosures. I define disclosure as related to the analyst's construction of his subjective reactions, which I think highlights the enormous importance for the analyst to treat disclosure as no more concrete a statement of truth than anything else he has to say. In describing the analyst's construction of psychic possibility, I also take up various debates within psychoanalysis about the degree to which patients' and analysts' psychic realities can be challenged and explored. An extended case example of a traumatized man in a long-term analysis is presented.

Part III, "The Conspiratorial Timeless Unconscious," explores how various theories examine and formulate about hope.

In chapter 9, "The Conspiratorial Unconscious: A Comparative Approach to the Problem of Limits in the Psychoanalytic Process," I explore a very complex way in which psychoanalysts and psychoanalytic theory may enact certain aspects of pathological hope, just as they have ignored some of its more routine and useful expressions of hope within the context of therapeutic action. I explore and speculate why analysis has become so lengthy and I raise questions about this issue as it relates to aspects of American ego psychology, developmental strategy models of Winnicott and Kohut, and American relational theory. I believe that each analyst, as well as each therapeutic model, has probably developed various kinds of avoidant compromises related to the tensions in psychoanalysis between possibility and limit.

In other words, we have had difficulty both theoretically and clinically integrating the tension between the romantic and limited part of the analytic process. This difficulty is hardly surprising since the tension between possibility and limitation is a large portion of what we try to work through in every analysis, indeed every relationship. Through an unremittingly hopeful attitude (expressed sometimes more through the vagaries of possibility than through well-articulated theoretical or technical stances), as analysts we have enacted the disavowed and probably dreaded part of our experience—those parts of us that feel less hopeful, those parts of us that are experts in the nature of repetition and the balance between old and new experience. As the understanding of defensive layering has been augmented, our appreciation of early development heightened, our understanding of narrative truth and mutual influence extended, we have to deal even more with questions about whether we offer a mode of therapy, a way of life, or both.

The final chapter of the book, chapter 10, "Concluding Remarks on the Logic of Hope: The Analyst's Concealed and Revealed Hopes in Psychoanalytic Theory," explores the analyst's subjectivity as it is expressed from an experience-distant or panoramic perspective through his choice of theory and formulation. At the heart of these choices is the analyst's view of the patient's psychic future, his hopes for the patient. The analyst is working toward a shift in the patient's experience of psychic possibility; in turn, every theory is essentially a theory of therapeutic action and a move toward broadened psychic possibility. Psychoanalytic theory, however, comprises assertions about both psychic possibility and psychic inevitability. In this chapter I examine the difficulty of learning new things as an analyst—how we are immersed in our own theory and why. Indeed, our choice of theory is embedded in our own hopes, metaphors, and experiences of change and growth, as well as our own important relationships with others. In this exploration of analysts' theoretical choices, I focus also on our variety of theories about the patient's sense of hope as expressed in relational choices and experiences with the analyst.

In psychoanalytic theory, our various kinds of logic of hope also include ways of indirectly accounting for or minimizing the analyst's hopes and wishes to influence (see also Mitchell, 1993, 1997). The book concludes with the sense that we have entered a new phase of psychoanalytic theorizing in which these attempts to minimize or avoid confronting our own wishes to influence have abated, giving rise to a new set of problems about finding ways to negotiate (Russell, 1973, 1985; Mitchell, 1988; Pizer, 1992) between the patient's and the analyst's psychic agendas—the ever-changing and evolving aspirations and limits of creating internal change within the social compact of analytic work.

ACKNOWLEDGMENTS

I OWE A HUGE MEASURE OF GRATITUDE to my patients for allowing me to know their struggles and to be a part of their growth. Every treatment that has gone well has involved a measure of change for both of us in ways that are challenging and exhilarating. I admire my patients' ability to work with both my strengths and considerable limitations.

My clinical work and thinking about clinical work have been nourished in diverse settings. During graduate school and my internship training I was fortunate to be able to work in a study group led by Merton Gill. I think that his transition from an ego psychologist to a clinician who embraced heartily the intrapsychic-interpersonal dialectic has shaped my work in many ways. He was encouraging to me about getting analytic training and after each paper that I published he sent a three- to five-page single-spaced, incisive critique of the paper.

When I moved to Boston, I was supervised by Gerald Adler who taught me a great deal and was extremely encouraging to me about my clinical work. I owe him a great debt for his confidence in me as a clinician.

During my analytic training and for many years beyond I was mentored by Anton Kris whose enormous generosity and support for my work has helped and nourished me as a clinician and writer. Our conversations over the years, with overlap and difference, and his willingness to participate in my evolution as an analyst are a model for me as I supervise and participate in the training of others.

My clinical work has also been shaped by my participation in two different peer groups at different phases of my analytic career in

Boston. First, a study group consisting of Ellen Blumenthal, James Frosch, Alexandra Harrison, Monty Stambler, James Walton, and Judith Yanof taught me a great deal from clinicians who were all more experienced than I. My current study group consisting of William Beardsley, David Berkowitz, George Fishman, Jonathan Kolb, and Elliot Schildkrout has been a pleasure, helping me develop my clinical work and my thinking about blending aspects of ego psychology, British Object Relations Theory, and American Relational Theory.

Many of my ideas have grown out of conversations with James Frosch, James Herzog, Mark O'Connell, and Elliot Schildkrout. In particular Elliot Schildkrout has been an invaluable friend and colleague for many years. I have learned from him about his ideas and he has helped me to shape mine.

Many people have read various forms of the writing in this volume in different stages of my career. I am especially grateful to Andrea Celenza, Jodie Davies, Diane Fader, James Frosch, George Fishman, Merton Gill, James Herzog, Irwin Hoffman, Jonathan Kolb, Anton Kris, David Levit, Christopher Lovett, Michael Miller, Stephen Mitchell, Mark O'Connell, Stuart Pizer, Owen Renik, Elliot Schildkrout, Malcolm Slavin, David Sloan-Rossiter, Martha Stark, and Jeanne Wolff-Bernstein for their willingness to read and critique my writing at various stages.

The seminars I have taught in comparative psychoanalyisis, therapeutic action, and Object Relations Theory at the Boston Psychoanalytic Society and Institute, the Massachusetts Institute for Psychoanalysis, and the Psychoanalytic Institute of Northern California have helped me to develop and integrate my ideas in ways that were quite instrumental in the writing of this book. I also owe a great debt to my individual supervisees at the Boston Psychoanalytic Society and Institute and the Massachusetts Institute for Psychoanalysis. My writing has also developed through teaching and supervising psychology interns at the Massachusetts Mental Health Center, the Cambridge Hospital, and the Beth Israel Hospital at Harvard Medical School.

I want to express my appreciation to Lewis Aron, my editor, whose critiques and encouragement during the writing of this book helped me to develop my ideas and complete the project. I want also to acknowledge my appreciation to Paul Stepansky, Nancy Liguori, Lenni Kobrin, Joan Riegel and the staff of The Analytic Press for their considerable help.

One of the most nourishing experiences of my adult life has been through a shared love of fly fishing with my friends Andrew Gill, Jonathan Kolb, Randall Paulsen, Elliot Schildkrout, and William Tapply. Through our various travels, days which combine time spent together and alone, we have experienced some of the most pleasurable tensions between intimacy and solitude.

Diane Fader helped make it possible for me to write this book, both in terms of her encouragement and her reading of my work. She shares with me a gigantic love for our objects of hope, Ben and Daniel, to whom this book is dedicated.

I am grateful to the periodicals cited below for permission to republish these articles with revisions: Chapter 3, "Old and New Objects in Fairbairnian and American Relational Theory," coauthored with David Levit, *Psychoanalytic Dialogues,* 8:603-624, 1998; Chapter 4, "Mutual Containment in the Analytic Situation," *Psychoanalytic Dialogues,* 10:169-194, 2000; Chapter 6, "Interpretation and the Psychic Future," *International Journal of Psychoanalysis,* 78:667-681, 1997; Chapter 7: "Countertransference Disclosure and the Conceptualization of Technique," *Psychoanalytic Quarterly,* 67:128-154, 1998; Chapter 10, "Facts All Come with a Point of View," *International Journal of Psycho-Analysis,* 77:255-274, 1996.

1

OBJECTS OF HOPE

A S EACH ANALYSIS BEGINS, I am aware of feeling a kind of ubiquitous, dense, textured conflict. The conflict is between possibility and limitation, what we will and will not be able to achieve. On one hand, I enjoy the sense of uncertainty about what will happen between the two of us. I know that neither of us can know the kinds of things that we will learn together. At the same time, there is also a sense of anticipation about what will happen and what we will learn together. In this mode, I think about what the patient wants to happen, what he is afraid will happen, what I hope will occur, what I am afraid will occur. This process and the conflicts about our different hopes are always present for me. As the analytic process proceeds, I think, more actively, about the limits of what we will do together. The tension between psychic possibility and limitation is a framework that constantly informs the analytic process for me; it is this framework that I probe in this book.

The tension I refer to is not static; it is different for each patient with whom I work. In addition to feeling excitement about things being uncharted, I sometimes wish a cartographer could come in and map things out, for I know that I am partly afraid of the process—afraid of the hard work, the intimacy, and the sense of uncertainty. I am reassured by my experience that we will become immersed in a process of trying to understand that is one of the most compelling things I have ever done. While I am suspicious of my urges to know in advance where we might go, I have also learned that, at least for me, imposing structure and expectation is intrinsic to the work. I think of this need for structure, in part, as informing me about my fantasies about what will happen; these fantasies are usually generative and not something simply to regret or avoid. Yet these fantasies and formulations also relate to what Bion (1977) referred to as the analyst's overvalued ideas (formulations and organizing ideas about what is being expressed), which are intrinsic to the nature of hope and formulation within the analytic process. Some aspects of formulation creatively organize and some tend to constrict meaning. The urge to promote freedom of feeling and creative thought and fantasy for both participants and the countervailing need to organize through constraint describe a portion of the analytic process not unlike what each of us does in relation to our inner life. Dominant metaphors constrict, just as they may in certain ways organize and expand. In the strict sense, a dominant metaphor is always partly defensive in this way.

As analysis proceeds, I am aware of this process in a very different way. The more I do analysis, the more I try to make explicit my thinking about what has and what has not happened at certain junctures because dyadic process and reality can, in some ways, distract us from thinking about the goals of psychoanalytic work. This imposition of my thinking runs counter to Bion's (1977) maxim that the analyst should be without memory and desire. On the contrary, as much as the analyst should try to fight expectations, these expectations are inevitable and there is no way around them. The work can be so involving that it is too easy to forget or deny the passage of time (see Hoffman, 1996, 1998; see also chapter 9). The timelessness of the unconscious has a magnetic pull for those of us who become analysts and many of us who become analytic patients. It fuels the process, but it can also conspire to make us lose focus about the goals of analytic work. I call this quandary, the "conspiratorial timeless unconscious" to refer to the ways in which the most compelling part of the process, its opportunity for freedom of expression and learning, can also conspire to deny the passage of limits and time.

Everything that we do together in analysis issues from the sense of emerging hopes and our various forms of reluctance, denial, and enactment of these hopes. In this chapter and the chapter that follows I begin to explore the nature of hope in the psychoanalytic process and, more explicitly, the tensions between hope and possibility.

JEFFREY: THE LOCATION AND RELOCATION OF DYADIC HOPE, POSSIBILITY, AND LIMITATION

Jeffrey was a patient in his early 50s who had been in one previous psychotherapy and two analyses when I began working with him. Each analysis had involved a chiefly negative paternal transference, one toward a female analyst and the other toward a male analyst. Jeffrey had always valued his analysts' efforts to help him understand his feelings of anger and disappointment toward his father and his analysts, though he never felt that he had become more able to trust someone in an intimate relationship as a result of his analytic work. Both his wives, before asking for divorce, told him that he was too distant for them to feel really cared for.

Jeffrey's father was extremely self-involved with his work, extramarital affairs, drinking, and mountain climbing, all of which took him away from his family. When his father was around he was often critical of Jeffrey for not being a good-enough athlete and being too interested in reading and games, especially chess. Theirs was a match made in hell. Jeffrey's mother was passive and anxious about the approval of her husband. She could be very admiring and supportive of Jeffrey when her husband was not around (which was a considerable amount of time), but things changed radically when he was around—at these times, she became more distant and preoccupied with the approval of her husband.

I had the sense that in both his previous analysts there had been some way in which the transference was viewed primarily in terms of its historical antecedents, as an experience of a negative relationship with his father. Yet there was no sense, at least as Jeffrey conveyed it, that the analysts had taken up the transference as a way to unconsciously, once again, create distance in his current relationship with his analyst. From early on I wondered if he felt that this distance was something he needed to maintain in order to protect himself from the deep sense of being inadequate and criticized by his father. I also wondered if it created an effect of distancing or irritation in the other person with whom he was engaged in a relationship. Jeffrey's compromises were not working well for him.

As he began analysis with me, Jeffrey felt anxious that he would be criticized for what he felt and thought and that I wanted him to be as I wished him to be, more than who he really was. Jeffrey said that this was quite like the feelings he had experienced in the transference toward his previous analysts and that nothing much seemed to happen over the course of these analyses. Neither of us was surprised that he would begin with this set of feelings. By his own report, Jeffrey had never felt challenged by his analysts. Additionally, both analyses had seemed foreclosed or interrupted by his wives' requests for a divorce. He had been bereft, confused, and hurt and his analyses had focused on helping him to regain his equilibrium. In each case, he left analysis after recovering from his loss, despite his analyst's encouragement that there might be a great deal more work that they might do together.

Jeffrey's fear that I would criticize him or be disappointed by him was to him like the air he breathed. He said that this was a "fact of life," an inevitable experience of his inner life. While I could feel Jeffrey's anxiety and concern, I was surprised to also feel impatient with him. I felt that there was something about the very act of analysis itself that partly colluded in a perpetuation of Jeffrey's pattern of avoidance and distance in his relationships with others. I felt guilty that Jeffrey was being a "good" patient. He was saying what was on his mind, and I certainly knew that he had come by these fears and transference experiences honestly.

I asked myself repeatedly if he was right in some sense about me. Was I critical of him? Did I have expectations about how he should be? More and more, as months went by, the answers I came up with were a resounding, yes! One part of me felt this was a problem. I should figure out why I was feeling so critical of Jeffrey's very understandable emerging transference. But the stronger sense was that my reactions to him might be related to his defensive refusal and anxiety about developing a different kind of relationship with me. I felt as though the regressive paternal transference might also be related to deeply unconscious retaliatory wishes toward his father. It was as if he had developed a method for getting back at his father by repeating this kind of relationship, again and again, and not knowing how, or refusing, to let a different kind of relationship develop. His regressive paternal transference was becoming more and more ossified, and it seemed to me that one more analysis following this pattern would constitute an enactment. Besides, I was uncharacteristically unable to feel genuinely sympathetic to his emerging paternal transference; I have the strong sense that this transference was not typically something I would feel difficulty receiving, empathizing with, and working through with a patient.

So for Jeffrey, if there was an unanalyzed aspect of regressive transference in this and his previous analyses, perhaps it was an element of how his angry feelings and need to protect himself from me might constitute an unconscious retaliatory expression toward his father. It was as if Jeffrey were repeatedly saying: "You're so critical of me, and it inhibits me. I'm no longer going to take risks. I'm going to be a good boy and do what you tell me and in analysis that involves saying what's on my mind and telling you about my transference. But that's as far as I'll go. I'm being a good boy, sort of. Really a kind of unassailable bad boy."

I began to challenge Jeffrey fairly actively. He was surprised by this and concerned that I might not be willing or able to tolerate his negative feelings about me that related to his father—an understandable concern. After a great deal of self-questioning about this possibility, and the fear of using my transference authority, I told Jeffrey that I thought he partly wanted to create an analysis that provided a kind of sanctuary from the bitter disappointment he had felt with his father. I told him that his stance toward change and participation with others in an intimate relationship reflected how angry he was with his father. If anything, rather than a creating a sanctuary, he was expressing his anger and disappointment again and again. I told him that, while I appreciated that he was doing the best he could to tell me what he felt and what was on his mind, I did not really experience him as *only* trying to understand himself as he reported his negative feelings and anxieties about me that reminded him of his father.

Over many hours, after his fear about my formulation dissipated, he was able to reflect on and explore this understanding. Jeffrey gradually started to feel connected to me and I to him in a way that felt substantially different than earlier in his analysis. He became much less articulate but much more expressive about a kind of dependency and uncertainty about who he was. He conveyed a much stronger sense of making efforts at growth and attempted responsibility. From my point of view, his analysis was beginning. I will not detail his complex analysis further here, except to say that his negative paternal transference was anything but circumvented. What we added was a close examination of his attitude toward it and how he also used it defensively. We spent years working on it together, as we did on the terror Jeffrey felt about being in new relationships in which others were allowed to make emotional demands on him.

If I can generalize at all from my own experience, I tend to think that many analysts are not sensitized, perhaps not well trained, to think about how unfolding transference serves multiple defensive functions. I would not have thought about this transference in this way, and particularly so early in the treatment, were it not that Jeffrey had already been in previous analyses. Patients like Jeffrey have led me to believe that there has been a kind of conscious or unconscious idealization of a particular kind of facilitating environment in analysis that sometimes seeks to avoid thoughtful challenge, and, at times, confrontation. Today, many analysts are not as likely to think about transference as Freud originally defined the concept as serving the patient's defensive needs to mitigate or avoid particular kinds of affect, memory, and especially new kinds of relatedness; I say this despite my belief that we should be aware of exploiting transference authority.

What I want to highlight in this brief vignette is the way in which my hopes for Jeffrey's analytic work and his own hopes and fantasies about therapeutic action were configured and changed. Jeffrey's hopes about change became clearer and clearer as his analysis progressed. What we learned was that Jeffrey's defensive use of the transference placed and expressed a limit on his capacity for intimacy in a way that interpretation challenged, trying to open up something new. We discovered that Jeffrey's unconscious ideas about hope and change were riddled with rage and disappointment. His was a kind of nihilistic hope that he would never be able to experience me as more than beset with disappointment in him, really a kind of hopelessness. He felt that the best he could do was express his disappointment in passive ways and that revenge, in the form of a good life through intimate relationships with others, was far beyond his expectations. Instead, he had developed an unconscious activity organized around decrying his father, but that did not allow for grieving, mourning, or pushing himself to try to do something different with his analyst or with others. Of course, conscious and unconscious expectations about change or hope are never that simple or one-sided. Jeffrey's investment in analytic work was also steeped partly in a heartfelt sense, a desperation, that something had to change! What was truly revelatory for him, however, was his discovery that his unconscious wishes to retaliate against his father through passive withdrawal and anger were taking up huge portions of his psychic experience and activity. Even more surprising was a kind of fetishistic use of analysis and the transference to aid in his retaliation (Feldman, 1993).

My hopes for Jeffrey changed as well. I seldom begin analytic work with a focus on the defensive aspects of transference. When a patient is beginning to elaborate loving or angry feelings toward me that I can easily identify as partly related to his earlier experiences with important objects in his life, I rarely think of much other than trying to understand and elaborate the nature of those experiences. Various types of psychic holding are required here. The analyst holds the patient's affects, fantasies, and experiences related to these objects. The analyst also tries to hold the inevitable ambiguities about not understanding fully his patient at this point in treatment. It is with the elaboration of these experiences over time that I can begin to get a sense of what is being repeated, what is genuine elaboration of experience differentiated from how transference configurations reflect defensive processes as well. My relatively early awareness of a defensive aspect of Jeffrey's transference as helping him to survive his father's criticisms as well as enacting his quiet revenge against his father was unusual, probably augmented by my recognition that his earlier analyses had been unable to help him examine this aspect of his inner life and his relationships with others. I found my sense of hope and therapeutic action moving from an investment in elaborating these negative feelings to a stance from which I wanted to point out to him how much his transference experience might prevent him from allowing other kinds of feelings to emerge. Thus Jeffrey and I began a long negotiation (Russell, 1976; Mitchell, 1988; Pizer, 1992, 1998) about how to talk about the multiple levels of our overlapping and different hopes for his analysis.

Freud (1912) introduced the idea of transference as resistance, a notion that has become less popular as psychoanalysts have become increasingly attuned to the ways in which transference is beneficial, informative, and ubiquitous in analytic work.[1] Reinforcing the value of

---

[1] I am grateful to Stephen Sternbach for reminding me of the tension in Freud's (1912) paper "The Dynamics of Transference" between a view of the transference as an essential dimension of treatment and as a source of resistance.

transference as an aid to the treatment, Freud noted that what is disturbing the patient cannot be changed in absentia. My analytic work with Jeffrey and many other patients has been influenced by the importance of attention to the patient's experience of the relationship, attunement to it, and resistance to it, and by my affective experience of the relationship. Jeffrey's transference also illustrates what I regard as a tension between resistance to something structural in the unconscious (a representational world organized partly around a set of affects directed toward his father and accompanying self-representations) and the experience of hope in the emerging relationship with me. I believe that there is much fertile work ahead within psychoanalytic theory that can integrate our thinking about the contemporary interaction, including the patient's and the analyst's mutual influence on one another, with the Freudian awareness that transference can serve as a source of resistance as manifested through relational configurations.

In the crucible of clinical work, these tensions are what make our work so difficult. For example, when a patient uses irony as an adaptation to manage overwhelming feelings of disappointment or rage toward parental figures, it is always difficult to determine when is the best time to take this up. It is one thing for a patient to understand at an abstract level that irony constitutes a kind of compromise between painful feelings of sadness and intense rage. It is another for the analyst to vigorously take this matter up in the relationship with the analyst. Doing so can often feel as though one is moving from the marinade, to the frying pan, and into the fire. In this process there are times when it feels like it is too much for the patient, and there is value in moving from the frying pan back into the marinade. The point at which the analyst feels a kind of nihilism in sitting with the patient's defensive irony or, as in Jeffrey's case, a hardened cynicism about intimacy is usually the point in analytic work from which there is no return.

This point of no return (if the analytic dyad is fortunate enough to reach this point) is often the place at which the analyst's creativity is most activated. For example, I have often used what I refer to as *perverse support* in trying to provide holding for patients during these moments of crisis. Consider a patient who lived with the conviction that he was nothing more than a projective receptacle for his mother's desires and fears and that to experience himself as a spontaneous wellspring of motivation and desire inevitably risked his feeling abandoned.

At a moment of crisis, this patient was beginning to take greater risks in actively experiencing his own desires but feared the loss of attachment to his mother. As we explored these feelings more deeply, he also revealed not only his anxiety about losing his attachment to his mother but also the fear that she would not know what to do without him (partly a dread and partly an unconscious wish that he were this important and essential to her well-being). Over time, I began to play with his fears through humor and, again, "perverse support." I said that I had a strong sense that, if he continued to make changes in his life, his mother would no doubt find ways to continue to use him as she always had (as her projective reciprocal) regardless of what he did—that, in fact, his mother's unconscious pattern rendered her a kind of Mrs. Magoo. The patient laughed and took comfort for a moment.

Deconstructing this clinical interaction for a moment, I think that what I was doing was providing support in the form of a compromise between holding hope for the patient as he visited a new experience of himself, on one hand, and, on the other, reminding him of his intense attachment to the experience of both his mother and himself in relation to his mother. The fear of losing his defensive attachment to his mother was terrifying, and through my cynical (or perverse) support I also held this attachment through humor. This was a moment of hope in the analytic encounter, a moment born, paradoxically, of my and the patient's awareness of how important it was to hold his nihilistic position, both interactionally and representationally, with his mother. Later, of course, further crises developed as this pattern of relating became a point of work between the two of us.

This blending of patients' tragic and romantic visions infuses analytic work both through our clinical interventions and through our varieties of psychoanalytic theory. Transference itself often constitutes the expression of both of these currents as it is manifested in relation to the analyst and others. Jeffrey's early transference blended affective expressions of hope and terror, which unfolded into a deeper and more complex amalgam of this pattern, as did my attempts to hold each side of this conflict. To "dismantle" this apparatus (Bromberg, 1998) requires the analyst's constant attention to the conflict. Support for the patient's nihilistic adaptation is no less crucial to change than is interpretation that attempts to probe the reasons why a patient is terrified to move into new psychic territory.

HOPE AND THE PSYCHOANALYTIC PROCESS

In Kierkegaard's (1983) words, hope is "passion for the possible." Hope has obviously been present in a broad variety of utopian and messianic social movements, both religious and secular (Averil, Catlin, and Chon, 1990). Psychoanalysis has a relationship to some of these social movements, for its goals are ambitious far beyond the therapeutic modesty inherent in clinical work. Psychoanalysis has a passion for the possible.

Simply as a theory, independent of therapy, its dramatic ambition, scope, and breadth of explanatory power has been expressed in asserting and explicating the powers of psychic determinism and repetition. Freud's (1929) message was anything but a naively hopeful message about "the shape of things to come," to borrow from H. G. Wells's brilliant title, which conjures up the future as an imaginary landscape. What intrigued so many diverse intellectuals about Freud's work was that he offered a way to pursue the comprehension of mental life. Freudian rationalism is characterized by an extraordinary power to explain our present behavior in relation to the past, a broadening of the psychic retrospective. The most tragic aspect of this view, one that emphasizes repetition and very little that is hopeful about Freudian theory, is dramatically summarized in Eugene O'Neill's dour and pithy admonition in *Long Day's Journey into Night:* "There is no present or future and the past happens over and over again, NOW!"

O'Neill's statement is an expression of despair, the withdrawal from hope and wish, the death of wishing, but it is also a statement of the tragic comprehension of our inherent conflicts and constraints in relation to wish and desire. Is it the statement of our relationship to biological entrapment in the form of the pleasure principle? Are hope and hopelessness rooted in structures of thought, affect, and action that are inflexible and absolute? Or are Freud's biological laws of psychic functioning a breakdown product of failures in object relating, as Fairbairn (1952) and much of subsequent object relations theory has put forth?

To suggest that something can change is an ambitious enterprise. Of course, all analytic theories boldly make such an assertion in one way or other, some by claiming the gradual ability of the ego to gain a modicum of control over id impulses or by asserting augmented capacities for observation and the neutralization of aggressive drive emphasized by American ego psychology. Others emphasize the detoxification of harsh superego introjects so that a new, more metabolized experience can be internalized and realized through the analytic relationship (Strachey, 1934); or the exorcism of previously colonizing bad object objects (Fairbairn, 1952); or a gradual relocation housing project for bloodthirsty ghosts with replacement housing starts for a more benign analytic introject (Loewald, 1960). Others promote an atmosphere of nonimpingement, which replaces narcissistic parental demands for a false self (Winnicott, 1969); or a psychic wrecking ball and reclamation project for a schizoid citadel through a transference and real relationship with the analyst (Guntrip, 1971); or a reequilibration of the balance between new and old objects (Greenberg and Mitchell, 1983; Greenberg, 1986; Mitchell, 1988); or through a renegotiation of how reality is constructed, including defining new balancing points between expressiveness and restraint, ritual and spontaneity in relating to others (Hoffman, 1983, 1991, 1994, 1996, 1998).

Thomas Mann (1936) described his association of hope and the future with Freud's vast undertaking as an almost involuntary response, one that occurred despite his awareness of how difficult the undertaking of psychic change: "'Future': I have used this word in the title of my address, because it is this idea, the idea of the future, that I involuntarily like best to connect with the name of Freud" (p. 230).

Similarly Einstein (1931), in a letter to Freud urging Freud to join him in forming a group of intellectuals to oppose war, spoke of the unique position of hope to the understanding of destruction and psychic determinism. Einstein intuitively grasped Freud's conviction that the only way to liberate mankind from war was through the gradual understanding of how powerfully combative and destructive instincts attenuate, limit, and are bound up with capacities for love and life. Part of psychoanalysis involves this capacity to work with and tolerate limits, and each psychoanalytic theory has differing conceptualizations of hope and limitation. For example, one of the most hopeful aspects of classical theory involves the ability to appraise limitation, the ubiquitousness of conflict, and the inevitability of wish and defense. Yet psychoanalysis, in general, has not done well in conveying the hopefulness of its world view. It has usually focused on hope as a defense against pessimism, sadness, and loss but has also seen hope as a part of adaptation that creates new possibilities and achievements.

Psychoanalysis has always been, in my view, singularly positioned to appreciate and detail both of these aspects of hope as well as the idea of pathological hope, the kind of outright evil suggested by the myth of Pandora. For Freudian psychology, hope constitutes a more implicit aspect of the theory because of the constant attempt to avoid transference cure and other more suggestive forms of influence. It is unfortunate that many classical analysts still associate the major tenets of American relational theory with a kind of naive hopefulness, the use of transference authority, an emphasis on suggestion, and a circumvention of defense and resistance while implying at the same time that American relational theory deemphasizes conflict as a ubiquitous intrapsychic phenomenon.

One of the premises of this book is that all psychoanalytic theory is a kind of logic of hope. We have a number of different types of logic of hope within psychoanalysis. Seen from this perspective, it is not surprising that psychoanalysis as a therapy and as a theory would have become so popular in America with the immigration of European analysts. While there are many factors involved in this earlier popularity, there is a long-standing dedication to the value of diversity of belief and faith in this country. The faith on which hope is grounded has not needed to be based on particular religions or social ideologies. There has always been latitude in the United States for faith in the progress of science as well as in the heterogeneity of religious and political ideologies. In fact, Bellah (1967) has called hope the "civil religion" of the United States. He has examined how, in the early years of the Republic, the United States was often described by leaders with imagery harkening back to ancient Israel. For example, Europe was likened to Egypt and America to the promised land. Psychoanalysis and its hearty roots in positivism were natural therapeutic repositories for hope in a postwar, technologically booming era in the United States.

It is also not surprising that psychoanalysis would decline in the worldwide popularity that it enjoyed during its first 75 years. The way in which psychoanalysis deals with and expresses hope is quite complex and not really very sexy. From the point of view of how outcome and process are manifested in psychoanalysis, hope is often expressed in being able to bear affect, ponder experience, integrate complexities in the form of conflict, or mourn and grieve for lost opportunities in relationships and work. A person is able to achieve pleasure, which is often attained at least as much through coping with the sobering realities of life as it is through its more direct forms. The social pact, mandate, or ideology of psychoanalysis offers a better future, but that future is most difficult to explain, and even harder to prove.

The Freudian view of liberation and hope is particularly difficult for most people to grasp, much less enjoy. Edmundson (1993), in an interesting exploration of Freud's body of work, summarized the nature of liberation within Freudian psychology:

> Normative psychoanalysis has habitually presented itself as a discourse of liberation. . . . By defying the taboo on speaking of incest, we engage in what seems to be a liberating exercise. But perhaps what we are chiefly doing is helping to consolidate the theoretical structure of the oedipal complex, which determines the forms of life stories and thus in some measure, of our lives. The personalized version of the oedipal narrative that each person engenders, or has engendered for him, helps render him more apparently stable, both to himself and to others. That is, it renders him more susceptible to domination, control, and limit. He becomes what Freud himself never was, a Freudian subject [p. 11].

How many people, learning about this view of therapeutic process and action, would say with enthusiasm: "Sign me up!"? Unfortunately, not too many. Yet any form of psychoanalysis, including the most classical approaches, acknowledges that being a patient has at its core a more lively discourse on liberation than that captured by Edmundson's summary.

Freud's power, for me and probably for many analysts, resides in his unbending capacity to combat intellectually our predilections for naive hope and unreasoned belief. Echoing Nietzsche's frequent refrain of the "herd" mentality, Freud (1930) struck a constant chord, reminding us of our inclination to avoid accepting responsibility for our own less than noble motives of greed, destructiveness, envy, and hatred.

Freud (1900) provided a kind of history of primitive cultures' reliance on the use of dreams for forecasting the future, a form of expressing a wish for or a fear of disappointment. Freud, in pointing out the relationship of dreams to wishes, was able to illuminate how wishes that emerge in dreams have been shaped according to a mold from the past.

Freud (1927a) repeatedly emphasized the value of rational thought and the difficulty we have in achieving it. Rational thought is slow and difficult and offers "unillusioned" hope (Bowie, 1993) in contrast to the avoidance of intellectual inquiry and the magnetic pull of thoughtless promises of a connection with an omnipotent other. Freud's positivism, also a part of his original élan and intellectual reach, provided a science or logic of the retrospective—a study of repression, symptoms, and defense as various kinds of compromise formation. The therapy, conceptualized as an attempt to oppose these patterns of cause and effect, followed as a logical continuation of this armamentarium.

Freud's theory represents a kind of tragic utopia in which conflict is ubiquitous. Perhaps it could be called a thinking man's utopia or, paradoxically, a realist's utopia. The excitement with Freud's theory as a comprehensive explanatory model has waned among many of its most ardent followers, as well as among biologically oriented psychiatrists and the public at large, partly because this naive positivism and this view of material cause-and-effect does not account for enough of what we observe. If anything, shifts in psychoanalytic theory have followed a natural-science paradigm for explanation—that is, that theory shifts, in the last 30 years in particular have been trying to fit the most data with the most logical explanation. We have moved from a kind of naive and infantile relationship to Freud's theory to include a quite different vision of human growth and possibility offered by a variety of types of object relations theory and, more recently, the exciting potential for analytic work offered by neurobiology and psychopharmacology.

Reconstructing the Future

One of the main sources of interest and motivation for this book is to redress what I regard as an imbalance between the way we understand the past and future in psychoanalytic theory and in practice. Freud and his followers have been extraordinarily skittish about examining both the role of hope and the concept of the future in psychoanalysis. They have feared, understandably, the potential connection that fellow clinicians and the general public would make between psychoanalysis and religion (Jacobi, 1988). Freud's brilliant rationalism directed analysis toward an understanding of the past and an attempt to reconstruct it.

Relational theory in Europe, the United Kingdom, and the United States, varied as it is, has tried to develop ways of understanding the dashed hopes of our patients through a metaphor different from, or at least in addition to, the encapsulated infantile neurosis. Winnicott, Balint, Guntrip, and later Kohut placed these wishes for a hoped-for object (and their revival) at the very heart of what motivates adaptation and change.

In fact, Kohut's (1984) definition of defense as the attempt to keep alive a responsive object from childhood and the opportunity to rework the revival of these hopes in analysis is at the heart of his view of therapeutic action. It is a paradox of the classical approaches' criticism of Kohut's work, that the reconstruction of the past, particularly in relation to regressive transference, often relies on the elaboration of the patient's attempt to revive buried, sequestered hopes and wishes as an implicit, unspoken affective clinical linchpin. Kohut's (1971, 1981) work provided profound insights regarding how we seek objects who will fulfill longstanding frustrating empathic failure. His understanding, however, was limited by the ways in which he reduced all defensive functioning to a singular motive involving the attempt to find a hoped for empathic object. Furthermore, his view of the analytic situation was embedded in a one-person psychology, ignoring the analyst's complex and helpful forms of countertransference. Some of these countertransference reactions help the analyst to understand the complexity of the patient's hopes and the various ways in which these hopes are avoided, just as they are expressed. Relational theory in the United States has, additionally, tried to elaborate the analyst's hopes and wishes about the analytic process (Mitchell, 1993; Renik, 1993, 1995; Cooper, 1996b, 1997).

Thus, while we usually think of reconstruction as involving a reconstruction of the past, this reconstruction almost invariably involves an attempt to revive hopes and wishes—it is often a kind of reconstruction of the future. Reconstruction substantially involves, in Bion's (1975) felicitous term, a "memoir of the future." Bowie (1993) asserts that for Freud the present in which the analytic subject speaks is poised, "uneasily between discontinuous time-worlds." He goes on to state: "The problem lies not in the fact that past and future are logically asymmetrical but the seeming flatness that afflicts one of them: the past has character but the future has none. Romancing the matter only a little, we could say that for Freud the past is 'a character,' while the future is a cipher and something of a bore" (p. 153). One of the most exciting things about recent attempts to integrate conflict and relational models is the attempt to spell out the character of the present and the future, which have always been at the heart of analytic work and change processes.

Bowie has tried to address the contrast between Heidegger's (1927) view of the future and Freud's and in so doing elucidates a clarifying perspective on how contemporary relational models see the future. For Freud, we are always in the desiring, wish-fulfillment mode. We are always in a kind of "if only" (Akhtar, 1993) pattern, which involves the accumulation of a succession of anticipated wishes and desires. Wishing in the present is for Freud always the accumulation of past experience from the infantile neurosis. In anthropological terms, Freud's infantile neurosis is akin to what Heilbroner (1995) terms the Distant Past. For Heidegger (1927), the present is already being shaped by the future. This statement, at first blush, may sound like a neatly packaged form of teleological reasoning. But Heidegger's "anticipatory resoluteness" is the highest form of experience and existence. Heidegger did not focus on the notion of the future as what has not yet become actualized. Instead, the view of the future comprises the height of "potentiality-for-being."

This idea seems to me to be captured in the final line of Rilke's (1907) dramatic poem, *The Archaic Torso of Apollo*. Rilke ends the poem with the statement that has always made quite an impression on me and has been quoted by more than one patient: "You must change your life." This statement is not just an expression of the need to translate desire and wish into action. The exhilaration of the poem consists in the way that desire and wish both signify and are intrinsic to experience in the present. For Heidegger, it is not even enough to say that this moment is intrinsic to the present—it need be said that it represents, to the fullest, an experience of the self. As Bowie (1993) has suggested, it is not far from Martin Buber's notion of "imagining the real." Imagining the real is not simply a statement of wish; it includes the capacity for reasoning, judgment, and, most important, elements of both mutuality and asymmetry (Burke, 1992; Aron, 1996) in a dialogue regarding psychic possibility. "You must change your life" is not simple exhortation from one person to another. It is embodied in every interpretation an analyst makes. Psychic holding, confrontation, interpretation of defense, and transference always suggest the wish that something can change or, sometimes, even that *something is changing if the patient can bear to see it.*

One element of the holding aspects of interpretation involves the analyst's holding of psychic possibility. This type of holding is not assurance that a new psychic position can be achieved. It is not an assurance that a defense can yield to a more supple flexibility or broader range of defensive organization. But this element of the holding of interpretation does assert or allude to a type of play related to the virtual or hypothetical psychic realm. For example, "What might it mean?" "Why is this something that you automatically assume?" "How do you get to that conclusion?" "What is the fantasy that you mention about?" I am emphasizing something about interpretation that Loewald stressed in his formulation about interpretation as involving one step within regressive ego functions and experience and the other in the realm of psychic change, both increased observation or potentially, behavioral change.

Much of our current interest in suggestion as inherent to interpretation is really the working through of this largely neglected inherent aspect of interpretation. We have gone from focusing more exclusively on the content of interpretation (as providing insight) to aspects of interpretation as providing holding (e.g., Winnicott, 1969; Modell, 1976). The holding metaphor has been useful in focusing on the aspect of interpretation which involves the analyst's containment of the patient's affect. However, the holding metaphor is limited as a dynamic explanation in that it fails to address the analyst's aim or push intrinsic to any interpretation. This push often involves simply our aim to help a patient observe something unconscious about what they are saying or doing. As a profession, we are taking more responsibility for our analytic push or nudge. I hope that this book explores even more about the exploration of the patient's psychic future intrinsic to analytic process.

If we were to translate Kohut's (1984) definition of defense into the language of Heidegger, we might find that the attempt to keep alive a hoped-for object is more than the preservation of a need or wish, or the accompanying opportunity for gratification. We would need to add that the act of preserving hope is itself one of the most gratifying things we can do under the psychic constraints we face at any particular time. It is a defense, interestingly enough, also related to Schafer's (1968) notion of defense functioning as a double agent—something that fends off a wish while simultaneously gratifying it. It might be said that Kohut (1984) suggested that hope imagines. This idea can easily be conceptualized as teleological in its approach to defense as I argued in an earlier paper (Cooper, 1989). But I am now more convinced that the way that hope imagines is not simply by waiting for the longed-for object, but by suggesting the multiple ways that anticipation of the psychic future is embedded in the way that we seek, as pleasurably as possible, to experience the present in the past and the past in the present.

It is fascinating that in other respects so much of relational theory is at odds with self psychology. In fact, I am inclined to think of self psychology as in many important ways more embedded in a one-person psychology tradition than in a two-person model. Kohut's self psychology remains in many ways a one-person psychology because, despite placing the issue of the hoped-for empathic object in the foreground, the other is conceived more exclusively as an extension of the self. At the most, the selfobject, or other, is an icon of possibility. The analyst/other is viewed as a selfobject, not a subjective object (Benjamin, 1988) who influences the very act of wishing and structures the construction and representation of wishing. Benjamin's work sought to illustrate the degree to which the "paradox of recognition"—how the child and the patient are influenced by the other's subjectivity—involves a change process involving reciprocal influence. Wishing is always in the process of forming, grouping, and regrouping, as the vignette of Jeffrey illustrates. In this sense the representational world partly mediates the experience of the other, but the representational world itself is anything but a static, internalized organization. It mediates experience and is constantly being influenced by experience.

Where most relational theory in the United Kingdom, Europe, South America, and the United States diverges from Kohut's is in the technical handling of the patient's preservation of hoped-for objects—in other words, in how defensive processes and their emergence in the transference are handled. In fact, I have often been fascinated by the shared and overlapping interests of both classical and American relational theory in attempting to interpret defense. The notion of defense, and particularly the analyst's use of countertransference to help understand disavowed experiences of the patient within American relational theory, is at great odds with classical theory. But classical theory makes use of the analyst's perspectives that differ from the patient's, a kind of use of self (deeply buried within the constraints of conceptualizing the analyst as a blank screen) that is not accounted for in the theory of technique because countertransference is only narrowly defined as the analyst's responses to the patient's conflicts.

All relational models, and here I include self psychology, have found limitations in thinking of object relating as comprehensively explained by the notion of reduction in drive tension. Equally important is the shared common notion that the future of self-as-subject is inherent to experiences of who we are and who we are becoming. The "future-self-representation," if you will, reciprocally influences the experience of the past, just as the past influences the experience of the present.

One of the most radical aspects of Freud's chronometrical approach to time was to construct temporality partly in accordance with wishes (Bowie, 1993). Yet this view, which focuses primarily on the timeless-ness of the unconscious, is in stark contrast to Heidegger's (1927) view of futurity and its influence on the present. Bowie (1993) cites an exception to Freud's usual approach to time: "Past, present, and future are strung together, as it were, on the thread of the wish that runs through them" (Freud, 1908, p. 148). But for the most part Freud would understand his comment as an elucidation of how a particular life history involves the succession and vicissitudes of wished-for states. For Freud, hope was essentially the conscious experience of wish and desire and functions in accordance with the pleasure principle to reduce drive tension.

Thus for Freud the act of imagination involved a kind of solitary, en-capsulated wishing. The notion of wishing as an encapsulated act reached its height with Freud's conceptualization of biological solitude, the assertion that an object is no more than the aim of an instinct. To be sure, classical models include the patient's representational world in discussing the act of wishing. In contrast, however, American relational theory conceptualizes hope as carrying the imagination, including the representational world, into an act of collaboration or mutuality with another. Psychoanalysis involves the act of imagining *with* someone else or at least that the possible will become a major issue for negotiation (Russell, 1973; Mitchell, 1988; Pizer, 1992).

Relational theory conceptualizes despair as embedded in the constriction of imagination into a private world, the "schizoid citadel" that both Fairbairn (1952) and Guntrip (1969) elucidated so clearly. Fairbairn emphasized this notion in its purest form when he suggested that the pleasure principle functions, as Freud described it, only as a breakdown product of deficient parental holding and frustrated dependency. But most relational models have tried in various forms to integrate conflict as an essential constituent of relating (Slavin and Kriegman, 1992, 1998). Conflict partly involves the confluence of hopes in a relationship that includes the dialectical tensions between intrapsychic and interpersonal dimensions of wish and hope.

OBJECTS OF HOPE AND HOPED-FOR OBJECTS

All psychoanalytic theories of development and therapeutic action address the question of how persons adapt to their environment and to some extent how hope and wish are maintained. Psychoanalysts hold hope and are objects of hope for their patients to be able to bear experience, to learn from experience, and to learn how to have new experience. Patients hold hope that their analysts will help them to do this, despite their reluctance or resistance to the process. On a moment-to-moment basis, some of our patients feel hopeful about the possibility of change and some feel more hopeless. Alexander Pope (1734) asserted that "hope springs eternal in the human breast." The aphorism "Where there is life, there is hope" speaks to a similar sentiment and level of discourse, which relates to the need to keep trying, persevering, pursuing, mourning, bearing pain and sadness, celebrating, living.

Freudian theory characterizes the human being as a wishing animal. Yet the most caricatured or stripped down version of Freudian psychology is somewhat at odds with the more humanistic implications of this assertion. For example, Eagle (1984) has suggested that within strict Freudian psychology their is no requirement that the object of a drive even be a human being. While this characterization places into focus Freud's notion of our biological indifference and the extent to which an object is the aim of a drive, I think it probably goes too far. From an evolutionary perspective, Freud wished to emphasize the extent to which the pleasure principle functions within a uniquely human environment and that in fact we have a capacity to seek highly creative, often highly disguised, secretive, methods involving multiple functions for preserving the pleasure principle. From my point of view, the thrust of some British as well as American relational models' critiques of Freudian psychology have questioned the notion that the pleasure principle is an overarching explanation for the nature of human relating.

I use the term objects of hope as a part of the way in which analyst and patient relate to each other within the contemporary context of the analytic situation and the multiple dimensions or axes within it. For example, Strachey (1934), Loewald (1960), and Greenberg (1986) have referred to the importance of the analyst as a new object working in conjunction with the patient's experience of the analyst as an old object. The historical transference (Cooper, 1987) overlaps with the patient's experience of the analyst as an old object and refers to the patient's experience of the analyst as in some ways congruent with important experiences with earlier caretakers. Analyst and patient asymmetrically, though mutually contain and regulate hope within the dyad in ways that I explore clinically in chapter 5. In particular, the analyst is a kind of symbol or icon of psychic possibility for the patient. There are also times when the patient holds and contains aspects of the analyst's hopes for the patient. As objects of hope, we relate to each other on multiple levels of reality and selfhood. These affective and cognitive experiences and attributions involve some of the relationships between the patient's and the analyst's views of each other with regard to social authority, hope, and the analysis of transference. Thus these experiences go far beyond the representational level of explaining hope though they are always being partially mediated through the patient's representational world.

What I call hoped-for-objects refers to a different level of theoretical discourse, namely, that which theoreticians call a level of longing and hope within the patient's development and representational world. This may take the form of concretized fantasies, including what Ornstein and Ornstein (1994) term curative fantasy or affective experience. Obviously these affects and fantasies often may be unconsciously held and may emerge in the process of analytic work. We have many different ideas about what patients are looking for and what they have done to protect, preserve, or perpetuate their longings. Often the two levels of discourse, which broadly represent the interpersonal and intrapsychic or representational realm that I have been discussing, equate the analyst and patient, as objects of hope, with the patient's hoped-for objects. This has been a problem for both the theory of psychoanalysis and psychoanalytic technique.

American relational theory has tried to bridge these two realms in a unique way that adds a great deal to the contributions of classical models, developmental strategies, and Kleinian theory. Within the American relational model, there is an attempt to conceptualize hoped-for objects as partly embedded within the representational realm while constantly being influenced by the contemporary analytic situation. The representational world and the immediacy of analytic engagement are always mediating the other and exerting reciprocal forms of influence on one another. For example, the current interaction is shaping what from the representational world of the patient will be in the foreground as both experienced and expressed, just as the representational world will partially mediate what is experienced in the immediate interaction.

REVISITING THE PSYCHOANALYTIC ATTITUDE: HAVING ATTITUDE (NOT TRANSFERENCE AUTHORITY)

One of the exciting and profoundly immodest things about the analytic attitude is that the two participants are *hellbent* on seeing if something about the patient that has been the same for a long time can change. Unfortunately there is not much room therapeutically and theoretically for capturing this determination without associating it with the ugly specters of the analyst's impatience, naiveté, reliance on suggestion, manipulation, or need to recklessly circumvent resistance. In recent years there has been an increased appreciation that the analyst's wishes to influence need not be mistaken for a lack of appreciation of resistance, repetition, and the need to respect the particular rhythm of a patient's growth processes. There has been a developing attempt to consider the analyst's wishes to influence in confluence with other modes of influence.

I enjoy the expression hellbent as a descriptor of both participants because it captures the determination and potential immersion and difficulty that are often a part of analysis. It is not an expression that captures the conscious attitudes of the patient and the analyst, who are often cautious, made wise by life and previous therapeutic experiences so that they know how difficult it is to change. For example, although Jeffrey was determined to try to undertake another analysis, hellbent is the last way I would describe his unconscious approach to change. What was helpful to him was his discovery of how hellbent he was to avenge his father through stagnation while unconsciously maintaining his attachment to his father. Moreover, Jeffrey found that a part of his attachment to his father was the persistence of a wish that his father and I could change and give him the approval he craved. This wish persisted so strongly that a great deal of our work revolved around Jeffrey's difficulty in selectively perceiving me as critical of him while excluding from his perception and experience the many ways that I held warm feelings and high regard for him.

I very much agree with Friedman's (1988) assertion that the therapist's capacity or need to see the patient's potential for change as a "necessary illusion" (p. 431). But I daresay most of us try never to lose completely a sense of how peculiar, unconventional, and ambitious the analytic enterprise truly is. Change, which tends to occur in small increments in analytic work, is a constant reminder of this fact. One of the things that an analyst has to learn to appreciate is that a seemingly small change is big stuff.

The patient is hellbent if he or she has undertaken an analysis. There are easier ways to approach making changes—not necessarily to make them but to approach them. Analysis is time consuming and costly and usually involves visiting and revisiting psychic regions that are painful. For some, it is the therapeutic court of last resort, and for others who are suffering less it is a very special and privileged opportunity to explore with another person one's curiosity and to nudge unturned stones. I would reserve the unlikely term hellbent even for patients who are consciously hopeless or dubious about the possibility of change.

In fact, most patients are usually not consciously hellbent. If anything they come to analysis with intense anxiety and guilt and feel inhibited or lacking control in some way. With some exceptions, many patients such as Jeffrey have seen enough of themselves to be skeptical about the possibility of changing. What can the analyst tell him that will make him able to hold on to a relationship, feel something more authentic about himself or someone else, feel less inhibited sexually, stop avoiding intimacy and self-awareness, stop feeling guilty, stop lying, start being able to enjoy himself, and the like? What can a patient feel or learn that will make it possible for new experiences to occur? Why indeed would I refer to a patient as hellbent in the face of all these forms of reluctance or resistance?

A patient is hellbent who knows or learns quickly at some level that every analysis is a radical experiment. The attempt to "woo nature" (Roth, 1987) is a risky climb. If the patient does not know this, trying to gain insight into why he does not is certainly a worthwhile effort. Anyone who would talk to an analyst three to five times a week at such great cost of time and money, enduring unknown and even sometimes untoward emotional rupture and disruption in his life and often for those around him is hellbent. Anyone who begins an analysis with some commitment is at least unconsciously looking to a possibility beyond the horizon of the present.

Transference itself is a representation of possibility, just as it reflects the cumulative affective and representational history of a particular experience. What is transference if not the amalgam of hopes and resistance to the experience of hope? The point in an analysis when a patient is able to work in the transference more actively and persistently not only inspires hope in the analyst but often represents a revived capacity for hope within a relationship. A patient who undertakes analysis is at least going to revisit the possibility for psychic change. He is going to experience the analyst holding psychic possibility with every interpretation (Loewald, 1960; Cooper, 1996, 1997). Holding psychic possibility goes beyond interpreting the patient's hopes in the form of wishes and fantasy; it includes the awareness that psychic possibility is not a static, encapsulated event with origins exclusively in infantile life. Possibility is constantly being forged through immediate experience and engages the dyad in the deepest kinds of interaction related to sexuality, desire, passion, frustration, envy, and anger.

The analyst is hellbent, even though his attitude is tempered by the awareness that, from everything that he has observed, this is going to be a very difficult undertaking. As psychoanalysts, we are schooled in the power and ubiquity of repetition and the forces that resist change. Yet it seems to me that we are hellbent in the sense that there is no other reasonable way to explain why we persist against those forces that oppose and fear change. Being hellbent signals that we have seen change, usually quite small, but often extraordinarily significant. It means that we have been trained in how to promote and hold psychic possibility, in subtle ways and sometimes in the face of apparent hopelessness; to appreciate that we all wish to change while staying the same (Bromberg, 1995); that change and stagnation often alternate in interesting and sometimes bewildering layering. *Being hellbent does not refer to an attitude that is based on suggestion and persuasion except as they are byproducts of the ways that interpretation is involved in, even inherent to, analytic influence.* Analysts are hellbent because, to some extent, consciously and unconsciously they are identified with their patients around the wish to change. They may also consciously and unconsciously identify with feelings of being stuck or, at more extreme levels, feelings of despair or aspects of hopelessness as well.

As Friedman (1988) described the analyst's capacity or need to see the patient's potential for change as a "necessary illusion" (p. 431), he also discussed the analyst's tendency to see change as inevitable rather than a result of his own "expectant intrusions" (p. 408). One of the ways to understand our current exploration into the analyst's subjectivity is that it marks a shift from our recent interest in epistemological questions about what the analyst knows to questions about what the analyst wants, his expectant intrusions. The analyst wants to broaden the patient's psychic landscape, to help the patient to "imagine the real" and to elucidate *how the patient unconsciously already imagines the real.*

Gradually we have been understanding the degree to which interpretation always and inevitably expresses aspects of the analyst's experience (e.g., Aron, 1991). Thus we need to shift from thinking about the analyst as "intruding" (though we have to think constantly about the possibility that at times we are) to thinking more about how the analyst and the patient inevitably shape the nature of hope within the dyad. While there is a wide range of affects potentially expressed by the analyst related to desire, dread, need, and wish, I believe that, to a large extent, these affects pass through a filter of hope. This hope relates to the broad concern of why an analyst has chosen to do analysis and the more specific concern of why he chooses a particular intervention with a particular patient. Most of the affects cannot be translated into the analyst's hopes for the patient—this would, indeed, make me the village reductionist analyst. Instead, I believe that many of the analyst's affects and experiences that are communicated through interpretation have been significantly influenced by the analyst's needs and wishes to influence. In turn these wishes and needs naturally draw from the analyst's own experiences of change as well as from his limitations and even inability to change within treatment and life.

Even more profound is that it is a highly selective group of people who choose to become analysts. We have not really come to terms with the notion that those of us who choose this profession were trained early, so to speak, to become analysts; we were often selected or trained at an early age to understand or reduce conflict, to take care of others around us, to resolve conflict, stir up affect where there was none, to provide emotional titration, and the like. I have often heard my colleagues say about their children: "If they decide to become analysts, I hope that they feel they had a choice." These declarations of hope and wish can come only from a sense of early indoctrination into the profession, albeit often with the sense of great pleasure and gratification that comes from the work. A humorous example of this phenomenon is illustrated in the recent film *Analyze This*. A psychiatrist father is listening to his young adolescent issue forth astute observations of his father's behavior, and the father seems to listen, knowing that his son has both benefited from and been afflicted by the constant exposure to his father's interpretive framework for understanding experience. But we need to contend with the knowledge that we analysts live in a kind of therapeutic community, what one very funny patient termed a sophisticated day hospital, as it were, in which we are indoctrinating our patients into a belief system that we have been experiencing for better and worse for a long time. It is a community that has given us pleasure, meaning, often a relief from old, conflict-laden patterns, and often a feeling of intimacy and relatedness.

At the most general or experience-distant level, the analyst's attitude is expressed through interpretation, which, in turn, is based on mounds of formulation that the analyst is aware of or not. Formulation is always in the foreground while a model of therapeutic action lurks close behind, pushing us to think about another person in a particular way. Patients are indoctrinated by our formulations and interpretations (Bion, 1967; Balint, 1968; Britton and Steiner, 1994), no matter how much we pay attention to our modes of influence.

Our view of our patients' future is an essential and underemphasized aspect of formulation and interpretation and is most visible in our theories of change and how we conceptualize our various modes of influence. This view of the future as contained in the analyst's formulations is still another aspect of the analyst's subjectivity, as I elaborate in detail in chapter 7 and chapter 10. Loewald (1960) wrote that psychoanalysts "fear too much the notion of molding the patient in our own image and that this fear has prevented analysts from coming to grips with the dimension of the future in analytic theory and practice" (p. 23). While Loewald's emphasis on the "mature" analyst's facilitating the patient's growth has been largely questioned and usurped in the context of the deauthoritarianism of the analyst's role, his concern with the relationship of the analyst's conceptualization of the future as it relates to his mode of interpretation and formulation is still minimized in many current discussions of psychoanalytic formulation and technique. In subsequent chapters I clinically illustrate this assertion.

In *Burnt Norton,* T. S. Eliot (1936) wrote: "Time present and time past, Are both perhaps time present in time future, And time future contained in time past." This view of the future is largely compatible with most psychoanalytic conceptualizations of the future. The importance of repetition is a crucial concept in psychoanalytic theory that focuses on how the unconscious past may explain the development of current and future life. Psychoanalytic formulation incorporates how the past is recreated in the present, particularly how its recreation forecloses new experience, both with regard to new affects and a new object experience in the transference. Interpretation of this pattern is hoped to increase the patient's access to these new experiences. Loewald (1960) summarized this aspect of formulation and interpretation succinctly:

Language, in its most specific function in analysis, as interpretation is thus a creative act similar to that in poetry, where language is found for phenomena, contexts, connections, experiences not previously known and speakable. New phenomena and new experience are made available as a result of reorganization of material according to hitherto unknown principles, contexts, and connections [p. 242].

Loewald emphasized that the analyst needs to retrace organizational steps that are organized on higher levels of sublimation so that the organizing process becomes available to the patient. Similarly, Sandler and Sandler (1994) describe the main aim of analysis as of broadening the patient's view of the past and the future:

> However, the main aim of analysis, in our view, is not to discover what went on in the past, not to release as recalled memories the repressed material of the earliest years, but rather to create a picture of the relevant aspects of the past in order to discover and understand better the present psychic structure and conflicts of the patient. We need to have a picture of the past in order to understand the present for the benefit of the patient's future [p. 1007].

Any attempt to understand something in either the present or the past entails the analyst's formulating within a context related to how he wishes to influence. Influence always involves a view of how the analyst wants the future to be shaped. How we wish to influence not only implies how we utilize formulation within a particular theoretical orientation or a particular theory of technique, but also enters into the area of our ideal view of how we wish to affect the patient. Sandler and Sandler (1994) poignantly address the issue of how analysts sometimes underestimate unreachable parts of the patient, which can lead to extremely lengthy and sometimes unproductive analyses (p. 1008). In this sense, the analyst's view of the future will, we hope, undergo transformation and revision over the course of an analysis, either with a view of the future as holding expanding opportunities, diminished possibilities, or both. I am reminded of something that Bernard Levin (1977) once wrote about the future that is applicable to the both analyst and patient over the course of analysis: "I have heard tell of a Professor of Economics who has a sign on the wall of his study, reading 'the future is not what it was'. The sentiment was admirable; unfortunately, the past is not getting any better either" (p. 17). In analysis, this is only part of the story. Fantasies and hopes for the future yield to more realistic perspectives on what is possible. This realization is often disappointing to both the patient and the analyst, just as what is possible is also energizing as it yields to new possibilities and new sources of vitality in the wake of discarded hopes and fantasies. At the end of analysis, it is not uncommon that the patient will feel that the past is not what it was cracked up to be, either not as good as one might have thought or not as painful as it was once was experienced.

But Sandler and Sandler's (1994) point implicitly raises issues related to magical fantasies held by both the analysand and analyst. Caper (1992) discusses a variety of aspects of the healing nature of psychoanalysis. He suggests that sometimes a patient's omnipotent fantasies for cure involve interpretation as magical and substitutive for the patient's need to solve the conflicts and problems he confronts in the analysis. I agree with Caper's questioning of the value of the concept of cure as an outcome of good analysis. The analyst may unconsciously hold these wishes in a similar fashion. Rather than formulation and interpretation broadening the observational field or, in Caper's words, attempting to "bring the patient into fresh contact with himself" (p. 287), the analyst's formulations can enact these magical fantasies of cure.

Thus it is essential to read every theory of psychoanalysis from the point of view of both how the analyst has observed change and how the analyst wants the patient to change. It is not surprising that many of us use analogies to marital or filial relationships in describing our use of theory (e.g., "He's wedded to his theory"). I have become convinced that this is why the metaphor or concept of neutrality needs to yield to new ways of describing how we must respect the limitations and power of our position. Part of our desire is expressed in why and when we look for important triggers for interpretation, i.e., important signifiers. Each psychoanalytic approach valorizes aspects of the analytic situation—defense that is close to the analytic surface (e.g., Gray, 1990; Busch, 1994, 1996, 1997), linearity and reconstruction (Faimberg, 1991); the patient's psychic reality (e.g., Schaber, 1983); and a variety of relational factors.

We also all have fallback positions when we feel hopeless, and this is another important function of theory. Theory in this sense provides a kind of holding environment to contain our uncertainty and the inherent vagaries and ambiguity of clinical work (Adler, 1989). Some of us think that a transference interpretation is what will restore hopefulness in the analyst or patient about the treatment or the reestablishment of meaning. Some move toward more linear thinking so as to reconstruct something that has happened in an attempt to explain where feelings come from and why for a particular patient (e.g., Faimburg, 1991). Some believe in the more expressive use of countertransference (Ehrenberg, 1992, 1995). These holding environments are not essentially compensatory in function. Theory serves a highly useful purpose, though most who adopt a particular theory are not familiar with the ways we become attached to our theories and resist modifying our stance and learning from different theories, sometimes in the face of contradictions to our model. I believe, for example, that my work with patients is usefully explained by a particular theory of technique but not with others. There are certain patients or phases of work in which the kind of defense analysis that I am doing is usefully explained by aspects of ego psychology, whereas other phases of work need to incorporate aspects of expressive countertransference in the analysis of reluctance and disavowed affect featured more heavily within various models of relational theory.

Analysts have been afraid not so much to have "attitude" but to take more responsibility for their wishes to influence through theory of technique. In some ways, the shift into examining the analyst's subjectivity, intentions, and wishes to influence (e.g., Aron, 1991; Hoffman, 1991, 1994; Mitchell, 1993, 1997; Renik, 1993, 1995) has required us to take more responsibility for these aspects of our analytic "attitude." Our theory, defined as a logic of hope, moves the wish to influence more into the foreground for us to examine and to try to take more responsibility. There is a powerful and implicit sense of "attitude" in Schafer's (1983) analytic attitude. For many analysts, though, analytic attitude is usually used interchangeably with essential kinds of restraint and modesty. At its best, this restraint involves a respect for the need to create a framework for the patient to be able to experience himself as fully as possible. At its worst, the restraint can become more globally an overemphasized fear of "interfering," which results in passivity. By using the term passivity I do not mean to focus on an analyst's tendency to be more quiet or even silent than is sometimes useful. There is naturally an important place for silence, restraint, and creating an atmosphere for the analytic process to emerge, as there are instances when silence reflects various kinds of countertransference withdrawal.

What I mean by the term passivity has more to do with both a specific aspect of technique in which the analyst tries "too hard" not to influence and a specific mode of theorizing that often places the analyst's wishes to influence in the background. The analyst is always influencing, whether intentionally or not. This influence includes my earlier reference to how we often conceptualize reconstruction as being pri-

marily of the past while minimizing reconstruction as an attempt to influence how these hopes and wishes can be reconciled with current and
future experience—a kind of reconstruction of the future. This reconstruction is a form of psychic holding or interpretation with which the
analyst is actively involved. I think of it as a kind of analytic function
that I call *holding the psychic future.* One of the most exciting things
about recent attempts to integrate conflict and relational models is the
attempt to spell out the character of the present and future that has always been at the heart of analytic work and change processes.

It is my view that while psychoanalysts have long understood the
many functions of holding affect within the analytic situation (e.g.,
Winnicott, 1958; Modell, 1976; Slochower, 1996), the concept of
holding the patient's psychic future has been discussed less fully. Loewald's (1960) brilliant and prescient view of interpretation emphasized
the analyst's ability to take a patient one step back into regression and
one step ahead to the future. Loewald meant by this that an interpretation tries to help facilitate exploration of something that is concealed
or protected through defense which, if understood, may allow the patient a new affective or ideational experience. For example, I believe
that when an ego psychologist or any other analyst points out a defensive shift, there is always some potential therapeutic action that revolves
around the interpersonal asking of a question—a request that asks the
patient to experience something different, new, or old. I underscore this
asking of a question because I don't believe there is such a thing as promoting observation for observation's sake. Those of us who believe that
analytic work attempts to promote introspective curiosity, understanding, and increased choice and responsibility know that this is as passionate and charged a value and belief system as any other. The wish to
help a patient "observe" is always embedded in sexual, aggressive, variously affect-laden interpersonal contexts.

The implicit request in each interpretation is anything but the use
of transference authority. In fact, it is the opposite because I view this
way of formulating our interpretive action as an attempt to account for
or to take responsibility for our therapeutic activity. The analyst's interpretation (or asking if you will) is experienced by each patient in a
different way. Using Loewald's paradigm, some patients will go more
in the direction of regression by fleeing or augmenting defense, while
other patients will falsely comply with the progressive direction of the

interpretation, and still others will be able to use the interpretation to experience themselves in a new (perhaps new because they can experience an old, repressed, suppressed, or disavowed feeling) way.

Another problem involves the way in which our accounts of therapeutic action are sometimes limited by the constraints of a theoretical framework that systematically evades aspects of the analyst's technical activity. In relation to theory, we have failed to take a more active role in revising theory in accord with what we actually do. I recently had a conversation with someone who said, in earnest, that the theoretical position that was taken in an article did not incorporate enough the technique that the analyst actually often employs in doing clinical work. I have every reason to believe that this problem is not unique to one school of psychoanalytic theory or technique, although I think the classical model, in particular, leaves less room than others for integrating the vibrancy and spontaneity of its most gifted practitioners.

There is nothing neutral about the invitation to ask another person to "take the risk of not knowing what you will say" (Phillips, 1993). It is a most unconventional suggestion, transgressing most every border of social discourse. The analyst's request is experienced by the patient as potentially reflecting all kinds of feelings and fantasies about what the analyst wants. Is it the analyst's desire that makes him ask this—his aggression, love, seductiveness, caring, wish to overpower and dominate, and the like? The logical question for the patient is, why should I take that risk? Ogden's (1995) decision to no longer ask patients to say what comes to mind was, I think, born of an attempt to take more active responsibility for his own wishes and values about the analytic process. He values his own privacy for thoughts and reverie within the analytic situation because it allows him to take risks in his associative process. Could we even say that among the many functions that reverie facilitates, *it allows the analyst to hope more fruitfully?*

I hope it is clear that what I mean by this opportunity for productive "hoping" by the analyst is a complex function, not related to naive or superficial hopefulness. What I have in mind is a process through which the analyst's reverie and reflection on what he thinks and says allows him to understand the confluence of conscious and unconscious communications, including defensive processes related to desire, sadness, anger, and affection. To hope more fruitfully is another way of saying that the analyst is trying to learn as much as possible about what the patient wants, what the patient is afraid of, how the patient protects himself, and the like. Again, the notion of the analyst's being hell-bent does not always refer to a conscious sense of being hopeful, but instead incorporates the multitude of countertransference experiences that the analyst tries to understand in doing clinical work.

One of the things analysts have to contend with is how out of place within contemporary culture is the request that the patient risk speaking without knowing what he will say. This in no way means that we have to retreat from the radical nature of what we do and what we see as prerequisites for our work. But we still have many vestiges from a time when authority was more trusted and accepted. The asocial nature of the analytic situation has been insufficiently explained to the public at large. This is another example of how our radical "attitude" has been sequestered while too many pine for a time when the asymmetry of the analytic situation was more consonant with other practices related to parent-child, teacher-student, worshipper-religious leader relations. It is not only our fallibility (Cooper, 1993) that needs to be explained but our attitude—our wishes to influence, our belief in a radical method of treatment, and, most important, the fact that the asymmetry of the analytic situation is not the binary relationship of other forms of relationship. All relationships have strong elements of asymmetry, not just parent-child, teacher-student, or sadist-masochist. Many people are able to find that there are useful, exciting, playful, and productive outcomes of asymmetry just as there are abusive, painful, and traumatic outcomes of highly asymmetrical relationships.

Thus in some ways we may have isolated ourselves from a part of our culture that is moving toward more complicated relationships to authority and asymmetry. We have the opportunity to apply psychoanalytic insights to the momentum of change around us within the realms of sexuality, longevity, international conflict negotiations, genetic engineering, and new art and music forms, which are increasingly based on participant-observer modes.

Unfortunately, some of us see change automatically as disguised repetition, superficial faddishness and the like. From this view, changes in psychoanalytic theory are also sometimes looked upon with trepidation and skepticism. The past is safe; the future is dangerous. However, Bowie's (1993) felicitous caricature—that the past is where all character and richness lie while the future is dead and "something of a cipher or a bore"—is only partially accurate. After all, classical analytic theory certainly emphasizes that homeostasis is maintained because of unknown terrors that must be kept at bay—the unconscious is partly the repository of wishes. But there is a way in which classical theory is much more focused on the past (Oedipus) and is dangerous. This formulation, which has great explanatory and therapeutic value, minimizes how the future is dangerous and defensively avoided while, in a sense, the "distant past" (Heilbroner, 1995) provides a safe distance for lively formulation. Much of contemporary relational theory has tried to move into the exploration of interaction and the possibilities that this exploration might hold for both elucidating unconscious conflict and promoting change. For example, Davies's (1994, 1998) recent work exploring postoedipal transference relates to how analysts sometimes focus too much on transferences to the unavailable oedipal object while minimizing aspects of postoedipal or more mature relatedness.

Psychoanalysis developed as a positivistic enterprise, a boldly pioneering study devoted to the retrospective explanation of psychic events. Any other relation to the future was to repeat the primitive attempts at prognostication that Freud (1900) so emphatically and forcefully denounced. Relational theory in the United States has helped to explicate the patient's act of wishing as intrinsic to and at times related to the analyst's hopes and wishes. The analyst's process of learning about his own hopes and wishes or lack of them is also a key source of potential information about the patient's affective and psychic life. The analyst attempts to find ways to shift the patient's conscious and unconscious hopes both in the immediacy of engagement and through the developmental history of the patient, born of loving and hostile feelings, gratification and disappointment, into a realm of playful dialogue and observation. His own hopes are constantly influenced by the patient and influence the progress of this effort.

PART I
INTIMACY AND SOLITUDE

INTIMACY AND SOLITUDE

Some Points of Comparison Between American and British Relational Models

IN MANY WAYS RELATIONAL THEORY in the United States has built upon the contributions of various schools of British object relations theory. Each approach uses the countertransference as an important source of information about the patient's representational world. Each model makes use of the notion of the analyst's containment of the patient's affects and unconscious conflicts. There are, however, some important differences. These differences include the ways in which the mind and the representational world are conceptualized as well as technical differences in approach to the types of analyst interventions, chiefly in the area of countertransference expressiveness.

Both schools of thought are interested in schizoidal experience. The work of Fairbairn (1952) and Guntrip (1969) has elucidated the patient's retreat from outer objects with a concomitant reliance on the world of inner objects, termed by Guntrip the "schizoid citadel" and, more recently, by Steiner (1993) as "psychic retreat." Bromberg (1998) has stated that for schizoid patients the analytic situation risks being a *dialogue* about the patient rather than an *analysis* of the patient (p. 58). Bromberg suggests that the patient's communication can take the form of free association's being unconsciously used to perpetuate distance and reliance on internal objects. Analysts within both traditions are aware of this danger and struggle to find ways to create an atmosphere in which the patient is able to peek out from this citadel with a degree of autonomy and self-generated motivation. Bromberg notes that, once out of this citadel and in order to stay out, the patient has to develop what Henry James called an "absorbing errand."

The British models usefully focus on the analyst's ability to survive the patient's "destruction" (Winnicott, 1969). This destruction refers to the patient's dread of external objects to the extent that they threaten the relinquishment and safety of a defensively insular internal object world. The analyst pays close attention to the vicissitudes of the patient's retreats from various aspects of external analytic events that symbolize for the patient the threat of an external reality (Steiner, 1993). The American relational approach sometimes makes a more directly expressive attempt to analyze this form of resistance, albeit honoring and respecting the patient's defensive insulation and self-sufficiency, while gradually trying to create with the patient an analytic reality that lies outside the patient's internalized world.

One of the major contributions of understanding the schizoidal patient from a contemporary Kleinian perspective has included a sensitivity to the ways that revenge and grievance contribute to the patient's withdrawal. While some case descriptions (e.g., Steiner, 1996) elucidate the dynamic nature of these impasses, there is less description of what happens interpersonally to help patient and analyst extricate themselves from these difficult circumstances in the treatment. It is probably safe to say that countertransference expressiveness in contemporary Kleinian analysis is more limited and less specific in clinical situations dealing with both hostile and erotic countertransference reactions than is the case for analysts working within American relational models.

The analyst's stance in these approaches implicitly differs with respect to the role of containment of affects. While both models emphasize the need to contain affects that are anathemas to the patient, the American relational model suggests more latitude on the analyst's part for various kinds of countertransference expressiveness. The purpose of these interventions is to analyze disavowed affects of the patient. Within Fairbairn's (1952) psychology, the analyst is essentially a new object to the extent that he is able to contain the patient's painful affects. Old object experiences are held by the patient to preserve a sense of safety and familiarity; new objects threaten these attachments. In contrast, in the American relational models, this containment is usually conceptualized as of only limited utility in promoting change. In this model, at particular points in well-developed treatments, the analyst actively contrasts the old object transference with resistance to taking in or experiencing new aspects of the analyst's presence. Interestingly, corresponding to Freud's (1914) initial definition of transference as a defense against other affects and unconscious experience, some of the analyst's countertransference expressiveness points to the patient's reluctance to see the analyst as a new object.

While these chapters examine primarily clinical approaches and case material, some of the themes I have outlined are constantly in the background.

2

INTIMACY AND SOLITUDE

I NTIMACY AND SOLITUDE are among the most dynamic of currents that carry the analytic process. It is one of the major paradoxes of the analytic experience that among the most intimate aspects of the relationship is a sense of solitude, limit, and separateness. Intimacy and solitude relate to some of the primary affective experiences within the analytic situation, tensions within any person and in any relationship. The complementarity of intimacy and solitude is just one of many ways to approach some of the most interesting and complex forms of tension within the psychoanalytic process and our points of various theoretical emphasis and debate about the process. The patient's and the analyst's experiences of intimacy and solitude are a major part of the background against which any exploration of hope is set.

It is partially true but overly simplistic to state that aspects of solitude are more emphasized in the strands and traditions of British relational theory and dimensions of intimacy more a point of emphasis in American relational theory. Instead, there are overlapping but also distinct ways that the two traditions weight these experiential dimensions within the analytic situation.

These traditions also relate to another way of thinking about the history of psychoanalytic theory, what Strenger (1989) has referred to as the romantic and classic traditions. To the extent that the classical and the Kleinian traditions emphasize the power of psychic determinism and repetition, it might be said that there is also more focus on solitude. I am using the term solitude here partly to connote a focus on an encapsulated, monadic unconscious. There is also a greater focus within the classical and Kleinian traditions on the developmental stage of symbiosis, which the infant is trying to integrate and in a certain sense recover from. Mourning is also an important part of developmental growth and a part of the therapeutic action as it is conceptualized both in Kleinian and Freudian analysis. I associate the Middle School and American relational perspectives with a more romantic view, emphasizing the potential for intimacy, newness, and spontaneity. In turn, particularly within the American relational model, there is greater emphasis placed on mutuality and the ubiquitousness of reciprocal unconscious influence both in the immediacy of analytic engagement and in the early parent-child interaction.

There are also differences between the Kleinian and American relational models regarding the expressiveness-containment continuum (Mitchell, 1995, 1997). The Kleinian orientation emphasizes the analyst's role in containing, metabolizing, and detoxifying the patient's affects. While this is an important aspect of therapeutic action within the American relational model, which I explore in greater detail in chapter 4, this model tends to focus on the analyst's expressiveness through interpretation more than does the Kleinian model. Each tradition emphasizes the importance of conflict, but conflict is conceptualized within quite different frameworks, as Mitchell (1997) has elaborated in great detail. The relational model has broadened the canvas for conflict to include interactional tensions that express and embody, as it were, dimensions of conflict.

It is especially through the concepts of expressiveness and containment that the lines between intimacy and solitude are interpenetrating, rather than opposites. Expressiveness on the part of both patient and analyst carries with it constraint and restraint. Containment (in both defensive and nondefensive contexts) is shared and expressed, often mutually, albeit asymmetrically, by both patient and analyst. If we think of the analytic space as a kind of canvas, there are many formations, transpositions, circles, breaks, and, as Rilke (1911) would put it, "marvelous curves" (p. 25).

The affective currents of solitude and intimacy, like the classical-romantic division, help to organize some of the different sides of conflict and experience within the analytic situation. An appreciation of solitude has to do with how the analyst's theory (even in more relationally oriented analyses in which patient and analyst are viewed as in a constant state of mutual influence) causes him to conceptualize himself as standing outside the patient's psychic reality. Intimacy relates to the way that the analyst, through interaction, is embedded in everything that the patient expresses about his experiential, motivational, and representational dynamics. Solitude involves the reality of limits within the interaction, including bodily experiences and ultimately death. Intimacy relates to the power of relationship, commonality, and mutuality along the way, including the *shared* realities of the finiteness of the analytic relationship. *Even the reality of limit* (see chapter 9) *or death is a shared terror and, in the context of much analytic work, a source of shared denial.*

Intimacy and solitude also relate to the ways in which analyst and patient will come to understand that their hopes overlap and collide with each other. The analyst's capacity for affect attunement does not imply that his hopes and wishes for the patient are identical to those of the patient. I think just the opposite is true. Analyst and patient hold each other's hopes in various ways that are explored throughout this book, but the process of holding hopes and wishes different from those of the patient are what is often most exhilarating and growth producing about the analytic situation. Interestingly, this is a value that is shared by both the classical and the American relational traditions. In contrast, most views of therapeutic action held by self psychology hinge more on the analyst's capacity to embrace more exclusively the patient's psychic reality regarding hoped for objects. Solitude partly involves the awareness that all hopes cannot be gratified and achieved, whereas the intimacy current is a part of the shared communication field that builds from this fact of human and psychoanalytic life.

Solitude also involves the awareness of the importance of psychic determinism and the sense of continuity about our experience, which we repeat and carry around with us—in Derrida's (1982) terms, our "already, ready" responses. Intimacy is about something new and surprising that can happen, even in the face of determinism, that influences interaction. Solitude concerns the analyst as an objective observer in Freud's positivistic enterprise or, as Bollas (1987) has termed it, as a "symbol decoder." Intimacy relates more to the shared affective field and the analyst as participant-observer. Perhaps solitude involves a part of what Mitchell (1993) has referred to as "the dismantling of hope." In many ways, the analyst's interventions straddle the line between the creation of psychic possibility and the dismantling of hope, what might be thought of as the transformation of hope.

I find these ways of thinking about intimacy and solitude (which I have in some ways artificially constructed) helpful only to a point because they are much too schematic. So many of our various analytic theories try to capture and embrace the complex interaction of each of these dimensions. The notion of a tension between intimacy and solitude contains a theory of both psychic possibility and psychic inevitability as essential elements in describing analytic process.

So, admittedly, this summary does an injustice to the complexity and power of classical as well as relational traditions. Some comparative debates about psychoanalytic theory devolve into what I regard as an ill-founded notion that interaction and interest in unconscious phenomena are at odds with one another. Implicit in this opinion is the notion that relational approaches minimize the aspects of solitude necessary for understanding unconscious process. In contrast, Mitchell (1997) has tried to examine clinically and theoretically the ways in which conscious and unconscious communications are inextricably woven into interaction. Classical analysts might feel equally criticized or misunderstood for their interest in the ways in which intimacy manifests itself in the analytic process. They would argue, I think, that there is nothing more intimate than "knowing one's mind" with another person.

Relational models vary on the dimensions of intimacy and solitude, as do classical models. The British object relations traditions of Klein, Bion, Fairbairn, Winnicott, Guntrip, and Bollas (I realize that I have in this list already alluded to at least three separate schools) have emphasized the importance of solitude as much as has any other psychoanalytic tradition. In my own version of relational theory, a distillation of American and British contributions as well as some aspects of American ego psychology, solitude has an important place, as does the opportunity to experience and understand the intense intimacy of analytic process. I think of solitude as an often important byproduct of the asymmetrical elements in the analytic situation. There is, however, a danger in taking too concrete an approach to how the asymmetrical and more mutual dimensions of the analytic setup are experienced. For example, some analysts (e.g., Adler and Bachant, 1996) equate the social-constructivism of Hoffman (1991, 1994a, 1996) or the perspectivism of Aron (1996) with diluting the patient's opportunity to experience solitude. In fact, just the opposite is true. Countertransference expressiveness, used actively to form and express interpretations need not imply that mutuality is valued any more than asymmetry. Nor need bearing solitude be seen as at odds with the analyst's continuous interest in the patient's way of seeing and feeling things. Nor does the relational perspective necessarily engender feelings of intimacy. Interestingly enough, sometimes the more an analyst wants to know how a patient sees things, the more the patient realizes that the analyst might also see things in ways that are different from the way he does. The more intimate a patient and analyst become, often the more separate they become. It is also true that it would be much too simplistic to suggest that the efforts within self psychology or Schwaber's emphasis on illuminating the patient's psychic reality will lead to less disappointment, anger or aggression on the patient's part than models that emphasize divergent psychic realities of both patient and analyst.

As analysts of differing perspectives communicate more with each other there is more opportunity to move away from the most schematic and polarized conceptualizations of these various traditions. This chapter is titled "Intimacy and Solitude" in an attempt to advance this discussion, especially what I regard as the very intimate ways that therapist and patient communicate about transference and relatedness and the very active ways they communicate about the limits of relatedness. As the book develops, I aim to explore how the dimensions of intimacy and solitude, expressiveness, containment, and mutual containment are often at work simultaneously and, as Hoffman (1994a, 1996, 1998a) has suggested, dialectically, in the clinical situation.

I deeply respect and appreciate the clinical heritage underlying the affective currents of intimacy and solitude as emphasized within varying aspects of psychoanalytic theory. While the notion of hope is a point of emphasis within this book, an appreciation of the tensions between intimacy and solitude, conscious and unconscious experience, expression and privacy can help us to understand the importance of hope as a source of influence in all theories of therapeutic action.

My favorite visual image for thinking about the analytic space and modes of influence between analyst and patient is of the more abstract work of Richard Diebenkorn. A painter of seemingly infinite space, like the Pacific Ocean and desert, Diebenkorn often used formations that resemble rectangles and colors that relate across shapes. There are distinct and overlapping, fusing colors. There is fugitive coloring. The shapes look solid at times and illusory at others, depending on whether we wish to distinguish by shape, color, light, or size. In psychoanalysis, the rectangles involve time in a number of ways. There are definable aspects of time, as agreed on by patient and analyst; yet time is a focus of subjective experience. Each session and each analysis begins and ends—sort of. What seems like the ending of a session or a theme may be the beginning of some new experience or piece of work. These rectangles or boxes also can signify the conscious and unconscious experience and representation of different people—patient and analyst and various people in the patient's experiential world. The notion of mutual influence is ubiquitous, as is the fact that analyst and patient have distinct lives and roles, which are also evoked for me in Diebenkorn's shapes. His inanimate shapes seem to be always in motion, interacting and influencing one another. It is sometimes hard to know where an idea, a color, or a shape begins. The shoreline and the horizon are always changing and interchanging. These shifting reference points are a little like Gadamer's (1976) notion that the historical movement of life consists in the fact that it is never absolutely bound to any one standpoint and therefore can never have a truly "closed horizon". The horizon is something into which we move and that moves with us.

INTIMACY AND SOLITUDE IN THE ANALYTIC SITUATION

At its best, psychoanalytic therapy actively deals with a tension between intimacy and solitude. Solitude resides in many aspects of the therapeutic situation, including asymmetry and mutuality, expressiveness, restraint, and containment. Intimacy and solitude cannot be likened to any one side of these dialectics. Yet our literature is replete with implicit and explicit attempts to liken the analyst's expressiveness to mutuality and the patient's "free association" with solitude (see Burke, 1992, for an example of this equation within the relational literature and Adler and Bachant, 1996, from a contemporary classical perspective). The experience of the body is compared to the realm of solitude, which is often considered synonymous with the domain of the unconscious. The analyst's expressiveness, particularly disclosure, is sometimes facilely represented as the analyst's seeking "egalitarianism." I have seen no evidence to suggest that unconscious meaning and body experience cannot be revealed and learned through a variety of interactions that occur in analysis, including many periods in which it is exclusively the patient who is associating as well as when active exchanges involve both the patient's and the analyst's associations. Affects, states of mind, and meaning are revealed and constructed in a variety of ways and types of interactions.

In other words, free association is a type of interaction. The analyst does many things to facilitate a situation in which the patient takes risks to say things in less formulated ways than is customary in conventional speech. This is not to say that there are not many times that the analyst needs to spend considerable time listening and allowing a patient to feel himself, to feel his body or a state of mind without the analyst directly speaking. But, again, this is a particular kind of interaction that allows for the deepening awareness of conscious and unconscious experience.

Experience is both separate and shared by analyst and patient, just as it is between artist and observer. Merleau-Ponty (1964) felicitously asked about the nature of aesthetic experience: "Where is the painting?" Analysts try to appreciate the paradox that solitude is more enjoyable if sometimes you have someone with whom to share it. The other side of that paradox was stated by Thoreau who said, "I have a great deal of company in my house, especially in the morning when nobody calls." Intimacy and solitude, then, exist with and are partly defined by one another. As Bion understood so well, very few things can be more intimate than sharing aspects of solitude. In one way, the body is the ultimate form of solitude, where one person begins and ends in relation to another—appetites, emotions, sexuality, excitement, malfunction, disease, death. The body is vehicle for intimacy and sharing with another and yet provides the ultimate form of solitude in death. Orgasm always occurs at the intersection of intimacy and solitude, mutuality and separateness, as it is experienced by oneself with another and as it ends.

Many analysts have written about loss and solitude and its relation to being with another person. Fairbairn's (1952) shift from Freud's emphasis on anxiety and guilt to the problems of early and later stages of dependence began the investigation of schizoid phenomena and defensively held isolation. Fairbairn's (1952) summary of the schizoidal dilemma as the fear that love will destroy is a pithy description of some of the ways that intimacy and solitude are always working together in our psychic life. Both Guntrip's (1971) elaboration of the schizoid citadel and Modell's (1975) elucidation of defensive self-sufficiency continued to elaborate on one's dread of need, vulnerability, and dependence. For such patients, the experience of dependence is anathema, and various kinds of self-insulated, solipsistic psychic bubbles develop to protect against the experience of the object. Analysis seeks to challenge the defensively isolated and insulated positions that patients have established so that they might experience a deeper sense of solitude and loss. In other words, if defensive self-sufficiency is challenged in a good-enough way, then a process of grieving can occur. One of the analyst's most daring and thus most intimate acts is finding ways to challenge this self-sufficiency. Yet finding these ways requires a deep appreciation of why patients seek refuge at almost any cost.

Winnicott (1958) defined the capacity to be alone as one of the most important aspects of health and creativity. He described this as a capacity to be alone in the presence of another. This is the capacity for two people to have an inner life, a fantasy life, an orgasm, and to be able to deeply appreciate this experience in another person, perhaps a loved one. He had a deep appreciation of the generative tension between privacy and interpersonal relatedness. He put it this way: "Although healthy persons communicate and enjoy communicating, the other fact is equally true, that each individual is an isolate, permanently non-communicating, permanently unknown, in fact, unfound. At the center of each person is an incommunicado element, and this is sacred and most worthy of preservation" (p. 33).

But, for Winnicott, aloneness is also dreaded during development because in its earliest form it symbolizes and evokes the experience of loss of symbiosis. While much contemporary infant research (e.g., D. N. Stern, 1985; Beebe and Lachmann, 1988) rejects both Freudian and Kleinian perspectives on symbiosis, Winnicott (1958) made the infant's loss of symbiosis a vital part of his theory. The transitional object is what helps mitigate separation anxiety as symbiosis is lost by allowing the infant to dose himself with the omnipotently held denial of that psychic reality. It is only with repeated illusory experiences of omnipotent control that the child learns to appreciate the reality of solitude, not to speak of the capacity to enjoy it. Here, I use the term solitude as Winnnicott (1958) did, to imply, paradoxically, the capacity to be aware of another's presence outside the self.

One of the most moving poetics of the analytic space lies in Bion's (1962) poignant summary, "We're both in this alone." This statement somehow captures the notion that I will try to understand your experience. I will even dare to try to explain why it is there, where it might come from, or how it protects against other aspects of experience. I will even dare, at times, to see if it can be modified. To do so, the contents of your mind and experience are going to get into me in all kinds of ways that we will try to make sense of. But you are alone and I am alone.

American relational theory has added a number of other crucial dimensions that were not a part of Bion's statement. These dimensions revolve around aspects of reciprocal influence that express conscious and unconscious phenomena and are elucidated through interactional tensions. Bion's statement is not about the interpersonalization of the patient's mind. It is instead about the analyst's efforts to accompany and witness the unfolding of the patient's essentially solitary associative experience.

For me, this idea, Bion's notion of the intimacy of solitude, is captured in an exquisite way, again and again in the poetry of Rilke. Here is a brief example in the short poem *For Hans Carossa*, especially as Rilke (1922) describes loss in the first lines:

Losing too is still *ours;* and even forgetting
still has a shape in the kingdom of transformation.
When something's let go of, it circles; and though we are
    rarely the center
of the circle, it draws around us its unbroken, marvelous curve.

This circle, with transformations of loss, is a way to think about the therapeutic process. It was described by Russell (1979) as a "spiraling staircase." Rilke is fascinated by the enormous intimacy of shared or mutual loss. In fact, for Rilke, love itself is partly defined by the capacity to understand the solitude of an other and in an other. In *Letters to a Young Poet* (1929) he put it like this: "And this more human love (which will consummate itself infinitely thoughtfully and gently, and well and clearly in binding and loosing) will be something like that which we are preparing with struggle and toil, the love which consists in the mutual guarding, bordering and saluting of two solitudes" (p. 73).

With every interpretation we analysts put forward, we are probing and pushing certain boundaries, and we are also protecting and hopefully respecting another's solitude. In a letter to a friend, Rilke (1922) wrote, "I hold this to be the highest task for a bond between two people: that each protects the solitude of the other" (p. 163). Again, in terms of method, the analyst paradoxically asks a patient to say a great deal that comes to mind and yet it is essential for the patient to know he is free to be silent or to speak. Ogden (1996) stated that "to privilege speaking over silence, disclosure over privacy, communicating over not-communicating" (p. 885) can violate both the patient's and the analyst's need for privacy. It is why, for example, Ogden objects to the fundamental rule of asking patients to say what comes to mind. He feels that both the analyst's and the patient's needs for privacy are a necessary part of any therapy, but, even more important, of any human contract. In my view, the privileging of speaking over silence can sometimes mean losing a grip on the tension between intimacy and solitude and the power of the analytic situation. It would be a little like a painter not using space. In an essay on silence, Reik (1928) quoted Beethoven as saying that the "most important thing in music is not in the musical notes."

Similarly, Wolff-Bernstein (personal communication) has suggested the importance of white spaces in Cézanne's watercolors for understanding the evocative potential of shape and color. Indeed, the artist is also holding this tension between communicating things that are incommunicado and holding inside things that may be inaccessible, consciously or unconsciously, even to himself or herself. The artist is like the patient and the therapist: for all three it is important to be able to allude to this private or inaccessible part, to try to communicate what is incommunicable in human experience. Reik (1928) wrote in the essay cited earlier that in analysis it is much more important to see what remains unspoken in language and to look for what is expressed in silence at the same time.

FREE ASSOCIATION AND THE TENSIONS
BETWEEN INTIMACY AND SOLITUDE

Whereas Ogden (1996) makes it clear that, for him, the invitation to say what comes to mind violates the essence of the analytic process—the capacity for both patient and analyst to develop and cultivate a sense of reverie—I do not believe that the analyst's request that a patient *try* to tell him as much as he can, even when he feels reluctant to do so, necessarily implies a disrespect for his patient's or his own need for privacy and reverie. Patients might have many different responses to that invitation, including an enormous sense of excitement or relief at the prospect. For many patients, this request does not threaten their conviction that their privacy can be maintained. Asking someone to do something in analysis does not mean anything until we find out what it means to the patient. Analysis remains dependent on speech—it is both a strength and a definite liability of the method.

Most important is how highly the analyst values the patient's saying what is on his mind. Anyone who deeply values and respects the patient's need for privacy, as well as his own, will convey this to the patient. But there is little question that the classical position, in which the mind is viewed in more monadic terms, relies on free association as a "technical requirement" (Adler and Bachant, 1996, p. 1024).

Many analysts have tried to capture the experience of both the patient's and the analyst's sense of solitude as it relates to the concepts of free association and neutrality. Adler and Bachant (1996) have stated, "Creating a situation that permits repressed imagery to *emerge* makes possible linkages to the body and bodily sensations that are often bypassed in approaches that give priority to the patient's subjective representation of relational experience" (p. 1024). Adler and Bachant repeatedly see the affective representation of relational experience as being at odds with the emergence of unconscious phenomena. In contrast, I see it is axiomatic that representation of relational experience expresses unconscious phenomena. Adler and Bachant tend to see interaction as a deterrent to free association and as a distraction from the elaboration of drive derivatives. Inderbitzen and Levy (1994) have also pointed out how external reality or perception can be used as a defense.

Kris (1982) has written extensively on free association and has influenced my work enormously. One of Kris's key contributions in his work on free association relates particularly to his methodological approach. He focuses on the patient's associations as providing a point of departure for the formulation of interpretations, an idea that has also been propounded by Gray (1990, 1994) and Busch (1993, 1995). Kris uses free association, especially the obstacles and points of derailment as an opportunity for exploration. This type of attention helps to alert analysts of all theoretical persuasions to listen for the nuances of shifts in affect, words, and, of course, dominant metaphors as a way of understanding aspects of defense.

In the following description, Kris (1982) emphasizes free association as a catalyst for the experience of solitude and the body:

> It is fundamental that the associations belong to the patient. They are derivatively a part of himself, especially of his body as they come to express feelings, needs and desires, and as they represent his self-image, symbolically. The analyst must take care not to dispossess the patient of them. They reflect not only the patient's investment in his body but his detachment from it as well. Where the patient can be helped to possess his associations more, by understanding more of his own meaning, he regains lost connections with his body and between constituent elements of his mind [pp. 4-5].

This is an elegant statement of the opportunity that analysis facilitates for reclaiming bodily experience. I agree with Kris that the analyst must help the patient to discover his own meaning, but usually that meaning is intertwined with all kinds of interactional tensions both with the analyst and, of course, within the representational world of the patient. The analyst should "take care not to dispossess the patient of his associations and experiences" as long as he does not take too much care. In other words, various kinds of interactions around constructed meaning, sometimes imposed by the analyst, are what allow the associations to make sense—that is, the associations are often coconstructed (e.g., Hoffman, 1991, 1992). Here-and-now experience, as well as more active interaction with the patient, is often deeply informative about the patient's bodily experience, state of mind, and new pieces of emerging unconscious material. Kris (1982) has in mind the need for the analyst to listen actively with an ear toward the unconscious. This view is compatible with the idea of actively interacting at times with the patient as well as the notion of paying considerable attention to how we inevitably enact various conflicts in the process of examining unfolding transference. Thus an interest in helping the patient feel connected to bodily and often unconscious experience and at the same time examining the complex aspects of interaction between patient and analyst are a vital part of analytic process. At times, the analyst has to listen to how the patient makes these connections for himself (or does not), while at other times the analyst may find that it is through a more active interest in the nature of interaction that he can better explore with his patient what these experiences are saying.

While analysts of varying theoretical persuasions may agree on the importance of patients experiencing and getting to know what their inner life is telling them, there is a great deal of variation of thought on whether or not mind can be described in strictly monadic terms. Mitchell (1997), who echoes much of Hoffman's (1991, 1992, 1994, 1996) work in the area of social constructivism, asks, "Is the mind uncovered or constructed?" (p. 19). Mitchell (1997) elaborates a kind of fundamental fallacy equating discernible processes "in the patient's mind" with neuropsychological events in the brain. For example, in the kind of reverie that analysis facilitates, associations are often shared by the dyad (Ogden, 1989, 1994, 1997, 1998). When my patients dream and begin to associate to the dreams, I usually associate too, and there is a way that the dreams become part of a shared intersubjective product (Ogden, 1996). Often in the literature (e.g., Adler and Bachant, 1996) the problem of whether the mind is uncovered or constructed is viewed in either/or terms. *In my view it is always both.*

Is free association by the patient the only method in analysis, the "technical requirement," or is free association but one important type of ritualized interaction that occurs between patient and analyst? This is not just a matter of semantics. Some patients' capacity to free associate or takes risks in speaking about unformulated experience (Stern, 1983) is facilitated by their lying down on a couch with relatively little input from the analyst for extended periods of time. Others in analysis need to hear from us a great deal, and we need to find out why, but more often than not through active engagement. One of the main problems of debates about these issues is that patients select their analysts the way they do. Analysts who are less interactive than others are not a magnet for patients who, for a variety of reasons, feel that they want an active engagement with their analysts so that they can take risks.

What makes these discussions so difficult is that they tend to leave out of the mix the particular ways that technical preferences are conveyed through personality and personal style. For example, an irrepressibly playful and engaging analyst who theoretically adheres to a classical position in many respects regarding technique (i.e., thinks of himself as a classical analyst while being unaware of all the ways he uses countertransference in imaginative and expressive ways) may be considerably more interactive than a somewhat inhibited or constricted analyst who subscribes to a more relational model.

I like the way that Phillips (1993) refers to free association as a way in which "the patient takes the risk of not knowing what he is going to say." This does not just happen de novo. Often that risk is taken by enacting all sorts of things. I sometimes think about someone's first attempt at parachuting out of an airplane and being reassured that someone is jumping with him. In analysis, the analyst often does not know he has been recruited to join in the patient's jumping until he is in midair and realizes it is time to pull the cord and begin trying to make sense (read: getting some control) of the situation. Many scary experiences incorporate the notion of falling. We fall silent. We fall in love. We fall for her. When something is beautiful or compelling, we think of it beyond falling—it is "drop dead" or "to die for." These expressions all convey the ways in which we give ourselves over to something.

Free association is anything but a free fall. It is a deeply interactive, interpersonal process partly because of the solitude that is stimulated by the asymmetrical arrangement, whether it be Stone's (1961) "mother of separation" (p. 86) or other background regressive experiences that have been stimulated. Taking the risk of not knowing what one will say is indeed to delve into the experience of solitude for both patient and analyst. Taking the risk of not knowing what one will say is also a deeply intimate experience, among the most intimate of any experiences *with another person.*

SOLITUDE, DEVELOPMENTAL CONTEXT, AND THE NATURE OF LIMITS IN PSYCHOANALYSIS

Stone's (1961) attempt to describe in broad and powerful strokes the "psychoanalytic situation" was replete with allusions to the kind of solitude that is evoked in analysis. Stone used the phrase "intimate separation" to describe how the analytic situation stimulates early longings for the gratification of the mother-child relationship. Adler and Bachant (1996) suggest that "the patient's relative physical and emotional deprivation in analysis, bridged only by verbal bonds of speech, inevitably links the analyst to the 'mother of separation'" (p. 1027). From this perspective, analysis both evokes these experiences of early separation and helps with the "taming of solitude" (Quinodoz, 1993, 1996). What is so striking to me in reading both Stone's and Adler and Bachant's conceptualizations is that their descriptions are not universally relevant to the experiences of many patients in analysis. These formulations leave out or minimize the constructed nature of emotional resonance for the patient. As I explore in depth later in the book, they also describe regression in a unidimensional way, leaving out not only the analyst's constructions around regression, but also some of the ways that new and old experience are invariably intertwined. Furthermore, their descriptions fail to account for aspects of mutual regression described by both Aron and Bushra (1998) and Coen (in press).

Another American analyst, Robert Caper (1992), who has been heavily influenced by Melanie Klein and Bion, has written extensively about the analyst and limits. I believe that this work is part of the tradition of appreciating the importance of solitude and the capacity to bear loss that psychoanalysis can engender. Caper (1994) emphasizes the importance of the analyst's always preserving the patient's experience of isolation and responsibility for what brought him into analysis, even within the context of the intimate analytic relationship. I would guess that his emphasis involves his own translation of Bion's (1962) words, "We're both in this alone." Phillips (1993) has also restated Bion's words in his typically pithy way: "Is it not, after all, the case that the patient comes to analysis to reconstitute his solitude through the other, the solitude that only he can know?" (p. 41).

To me American relationally oriented analysts are no less interested in the experience of solitude in analytic work, but there are some very interesting questions to consider. For example, social-constructivists (Hoffman, 1991) and most American relational analysts identify analyst and patient as cocreators within the analytic process. While American relationally oriented analysts also attempt to help patients take responsibility for their conflicts and their own centers of subjectivity, including disavowed affects that the analysts may be keying into over time, we are also devoted to the notion that, as participant-observers, we learn about our patients' conscious and unconscious processes through our own experience. Hoffman (1996) noted:

> Stated succinctly, and summarizing the movement from the beginning until now, we have traversed the distance from analysis as solitary reflection to analysis as relational struggle. In the latter, against the backdrop of the ritualized asymmetry of the psychoanalytic situation from which draw special moral power, we participate as intimate partners with our patients as they wrestle with conflict and as they choose from among, and struggle to realize, their multiple potentials for intimacy and autonomy, for identification and individuality, for work and play, and for continuity and change [p. 133].

To state a question overly simplistically, Does a patient whose analyst conceptualizes conscious and unconscious mental processes through a "process of interpretive construction" (Mitchell, 1997, p. 217) feel separate from the analyst in a different way than he would from a classically oriented analyst who interpreted the patient's affect as a largely intrapsychic event? One would think so. Does the patient's experience of an analyst using countertransference in a more expressive and at times active way change the experience of solitude? Hoffman (1996) seems to raise these questions: "The asymmetry makes our participation in the spirit of mutuality matter to our patients in an intensified way, one that helps to build or construct our patients' view of themselves as creative agents and as persons ultimately deserving of love" (p. 121).

While I agree with Hoffman's description generally, I think that patients' experiences of the tensions between our positions of asymmetry and mutuality are quite complex and varied. Hoffman's description seems to be a kind of summary of what he sees as an end point of analytic process. Along the way, mutuality and asymmetry resonate in all kinds of interesting ways, through fantasy and memory, with other important objects in the patient's life.

If we think in Kleinian terms about the symbolic value of interpretation as a mode of intervening, how is the act of using countertransference expressively symbolized for the patient? Is it a breast that is given? Is it a breast that is taken away? Is it forced? Is it given lovingly? These are questions that I am constantly struggling to answer for myself in my clinical work. It is an area about which contemporary Kleinian and American relationally oriented analysts can richly collaborate (see e.g., Mitchell, 1995). While, of course, these meanings are always individually and uniquely meaningful for each patient, we also have to step back and think about our own modal experiences when we do analysis. Does one type of work, and the way one's particular style expresses a given technical stance, engender more experiential understanding of grief and mourning than another, or more about fears of dependency, closeness, and intimacy?

Caper's (1992) use of the term alone connotes the patient's intrapsychic structure, defense and conflicts in the context of an analytic enterprise that seeks to help the patient come into a new form of contact with inner experience and a new understanding of motivation. Bion's (1962) statement acknowledges the intimacy of the analytic situation, but "both" refers to each participant's being alone. Caper perceives his role as "simply to help the patient experience neglected aspects of himself and his objects as fully and accurately as possible" (p. 290). Caper's position is similar to Kris's (1982) that the analyst's job is to help the patient "possess his associations more, [and] by understanding more of his own meaning he regains lost connections with his body and between constituent elements of his mind" (pp. 4-5). For Caper, becoming a transference object implies that the analyst is what he terms "an external fantasy object." Interpersonally influenced approaches of all kinds emphasize that intrapsychic functioning can never be entirely disentangled from the relational and interpersonal context. Most important, interactional and relational patterns express some of these connections to one's body. Affect and representation are inextricably related both in development and in immediate engagement.

Another aspect of solitude in the analytic situation has to do with the patient's and the analyst's sense of limitation and therapeutic modesty. For Caper (1992), as was true for Klein and Bion, once again, this means that the analyst has to become an external fantasy object or transference object if the analysis is to proceed. Thus, when the patient projects his wishes for the analyst to be omnipotent, the analyst has to remain outside this fantasy by maintaining a realistic sense about the varieties of change or healing that can occur. Freud's (1912a) surgeon analogy—to dress the wound, not heal it—is aimed at establishing a therapeutic position for the analyst that maintains these distinctions. Bion (1959) noted that the analyst's abstinence produces what he called "the sense of isolation within an intimate relationship" (p. 73). This sense is a direct outcome of the analyst's awareness of his own limits. Quinodoz (1996) has similarly argued that, in his relationship with his analysand, the analyst must be able to tolerate a sense of solitude in the presence of someone else. Like Ogden (1994, 1996), Quinodoz argues that it is this capacity which, in turn, promotes the analyst's capacity for reverie.

I think it is universally true that the analyst has to respect the limits of his or her method and that responsibilities and choices are always in the hands of the patient. Most analysts would agree that rarely a day goes by when they are not reminded of the limitations of their method. In some ways British relational theory has probably been especially oriented toward the analyst's limitations and the need for both participants to bear, grieve, and mourn affect states related to these limitations. Sandler and Sandler (1994) have written movingly and in a challenging way about the reluctance many analysts have in accepting the limitations of their work and how it is worth appreciating the degree to which this reluctance may be operant in analyses as they seem to get longer and longer. Again, in the stereotypes of comparative analysis, I think that American relational theory has in a way been more ambitious than other approaches about what we can do. Part of the history of analyst disclosure has revolved around our trying to provide possibilities for change and movement at points of impasse or apparent stalemate. There are probably some ways in which the theme of heroism has played a part in American relational theory. I have been particularly interested in how to move the heroic into the routine and vice versa in theory development. For example, I think comparative psychoanalytic debate would be advanced by writers in the American relational tradition describing more routine or modal clinical moments and less about points of impasse. I would further suggest that sometimes the heroic motives of the analyst as he represents and tries to foster psychic possibility are no less a part of classical theory—they are just veiled within the demands of the blank screen and anonymity stance.

SOLITUDE AND SCHIZOID PHENOMENA:
THE INTIMACY OF REVENGE

The British relational model includes Fairbairn's emphasis on the schizoidal elements in each of us and Klein's delineation of mourning and the depressive position. British object relations theory has adopted the part of Winnicott's theory that focuses on problems of aloneness and solitude, whereas the American relational model has been more interested in Winnicott as a transitional theorist, beginning to move toward a conceptualization of the mother or analyst as subject rather than exclusively as object (Benjamin, 1988).

The other side of solitude as underscored in British object relations theory—the schizoidal defenses, colonization of bad objects as a way to fend off abandonment, the normal developmental process of obtaining and creating auxiliary objects to soothe anxiety in the context of infancy and early childhood—is the wish to recover from a lost or dashed opportunity for successful dependence, closeness, and intimacy. All schizoidal defenses, be they Guntrip's (1969) schizoid citadel or Modell's (1975) cocoon of self-sufficiency, reflect a reverberating cycle of the wish for dependence and intimacy and a sense of loss and failed dependency leading to one or another version of "psychic retreat" (Steiner, 1993). In this sense, intimacy and solitude are part of a spiraling psychic edifice, representational and interactional, though probably more like a mobile edifice or home, as we experience one or the other side of dependence and aloneness.

British and American authors alike have written extensively about schizoidal experience. The British approach, chiefly the work of Fairbairn (1952) and Guntrip (1969), has elaborated the patient's reliance on the world of inner objects and retreat from outer objects. Guntrip's term (1969), the schizoid citadel and, more recently, Steiner's (1993) notion of psychic retreat refer to the ways in which a patient is ensconced in "an area of relative peace and protection from strain when meaningful contact with the analyst is experienced as threatening" (p. 1). Bromberg (1998) has stated that, with schizoid patients the analytic situation risks being a dialogue about the patient rather than analysis of the patient (p. 58). Bromberg suggests that this state can take the form of free association being unconsciously used to perpetuate distance and reliance on the world of internal objects. Steiner (1993) suggests a similar problem: that some borderline and psychotic patients find a kind of habitual residence in retreat within analysis. Analysts within both traditions describe a clinical process that needs to focus on the patient's vicissitudes of avoidance and retreat. Such avoidance can take the form of using free association to, in a sense, say nothing. Cold disengagement, feelings of superiority, quietness and deadness in the material, and the use of fantasy to replace discussing actual daily life all reflect ways that such patients cling to the schizoid citadel.

In Steiner's (1993, 1996) approach, the analyst pays close attention to the patient's retreats from various aspects of external analytic events that symbolize for the patient the threat of an external reality outside the patient's internal world. The British models usually focus on the analyst's ability to survive the patient's "destruction" (Winnicott, 1969). This destruction refers to the patient's dread of external objects to the extent that they threaten the safety of a defensively insular internal object world. Steiner (1996) has also shown how much psychic retreats can be based on resentment and grievance, another form of destructiveness. This resentment can often lead to impasses in treatment that Steiner is quick to suggest are extremely refractory to change.In a moment of great candor and courage, Steiner (1996) writes:

> I am ashamed to admit that I could not find satisfactory clinical material of an instance where a resentful impasse can soften to allow a successful move towards a depressive solution of the "Oedipal" conflict and this is why I turn to literature for an example. Nevertheless, I believe these instances are clinically real and important although very difficult to describe. Often they are fleeting and both patient and analyst may come to doubt whether they are genuine. Sometimes after a more than usually virulent attack the patient may notice that I look tired or even unwell. A recognition that I am considerably older than the patient has realized has produced another shift that has led to a lessening of resentment and envy.

> These moments often follow periods of intense hatred in which the analyst has been cruelly attacked. If the attacks can be tolerated and properly analyzed rather than condemned, resentment can give way to remorse and a move towards reparation can begin.

Often this takes the form of forgiveness both on the part of the patient for the analyst's faults and shortcomings and on the part of the analyst, who must share this process and give the patient the sense that psychic reality does not have the moralistic unforgiving quality that it so often acquires. In the same way an open attack by the patient may enable to analyst to escape from a paralysis of guilt and defend himself more vigorously. The may in turn enable him to feel regret and guilt, allowing him to climb down and initiate a more forgiving atmosphere [p. 438].

Steiner is talking about the importance of the analyst's surviving the patient's destruction, but he is also suggesting some of the very important, sometimes subtle, sometimes not so subtle ways that patient and analyst get to know each other in these demanding circumstances. It seems to me that Steiner is moving toward elements of analyst-expressiveness within this paper without necessarily feeling comfortable or having the theoretical scaffolding to support his clinical descriptions. It is probably safe to say that countertransference expressiveness in contemporary Kleinian analysis is more limited and less specific in clinical situations dealing with both hostile and erotic countertransference reactions than is the case for analysts working within American relational models. Steiner is also quite sensitive, as he should be, to the possibility that an analyst, by making some of his countertransference known to the patient, can make the patient feel guilty about expressing destructiveness, revenge, or envy. On the other hand, I have been struck in reading some of the contemporary Kleinian literature (e.g., Steiner, 1996; Spillius, 1999) that there are points of transference-countertransference impasse in which the patient may very likely have a pretty good read on the analyst's struggle anyway. In such instances, it may be helpful for the patient and analyst to discuss what is going on between the two in more direct terms in trying to understand what is being enacted.

Steiner's contributions to understanding the important role that revenge plays in both oedipal and schizoidal conflicts remind me of several patients with whom I've worked, some under routine and others under heroic analytic circumstances. More specifically, when severe hatred of parents and others is a feature, revenge can play such a large role in personality that the analyst has to work hard to make the analytic experience "real." In other words, prior to the analyst's surviving the patient's destructiveness, the analyst has to help the patient to move from an abstract expression and experience of hatred into more heartfelt states of vulnerability and need.

This work occurs more easily for some patients than for others. Some of the most meaningful work I have done with such patients has involved the patients' gradual and natural movement from positions of quiet, isolated vengeance to the experiences of sadness and need. One such patient was an unusually gifted man who loved and felt love by his parents, but from a distance, and who was somewhat unknown by them for his particular intellectual and emotional resources. Into his late forties he had spent most of his time in relationships feeling isolated and misunderstood by his girlfriends. In adolescence, he had felt relieved that his parents gave him so much room. He would often say: "I was relieved that they didn't want to know me too much. My friends had parents who were pushy and intrusive." Yet as analysis developed, he became more and more aware of how much he had tried to turn a sow's ear into a silk purse. His needs for autonomy which began to ossify in adolescence were pseudomature adaptations to earlier disappointments about feeling isolated and somewhat unseen. The more I saw him, the more he felt a sense of great sadness about the degree to which his quiet revenge toward his parents was unconsciously enacted with girlfriends. Again and again, he felt they would never be as interested as he in deep knowing. What he began to learn as he could experience his longings was the way in which this underlying and persistent motive created a huge distance between his girlfriends and him.

Another patient had constructed a self organized around a sense of what her older sisters and mother had wished for her. She was a highly successful woman who never felt that she could say what she wanted, only what her boyfriend or mother wished for her. While quite aggressive in her work, she struggled internally and externally with the use of sarcasm as a kind of compromise between her sense that she had to comply with the wishes of others and her anger toward them. With an earlier analyst, she had secretly invented dreams in order to see if the analyst would be able to detect their falseness or inauthenticity. When she began with me it was very difficult for her to see the complexity of meanings involved in this act of invention. I thought that, in part, it was an attempt to find an authentic self or a dream that could be hers without her mother's laying claim to it. On another level, her dream inventions expressed revenge and hostility. The act of invention expressed her hopelessness about whether someone could know her. She was loathe to let herself feel how much she wished to be known. We did a great deal of work together to discover if she could tolerate ambiguity in her affective states, something that was anathema for her. During sessions with the patient, I often associated to Edward Hopper's paintings of isolation and solitude (which often featured women alone in hotel rooms and apartments). My patient's appearance ensured that she was never without suitors, but her sense of isolation was becoming more apparent to her in the analytic work. She had become so used to being told what to do, that it seemed beyond her imagination to consider that something useful could result from giving herself time and room to experience her thoughts and feelings. The feeling of being alone became more accessible to her as she was able to tolerate not immediately doing what she thought someone wanted her to. Eventually the transference evolved in such a way that she experienced me as a mother who wanted her to do things. She was, of course, right—I did have an agenda of growth and understanding, tolerance of affect, and the like. During the most vivid and painful points of transference, it felt to her as though her goal (to feel free of others' demands and directions) was incompatible with my goals for her related to working through these conflicts much as Spillius (1999) has described.

Sometimes the kinds of movement I am describing involve more than helping someone to feel sadness lurking beneath rage. For some patients, an important aspect of defensive self-sufficiency (Modell, 1975) or "talking about" things (Bromberg, 1998) takes the form of keeping abstract everything in psychic life. In these circumstances, the analyst can sometimes usefully express aspects of countertransference that help inform the patient of disavowed experience.

Thomas, with whom I worked in analysis for many years, said "my only hope is to be an asshole." He sought to avenge his mother's alternating seductiveness and abandonment. She was quite rejecting and critical of the patient's father in ways that both excited and frightened my patient. Thomas felt his oedipal conflicts in a concrete rather than symbolized way, not unlike what Rothstein (1979) described in a paper dealing with oedipal conflicts in narcissistically disturbed men. In these cases, a boy's oedipal wishes are made more real and terrifying by dint of the father's inability to set limits or establish the "universal law" (Chasseguet-Smirgel, 1983). His analysis had become what he termed "anal-ysis"—an attempt to reduce and depersonify both of us into parts, into assholes, as a way to avoid the terror and rage he felt at the hands of his parents. Shengold (1985) has described vividly a number of such men in his analytic work.

It took me a regrettably long time to trust the sense I had with Thomas that there was something unreal, overly dramatic, "about"-like in his prolific and dramatic free associations. For a long time I made interpretations about the nature of Thomas's preoccupation with anal phenomena and his hatred toward any of his many girlfriends who could have orgasms when he wouldn't allow himself to have one. What I neglected too much, however, was the as-if quality to Thomas's relating to me. While he was trying to seduce me and disarm me, thereby enacting his mother's role with him, what was more important was the way in which he attempted to encapsulate himself, solipsistically within his associative bubble, much like Volkan (1973) described. Volkan suggested that for some narcissistically disturbed individuals, free association itself can be used as a kind of transitional object to provide a solipsistic realm within which the patient can dwell.

I have found that a degree of countertransference-expressiveness in this work is essential for the analysis to become viable. The interpretive action in operation in my countertransference expressiveness with Thomas involved trying to take up his defensive depersonification of himself and me in our analytic work.

Relationally oriented analysts in the United States sometimes make a directly expressive attempt to analyze this form of resistance, albeit honoring and respecting the patient's defensive insulation and self-sufficiency, while gradually trying to create with the patient an analytic reality that lies outside the patient's internal world. In the United States, the attempt to interpret and analyze these sources of resistance is what differentiates such analysts as Bromberg (1998) and Mitchell (1992) from Trop and Stolorow's (1992) approach to the analysis of schizoidal and highly narcissistic patients. Trop and Stolorow feel that interpreting these defenses as sources of resistance will deter the progress of the analysis and possibly even catalyze the patient's further retreat. Interestingly, the active use of interpreting schizoidal defenses is also sometimes compatible with classical analytic approaches (Richards, 1994). In a fascinating discussion of a highly narcissistic person analyzed by Trop and Stolorow (1992), Richards (1992) and Mitchell (1992) each took a more active approach to the analysis of resistance. Richards and Mitchell agreed that a point of interpretive focus might be on the patient's unconscious identification with aggressive objects, but they disagreed on how to understand and voice these understandings. Richards suggested taking up these identifications as a kind of disavowed aspect of the patient's experience, whereas Mitchell pointed to particular aspects of interactional tension between the patient and analyst which reflected some of these identifications.

Some of these differences in approach to the treatment of schizoidal patients relate to a few points of misunderstanding about American relational theory and the ways it deals with tensions between intimacy and solitude as well as between mutuality and asymmetry. I refer to these misunderstandings as the "fallacy of intimacy in American relational theory." One misunderstanding is the notion that an interest in mutuality and reciprocal influence means that there is some sort of superficial attempt at establishing an "egalitarian" atmosphere in the analytic situation. The term egalitarian is often used as a blanket dismissal of a more complex view of therapeutic action, much as Mitchell (1997) has described the dismissive use of "corrective emotional experience." I describe this characterization as superficial because there is a conflation and blurring of two distinct levels of theoretical discourse. At one level, the mind is conceptualized as something other than the distinct, closed system hypothesized in Freudian theory. The other is the clinical level of relating to a patient. *A belief in reciprocal influence and the value of constructed meaning need not necessitate a belief in the dissolution of aspects of separateness, distinctiveness, and asymmetry between patient and analyst.* The analyst and patient are not equidistant from the patient's conflicts (Schafer, 1983), no matter how much we believe in intersubjective influence.

Another point of confusion has to do with conflating the importance that American relational models place on the active and expressive use of countertransference with another kind of naive translation of self-revelation for the purposes of, once again, establishing egalitarianism. For a moment I will take a closer look at each of these problems and areas of confusion.

THE FALLACY OF INTIMACY IN COUNTERTRANSFERENCE EXPRESSIVENESS

Among the most critical stereotypes of relational approaches in the United States is that there is too much emphasis on a kind of superficial intimacy created by the loss of asymmetry. The argument goes that egalitarianism is the underlying motive behind countertransference expressiveness, rather than providing an additional inroad into understanding and illuminating disavowed affect and unconscious experience. Interaction is juxtaposed against an interest in the unconscious dimension of experience. From a Lacanian perspective, it might be expressed with no small degree of concern or criticism that the American relational approach sometimes focuses more on the Imaginary than on the Symbolic.

The issue of disclosure is worth examining briefly in relation to some facile equations between relational theory and intimacy or egalitarianism because in some ways it crystalizes the most dramatic aspects of the analyst's countertransference expressiveness but also, as I try to illustrate later in the book, constraint. Despite the fact that the subjectivity and personal engagement of the analyst are at the heart of the technical use of disclosure, I believe (Cooper, 1998a, b) that there is value in thinking of our disclosures as analyst based ("analyst's direct disclosure") rather than the commonly used term "self-disclosure." I suggest this distinction because the subjectivity of the analyst is central to all kinds of interpretive processes in analytic work. Despite the fact that, superficially, disclosure appears to be more "self"-revealing, I do not think that it is any more expressive of the analyst's "self" than is any other kind of analytic intervention or interpretation; instead it is expressive differently from some other kinds of interpretation. Disclosure is intended to be more directly expressive only of the analyst's construction of experience, often "unformulated experience" (Stern, 1983) at a particular moment in treatment. It is no more or no less compelled by unconscious factors than is any other kind of intervention. To be sure, the analyst's direct disclosures may catch more of the patient's and theorist's attention, particularly within a climate of a particular mode of analysis and historical biases in our theory in which intentional disclosures have been used more sparingly.

The term self-disclosure developed as a byproduct of the need for psychoanalytic theory and technique to find a way for the subjectivity of the analyst to break through the historical constraints of an analytic stance that had centered on the concepts of the blank screen and anonymity. Relational theorists observed the centrality of the analyst's subjectivity and needed a way to place this subjectivity into the equation. More particularly, relational theorists have emphasized the importance of understanding the patient's perceptions and experience of the analyst's subjectivity (Gill and Hoffman, 1982; Hoffman, 1983, 1991; Aron, 1991) and the analyst's sense of his or her own experience in coming to terms with mutual influence in the analytic situation. Yet any analyst who takes seriously the value, power, and limitations of analyst disclosure is operating well within the purview of any other intervention.

Thus, in my view, what distinguishes the subjectivity of the analyst in disclosure is *the analyst's conscious or deliberate attempt to reveal to the patient a construction of the self—either an aspect of his or her subjectivity or a "fact" (a piece of information about himself or herself)—so that something new can be explored or understood.* The aim of such an occasional intervention is not necessarily to establish mutuality or dissolve asymmetry, even though it can potentially be temporarily consciously experienced that way. Usually the aim of this type of intervention, like that of many others, is to create a form of psychic possibility that patient and analyst can try to explore. But, at times, disclosure can appear to have fewer secondary-process properties than interpretation does. When used judiciously however, disclosure, like many other kinds of interventions, is at the margin of what the analyst does and does not know about the patient and himself or herself. More often than has been appreciated, other kinds of interpretation also integrate unformulated experience and constructions of the analyst's experience. As is true of any intervention, part of this assessment involves considering the applicability of Gill's (1983) admonition that the analyst's subjectivity may be as defensive, and thus unconsciously held on his own part, as any other piece of data revealed by patient or analyst.

The purpose of any expressive use of countertransference is not to establish mutuality or reciprocity. Rather, its use grows out of conceptualizing unconscious processes as mutually influenced. Thus, there is value in using the analyst's experience as a resource in illuminating disavowed affect. I have come to believe that we have taken a rather concrete perspective about how disclosure relates to other interpretive processes. If we take Hoffman's (1991) paradigm seriously—that is, that every interpretation involves a construction of the analyst's and patient's participation—then disclosure is best regarded as an attempt to place a construction of the analyst's subjective participation more plainly in view than is the case for other kinds of interventions. If we take a Kleinian view as well, do we not have to find out how the patient, through his associations, experiences and expresses the symbolic meaning and value of all interventions? The use of the term self in self-disclosure minimizes the selectivity of the analyst in employing disclosure and approaches the subjectivity of the analyst as a concrete entity rather than as something the patient will have all kinds of fantasies and experiences about during the analytic process. In later chapters I examine in much more detail why and how it is that the subjectivity of the analyst, as it is applied in analytic work, is usefully distinguished from the "self" concept.

Another misconception, criticism, or concern levied against relational models is that the analyst's interest in "authenticity" signifies a kind of superficial approach to interaction rather than an interest in unconscious process. It may seem contradictory to argue, on one hand, that the concepts of self and subjectivity of the analyst are distinct, though overlapping, domains and, on the other, that the analyst's authenticity is vital to the analytic process, as I suggest. Yet I maintain that authenticity and the concept of self are not synonymous, just as the analyst's self and subjectivity are not synonymous (Cooper, 1998b). Consider instances when the analyst shares a piece of countertransference experience as what Racker (1968) referred to as a concordant identification. In other words, the analyst might suggest to a patient who is repeatedly late that perhaps he fears exploring how much he dreads the analyst's keeping him waiting or making him feel abandoned. Part of why these situations can be so potent for patients may be that they feel our authentic involvement just as they perceive that there may be something insightful about the interpretation or query. I would say, however, that these examples call upon the analysts' ability to use themselves in the context of interpretive work. We do not know in advance what an analyst might feel about a patient's being late. He might feel hurt or relieved, angry or gratified, or many of these feelings simultaneously. But we do know how he is using his experience both in the present and how he has come to understand the representational world of the patient.

I believe that analytic authenticity is embedded in all interpretive activities as a precondition of interpretation. My definition of authenticity overlaps a great deal with Renik's (1995) description of an effort to communicate everything that in the analyst's view will help the patient understand what the analyst thinks about what the patient is saying and where the analyst is trying to go with the patient. I would, however, underscore the caveat that the analyst's attempt to communicate what in his or her view will help the patient is *always a construction*. A part of the analyst's construction is the possibility that he may be surprised by what he finds out about himself or herself in the process of reflection and interaction (Hoffman, 1991). This surprise is also a part of interpretive or exploratory efforts to learn about the patient's experience of the analyst's subjectivity and is embedded in, and central to, any definition of the analyst's authenticity. At the same time, through each formulation and interpretation, the analyst is always consciously and unconsciously directing where the patient might go, whether or not the analyst likes this directional power.

A capacity for surprise and spontaneity is also applicable to what Hoffman (1994) has usefully described as the dialectical tension between the analyst's authority and personal expressiveness. He suggests that there is no "book" that can be prescribed regarding this equation. Rather, he surmises that the analyst's struggle to learn about both the patient's and the analyst's participation makes for an "overarchingly authentic engagement with the patient" (p. 193).

Mitchell's (1995, 1997) recent attempt to compare and reconcile the technical contributions of interpersonalists and Kleinians has important implications for understanding the analyst's authenticity and its relation to intimacy and solitude. He suggests that interpersonalists are more likely than others to feel free using aspects of personal expressiveness, such as immediate affective reactions and, at times, disclosure. While he is positively disposed toward the spontaneity and freedom that the interpersonal model affords the analyst, he is also in agreement with the Kleinian analysts' attempt to contain countertransference in order to understand and process affect. Mitchell warns that Kleinian analysts are often sensitive to the pitfalls of immediately interpreting or commenting on a disavowed affect through projective identification, which can have the effect of overwhelming the patient and causing further disowning of disavowed affects. Mitchell suggests that "authenticity in the analyst has less to do with saying everything than in the genuineness of what actually is said" (p. 146).

I find Mitchell's emphasis on the tension between expressiveness and spontaneity, on one hand, and the need to contain particular affects for affective processing, on the other, important because it moves toward a supple, practical, and useful definition of analytic authenticity. I also agree with Aron (1996) that the concept of genuineness is as difficult to determine as is authenticity. In my view, one of the problems is that genuineness and authenticity are concepts that can be only *partially* elucidated by describing the analyst's position—the patient's experience of the analyst is a part of what defines authenticity or genuineness. Furthermore, the attempt to be genuine can obviously be as infiltrated with defensiveness on the analyst's part as can more overt attempts to foreclose exploration of the patient's experience. Along these lines, Mitchell (1993) states: "Honesty, truth, openness, and genuineness are always highly ambiguous. Subjectivity is not a simple or singular essence like 'true self'" (p. 31).

Thus, sometimes misconceptions of American relational theory highlight the analyst's authenticity as an overriding need from the analyst pressuring or biasing the interaction. Authenticity is something defined by the analyst, the patient, and the dialogue between the two. It is, in part, an intersubjective process, not an outcome of the analytic situation.

A related concern is that there will, in the American relational model, be a minimization of or impingement on the patient's potential space within the analytic situation. The preservation of potential space may be thought of as providing the opportunity to explore and experience elements of solitude. Classical analysts would value potential space as a location for the experience of solitude. For example, Adler and Bachant (1996) fear that a two-person psychology might mean a "two-person neurosis." Within this concern is the notion that an analyst who sees the mind as generated in the context of reciprocal influence, and thus partly informed by his countertransference, will expect the patient to help him out with his own neurosis.

I place a great deal of importance on preserving potential space so that both patient and analyst can feel and work. Potential space can be determined only through the experiences of patient and analyst. At a more experience-distant level, it is a mighty difficult concept to get a handle on. Mathematicians apply the term "surreal number" to that category of number which has no "real" computational value. For example, the number, "infinity squared," lies within the realm of the conceptual rather than being a number to which we can ever assign computational value. It has struck me that the concept of potential space within the analytic situation bears some similarity to the concept of a surreal number. This in no way mitigates the value of the concept in understanding the analytic situation, and especially the impact of both the variety and timing of our interventions. It does, however, require that we think even further about how this concept can be made as functional as possible.

The attempt to maintain the potential space of the analytic situation is what many analysts commonly hold as a value or ideal in pursuing analytic work. In the rich dialogue that ensued between Davies (1994) and Benjamin (1994), and Gabbard (1994), and more recently in a dialogue between Davies (1998), Hoffman (1998b), Gabbard (1998), and me (Cooper, 1998b) regarding the analyst's disclosure, a central point of discussion involved the concept of potential space. When do the analyst's disclosures or other interpretations open up the observational field? When do they seem to foreclose pathways for exploration or experience of affect and ideation? When do disclosures interfere with the development of transference or help in the understanding of what has already developed? From a contemporary American ego psychology perspective (Inderbitzen and Levy, 1994) when do various kinds of interventions "distract" from the emergence of drives and their derivatives?

Most examples of interpretation, including expressive uses of countertransference, point to how various sound bites from an analysis make it difficult to evaluate when potential space has been expanded or constricted. It is often only by assessing an analysis over a period of time that we can know how an intervention has expanded or foreclosed the potential space of the analytic situation. Just as it is also difficult to isolate the effect of an analyst's intervention from that of the amalgam of technical procedures used by the analyst, potential space is a process that, except in frank enactments of boundary violations, is not usually a discrete phenomenon or a clinical moment that can be easily isolated.

Renik's (1995) numerous illustrations of varieties of disclosure sometimes reveal instances when he decided to share with a patient some of his perceptions of himself that were different from those attributed to him by the patient. While it could be argued that this form of disclosure might constrain aspects of potential space by minimizing the patient's perceptual and psychic reality, it could also be argued that these interventions open up pathways of association previously unavailable to the patient. Again, it is part of the analyst's job to assess the impact of an intervention on the patient and the overall progress of the analysis. Has the analyst opened up new modes of inquiry and negotiation or unwittingly (or wittingly) imposed a unilaterally defined truth?

There are obvious kinds of impingements on potential space that we can (should) recognize as such, for example, ethical violations between analyst and patient such as sexual abuse (see Celenza, 1998, for a review). However, as Renik (1996) has pointed out, we are on thin ethical ice if our main considerations related to obvious ethical violations involve the risk of impinging on the potential psychic space of the analytic situation. The ideal of analytic anonymity (Renik, 1995) is often the subtext for a readiness to view the analyst's interpretations involving expressive use of countertransference or disclosures as impinging on potential space within the analytic situation. I believe that thinking of the analyst's interpretations involving expressive use of the countertransference as not synonymous with self-disclosure, and as similar to a variety of other analytic interventions, perhaps provides a fair basis on which to evaluate this issue. I take it as a given that almost every transference or resistance interpretation risks impingement on potential space. Balint's (1968) admonitions about the hazards of consistent interpretation emphasized how interpretive style and theoretical predilections almost inevitably lead to forms of indoctrination, even though he singled out the Kleinian school in particular. If the analyst is willing to consider his or her impact on the patient, then the criteria for assessing the degree to which disclosure may impinge on potential space may be more easily evaluated. Thus, the surrealness of the concept of potential space does not preclude its utility in evaluating the efficacy of the analyst's disclosure. We are often on rather speculative ground, however, when we evaluate a clinical moment without extensive information about what both preceded and followed from the interventions.

Among the most complicated factors in assessing potential space is that many of our aims and the effects of our interventions do not fit neatly into one category or another. Potential space is experientially defined by both patient and analyst. For example, sometimes the analyst's interpretation will be experienced as an impingement and require analyzing a repetitive aspect of the patient's earlier experience that has led him to experience the intervention in this way. Sometimes the patient feels immediately that potential space has been negatively influenced and yet later comes to appreciate what has been learned. Naturally, this appreciation could involve the possibility that the patient has complied with a style of the analyst, but this is no more likely an outcome than with any other kind of interpretation. Or sometimes a patient may feel that the analyst's interpretation is helpful in expanding the potential space, and, over time, one or both of the participants may come to feel that they have become importantly derailed from the aims of analytic work.

Friedman (1988) and Mitchell (1993, 1997) have elaborated one of the central paradoxes at the heart of psychoanalytic treatment. The ritualized asymmetry of the analytic situation and the power invested in the analyst as a figure of social authority are important tools within the analytic process. The analyst uses this authority—indeed a large portion of the transference is comprised by this authority—in creating psychic possibility. Yet the analyst also attempts to analyze to as large an extent as possible the complexity and necessity of this hope for the patient as a form of adaptation in the past and present—the basis for psychic inevitability in the conscious and unconscious life of the patient. One of the most important outcomes of analysis is learning to live with the ways in which hopes are by their very affective nature both achievable and unachievable. The ability to create, resurrect, challenge, modify, and even renounce our hopes is as good as any other definition of health that I have come across.

There is another side of this paradox, a related paradox. The analyst also hopes for the patient, and yet his job is to analyze this influence. He is not only the recipient of the patient's hopes for the analysis and for him to provide something in all sorts of ways and at all sorts of levels. He also has a variety of needs and wishes for the patient, one being that something useful will come of the work. The analyst's needs for the patient contribute as a dimension of the mutuality of the analytic situation, but it is also an element of isolation or solitude. Patient and analyst share hopes, but there is inevitable and necessary conflict regarding hope, just as there is about desire, love and hate. Conflicts regarding hope involve disjunctions and differing expectations between analyst and patient as well as internal conflict. These conflicts create feelings of solitude, just as they are experienced as a part of the shared, intimate, affective structure that houses both patient and analyst within the analytic process.

3

OLD AND NEW OBJECTS IN FAIRBAIRNIAN AND AMERICAN RELATIONAL THEORY

I T IS USEFUL TO THINK about the nature of hope and influence in the analytic situation as related to the balance between the patient's experience of the analyst as an old and a new object. In this chapter I take up a few points of technique and theory related to specific conceptualizations of new and old objects and the implications for working in the analytic situation. These issues involve some interesting points of divergence and convergence between American relational theory and British object relations theory.

To its credit, American relational theory has asserted the importance of the analyst's emerging experientially as a new object, in contrast to the historically held object, through a variety of interventions, including interpretations of transference and defense, as well as expressive uses of the countertransference. Currently, there is tremendous variability within relational theory (Tansey and Burke, 1989; Mitchell, 1994; Stern, 1994) as to whether the patient looks for newness in the old or whether the search for newness emerges out of repetitive patterns with the old. These differences relate to a number of other important dimensions of the analytic process, such as theories of development and the value of regression. Nevertheless, relational theory holds that the patient is looking both to repeat old experience and to be exposed to new experience (Hirsch, 1994).

Much of the patient's experience of the analyst as old and new has more to do with the subtle nuances of the interaction between patient and analyst than with specific technical procedures on the part of the analyst. At times, the way the analyst emphasizes or constructs himself is closer to how the patient has experienced past objects and, at other times, closer to the contrast between the analyst's purpose, activity, or behavior and that of past objects or historically held transference. At still other times, the interaction points to something about who the patient or the dyad might become—a kind of anticipation of the patient's psychic future. Interestingly, as a regressive aspect of transference, who the dyad is becoming (or who the patient is becoming) may reflect old patterns of relationship. Some of the ways the analyst poses these constructions refers to modality of intervention (traditional interpretation, disclosure, inquiry) and some relate to a style of intervening seriousness, humor, play, schtich. In a sense, negotiation augments the patient's internal dialogue regarding these old and new experiences as well as to interaction between analyst and patient (Russell, 1985; Mitchell, 1988, 1991; Pizer, 1992).

The notion of the new object was introduced by Strachey (1934) to describe how the patient, having become aware of the lack of aggressiveness in the real external object (in contrast to the patient's archaic internalized fantasy objects), is able to introject a new, more benign object. Subsequently, the aggressiveness of the patient's superego is diminished. Strachey wrote that the analyst's newness consists of the detoxification of troublesome affects before being communicated back to the patient. Loewald (1960) similarly referred to the ways in which the analyst, through systematic analysis of the transference "distortions," is gradually experienced and observed as a helpful and therapeutic agent of change for the patient. For Loewald, the analyst is conceptualized as a new object to the extent that he or she offers the opportunity for rediscovering the early pathways and patterns of object relations, leading to "a new way of relating to objects and of being oneself" (p. 229). Newness includes the analyst's vision of the patient's future (Loewald, 1960), comes to represent psychic possibility, or both.

While a new object experience is a major focus for all contemporary relational theorists, there are diverse perspectives on how newness develops. For example, a positive new object experience may be facilitated by the analyst's monitoring and assessing the relative degrees of safety and danger in the patient's transferential experience (Greenberg, 1986) and elements of repetition that threaten stagnification or impasse.

Newness may also include the possibility that the analyst will make more of his subjectivity known to the patient so that a contrast may be established or developed between experiences of the analyst that at least correlate with historical experiences and those which provide or represent new and different relational experiences. In a sense, the patient cannot allow himself to trust that the new object is different from the old object.

Another form of newness emphasized in the American relational tradition occurs when the analyst acknowledges to the patient ways in which he or she behaved very much like the old object. Here, the analyst offers what may be a new opportunity for open mutual exchange and dialogue about such an occurrence (i.e., where the analyst engages in a repetition of a problematic old object experience).

Sometimes this newness is established less directly by drawing the patient's attention to his own revealed and concealed ideas and perceptions about the analyst's subjectivity (Aron, 1991, 1992). At other times, newness comes in the form of the analyst's expressing or disclosing aspects of psychic possibility that may catalyze new realms of experience of self and other. To some extent, any interpretation "virtually discloses" (Cooper, 1996a) some aspect of the analyst's view of psychic possibility.

In contrast to these various routes to potential newness portrayed by American relational theories, British object relations theory, particularly Fairbairn's work, has emphasized the attachment to old figures in order to control toxic affects and environmental failure. The old object, abandoning, persecutory, or exciting in nature, is internalized so that it can be controlled. To the extent that it is internalized and clung to as familiar, it is good because it brings with it safety and has adaptive value. The new object, in the form of the analyst, is bad or threatening, for it represents the unfamiliar. One aspect of interpretation in this context expresses the psychic possibility that the patient is capable of renouncing an old object experience or can transform it from a persecutory or hurtful one into something that can be grieved or mourned. The patient's resistance or reluctance can take the form of the patient either seeing the analyst as new object from the get-go, and being threatened by it, or clinging to a bedrock experience of the analyst as an old object despite surface rumblings of newness.

The question explored in recent developments in American relational theories partly involves how and why this new object is able to become less threatening so that the old object ties can somehow be relinquished or substantially mitigated. The patient's potential relational pathways have become constricted or collapsed into a one-lane road. The analyst is presenting to the patient a vision of how there can be or are many roads and connections. The patient sees or experiences that the relationship can be affectively colored in only one way. The analyst sees more than one color, though the colors sometimes seem faint or fleeting—fugitive coloring that quickly moves back into one color, the color of historically held transference.

Several authors have begun to delineate these differences between British object relations and American relational perspectives. Mitchell (1995, 1997) has usefully examined various modes of interaction between patient and analyst within British and American relational theory. He discusses, in particular, the analyst's processing and containing affect, as emphasized in contemporary Kleinian theory, in contrast to the analyst's personal expressiveness and participation within interpersonal and American relational theory. Interestingly, Steiner (1993), writing from a contemporary Kleinian perspective, has also discussed the value of the analyst's maintaining a certain tension between expressiveness and restraint within all interpretive processes. Each of these models differs in some ways from the "developmental tilt" models of Kohut and Winnicott (Mitchell, 1988, 1991, 1993), which highlight the need for the analyst to meet certain aspects of the patient's experience of impingement and deprivation.

As is so often true, looking at the analytic stance in a broad sense (i.e., expressiveness/containment/provision) necessitates looking more fully at a variety of central relational issues, such as the construction of new and old objects, safe and dangerous experiences, mutual and asymmetrical arrangements, all of which have many implications for understanding interaction. From a constructivist perspective, the construction of new and old, like "need and wish" (Mitchell, 1991) have to do with both the patient's and the analyst's experience. The work of Fairbairn (1952) and the recent developments in American relational models can assist in these complex constructions of affect and idea for the analytic dyad.

In a sense, in all our theoretical conceptualization we have a tendency to characterize what is new and old, mutual and asymmetrical, safe and dangerous more in terms of the analyst's intentions than through the amalgam of the analyst's and the patient's conscious and unconscious experience. For example, in the concluding section of his paper on therapeutic action, Strachey (1934) schematically attempted to characterize a variety of interventions by focusing on the analyst's intentions, without considering that any of these interventions may be experienced in any number of ways by the patient.

In more contemporary literature many authors have fallen into a similar pattern, describing the analyst's intentions as a way to characterize an intervention. For example, much of the recent literature on disclosure has examined disclosure as an avenue for constructing the analyst as a new object differentiated from the historical transference object. Burke (1992) explores disclosure as related to aspects of mutuality, while relative degrees of anonymity are associated with asymmetry. I agree with Aron (1996), however, that this equation of disclosure with mutuality can be problematic because, like Strachey, it overemphasizes the analyst's intentions. Accordingly, an analyst may disclose with conscious intention to augment a level of mutuality that is not necessarily matched to either the analyst's unconscious motivations (Gill, 1983) or the patient's experience of this intervention. In fact, there are aspects of privacy, boundedness, and solitude within the analytic situation that are among the most mutual aspects of the analytic situation (Ogden, 1996), just as disclosure can resonate in experiences of asymmetry for particular patients. Not all circumstances in which disclosure proves useful can be explained as being so because of the analyst's mutuality with the patient.

Thus, there are useful tensions between, on one hand, Fairbairn's emphasis on our attachment to bad and old objects and our refractory clinging to these bad objects in the face of receiving something new and, on the other, a construal of a push or willingness toward integrating externality and newness of objects (Winnicott, 1969; Stern, 1985; Benjamin, 1988). There are a number of ways to understand these divergent formulations of basic developmental processes and their implications for psychoanalytic treatment. One is that each of these formulations is to some degree accurate and has greater or lesser degrees of applicability to particular types of patients. Another, which I tend to favor, is that each describes aspects of a universal process that needs to be integrated by the analyst.

CONSTRUCTIVISM AND THE NEW-OLD OBJECT CONTINUUM

It may seem a commonplace to assert that the patient's and the analyst's experiences of the analyst's newness or oldness are constructed by each analytic dyad. Yet analysts from widely divergent theoretical orientations have a tendency toward somewhat concrete constructions of newness and oldness and safety and danger.

The Analyst's Obstacles to Seeing Newness

Analysts who begin with an appreciation of Fairbairn's (1952) theoretical perspective that the old object is clung to for familiarity and safety have many ways of trying to integrate the puzzling tendency for many patients (for example, masochistic patients) to hold on to what seem to be exceedingly painful object attachments. Yet this perspective might also create a certain liability in minimizing instances in which new object experience is sought or expressed. Perhaps, at times, a patient engages in "object probing" (Ghent, 1992), which is overlooked by the analyst because the patient's affects or projections onto the analyst seem familiar when assessed against the patient's parental objects. For example, patients who express negative feelings toward their analysts often seem to be seeing or experiencing something in relation to the analysts that resembles what they have felt toward a parent. What can be overlooked in such formulations, however, is the previously unavailable opportunity for expressing feelings with such an object. For example, in the case of Sarah (to be discussed later), a new opportunity emerged that allowed her to express her negative transference toward me in ways in which she had never experienced it before. At other times, the analyst is likely to focus on certain ways in which the patient seems identified with the parent by identifying with the aggressor or the victim. While this identification may be useful in understanding old and familiar processes, sadomasochistic identifications may also occur simultaneously with the new opportunity for communication patterns with others.

Winnicott (1963) and Casement (1985) have each emphasized how the patient creates a "real" or new opportunity in the present to use an analyst to represent old object experience.

> Corrective provision is never enough. What is it that may be enough for some of our patients to get well? In the end the patient uses the analyst's failures, often quite small ones, perhaps maneuvered by the patient . . . and we have to put up with being in a limited context misunderstood. The operative factor is that the patient now hates the analyst for the failure that originally came as an environmental factor, outside the infant's area of omnipotent control but that is now staged in the transference. So in the end we succeed by failing—failing the patient's way. This is a long distance from the simple theory of cure by "corrective experience" [Winnicott, 1963, p. 258].

It is only over time that the analyst can come to see whether a particular kind of enactment of the transference is as Winnicott described. During this process, however, it is easy to see these forms of repetition as only part of the old object experience. Stern (1994) has described this kind of experience with the analyst as the "needed" object experience (even when it appeared initially as a repeated experience). The problem with Stern's formulation is that his descriptions can become teleological, as if the patient somehow knew how to work something through in which he or she was stuck. An alternative explanation is that, as old object experiences are worked through, new object experiences are more accessible (Tansey and Burke, 1989; Mitchell, 1994). The ability of patients to do the best with what we have to offer is, I think, different from saying these are "needed" relationships. My emphasis on patients' capacity to both use and preserve hope in their modes of object relating and defending is different from suggesting they somehow know (consciously or unconsciously) that they need these. I want to emphasize how much the analyst's theoretical biases influence how he or she constructs these experiences and how these constructions, in turn, determine what might be experienced as new by the patient's expressions.

For example, Sarah was a 25-year-old woman who had been frequently depressed when she began analysis several years earlier. Although her academic work proceeded well, she often felt that she should be doing something more exciting than her graduate studies. She also felt this kind of restlessness when she began a relationship with a potentially interesting man. She was now in a phase in which she had been able to work through a great deal of her anger and sadness related to feeling rejected by her father. She had experienced him as always "too objective" rather than effusive about her appearance and her intellect. In her current situation, we were examining her predilection for involvement with married or otherwise unavailable men and her avoidance of men who might be more readily available for a relationship. We agreed that, despite her frustration with the unavailable men, she remained attached to a fantasy that she could persuade her father to think differently about her and throw all caution to the winds to be with her.

In the earlier phase of analysis, she had experienced me as globally unavailable and rejecting toward her. Over time, we developed a warm, friendly way of being together, albeit one in which she was still visited by feelings of my rejecting her though in more specific ways. Sarah would adamantly tell me about my unsatisfactory wording of interpretations or observations, and she would propose comments that would be more affirming to her. At one level that was quite accessible to her, she recognized her readiness to respond to me as her unavailable and critical father. We also understood her instructions as expressing a kind of nihilistic and despairing display of her sense that if she did not tell me what to do, I would never comply with her wishes and needs to be affirmed. There were elements of punishment and sadism in the ways in which she would hypervigilantly discover one example after the next of my tendency to be critical or more reserved in affirmation than she wished. She was able to experience her wishes for retaliation against me, including wishes to hurt me and make me feel as rejected as she felt by men. Often, as we spoke of these feelings, she would smile or laugh uncontrollably as she recognized the intensity of her anger.

Sarah agreed with my sense that she selectively perceived and experienced my remarks in terms of what was less affirming or supportive and at times minimized my acknowledgment of her achievements and strengths. She also agreed with my observation that at times her selective perception represented a repetition of her relationship with her father, which she painfully held on to, a kind of holding on to an object experience as described in Fairbairn's (1952) theory. Even as we took up something about her selective perception, there were times when I conveyed to her my agreement that she had a good point to make about my insensitivity to her need to feel affirmed.

As Sarah became increasingly able to tell me about what she wished for in her relationship with me—which took the form of criticizing the wording of my interpretations and observations—she was able to recognize her ready responsiveness to me as her unavailable and critical father. Over the course of our analytic work, however, she also began to understand her instructions and corrections of my interventions as new opportunities to express her feelings of anger. Moreover, her newly found ability to correct my interventions allowed her to express more clearly her wish to have had a father who was less objective and more enthusiastic or passionate about her developing body and mind.

In this phase of analysis with Sarah were a number of threads of experience and enactment that help in thinking about the complexities of new and old object experience. One complexity relates to enactment and the likelihood that the analyst will repeat painful aspects of the patient's earlier experience. Thus the old object is reexperienced and repeated in the present. The patient's expectations and tendencies to repeat are forged onto the new experience with the analyst, and the analyst is likely to respond to or cocreate these repetitions. Enactments often involve the ways in which we unconsciously participate in a repetition of an earlier failure that was close to the patient's experience of an earlier trauma (Casement, 1985). The patient is skeptical that the analyst can become a new object partly because she sees the ways in which her analyst is the same as the old object through repetition and enactment.

Our tendency to see repetition may, however, blind us from seeing how new opportunities for relatedness are emerging. Sarah's ability to feel safe enough with me to criticize, correct, evaluate, and complain constituted part of a new object experience. This observation is very much in keeping with the notion that negative transference often involves the deepest kind of trust and safety (Greenberg, 1986). At the same time, there are many instances in which positive and, especially, erotic transferences involve intense sadistic and negative affective experiences (Stoller, 1979; Gabbard, 1994). It is easy to see how our theoretical constructions of Sarah as holding on to the old, bad father (safe) so as not to be threatened by the new might deter one from viewing Sarah as exploring a new opportunity and pathway, as she gave repeated expression to very familiar feelings of rage and sadism toward me. Analyzing how she was holding on to the old could potentially minimize how she indeed was taking in something new.

It is not uncommon and may be inevitable for us to repeat aspects of the old object whether we focus on what seems to us old or what is new in what the patient is expressing or feeling. For example, if an analyst rigidly sustains a stance of emphasizing the newness in the patient's expression of negative feelings toward him as something not previously allowed within the parent-child dynamic, then the analyst may be repeating aspects of the old. On the other hand, the relentless interpretation of Sarah's attachment to the old might have similarly constituted a repetition of Sarah's sense of being unrecognized by her father.

The case of Sarah raises an interesting question about the extent to which sadism directed toward the analyst derives from the patient's feeling threatened by the new object or from expressing old feelings toward the new subject? I believe it is useful to think of an object representation as containing aspects of self and object. I have already posed the familiar question raised by Fairbairn (1952), namely, whether or not the patient's sadism is a response to the threat posed by a new object on the horizon which disrupts a tenacious gravitating toward the old. Both British and American relational models have highlighted the ways in which a patient may enact aspects of the old object, thus requiring the analyst to adopt aspects of the patient's self in relation to the object. In these circumstances, the question is always whether or not the analyst will be or can be a new object, a new subject, or both. Will the analyst feel beleaguered, helpless, sad, furious, or retaliatory in response to the patient's communications? If the analyst does experience these feelings and express them, can he do so in a way that differs from how the patient did so? This intervention can be accomplished through either the analyst's containment and reintroduction of these feelings (speaking from an effectively processed internal emotional state) or judicious self-disclosure.

While it is difficult to formulate general guidelines about determining which patterns of old or new object experience are more dominant at one time or another, it is probably a good idea to keep each possibility in mind. The analyst needs to balance the need to stay with the experience of the analyst-as-old-object in effigy, while remaining attuned to possible ways in which the analyst may emerge from the old object experience as a new object. In Freudian analysis, there is probably too much resistance or reluctance by the analyst to interfere with the development of the old object experience. This position minimizes the value of 1) the analyst's drawing attention to the ways in which the patient might be using the analyst in a new and different way as opposed to holding on to the old object for fear of mitigating or diluting the power of the historically held transference; 2) the analyst's using disclosure to differentiate himself at times from the old object; or 3) the analyst's using aspects of his subjectivity as a construction that might allow further interpretation (Cooper, 1997, 1998a,b). Furthermore, the classical position paradoxically minimizes the refractoriness and resilience of transference phenomena; that is, the transference is not necessarily diluted by addressing old and new object phenomena at the same time.

The points of reluctance or resistance for analysts within the relational model have the potential to determine too quickly that the analyst needs to do something to act as a new object. Speaking about patients and analysts, Greenberg (1986) drew attention to the potential of patients and analysts alike to embrace defensively aspects of the new object. It is quite understandable to seek relief from the unrelenting repetition of problematic relationships. The problems here, well documented by Gill (1983, 1994a), relate to the possibility of either diluting or diverting aspects of transference or being influenced by a number of unconscious factors. There is value in the patient's being able to find and create the object (Winnicott, 1969) in the form of the new-object/analyst. If the analyst harps on the theme of newness, the patient's experience may shift to staleness or compliance.

Thus, it is not surprising that relational theory can help or hinder in determining the balance of new and old. Relationalists are quite aware of contemporary factors in the analytic situation. Relationally oriented analysts are likely to pay attention to how much the patient observes, perceives, and experiences about them that might influence patients' reluctance to trust their analysts. This is also true of revisionist approaches to classical technique, such as that of Schwaber (1983, 1995), which underscore the patient's psychic reality. A patient's overattention to the analyst's contribution could, however, also indicate a reluctance to shift his relationship to the internalized bad object.

Generally speaking, I try to explore with patients what they have noted in my behavior that has led them to a particular transference experience or construction. But, sometimes when I do this, I begin to sense that we are both avoiding what we know to be a particular experiential predilection of the patient. It is at this time that I am likely to shift from my exploration of what the patient has noted to a more assertive probing about how often the patient tends to see this in me and others.

For example, Donald was a middle-aged man who felt that women were controlling him in most of his relationships, including his relationships with his two previous wives. He had felt dominated by his mother and disappointed by his father, who was unable to stand up to her frequent complaints and the orders she issued. It was easy to empathize with Donald's sense that he had often felt pushed around by his mother and hence was trying to develop a different relationship with his lover based on mutuality, compromise, and conversation about differences. Donald felt that when he was speaking, others interrupted him when he was just beginning to make a point. As the analysis developed and an initial positive transference began to wane, Donald felt interrupted by me as well. We often understood this feeling as a repetition of his experience with his mother, but he was not particularly curious about his contribution to the process. In relation to both his mother and me, Donald felt that what he had to say was not as important as what she wished to say and how she wished to influence decision making. He felt that his opinion counted far less than ours.

As the analysis progressed, I noted to myself that Donald had a very striking cadence to his style of speech. He would make a point that led me (and I imagine others) to believe that he had finished speaking. Sometimes, unwittingly, I began to make a point or observe something, only to find that Donald was just getting started. My behavior was egregious to Donald, as was similar behavior by his mother, his wives and several close friends and colleagues. As this pattern began to develop, I came to empathize with Donald's sense of being hurt and violated. As the analysis progressed, however, I also found myself becoming impatient with this kind of interaction; I began to feel that there was something really quite ill conceived about probing Donald's perceptions around what I had done when I "interrupted" him. I started to think about what I regarded as a complicated and upsetting verbal pattern that Donald got into with me and others. Convinced that I and others would interrupt him, he had built into his speech a kind of expectation and cadence that were likely to bring about his worst expectations. I tried to probe what seemed available to him about expecting to be hurt and how angry he was most of the time. He had a fight inside that was waiting to happen. My attention moved away from the observable aspects of the interaction to what I was feeling about Donald as he spoke. I began to let him know more about how I experienced him at these times—hurt, expectantly angry, brittle, and fixing to rumble. This shift in my stance was not easy for him but eventually led to his sense that he could really get into his anger with me. He wanted me to apologize to him, and yet he could also feel that there was something useful about what I was observing in him. We began to realize how I would repeatedly enact these feelings like his mother at an experiential level, but that he had had a great deal to do with creating his perceptions of me. Interestingly, I gradually became able to stop enacting my cocreated drama with Donald by waiting longer or by checking with him to determine if he was still in the middle of speaking. Thus we were able to create an atmosphere that allowed Donald to explore his internal readiness to feel interrupted.

Inderbitzen and Levy (1994) have made a valuable point about instances when exploring the patient's perspective and perceptions of the analyst may "distract" from what they term unconscious derivatives related to these perceptions. They argue that focusing on patients' perceptions of the analyst may result in a failure to note how patients sometimes use external reality as a defense against exploring unconscious derivatives. I would be far more comfortable with their argument if they had given equal weight to the frequent tendency for analysts to collude with patients' defenses by focusing on unconscious derivatives and not seeing the observable defensive functioning within the interaction. Thus, not paying considerable attention to the patient's perceptions and construction of events has its own hazards, hazards I earlier outlined regarding the analyst's insensitivity to the patient's communications about experiencing the analyst as a new object or, at times, the need for the analyst to acknowledge (to himself and the patient) that he has been enacting patterns related to the old object. As Donald was able to talk about my "interrupting" him, I was able to behave in a different way, which, in turn, allowed us to examine his anger and readiness to see me as an old object.

Keeping in mind these complexities may help the analyst to determine whether it is useful to make interpretations or constructions that contrast the analyst with the historically held object in order to examine the patient's reluctance to experience newness or dread and anxiety about this possibility. The question is whether these interventions seem useful or whether interpretations that relate primarily to the patient's experience of the analyst as an old object may be more resonant or generative.

The Patient's Inner Obstacles to Seeing Newness

There is a variety of components to the patient's clinging to the safety of the old object and reluctance to accept the new object, in addition to those posited by Fairbairn's (1952) theory. These aspects relate more to immediate, contemporary experience and to the person of the analyst portrayed in interpersonal and relational-conflict theory and much less to early experience and mechanisms of internalization that were a point of focus for Fairbairn.

Most analysts would agree that a patient is likely to see the analyst as similar to the old object because of the power of transference and the likelihood that unconscious enactments will affirm the patient's worst fears about the resemblance between the analyst and the parental object. This view is essentially consistent with Freud's (1914) descriptions of transference and his originating the term. Freud suggested that the transference is always initially enacted before it can be put into words. My work with Donald illustrates both his transferential readiness to experience me as his mother in certain ways and the ways I unconsciously repeated and enacted these expectations.

Two other factors seem salient here. The first is that everything we know about the tendency to repeat should lead us to the consideration that a patient will unconsciously choose an analyst who may in some ways psychologically resemble the parental object. In this way, the patient may be attuned to all sorts of things seen before. A second factor may relate to the "He (or she) can't be as good as he (or she) looks" phenomenon. Regarding the first point, it is easy to repeat neurotic aspects of object choice in every relationship—romantic, professional, analytic. Particularly perplexing for all of us in making choices is that we often believe we are choosing only on the basis of consciously experienced and observed phenomena. A man chooses a lover who is more easygoing and quiet than his intense and intrusive mother but then discovers that she is just as intrusive as the mother—she just takes longer to reveal it. This is a good example, because it brings up the complexity of how, in analytic work, analyst and patient ask themselves whether this configuration reflects repetition in object choice or how the patient's experience of his intrusive and demanding mother is likely to rear its head in any romantic relationship. The lines are seldom clear, particularly because the repetition in object choice may not necessarily be a choice of the same kind of object, but rather an object who is willing to accept the processes of role induction and role responsiveness that the patient needs or is likely to enact. In addition, the patient may "be able" to find a familiar position for the self in the relationship, even when there are significant differences between internal objects and the current other. The issues discussed here are often confusing because they are likely to reflect overlapping and concurrent processes.

All these processes are obviously applicable to transference in the analytic situation. The patient's experience of the analyst is colored by aspects of the historically based transference. The analyst sometimes acts in ways that confirm the patient's expectations that the analyst is like the parent. Then, to make matters even more confusing, the patient may often actually choose an analyst that resembles some of the most problematic aspects of the parent. These circumstances present great obstacles and opportunities for any analysis. Summarizing many of these observations, Greenberg (1986) writes:

> Unless he [the patient] has some sense of the analyst as a new object, he will not be able to experience him as an old one. The inability to achieve this balance is responsible for many analytic failures. If the analyst cannot be experienced as a new object, analysis never gets under way; if he cannot be experienced as an old one, it never ends [p. 98].

The resemblances help create the potential to experience the analytic situation with great depth and authenticity. Here, the inverse of

Greenberg's statement is also relevant—unless the analyst is enough of an old object, treatment cannot begin. For some patients, however, the similarity between the analyst and parental figures makes it difficult to experience the new opportunity the analytic situation offers for symbolic and interpretive play. In this case, Greenberg's original statement applies—unless the analyst is enough of a new object, treatment cannot begin.

Another factor in a patient's reluctance to experience newness in the analyst derives from his skepticism about whether the analyst can really be as good as he seems. Hoffman (1994a) has suggested that the analyst's "self" is in most instances relatively unknown to the patient. He states that one of the aspects of ritualized asymmetry in the analytic situation is "fostered partly by the patient's knowing so much less about him or her than the analyst knows about the patient" (p. 199). Hoffman further argues that the analyst is in a relatively protected position, one that is likely to promote some of the most tolerant and generous aspects of his or her personality. This protection exists despite the analyst's authentic participation and sense that he or she has specific feelings or experiences with the patient. Hoffman emphasizes how this relatively protected stance tends to foster idealizations in the patient. Renik (1995), in contrast to Hoffman, sees these idealizations of the analyst as potentially problematic if they are insufficiently analyzed. Hoffman (1994a, 1996) sees these idealizations as potentially an aspect of the analyst's authority and influence and facilitative of the patient's use of the analyst.

The radical nature of the social context in analysis is one in which personal participation is an inevitability, but one that is inherently contextually defined by the work task, both unique and overlapping with other social contexts. Thus the interactive matrix (Greenberg, 1995) borrows from and is partly separate from the larger social context. This view is compatible with Hoffman's (1994a) elaboration of the asymmetrical arrangement that partially protects the analyst's anonymity, and how he or she will be known by the patient.

However, the tensions between what is unique about the analyst's participation and the overlap with the larger social context are of key importance in understanding another element of the patient's reluctance to experience the analyst as a new object. It is my sense that the patient is always partly aware that the analyst's usual responsiveness cannot really be as good as he or she is able to be with the patient. In fact, in instances when the patient cannot let this awareness move to the foreground during some phases of an analysis, it is usually for reasons that bear taking a look at. I agree (Cooper, 1998b) with Hoffman that the analyst is in a sense protected by the patient and that many aspects of the analyst's self, despite the analyst's authentic engagement, remain in the background or are simply not well known by the patient. Yet in contrast to Hoffman (1996, 1998a) I believe that patients are often aware that there is much about the analyst that they do not know. While illusion is a necessary part of every analysis, many patients are aware of the tensions between the real and intimate and the illusory nature of analytic engagement. Many analyses pursue understanding the patients' inability to form such illusions in the analytic and in nonanalytic relationships, just as for some patients it is the work to comprehend how easily they form such illusions.

I am suggesting that in many analyses the patient, even as he suspends disbelief, is aware of the possibility that he is getting some of the best of the analyst. Part of the patient's trepidation in moving to a new object can be alleviated by applying this awareness to the patient's reluctance to seize the possibility that anyone can be new, different, or this good. For example, part of the work involves exploring why anyone has to be *that* good in order to engender trust, love, wishes for intimacy, and the like. The patient's inability to trust the new, or even see the new, is never entirely separable from his or her attachment to the old object or the old representations. Yet there are built-in dimensions in the analytic set-up that are part of the patient's attachment to the old. It is important to note too that, given the tremendous vicissitudes of everyone's emotional states and of interpersonal relating, the patient is bound to have had experiences of the parent's being different from some position that became crystallized as a central old object position. Thus patients have experienced parents as displaying a range of experience. Often this variation was followed by the parent's resuming a central or primary (modal) affective stance. With repeated experiences of being seduced by the appearance of a "new object" in the parent, only to be disappointed, the patient would be much less likely to trust any fresh signs of "newness" in the analyst. The patient sustains the tension around the question, "When is the other shoe going to drop?" The analyst's awareness of this dimension can be helpful in analyzing the patient's attachment to the old. For example, an additional complexity involves how the newly found hope expressed toward an object often leads to retreat to a more suspicious or paranoid/schizoid position and hence produces enactments.

Thus, the Fairbairnian (1952) model in its pure form may at times minimize contemporary factors that further contribute to the basic Fairbairnian appreciation of the individual's need for attachment to the old object. In other words, there are ways in which the contemporary American emphasis on relational processes in the immediacy of analytic engagement has elucidated factors that reinforce an understanding of the patient's wishes to hold on to the old object. The patient is aware at some level that the newness or goodness of the analyst is related to the analyst's function, his role within the asymmetrical arrangement of analysis—so he is not entirely to be believed. While Hoffman (1996) articulates so clearly the ways in which we are idealizable and not real, ways that foster idealization, there is also a question about whether or not the patient ever fully believes this to be real. This is one of the forms of play in analysis involving the transference and countertransference. The patient is reluctant to take in a new experience, which is viewed as artificial and not real. (Obviously this discussion is at the level of discourse involving generalities. We know that some patients are prone to idealization, others prone to cynicism about whether the analyst can be a good object. Most of us operate on multiple levels of reality in the analytic situation [Modell, 1991], suspending our disbelief more in some instances and less in others.)

American relational models reflect a great deal of awareness of how much the patient observes, perceives, and experiences about the analyst that might influence the patient's trepidation or reluctance to trust the analyst. As I have suggested, the danger in this model is that the patient's "need" to repeat, or his predilection to impose the old object situation, could be minimized if the analyst becomes overly focused on the patient's immediate perceptions of the analyst as behaving in particular ways and especially if the analyst valorizes newness for therapeutic action. For example, had I continued to explore exclusively Donald's perceptions and experience of me as "interrupting," we might have been compromised in being able to explore his wanting interactions that allowed him to voice his grievances. Obviously, there are many instances when the analyst responds in ways that confirm the patient's expectations but that are not role-induced. There are other instances when the analyst may even be inducing certain roles and behaviors in the patient. There are, however, also many instances when, in line with classical views of transference, the patient repeats the old object experience with the analyst.

DISCLOSURE AND THE NEW-OLD OBJECT CONTINUUM

Another issue related to constructivism and the old-new object continuum is the analyst's assumptions about the stimulus value of his interventions (if, indeed, there ever is such a thing in analysis apart from the patient's and analyst's psychic view of reality). For example, disclosure offers the patient a view of the analyst as a potentially new object. There are instances when aspects of disclosure resonate for the patient with mutual aspects of the analytic situation, as Burke (1992) has noted. In most cases, however, disclosure by the analyst is fairly selective and remains at quite a distance from how intimately the patient might want to know the analyst. I like to think of disclosure, when it is used for a good purpose, as involving and maintaining a tension between mutuality and asymmetry in the analytic situation. When a patient is unable to tolerate the ambiguity of the analytic situation, there is not a useful tension being maintained regarding asymmetry and mutuality. This does not mean that the analyst should disclose something that he wishes not to.

Similarly, sometimes aspects of the analyst's anonymity resonate for the patient as having aspects of mutuality—that parts of both patient and analyst are separate; that they have secrets from each other; that there is boundedness and privacy. Bion's (1977) statement about the analytic situation points to these aspects of separateness, even if it is embedded in particular assumptions about the degree to which personalities involve separate intrapsychic structures rather than intersubjectively intertwined organizations: "We're both in this alone" (p. 37). Ogden (1994, 1996) has repeatedly emphasized the privateness of analyst and patient as part of their overlapping aspects. It is overly schematic to say that disclosure involves mutual aspects of the analytic situation, just as it was for Strachey (1934) to draw clean lines of distinction between interpretation and suggestion.

Similarly, disclosure can be used to reveal the analyst as either a safe or a dangerous object. Disclosure often involves a presentation of the analyst as a safe new object in contrast to the dangerous or destructive feelings associated with the old object. This use of disclosure can be especially helpful if the patient is prone to experience the historically held transference in a way that is so extremely scary or depressing that the analytic process can become limited or stagnated. The analyst essentially uses a form of clarification or differentiation of himself from the parental object embodied in the transference with the hope of supporting the patient's capacity for self-observation, titrating or modulating affect. Of equal value, however, is using disclosure as a way of presenting danger. The analyst often interprets or queries, directly or virtually disclosing a construction of himself, in order to pose what is most threatening for the patient to consider. For example, the analyst says, "As angry as you are that the only reason I see you is so that I can charge you money for our visits, perhaps it is threatening to think about any other reasons that I might talk to you."

It is not easy to assess the effects or implications of the analyst's holding these biases in understanding interaction. One reason I emphasize that disclosure or constructions of the analyst as a new object cannot be prospectively categorized is that the patient usually experientially integrates, uses, or rejects our constructions in accordance with his or readiness to visit new and old object experiences. In chapter 7 I examine how some constructions of our self as a potentially new object often recapitulate for the patient aspects of the historically held transference. One possible implication is that, if the analyst approaches these disclosures as intertwined with aspects of mutuality and asymmetry, there may be more readiness to work with the complex texturing that the patient experiences in response to this or any other intervention.

HOLDING THE PSYCHIC FUTURE:
THE FUTURE OBJECT AND SELF

Every psychoanalytic theory of growth, either in describing development or the analytic process involves aspects of benevolent disruption.

Even "developmental tilt" theories (Mitchell, 1988) emphasizing the analyst's need to stay as close to the patient's psychic reality as possible stress the inevitability of failing the patient and the resultant tensions that can at the same time be productive of growth. Other theories, including classical, interpersonal, and relational-conflict theories, have built-in conceptions of how tensions between the participants produce change—it is just a question of how you go about the process and what unit of analysis is addressed (e.g., a mind or an interaction) and what your goals for analysis are.

In a sense, every theory has a mode of benevolent disruption that partially constitutes the new object—either through survival of the patient's reactions to these failures or through the psychic possibility that emerges through interactional tension or shifts in intrapsychic organization. In Kohut, the new object is one that will not empathically fail around the responsiveness of healthy narcissistic needs. Winnicott's new object is able to meet the moment of hope expressed in the patient's authentic or true self. In the classical view, the new object is one that can offer a crucible for the patient's old experience, an opportunity for repetition to become visible, heartfelt, and tamed through neutralization of drives. In most relational models, analysis involves the opportunity for a combination of new and repeated relationships. Relational models offer ways of thinking about the balance of new and old as well as technical approaches that help to construct the analyst and the interaction.

I view the new object partially in Loewaldian terms, as holding a version of psychic possibility for the patient. In most ways this idea is akin to Greenberg's (1986) emphasis on the analyst's needing to strike a balance between safe and dangerous, old and new. Loewald, however, did not address the complexity and variety of ways that the analyst needs go about holding psychic possibility except through classical interpretation. I have tried to demonstrate that it is not universally useful to equate the newness of the object with safety. While Fairbairn's (1952) theory allows for a deep appreciation of this observation, his theory is less attuned to the interpersonal and immediate aspects of analytic interaction that can help the analyst attend to how the new object is unsafe. Sometimes psychic possibility is provided or maintained by containment and restraint on the analyst's part, allowing the transference, in the form of the old object, to unfold. At other times, providing or underscoring psychic possibility involves the analyst's attempts to construct a view of how the analyst can be distinguished from the old object. At yet other times, this may involve drawing attention to the patient's reluctance to let the analyst be viewed as an old object.

Donald's treatment illustrates how I tried at some point to distinguish myself from his maternal transference object by both challenging his aggression and readiness to fight and by learning how I had enacted the very thing that he feared. I could become a new object only over time and in contrast to his transferential experience of me as an old object. Importantly though, I actually enacted the role of the old object, which was also inextricably tied to his own unconscious need to fight and to create circumstances in which it seemed that a fight was called for.

Sarah's treatment was characterized by a tension between my consciously experienced hopes for her—an opportunity for her growth and her capacity to form a relationship that would be more satisfying to her—and a kind of enactment of the old object, coconstituted by the two of us. My enactments were often manifested by my saying things in ways that seemed overly evaluative to her. At times she was quite right (i.e., her identifying an evaluative attitude in me in a given moment, which I later could see as well) as was her hypervigilance to how I and others approached her. In fact, we were able to understand over time her intense reluctance to believe either that I was not critical of her or, if and to the extent that I was, that my criticisms need not overshadow many other feelings and attitudes toward her, including that I cared for her a great deal. Of note was her readiness to experience me as a familiar object and my tendency, at times, to act in ways that would elicit this feeling in her. The analyst's inevitable participation in aspects of repetition can sometimes fuel the patient's tendency to cling to attachments even though the analyst might at other moments be doing something quite new.

The analyst's interpretive anticipation of where the patient might go also often enacts an amalgam of the old and new object, coconstituted by patient and analyst. Thus, holding on to the notion of the patient's psychic future often combines aspects of the old and the new objects. This holding mirrors the ways in which the patient's experience of the old object may sometimes involve something new, in Ghent's (1992) terms, object probing. I am again emphasizing the ways in which the new object functions to hold a view of psychic possibility for the patient. For some patients, psychic possibility has less to do with consciously experienced hope than with the capacity to face and integrate painful experience that underlies consciously experienced hope. For others, psychic possibility has much more to do with the threat of trying to be consciously hopeful in the face of loss or disillusionment.

The relational model not only emphasizes ways in which the newness of the analyst can be helpful, but also has the potential to deepen our understanding of why patients remain attached to the old. To some extent, examples of disclosure and constructions by the analyst in our literature portray the analyst as a new object who is safe, relative to the historically held bad, dangerous object. Yet sometimes disclosure conveys useful constructions of ourselves, as distinguished from the old which are threatening and unsafe (Fairbairn, 1952). For example, it can be terrifying for a patient who has never trusted, to increasingly confront an object who seems worth trusting, thereby imperiling all his extant systems and patterns of defense and withdrawal.

There is a fundamental paradox in Fairbairn. Despite his radical assertion that there is a drive called object relating, Fairbairn, like Freud, viewed the individual as not wanting to recognize a new person for fear of threatening an attachment to an old object. Obviously, for Freud (1905a), the old object is clung to because it reduces instinctual tension—there never really is a new object, only the refinding of an old object. For Fairbairn (1952), the individual wants to hold on to the object he has known and internalized in order to create or maintain safety. Furthermore, the object with whom he visits and revisits in therapy is in many ways a bundle of the projected, previously internalized object images. Contemporary relational theory describes the hoped-for negotiations that can go on between the patient/subject and the analyst-as-new-object, amidst the collaborative experience and clarification of the analyst-as-old-object in the transference. American relational theory contributes to a Fairbairnian view particularly in its elaboration of the variety of factors that make the renunciation or exorcism of the old object so difficult.

That the patient can really trust someone new in the face of bedrock patterns of relating is indeed an ambitious goal. The patient works and learns to play with experiential and transferential tensions in believing that the analyst can be different from the person whom the patient has known and that, at the same time, the analyst is also similar in some ways to the patient's objects—similar either because the analyst repeats and recreates what has happened or because the patient's experiential overlay inevitably comes into play. The analyst is always partly a construction based on whom the patient has known and whom he wishes to know, as well as who the patient is and who he wishes and strives to become. Through these tensions and multiple levels of reality, the analyst has the opportunity to influence. Psychoanalysis tries to help people engage in deep experience. It explores their inclination to trust or mistrust others, to construct playfully the real and the illusory, the old, new, and future self and object.

4

MUTUAL CONTAINMENT
IN THE ANALYTIC SITUATION

SINCE THE CONTAINING FUNCTION of interpretation is essential to so many aspects of analytic work, it has received a great deal of careful and thoughtful attention by a number of psychoanalysts. Strachey, Bion, Winnicott, Guntrip, Balint, Loewald, Ogden, Modell, Casement, Slochower, Mitchell, and Steiner, among others, have described some of the primary features of the analyst's containment of affect for the patient. Strachey's (1936) description of how interpretations detoxify harsh superego aspects of the patient's psychic life marked the beginning of the transition from conceptualizing interpretation strictly as a method for conveying content to a process of communicating and holding affect. Winnicott (1963, 1969) and Modell (1976) elaborated the idea of holding as a major function of interpretation and therapeutic action. Winnicott's (1960) work related to the complex ego and object maternal functions during development and analysis that are essential to a great deal of my analytic work. A great deal of Bion's work can be understood through the lens of containment that is provided by the analyst through the analytic process. Most recently, Slochower (1996b) has described in great clinical detail the ways in which analysts hold and contain patients' affects through interpretive process. Slochower (1994, 1996a,b) and Wrye (1989, 1997) in a series of very interesting papers have been elaborating a variety of maternal transference/countertransference developments in analytic work as related to psychic holding and the exploration of desire.

Mitchell (1995, 1997) has highlighted the British (especially Kleinian theory) emphasis on containment and metabolization of affect, whereas American interpersonal theory emphasizes the analyst's functions of expressiveness and spontaneity. He describes how these traditions might work in complementary ways.

Understandably, we have developed a much larger literature on how the analyst provides containment for the patient than on how the patient helps contain affects of the analyst. By focusing on the patient's containment of the analyst, I hope not to minimize the importance of the more frequent current involving the analyst's containment of the patient. Nor do I want to suggest that we can look at the patient's containment of the analyst without looking simultaneously at the vicissitudes of the analyst's containment of the patient.

A patient's containment of the analyst occurs in a broad range of situations that extend far beyond the visible instances when analysts are directly expressive of their own affects. In response to this imbalance, I explore how patients help analysts contain various kinds of affects within the analytic process, particularly more routine and less heroic types of containment. While this containment is generally a far less prominent feature of analytic work than is the containment provided by the analyst for the patient, it is omnipresent. The routine elements of containment that the patient provides for the analyst involve working with the knowledge of the limits of the other, including the possibility that in a long-term treatment the patient will often get to know quite well the quotidian aspects of the analyst's personality, as well as elements of his neurosis and its relation to the patient's conflicts. Mutual aspects of containment are extremely important in the expression and titration of hope and the negotiation of psychic possibility within the analytic dyad. Aron (1996) illustrates that mutuality and asymmetry are highly complementary components of analytic work. That a patient provides containment for his analyst does not mean that he does so in a way that is equal to or identical with that provided by his analyst.

Understandably, a likely concern about this area of exploration is that many analysts may think that it is only in problematic countertransference enactments that the patient should become particularly or strikingly aware of elements of his analyst's personality. Yet I think that anyone we get to know reasonably well, including in the unique and peculiar arrangements of analytic work, comes to know things about us, particularly when strong affect is at play. I know very few analysts, including a number who were extremely happy about and grateful for their analyses, who do not convey a sense of how they worked around one or another personality feature of their analyst. More important, it is possible that, over time, the patient's experience of the analyst's limitations is an important part of the therapeutic action. The patient has to be able to use the analyst's limitations. It is true that, for many schizoid patients, the analyst's shortcomings and limitations may stimulate further psychic retreat and justification for staying in that position (Steiner, 1993). But for patients who are able to have an analysis "of the patient, not about the patient" (Bromberg, 1998, p. 58) the ability to observe and work with the analyst's limitations may be usefully regarded as a necessary part of grieving and mourning about the nature of limitations in relation to analysis, the analyst, and self-experience.

Hoffman (1996) and I (Cooper, 1998b) have discussed how the way patients get to know us is not identical to the way others get to know us outside analysis. Yet there are elements of our personalities that most analytic patients will get a feel for, albeit those aspects are filtered through whatever he or she brings to the situation. In particular, patients get a sense of how analysts deal with specific affects, conflicts, and transference projections attributions. Some obvious examples might be: "He would get anxious about dealing with my sexual feelings toward him or his toward me" or "I felt like I had to show him that I could deal with those feelings" or "He could help me be angry at him, but he got anxious whenever I expressed anger toward my father." Other, more subtle examples might be: "During the time that we were finishing, he seemed to be more active in a way that I thought he was reluctant to be in the earlier phases."

No doubt, these perceptions of the analyst's vulnerabilities or characteristic ways of dealing with or avoiding conflict are informed by the patient's conflicts, but I think that one of the really good outcomes of analysis is the patient's heightened ability to get a sense of the analyst's functional person, his strengths and weaknesses. In so doing, the patient can relinquish an infantilized, idealizing position in relation to the analyst. Many of these observations are in the background during analysis and move to the foreground during postanalysis years. Yet these dynamics are always operating—it is just a question of if the patient and analyst are able to look at the elephant in the room. I think that we, as analysts, can become ever more aware of how our patients routinely need to work with and around us to attain some benefit during analytic process. Some of this work is most conspicuous in a phase of treatment that Davies (1998) has discussed, namely, the postoedipal phase. During this phase, the patient may be most likely to see the limitations and strengths of the analyst, as well as the constraints of the analytic situation in a less affectively stormy climate.

CONTAINMENT AND MUTUAL CONTAINMENT BETWEEN ANALYST AND PATIENT: ALLEN AND GOOD-ENOUGH RETALIATION

Probably the easiest way to begin discussing mutual aspects of containment is to start historically with the transition in theorizing about projective identification from a strict focus on metapsychology in Kleinian theory to the clinical levels of interaction that were the contribution of Middle School object relations theory, American relational-conflict theory, and interpersonal theory. The concept of projective identification had its origin in the representational world of the patient within Kleinian theory. Unacceptable drives and affects were located within representational images of the object. By dint of retaliatory anxiety (Klein, 1946; Kernberg, 1975), the patient feared the object (representationally encoded) and thus maintained a hypervigilant stance. As the concept of projective identification became interpersonalized within middle school relational theory, interpersonal theory, and, more recently, American relational theory, as described well by Tansey and Burke (1989) and more recently by Mitchell (1997), the focus turned to the analyst's responsibility for feeling, sometimes enacting, and holding these dreaded affects, detoxifying them, and metabolizing them before placing them back out into the psychic space between patient and analyst. The analyst needed to contain the dreaded affects of the patient for a long enough time and in a good enough way so that a helpful reinternalization process could occur.

Most discussions of the patient's role in this process have focused on the importance of reinternalizing these affects and attributions without specific mention of how the patient needs also to reinternalize aspects of the analyst's anxiety, anger, needs, and wishes. There has been less explicit discussion of the patient's role in the reinternalization process in the context of the analyst's limitations in sufficiently holding and containing affects prior to making interpretations to the patient. Instead, most discussions usually center on the analyst's need to recover and get back on track when he or she has been insufficiently able to contain the patient's projected affects. This model suggests that containment works in only one way. The analyst contains the patient's affects, but what is minimized is the value in reciprocal processes and in affect exchanges through which the patient learns to trust her experience of her analyst, including the disappointing experiences.

To be sure, most psychoanalytic theory, especially object relations theory and self psychology, hold benevolent disruption as a part of the therapeutic action. But this has more to do with misattunement than with the patient's everyday experience of abiding and containing the analyst's quotidian personality features, including his neurosis. Thus, little has been written about ways in which patients contain the affects, experiences, and even formulations of their analysts.

One of the things that a great many contemporary psychodynamic clinicians have been trying to understand is how to reconcile this necessary aspect of containment, or respect for the patient's dread of experiencing old and new affect in a relationship, with the analyst's expressive use of the countertransference. There are patients who probably cannot ever tolerate holding that involves the mutual and reciprocal process of affect exchange—that is, working with the analyst's conscious and unconscious expressiveness. I think, however, that many of the most hurt of our patients (perhaps not all) can learn to find ways to take in the experiences of dreaded affect that they push away. But, even more important, *most patients can learn to see how they are already doing it whether they like it or not.* In other words, no matter how much we provide a holding environment, we are asking patients to engage in reciprocal holding. I fear that to claim otherwise is grandiose and, perhaps even worse, sometimes regression inducing in ways that prolong treatment.

We all know that patients do a great deal to contain our affects even when there are less dramatic circumstances than filling up the leaks in the therapeutic holding vessel during projective identification. Even when analysts are successfully maintaining a holding and containing function during projective identification, a patient will begin to know that the analyst is holding on to dreaded affects—usually dependency, need, vulnerability, or anger—and, in the best of circumstances, the patient begins to take more and more responsibility for holding and owning, as it were, these experiences. The patient's vigilance toward the analyst moves from retaliatory anxiety (Klein, 1946; Kernberg, 1975) to a not uncommon experience of concern or even curiosity about how the analyst is doing, holding on to all this affect. In the best of circumstances, the patient begins to feel a wish for reparation and even gratitude, though naturally these experiences can often be born of fear and guilt about being too much for the analyst. In this process of projective identification, the patient often feels simultaneously two divergent affects, a kind of "divergent conflict" (Kris, 1982) in which he is pulled in two different directions. In this instance, there is the wish to keep dreaded affects external and the growing sense that the analyst has a point about the fact that these are warded-off experiences of the self. This divergent conflict may partially overlap with what Bromberg (1994) has written about moving from dissociated affective states to a position of conflict. It is at these moments that the patient and analyst can hold and contain affects and take more responsibility for their exploration.

In reference to the process by which affects begin to be expressed before being more easily metabolizable, sometimes in the context of projective identification and sometimes in other therapeutic situations, I have become interested in what I call *good-enough retaliation* or *good-enough impingement* on the part of the analyst. What I mean by *good-enough retaliation* is the kind of unformulated experience that the analyst conveys to the patient during the process of containment. Often these communications involve unconscious and sometimes conscious ways of retaliating that express the limits of the analyst's ability to hold and contain affects. Good-enough retaliation is not based on an intervention through which the analyst is intending to retaliate. It is, however, often experienced by the patient as a form of retaliation and may feel to the analyst as though he can no longer hold on to particular kinds of affect. It is a form of retaliation that the patient ultimately can survive.

When the analyst is exhausted by holding on to affective experiences that the patient wards off and starts making interpretations, there are often a number of processes occurring. One process has to do with the analyst's need or wish to be able to interpret and help the patient observe disavowed experience and conflict. But there are many instances when by doing so, the analyst is virtually expressing discontent or even unwillingness to continue in the previous mode of holding on to these disavowed experiences. There are many ways in which the process of beginning to interpret these experiences may be experienced by the patient as exclusively retaliatory, even though the analyst may view these experiences as largely interpretive. There are also times when the analyst is aware of expressing intolerance for the previous patterns of interaction but that he may still view as part of an interpretive process, although, once again, the patient may experience them very differently, as punishing or in some way hurtful. The line between what is being expressed through interpretation versus more frank retaliatory expressiveness by the analyst is sometimes thin and requires a great deal of work to clarify both for the analyst and within the dyad. These experiences overlap with what Mitchell (1997) has referred to as therapeutic outbursts, but I prefer to think of them as retaliatory and impinging in order to capture what are often specific affects as experienced by the patient.

I once worked with a patient, Allen (whom I will describe in much greater detail in chapter 8, "The Analyst's Construction of Psychic Possibility"), who for the first few years of analysis objected to my making interpretations because he experienced me in a way as his intrusive and controlling mother. Over the course of a few years I shifted from feeling deeply sympathetic and understanding about why he would experience me this way to wanting to find a way for my understandings to be placed in our interaction. I felt as though I wished he could experience my listening as a kind of holding. Instead, my very presence made him feel agitated. My attempts to understand his fear and experience of impingement seemed to irritate him even more. For the first few years of analysis I tried to bear these experiences with the hope of creating a feeling of safety for Allen.

As he continued to experience me as intrusive and controlling, I began to retaliate unconsciously in ways that involved more disengagement. Clearly, I felt that if I could not engage with him as I "needed or wanted" him to be able to do, I was not going to be as engaged with him as he "needed or wanted" me to be. Mitchell's (1991) discussion of the constructed nature of need and want is highly relevant here since Allen and I were beginning to negotiate the nature of what he needed.

I justified this therapeutic development by noting that in a sense I had struck a compromise. On one side, I wished to interpret Allen's massive defensive structure organized around a consciously and unconsciously protective and retaliatory survival mode to which he clung for dear life. On the other side, I was having difficulty tolerating his massive feeling of hurt by his mother as well as his fear. The two sides were becoming emulsified, so that I did not know which was his survival and which was his unconscious hostility toward both me and his mother. Naturally, both sides were important. Although I felt myself losing the capacity to tolerate his pain, I had not completely given up either. These experiences go to the heart of how a "crunch" (Russell, 1973; Mitchell, 1997) is felt and thought about by both patient and analyst. The essence of a therapeutic crunch, as Russell (1973) noted, lies in an uncanny sense of lack of resolution of the problem of who is doing what to whom within the dyad. To make matters even more difficult, it is often a time when the analyst no longer feels a sense of genuineness and authenticity in understanding the patient's experience of the analyst.

As I became aware of this form of retaliatory withdrawal on my part, I hoped that it was a signal that deeper and different types of negotiations might be possible. I felt that it would be condescending for me to assume that my expectations necessarily impinged on Allen, particularly when I no longer felt a genuineness about my experience of Allen's formulation. I was looking at my limitations to being the kind of object he wished me to be. I was also looking at the types of retaliation that were becoming a feature. I could continue to disappear, or I could become more vocal about what was happening between us. Since I saw my disengagement as a kind of compromise between his needs and my anger, between his theory of therapeutic action or cure and my own, between his sense of victimization and my sense of his unconscious victimizing, between our terror of hurting and being hurt, between his trepidation and my wishes for him to have a new and different kind of relationship with me and others, I decided to try to get out of my own temporary schizoidal pup tent and see if Allen and I could do some building on a new, more permanent psychic housing. Could there be room for my subjective experience to be something other than an intrusive and critical presence? I hoped so.

My hope could have been pathologically pushy and disrespectful of his traumatic past. My hope could have been part of a disavowed aspect of his adaptation, that is, the pushing away of his hoped-for experience with a less intrusive, more empathic parental figure. My hope could have had a great deal of masked aggression and hostility toward his hopeless and nihilistic strategy of relegating me to a silent yes-man or, as we began to term it, a "yes-mom." My hope could have expressed my own anxiety about Allen's regressive longings and wishes. I believe that my hope also reflected the warded-off, wished-for paternal presence that Allen did not have when he was growing up but that might have provided a counterbalance to his experience with his mother and a kind of protection from her. I think that all these meanings and motives were a part of my wish to nudge Allen into a different kind of experience or psychic possibility—not one that circumvented his experience of being on the receiving end of his mother as felt in the maternal transference, but one that tried to incorporate still unconscious aspects of his experiences of identification with her.

The point of this clinical moment, which I imagine is quite familiar to most analysts, is that there is a wide variety of types of retaliation and fallibility to which the analyst exposes the patient in the process of analytic work. There are ways in which our limitations in containment can be good enough, that is, not so destructive, so that both patient and analyst can hold the level of disillusionment, anger, and frustration and new learning and experience can occur. Allen had to do a great deal of containment of his own rage and suspicion as I began more actively to express my wishes and needs that were alien to Allen, so that I might highlight a kind of potential experience of me as object different from his historically held maternal transference. There is little doubt that I was virtually and actually expressing my wishes and needs that I might become a different kind of object to Allen and that he be able to experience new and different aspects of himself in relation to me. He not only had to contain a new kind of experience with me in what I hoped was the therapeutic trajectory, but he also had to contain his disillusionment that I was not patient enough to, as he put it, wait a decade or perhaps even more until I began to make interpretations. I was not necessarily complying with his fantasy of therapeutic action or, in the words of Ornstein (1995), his "curative fantasy," although I did want to try to understand his. I was trying to analyze this fantasy rather than simply enact it, although, of course, I was constantly trying to understand how I might be enacting aspects of his relationship with his mother.

In a sense, I was trying to create circumstances in which I thought I could better understand his fantasy as both a wish about what was and reluctance to explore what could be. It seems to me that part of what happens during the crunch is that both patient and analyst become a wrecking ball toward the other's experience in the service of trying to make it more understandable to the other. Protecting the solitude and privacy of the patient is essential to analytic work (Bion, 1962; Ogden, 1996). Indeed, this protection of potential space and sensitivity to the generative aspects of solitude are a bit like Rilke's leitmotif throughout his poetry on the "mutual guarding and protecting of the other's solitude" as the highest form of love. Yet this dimension of analytic work is only one part of what is generative. It is an ideal but is, in the best of circumstances, benevolently transformed through disillusionment and good-enough transformation or even "good-enough" wrecking or retaliation.

To be sure, an analyst's expectation of mutual containment from the patient can easily involve a countertransference enactment, particularly if the border between containment and more frank taking care of the analyst's needs has been crossed. The patient's ability to absorb and work with the analyst's limitations can and often does involve ways in which he or she has taken care of a parent that may repeat aspects of childhood and thus involves an enactment within the dyad. With Allen, I had to consider constantly whether my wish to be experienced differently or as what Kleinians might term an object "external to the transference" (Bion, 1977b; Caper, 1994) had to do with my own impatience, my own need to be seen. In other words, the patient may feel that he has to accommodate to the analyst's needs. When this is a feature in an analysis, it is important that the analyst become aware of it over time and try to analyze it if it becomes a persistent feature of the treatment. During periods of affective intensity or the crunch, it is especially difficult to differentiate between these transgressions and routine aspects of mutual containment during periods of affective intensity that I am elucidating. I am thinking here of quotidian moments when there is less frank enactment; instead the analyst needs to finds ways to accept and work with the patient's containment of the analyst's heightened affective expressiveness as a part of the treatment process. The analyst cannot ask to be taken care of by the patient any more in a model that uses countertransference expressively than he can in any other model. This requisite restraint is a far cry from taking a good hard look at how much our patients are always containing aspects of what we say and do. The point of occasional expressive use of countertransference is not to legislate perspective and authority, but to alloy it so that a new psychic metal can emerge.

Many aspects of mutual containment become a feature in dealing with other forms of sustained negative transference. I have been amazed at times at my patients' ability, even in the context of intense and sustained negative transference, to help me stay on course. For example, if a patient expresses hopelessness and I take it too concretely, the patient can remind me about the transferential nature of why I am experienced as too ineffective, too uncaring, too caring, too needy, too remote, and the like. In effect, the patient is reminding me that I am taking the transference in too concrete or literal a way. One patient became very relieved at my calmness in the face of her repeated conviction that something had gone on between us that spelled doom. She repeatedly was heartened that we could make sense of horrifying, catastrophic experiences and dread about where things would go between us. Yet, at a certain point, it was I who became fearful that something was really problematic in the face of the negative transference, and it was she who had to remind me that these were feelings held in the complex amalgam of the real and the transferential. She essentially said to me, "Hello, have you ever heard of transference, Dr. Concrete?" These moments can also mark the beginning of a shift from a position in which I have been the sole holder and container for hope and she the sole container for hopelessness; she begins to hold a bit more of the hope and I am now holding more of the hopelessness. Not only are these experiences powerful as beginning changes in a therapeutic process, they also provide sustenance for the desperate and exhausted dyad trying to survive a negative transference.

Some Routine Elements of Containment of Desire in the Erotic Transference-Countertransference

The good-enough holding and containing that the patient does for the analyst occurs in a broad variety of circumstances, far beyond absorbing what seeps out around the analyst's unconscious retaliation or fear and exhaustion with the patient's hostility or hopelessness. In many of these circumstances, there is a sense of familiarity with the analyst's limitations and, as in any good, long-term relationship, a capacity to tolerate disillusionment and limitations in the other person. Patients learn about the ordinary aspects of the analyst's personality and neurosis and how these are manifested in the analyst's ways of experiencing and managing a variety of affects. These include how we deal with money, sexuality, guilt, our own excitement, our ability or limitations in dealing with time, and the like. Sometimes I have an image of a couple who know each other well, the good and the bad, and especially how to get the best out of what each other can give. Another image is of orangutans picking knotted fur and bugs off each other's back—they come to know what bugs them. Analyst and patient come to do this around relational and emotional knots (Pizer, 2000), tangles, and the like. They learn when to do this and when not to, and they learn how to change.

In my work with some patients over a long period of time, they have described the ways in which they dealt with particular kinds of character traits of mine that seemed quite familiar to me. Rarely are their observations without various transferentially influenced meanings that the patient has combined with his own perceptions. In highlighting this dimension of analytic work, I do not mean to minimize the power of transference and the experiences I have with patients' experiences of me that do not feel like familiar aspects of my character or behavior. In the best of circumstances the patient's accommodation should not be viewed as catastrophic or even, necessarily regrettable, if the analyst knows himself or herself well enough to be able to take seriously what the patient is observing and learning about regarding his or her limitations. To expect otherwise is to expect the impossible. This model of analysis, this heroic effort or expectation of being so good—so good that the analyst's warts are not showing—can actually become destructive to a patient and to others in his or her life, particularly if it becomes a template for what the patient expects from others in a relationship. Most people who complete successful treatment have been *aided* in seeing and trusting their sense of their analyst's limitations, not through revelation, but through therapeutic work. Indeed, to me this ability to see the analyst as a more whole person is one of the hallmarks of a good treatment.

In a long-term treatment in particular, the patient gets to know the analyst's everyday ways of dealing with desire, intimacy, and dependence. Each analyst feels particular kinds of conflicts around the emergence of erotic transference or preoedipal transference that the patient will often come to know or at least sense. Sometimes this is a real problem in an analysis. For example, if a female patient comes to know that her male analyst cannot deal with the intensity of her sexual feelings, she may feel that she has to back off. If, in turn, her analyst is unable to pick up on this unfortunate adaptation to his limitations to the point that he cannot analyze it within himself and with the patient, pieces of work will never be accomplished. Similarly, if a patient gets to know her analyst's exhibitionistic needs and works around them to her detriment, accommodating in ways that are familiar and painful for her in terms of her own growth, then this is similarly problematic.

But there are some ways in which we tend to minimize that aspects of the patient's accommodation to the analyst's conflicts are a part of most treatments. Some patients learn how to say to the inhibited analyst in one way or other, "Come on, buddy, I need someone to engage with and play with so I can get this stuff worked out." The other side of this is the patient who sometimes has to say to an analyst who can get a little wound up, in effect, "Down boy." It is important to elaborate what I mean by the "patient's saying" something about these matters. I am referring to a broad range of ways that the patient may consciously or unconsciously allude to his or her perceptions and experiences of the analyst, many of which are also filled with fantasy and transference expectations. But many of our patients learn how to help us to work with them. It is as if the patient who has felt so helped by her analyst in a number of other ways is able to say to her analyst, "Come on, work with me here."

In not too drastic circumstances, the patient might engage in these processes through a sense of humor. For example, one patient who became aware of the pleasure that I often take in associating to some of my patient's dreams (not my own, private associations) would sometimes interrupt me and say something like, "Do you think that I might be able to finish associating to my dream? I know it's a radical proposal." We laughed and tried to use his helpful supervision. Naturally, these moments are complex in meaning—they do not only necessarily involve the patient's providing containment for the analyst's excitement, inhibitions, or exhibitionism. The patient might be unable to feel engaged in the process of associating until his analyst "interrupted" him. He could be involved in a kind of displaced sexual activity, such as unwittingly conveying that he had stopped associating for the moment, but then feel angry about being interrupted. Perhaps this kind of process can be a displaced form of sexual activity, such as "I want to have my orgasm first" or "I want to be on top." The patient and the analyst could be recreating particular kinds of ways that the patient's family members neglected and interrupted him in their discussions. There are also the ways in which the patient requires us to fail. Winnicott (1971) stressed the importance of learning about failure in the process of being "good enough."

In a series of papers related to erotic transference and countertransference issues, Davies (1994, 1998) has attempted to find a place for a theory about the nature of adult sexuality and particularly what she refers to as postoedipal development. While the asymmetry of the analytic situation often mobilizes the experience of the analyst as an unavailable oedipal object, there is no doubt that as analysts we have minimized the complexity and diversity of sexual feelings and desires as we understand developmental and transferential processes. Thus Davies has begun to explore the application of a complex developmental line to erotic interest within the transference relationship in analysis. This developmental line relates to the present discussion about containment because I believe that the reasons why we have focused so strongly on the analyst as an unavailable oedipal object go beyond the universality and power of Oedipus. It has also provided a kind of built-in containment, a cap, or even an avoidance of the complexities of postoedipal issues and related countertransference experience. Speculatively, it may also be an area where we have sometimes unwittingly contributed to lengthier analyses than might be necessary.

Davies (1994, 1998) not only explores the nature of these developmental lines; she also deals with basic issues about what traumatic experience does to one's capacity for play and the appreciation of reality and paradox. Davies invites us to think about creative ways to differentiate between dyadic and triadic experience and the ways in which we can and cannot apply formulations of optimal oedipal configuration to persons who have experienced considerable trauma. This discussion raises fascinating questions about the nature of containment and expressiveness, safety and danger among patients who have been traumatized. How much do we contain psychic danger for the traumatized patient and how much do we try to hold them psychically as they revisit these experiences?

This complexity is welcome if we allow ourselves to see how equating the analyst with the unavailable oedipal object is an overvalued idea (Bion, 1977a) that the analyst needs to contain in order to be more open to other formulations.

MUTUAL CONTAINMENT AND THE EXPERIENCE OF TIME IN THE ANALYTIC PROCESS

Another really interesting aspect of how patients contain for the analyst involves their capacity to interpret aspects of new experience. Analysts are trained to see and understand aspects of repetition; we are trained less to look for newness in the repetition (see chapter 3). I am often struck by how often patients are, at particular times, much more adept at providing this vantage point than are their analysts and how they can aid in this process. At such times, patients may contain our tendency to see repetition and to focus too much on historical transference as a kind of one-dimensional surface. The tendency to develop a formulation about how and what transference patterns are forming and stay too focused on these at the expense of other emerging material is just as powerful a force for the analyst to contend with as are our well-documented tendencies to avoid transference (Bird, 1972; Schlesinger, 1997). Just as patients need to learn how to observe the transference as it unfolds in the interaction with the analyst, analysts need, at times, to learn from their patients how to see new aspects of interaction.

My main point here is that, once again, the patient serves an interpretive and containing function in relation to the analyst's limitations. For example, the patient might say, "How come you don't see that by not needing you, I'm able to stop acting in the same erotically masochistic way I act with unavailable men? You keep seeing it as a fear of my needing you." What is often the case, and sometimes a point of shared humor for patient and analyst, is that the experience of "How come you don't see how different this is for me" sometimes has, in fact, elements of repetition as well! Far from humor, however, was my work with Allen and the tormenting, exhilarating, unsolvable experiences of the crunch that raised an interesting question: to what extent did his anger toward me derive from the sense of threat from me as a potentially new type of relationship, or was it an affective expression directed toward the old object conveyed through new self-experience?

The analyst's use of containment and expressiveness sometimes draws attention to how the patient might be using the analyst in a new way, different from the way he used the old object. At the same time the analyst must monitor and contain the possibility of mitigating or diluting the power of historically held transference. The analyst sometimes differentiates himself from the old object experience but often also needs to contain the urge to point out to the patient how different he is from the emerging and potentially beneficial transferential picture of the analyst. We can easily defensively embrace aspects of the new object. Doing so essentially involves our inability to contain affects related to the unrelenting repetition of problematic relationships (external and internal) in the patient's psychic life. The analyst's subjectivity in such instances has to be contained, as Slochower (1996) has illustrated.

Russell (1973) had a great deal to say about the ability of both patient and analyst to sustain and contain uncertainty and ambiguity during periods of affective intensity, or what he termed the crunch. In his description of the crunch, Russell made it very clear that the uncertainty about what is what, what is old and what is new, and even, at times, who is who is a shared uncertainty, or at least it should be.

I would add to this evocative description of the treatment process another dimension: that both analyst and patient are constantly trying to look into a new psychic realm, the psychic future. The analyst is constantly promoting a psychic agenda, or at least I hope she is—and this is true even for analysts who say that their intention is to "match" the patient's psychic reality as much as possible. Every intervention, question, interpretation, and silence emerges from the analyst's wishes (and conflicts about wishes) for the patient to see or understand something, to bear experience. That we are always hoping that our patients will find new possibility in their lives continues to be one of the largest dimensions of the blank screen that we continue to evade.

The analyst has to contain his hopes and wishes, many of which are in concert with those of the patient, just as he has to allow himself to express them, even, at times, those which differ from the patient. The patient has to learn to understand how the analyst contains these hopes and wishes, and each has to learn to identify with the hope for psychic change and movement that comes from the other. To be sure, patients have to contain their hopes and wishes; otherwise they would soon lose patience with the sometimes slow and arduous process of psychoanalysis.

It is helpful to think about these experiences with the idea that the patient makes the analyst feel the "uncanniness" of the unsolved problem between them (Russell, 1973), about what is old, what is new, and what is in the hopper and trying to be generated. The analyst has to feel and contain his uncertainty about what is old, new, and possible, and it is often only with the patient's help, no doubt defensively and conflictually determined, that he is able to find out.

The analyst also actively makes the patient feel this unsolved problem in a new and vivid way. The analyst constantly provides elements of containment around the wish that the patient will be able to move and shift in various affective positions and conflicts. The patient will to some extent always automatically contain the analyst's wish for the patient to shift in all sorts of ways, most naturally and powerfully through some of the patient's own processes of defense and maintaining homeostasis and external processes of affect regulation with the analyst. The patient is sometimes telling the analyst in one way or other to "hold your horses, buddy" while at other times trying to catalyze possibility for change. We analysts are also each quite different in how we encourage or not. Some of us worry so much about pushing or impinging that what can result is a treatment in which, as one of my colleagues likes to say, "Nobody laid a glove on him." Others of us may be too aggressive and need help with the appreciation we each must have about how difficult it is to change. We try to notice the vicissitudes of our hopes and wishes regarding treatment in various kinds of dynamic tension and in relation to our patients' conflicts and our own. Through the process of analysis, these wishes are always being expressed, enacted, contained, abided, and defensively regulated.

I sometimes wonder whether the brilliant and much-needed work of such analysts as Winnicott and Kohut has attuned us so much to patients' attempts to preserve hope and longed-for object responsiveness that we may tend to equate the analyst's activity with aggression or interfering with the emergence of hoped-for objects (Cooper, in press).

Benjamin's (1988) elaboration of the "paradoxical role of recognition" underscores the analyst's experience as subject relative to his role as an object in meeting the needs and experience of the child during development. Benjamin emphasizes the degree to which analysts minimize the generative potential inherent in colliding subjectivities. In a sense, the minimization of the role of the mother's subjectivity may be a part of a more general discomfort with the parent's aggression and activity and its instrumental role in the child's development. We may also sometimes associate analytic activity with the impinging bad parent, particularly within more developmentally based analytic theory, which focuses on the parent as object rather than subject.

Perhaps too we associate our awareness of time and limits with impingement. As I suggest in chapter 9, we may have become so absorbed in the timelessness of the unconscious in analysis that sometimes we too easily forget about time passing, what I earlier called the conspiratorial timeless unconscious. This is a point that has been well articulated by Hoffman (1996) as the tendency of patient and analyst to collude in a denial of both death and the passage of time. It is the analyst's job to help contain the tendency to deny the passage of time.

The analyst's attention to the timelessness of the unconscious is essential to how he conceives of the role of regression in analytic work. Even the necessary and inevitable aspects of regression should always be contained and juxtaposed against the present through interpretation. Loewald (1960) captured this idea beautifully when he described interpretation as always having one foot toward regression and another toward newness, growth, and an anticipated future. The road to new relational pathways and new choice almost always encompasses the regressive experience as well. Loewald's "ghosts of recognition," though, sometimes have to be coaxed to come out of the psychic walls.

The developmental approaches have brought an influx of romantic energy to the process, most vividly in elaborating how our strategies of survival help us to preserve hopes and wishes for empathic objects, even if our initial objects of hope have been disappointing or even woefully lacking. Any analysis that is useful helps to catalyze the experience and recognition of these hoped-for objects. Yet it is possible that these models have not only replaced the blank screen with a new version, the "generic analyst" (Mitchell, 1997), but also have oversimplified the multiple, complex, and reciprocal ways in which analysts contain and influence their patients and are contained and influenced by their patients through the analytic process.

The crunch, as both Russell (1973) and Mitchell (1997) have described, is about the uncanny perplexity of past unsolved problems and how they are remanifested in the therapeutic situation. The crunch is also an expression of the affective mass that surrounds the conscious and unconscious mandate or social compact of every treatment. The analyst's position treacherously combines respect and modesty along with the necessary therapeutic attitude of being hell bent to try to facilitate change. Rilke (1907), in one of his most dramatic statements, at the end of his poem called *The Archaic Torso of Apollo* exclaimed, "You must change your life." The analytic crunch is mobilized, energized, and catalyzed by this social, relational compact. It is what causes both repetition and the possibility for newness or what Martin Buber (1970) called "the imagined real." Containment governs both the tragic experience of foreclosed possibility and the inevitable, reopened feelings about possibility for all patients, alone and together with their analysts, intimately and in solitude. Containment is indeed among the most intimate ways in which two people can interact, open up, and excite possibility and limitation with each other—in analysis and in every other relationship.

PART II

THE SHIFTING SURFACE

THE SHIFTING SURFACE

A Comparative View of Sources of Influence in American Relational Theory and Ego Psychology

I N THE NEXT FOUR CHAPTERS I explore the concepts of regression, defense analysis, and countertransference expressiveness. In the way that I practice analysis, I see a great deal of overlap and usefulness in trying to integrate the contributions from each of these perspectives. I am largely in agreement with those theorists (e.g., Greenberg and Mitchell, 1983; Hoffman, 1983) who have described ways in which these perspectives provide fundamentally different views of both mind and various aspects of the analytic stance. These differences relate to whether the mind is viewed as monadic or subject to mutual influence, whether defense is conceptualized within a one- or a two-person model, and how the countertransference is used in the analytic work. Yet there are also interesting points of overlap. For example, in recent years I have become interested in how classical models and relational models are more free than some developmental-tilt models in using clinical moments in which the analyst notes affective experiences and views of psychic reality as differing from or complementary to those of their patients. To be sure, analysts within these models use these moments in quite distinctive ways. Each model also focuses on different phases of clinical work, which highlight some of the profound differences within the models.

Some interesting questions coalesce around whether differences in the types of clinical situations chosen for illustration in clinical papers also in some ways obfuscate or cloud over aspects of overlap in clinical work. For example, I think that our relational literature has focused on points of impasse, whereas ego psychology has tried to illustrate modal moments of analytic work. This observation raises questions about how ego psychologists work at points of impasse, and how relational analysts work in situations involving less threat of stalemate or impasse. From the narrative and clinical illustrations of such issues as regression, interpretive influence, and countertransference disclosure, I hope the reader will be able to explore some of the ways in which the models provide differing and overlapping perspectives.

I will try to provide some ways of integrating the insights of relational and ego psychological models. Hoffman (1996) has suggested that to some extent we replace free association as the central focus of analytic attention with the "free emergence of multiple transference-countertransference scenarios, a sample of which is more or less reflected upon and interpreted over time" (p. 113). In my clinical examples in this section of the book, I try to illustrate how the analyst's attention to the surfaces of the patient's associations, emphasized by ego psychology, inevitably involve our participation in conscious and unconscious transference-countertransference enactments. Attention to both domains is helpful both in our analytic work and in integrating the contributions from each of these theoretical models. Questions are raised about the value of the term surface in psychoanalytic theory, particularly in conceptualizing a shift from topographical approaches to affect and associative content to a view of clinical moments as points of transference-countertransference experience between patient and analyst.

The implications for this shift are also important in integrating the theoretical perspectives offered by ego psychology and relational approaches regarding the therapeutic action of psychoanalysis. I suggest that in making what ego psychologists view as defense interpretations, we are often "holding" a view of the patient's psychic future. Loewald's (1960) view of interpretation as having one foot in regression and another in anticipating the patient's growth, comes close to the way I will try to reconcile the ego psychological and relational perspectives on interpretation. Loewald did not, however, explicitly reconcile the intrapsychic and interpersonal functions of interpretation. Some defense interpretations of disavowed affect that involve what I call "analyst disclosure" function in similar ways to what ego psychologists refer to as the interpretation of defense.

5

REGRESSION AND THE OLD-NEW
OBJECT CONTINUUM

Molly and the Problem of
"Antiregression" and Progression

In this chapter, I explore some of the ways in which productive regressive transference and new experience are held in complex interaction with one another. A case example illustrates some aspects
of my struggle to see new experience emerging from analytic regression. This case may also be usefully understood as involving some aspects of what Sandler and Sandler (1994b) call "antiregressive"
dimensions within the transference. Antiregressive phenomena refer to
patients' fears of allowing themselves to play with transferential aspects
of experience. I, however, would like to extend their work to highlight
how an analyst's views of the patient's fears of regression may sometimes
reflect the analyst's limitations in observing other, less expected aspects
of transference. This dimension within the countertransference refers
to what I call "mutual antiregressive" dimensions within the transference and countertransference. I allude to the analyst's resistance to seeing something new that the patient is expressing and experiencing,
often unconscious in nature. This work may complement some of the
recent territory explored by Aron and Bushra (1998) in their paper on
mutual aspects of regression in the analytic situation.

A BRIEF REVIEW OF CURRENT CONTROVERSIES
RELATED TO REGRESSION

It is a daunting task to integrate the two fundamentally different views of regression that I hold. One relates to the value and inevitability of a developmental atmosphere engendered by both the invitation to speak as openly as possible and the asymmetrical arrangements of the analytic situation in which the patient is likely to attribute to the analyst aspects of parents and earlier caretakers. Analysis offers the extraordinary opportunity to discover and experience elements of psychic and somatic life previously unknown, or perhaps new, akin to Bollas's (1987) "unthought known." The other perspective, however, is that the patient can sometimes be infantilized by the analyst, and an opportunity for growth can easily be overlooked. These days, classically trained analysts need ask about the potentially destructive aspects of viewing patients as naive participants, whereas relationally oriented analysts need ask whether they are too readily inclined to overemphasize the maturity or pseudomaturity of the patient. It is in the area of regression that both approaches are indispensable in understanding and analyzing affect and unconscious process in clinical analysis.

All analysts have particular strengths and weaknesses in the use of regression. Some are able to promote it or facilitate its emergence and use it well. The capacity to create safety (a safe feeling for patients to express themselves) does not mean that the analyst necessarily knows how to confront patients in a safe manner in relation to conflict. Some analysts know how to promote regression but do not necessarily know what to do with it once it develops. In other words, some know how to interpret deeply preoedipal longings and wishes, striking resonant chords for a patient. But they do not necessarily know how to interpret aspects of character defense that move the analysis out of the most regressive experience and into some of the issues that are engaged in more frequently by those with whom the patient relates. Similarly, some analysts are unable to confront patients with the use of transference as a defense against other experiences. Usually we each have our strengths in dealing with particular affects, such as love, sadness, anger, or excitement, as well as our ability to interpret a patient's reluctance to experience these affects.

Relational theory in the United States has usefully challenged some of the most concrete interpretations of the developmental metaphor in analytic work, particularly within the "developmental tilt" (Mitchell, 1988) models of Winnicott, Kohut, and, to some extent, Loewald. Yet I agree with Slochower (1996a) that, despite the many complexities of regressive experience in analysis, we need a perspective that encompasses the inevitability and utility of regression in doing analytic work. Regressive experience includes both the value of the patient-as-baby metaphor of developmental tilt models as well as the subtle notion of defensive regression of many ego psychologists (e.g., Gray, 1990; Busch, 1995; Schlesinger, 1997).

This perspective helps balance what has been emphasized in American relational models—an awareness that old and new experience often occur in complex patterns and that we can easily take the baby metaphor in too literal and concrete a fashion. In particular, Slochower (1996b) has elaborated holding as a psychological metaphor and set of technical principles that are necessary in working with some analytic patients. To Slochower, the holding process involves both the adult patient's struggle with the current residue of early trauma and the patient's experience as a child. She agrees with Ghent (1992) that *the paradox of the patient as baby and adult is better tolerated than resolved.* This idea seems to me to be consistent with the prominence Loewald gives to the constant marriage of progressive and regressive elements of experience in our functioning. Bromberg (1991) echoes Loewald's (1960) and, earlier, Anna Freud's (1936) understanding of the tension between child and adult within the patient. Bromberg adds that the analyst has to maintain an analytic attitude toward the "child" in the patient as simultaneously real and metaphorical.

These psychic positions and tensions are linked to the vicissitudes of hope for the future, including the emergence and resistance to experiencing such hopes in analytic process. Controversies and debate among psychoanalysts in recent years often surround the issue of how and what forms of regression are valued as well as the degree to which regression is seen as inherent to the method or the practitioner's theory and expectations.

Consider some of these views about regression which are filled with tension and paradox. Regression is useful and inevitable in the process of many analyses, yet some versions of regression are highly iatrogenic and problematic. The invitation to risk saying anything that is on one's mind opens up a vast expanse of wishes and needs as well as anxieties about doing so. The same is true for the analyst who is invited into the interactional, representational world of the patient. Although there is a developmental atmosphere in the analytic setting, the developmental metaphor can be taken too concretely by the analyst. It can be stultifying or could engender a malignant regression. For some patients, being permitted *not* to regress is what makes an analysis different and productive. While the patient needs to be able to experience the analyst as an old object, the analyst needs to be experienced as a new object as well. The attempt to understand the analyst as a new object risks diluting the patient's experience of the analyst as an old object; the attempt to analyze repeatedly the patient's reexperience of the analyst as an old object can divert from or minimize the patient's ability to use the analyst as a new object. At times the analyst's using overly concrete developmental models of regrowth can both infantilize the patient and mask aspects of the analyst's unconscious aggression and sexual feeling.

One of the ways in which regression can be misunderstood is in the meaning attributed to the relationship between regression in analysis and regression in life. Anna Freud (1936) and later Holzman and Ekstein (1959) described how regression is often a necessary element of development. In particular, Anna Freud appreciated that children and adults backstep in order to progress in accomplishing developmental tasks. Adults coping with radically shifting conditions in their lives are also often able to use aspects of regression in the service of adaptation. Nowhere is this coping clearer than in the brutal accounts of daily life in the concentration camps that were so vividly described by Levi (1995). The constriction of mental and emotional life and the return to childhood rituals in some ways served the function of denial, adaptation, and survival. This was also detailed by Bromberg (1979) poignantly as he described to interpersonalists the natural pull for regressive phenomena in the course of analysis.

It is my sense that classically trained analysts are accustomed to useful aspects of regression but are not always taught to look for progressive aspects of the patient's so-called regressive phenomena. Yet, even among classically trained analysts, there are many ways in which useful aspects of regression can be discouraged to the patient and opportunities overlooked. For example, Schlesinger (1997) points out that beginning analysts often ignore or minimize the useful instances of interpreting conflict that appear around the emergence of regressive transference. As both a superviser and a clinician, I am aware of how we sometimes tend to discourage the patient's emerging transference and regressive elements in communication that express it. Schlesinger writes:

> The technical problem at this early point in the interpretive process is to help the patient appreciate the importance of experiencing the anxiety rather than quelling it—since, like all affects, it will fade of its own accord, requiring no special efforts. On the other hand, if the patient would remain with the anxiety and "appreciate" it, it might permit the underlying conflicting messages to come through in clearer form. The first specific interpretation should attempt to link the patient's "regression" to its immediate, proximal cause, most often something the analyst has just said or done [p. 6].

Schlesinger's point is that often the most productive work can be done on the edge of the patient's regressive moment by the analyst's trying to understand something about what is emerging without foreclosing this experience. There is a tension between interpreting and supporting defenses against the emergence of transference.

To their credit, ego-psychologically oriented analysts such as Kris (1982), Gray (1990), and Busch (1995) use the concept of regression in circumscribed and well-defined ways. They are interested in the movement of the ego back and forth between expressiveness and defense, and they try to analyze the most manifest, directly observable instances of when a patient moves away from a particular affect or idea. These analysts demystify the concept of regression and do not fall into the vagaries of the concept of regression in presenting a methodological approach to using the concept in clinical work. As I explore in chapter 7, however, on countertransference disclosure, I wonder whether the analysis of defensive regression can sometimes fail to take into consideration important transference-countertransference enactments that occur while the analysis of defense is taking place.

I believe that classically oriented and relationally oriented analysts are probably in pretty strong agreement that there is not an isomorphic relationship between childhood experience and the kind of regression we observe among adults in analysis. Balsam (1997) has stated that regressive experience, as a communication of emotional forerunners to the present tense, helps to restore what Loewald (1978) referred to as the historicity of the individual. My sense of this historicity includes a broad range of phenomena, including narrative truth (Spence, 1982; Schafer, 1992), the reconstruction of a relationship between a present state and an earlier variation of this state in development, or a deeper and more vivid sense of the here-and-now that the patient does not consciously relate to some earlier time yet nevertheless now understands in relation to present and future contexts. There is always a tension between growth and regression, between change and stasis.

Loewald (1978) appreciated the ways in which more mature development are inextricably linked to an awareness of our most primitive experience:

> To own up to our own history, to be responsible for our unconscious . . . means to bring unconscious forms of experiencing into the context and onto the level of the more mature, more lucid life of the adult mind. Our drives, our basic needs, in such transformation, are not relinquished, nor are traumatic and distorting childhood experiences made conscious in order to be deplored and undone—even if that were possible. They are part of the stuff our lives are made of. What is possible is to engage in the task of actively reorganizing, reworking, creatively transforming those early experiences which, painful as many of them have been, first gave meaning to our lives. The more we know what it is that we are working with, the better we are able to weave our history which, when all is said and done, is re-creating, in ever-changing modes and transformations, our childhood. To be an adult means that; it does not mean leaving the child in us behind [p. 22].

What is really interesting about Loewald's characterization is its relevance to both sides of the debate about the value of regression in clinical analysis. It means that analysis provides a unique opportunity to engage safely in exploring early experience. The concern among classical analysts would be that in relationally oriented approaches there is too much emphasis on the mature aspects of the individual rather than creating a developmental atmosphere that promotes the emergence of unconscious affect. On the other side of the debate, it might be argued that there is nothing about engaging the patient as a mature adult that precludes the emergence of more regressive aspects of defense and character. As Loewald said, "To be an adult . . . does not mean leaving the child in us behind."

Merton Gill's shift in position regarding regression is relevant to the discussion of how regressive and new phenomena are a constant part of analysis. Gill changed his 1954 position regarding regression quite dramatically over the years. Gill's (1954) frequently cited definition of psychoanalytic technique emphasized regression as one of the central and essential concepts and developments within analytic process: "Psychoanalysis is that technique which, employed by a neutral analyst, results in the development of a regressive transference neurosis and the ultimate resolution of this neurosis by techniques of interpretation alone" (p. 775). In this paper Gill attempted to clarify that he believed that regression is not a "spontaneous" occurrence in the analytic process. Instead, he stated, "The analytic situation is specifically designed to enforce a regressive transference neurosis" (p. 778). He went on to show how the "trappings" of analysis attempt to induce, accelerate, and deepen the transference.

By the late 1970s and early 1980s Gill (1982) felt that too many analyses had become too intellectual, too sterile, and too devoid of the deeply experienced affects that both he and Bird (1972) believed to be crucial for the analytic task. The element that Gill felt made analysis most intellectual was a predilection for some analysts to be too focused on the reconstruction of the past while being relatively less focused on the here-and-now.

Gill (1994a) changed his position about regression's involving the revival of the oedipal neurosis as an essential aspect of psychoanalysis. He believed that what we construe to be regression may often be usefully seen in other ways. He wrote, "While one can think of this as regression (the appearance of formerly repressed contents), it is at least equally reasonable to think of it as progression in the sense that the patient is able to confront increasingly distressing issues" (p. 75).

I believe that in its first 80 years, and particularly in the last 40, psychoanalysis may have evolved with some aspects of a particular kind of regrowth fantasy for the patient, both consciously and unconsciously held. Particular "developmental tilt" theories (Mitchell, 1988), such as those proposed by Winnicott (1969) and Kohut (1982), focused more on the patient's opportunities for regrowth, whereas many other theories have probably held more *implicit* expectations about the opportunity for regrowth. Much of psychoanalytic theory proposes that, through a regression to points of infantile conflict, the patient will be met by the analyst in a new way, one that creates new psychic opportunity. Winnicott emphasized meeting the patient's moment of hope that had earlier been dashed. Kohut (1984) echoed this idea by highlighting the analytic reactivation of defenses that were originally erected to preserve a hoped-for selfobject. Some would argue that contemporary relational approaches have minimized the "developmental atmosphere" (Stern, 1994) of the analytic situation by emphasizing the maturity of the patient and the patient's ability to integrate the analyst's subjective reactions as an important aspect of growth during analysis. Those most critical of the relational model might go so far as to say that, in conveying and using the analyst's subjectivity, we have gone from a naive or infantilized patient to a parentified patient—one who is asked to be pseudomature before his time.

To my way of thinking, relational and classical models have a great deal to teach each other regarding matters of regression. Aron and Bushra (1998) seem to have come to a similar conclusion. They discuss some aspects of mutual influence in regression that might be minimized with a classical emphasis. Yet they also suggest the value of the state concept for relationally oriented analysts to consider more actively in their clinical work. I am exploring, additionally, the analyst's need to consider certain kinds of new behavior and relatedness within regressive states and particularly transference.

I do not believe that there is value in thinking about regression in terms of whether or not it is iatrogenic. Regression is a by-product of the unusual arrangements of analytic work as well as a ubiquitous part of emotional life. I think of analysis as partly a regressive context, somewhat analogous to what the art critic Peppiatt (1997) stated about Jackson Pollock's painting: "Pollock's paint-slinging created swirls of color that draw the imagination into a region of boundless space" (p. 18). In some ways the analyst provides a canvas onto which the patient slings, delicately drips, smudges, or dribbles paint. The experience of analysis, the experience of subjectivity itself, and particularly someone listening to it invites our imaginations and psyches into a region of seemingly boundless space. One of the things that is most extraordinary about this space is the invitation to talk about one's feelings, one's body, with a great deal more abandon than in most other verbal settings. I say "seemingly" boundless because, while the invitation opens up fantasies of unlimited wish, desire, and gratification, it also opens up experiences of limitation and disappointment. All these experiences constitute what we commonly think of as regression.

But while it is important to say that regression occurs descriptively and not prescriptively, it is also important to distinguish between types of regression that occur naturally and those that are in many ways brought about by the analyst. Gill (1994a) discussed the reluctance by some analysts to take seriously the notion that when we are taking something syntonic for the patient and trying to create a level of discord or curiosity, we are probably engaged at the same time in creating or inducing a level of regression as well. What would happen if the patient could stop putting on a happy face, verbally or behaviorally, when she is angry? What would happen if she could stop acting impulsively through withdrawal whenever she began to feel tenderness toward another person? Why does my patient ask me so many questions at the beginning of an hour when he is unconsciously feeling so anxious about whether I really care about him? All these interventions seem to me quite consistent with the idea of interpreting habitual or characterological defensive configurations and adaptations. These interventions, taken cumulatively over the sessions, seem to me quite consistent with the idea of interpreting habitual or characterological defensive configurations and adaptations. These interventions, taken more cumulatively over the course of analysis, are likely to have the effect of stripping away familiar behavioral and psychological modes of adaptation. This kind of regression does not happen; it is induced. To be sure, each patient responds in quite different ways to the analyst's actions, but there is a common assumption that the analyst is performing a common function of interpretation—to take something familiar and make it unfamiliar. We all lose our bearings when something is made unfamiliar, but there is also opportunity for learning.

Sometimes making the familiar unfamiliar involves confronting the patient with evidence of how he uses habitually "regressive" modes in order to avoid feeling or thinking things that cause discomfort. At some level, these kinds of interventions are aimed at helping a patient to feel or think on a different, shall we say, "more realistic" level. This kind of defense interpretation interferes with what we more superficially term regression. For example, a male patient is trying to stop a female friend from trying to seduce him and he, her. He wants to do so because it is his sense that, through this behavior, they avoid getting to know each other better. It is a struggle for him. Whenever the friend engages in a kind of nonflirtatious discourse, my patient interprets to her some underlying meaning to her behavior; he is enacting his wishes to penetrate, play, have sex with, and probably as well, to hurt her. A natural question follows: What might be avoided by taking her in as she was recently inviting and that he consciously says he wants—a friendship in which seduction is not reflexively featured? Or what is keeping him from seeing that his difficulty resisting their seductiveness toward each other is an indication of strong feelings worth pursuing more seriously? For this particular patient, whether or not to seduce or be seduced kept him from experiencing deeper aspects of his mistrust and wishes for closeness with a woman.

One of the most confusing and interesting aspects of regression is that, on one hand, regression exists as a universal, natural tendency or outcome of the analytic process, and, on the other, it can also be a response to the expectations of the analyst (Mitchell, 1991). For many analysts, the arrangements of analysis offer many parallels to those of the parent-child relationship. The asymmetrical arrangements of the analytic relationship engender certain aspects of desire, hostility, needs, longings, wishes to be loved, competitive and rivalrous feelings, wishes to rebel, and others reminiscent of the child-parent relationship. Most analysts agree that, while ideally there is a developmental atmosphere in analysis, what gives analysis its power is that it is both similar to and different from the parent-child relationship.

These observations about the developmental atmosphere of an analysis can never be fully separated from the degree to which the analyst is prepared to see the analytic relationship as an analogue to the parent-child relationship. It is useful for any analyst to consider his own assumptions (or observations) about the extent to which the developmental metaphor is operating in his viewpoint or observing stance. How important to the overall success of analysis is it to reconstruct what happened during childhood? How much do we take the developmental metaphor literally? Considering how we use the developmental metaphor is important because some analysts are reluctant to interpret highly avoidant aspects of regressive transference for fear of impinging on what they construe to be, or hope to be, an unfolding process. How much is the analyst oriented to such varied and complex uses of reconstruction as how childhood experience applies to the *new* analytic relationship and "interferes" with various psychic possibilities of self- and other experience. Loewald emphasized how interpretation involves one step toward regression and one step toward what I have called the psychic future (Cooper, 1997).

A fascinating argument has been brewing within the American relational conflict literature about the nature and importance of regression in clinical psychoanalysis. Some (e.g., Stern, 1994) have suggested that "a developmental atmosphere" is inherent to the analytic setting. This assumption implies that the analytic setting engenders certain kinds of regressive pulls related to the hierarchical and asymmetrical arrangement. These forces include the mobilization of archaic, characterologically constricted modes of relating and complex defenses against reexperiencing early trauma or modes of relating. Not in place of, but in conjunction with, this view of analysis, others, such as Mitchell (1991), have underscored analysis as an encounter between two psychological adults. Rather than minimizing the inevitability of the patient's reexperiencing of early traumas or dependent modes of relating, Mitchell's (1994) view of regression focuses more on regression to earlier interpersonal contexts than to thwarted developmental fixation points. These interpersonal contexts are associated with reparative forms of interaction, new kinds of experience that differ from the earlier types of interaction, which were stultifying or traumatic.

I find that the points made by both Stern and Mitchell have a great deal of merit. Process viewed as developmental unfolding can be extremely helpful if it is done in a way that does not assume an isomorphic relationship between analytic process and childhood development. Developmental metaphors can also be extremely helpful as long as the analyst maintains a sense of their being tools used in constructing meaningful affective and ideational narratives. The analyst has to be aware of the inevitability of projecting onto the process certain kinds of expectations regarding developmental models and fantasies (Balint, 1968; Mitchell, 1991). Bromberg (1993) summarized these tensions well:

Therapeutic regression refers to the "raw" states of cognitive disequilibrium allowed by an analytic patient as part of the progressive, self-perpetuating restructuring of self and object representations . . . the deeper the regression that can be safely allowed by the patient, the richer the experience and the greater its reverberation on the total organization of the self. . . . The "child" in the patient is a complex creature; he is never simply the original child come to life again, but always an aspect of an aware and knowing adult. In this respect it is fair to portray the relationship between analyst and "child" as simultaneously real and metaphorical. Regression in one respect is a metaphor, but not *only* a metaphor. It is also a real state of mind . . . [pp. 416-417].

One of the most confusing aspects of attempting to appreciate the child and adult in the context of discussions of regression in the literature is that it can sometimes be thought of as the patient's transition to earlier periods of development. For example, Gill (1994) wondered if becoming increasingly aware of repressed material indicates deeper levels of regression. If a patient is better able to face distressing issues that were previously omitted from awareness or repressed, then there is reason to believe that the patient is becoming stronger. Perhaps sometimes we confuse the patient's need for relational contact or accompaniment with the repressed material with regression to an infantile state.

For example, Josh, a man in his late 30s, began to feel a deep sense of desire that had been previously repressed. Josh asked me to help him see the danger signs if he were to act on any aspects of his desire. Feeling overwhelmed by his wishes to have sex with every available woman made him feel that he needed a man to tell him to slow down, that there could be some difficult repercussions if he were to pursue all his romantic interests. I understood this request at a number of levels of psychic reality. There was a wish to have me be established as "the law," setting limits on his desire in ways that he did not know how to do or want to do for himself. Josh wanted this alliance also to obscure competitive feelings between the two of us. I felt as though the fantasy and expression of wish was of a very deep kind, one that he had never expressed so directly to me before and one that was a source of huge disappointment and sadness in relation to his father. In this regressive context, Josh may have revisited points of interruption or conflict with his father. Additionally, however, the newness of the analytic situation recalled a broad variety of limitations with his own father. Josh may have been guilty about his own oedipally based desires that related to the conflicts prohibiting him from seeking more from his father. But I would have been more comfortable with general conclusions focusing on affective states and points of conflict. I view this kind of moment as incredibly complicated in the matter of regression because there are concurrent affective lines being expressed and enacted all the time. Josh was exploring wishes and needs that had not been previously explored. Partly in that context, he asked for a kind of psychic holding in relation to those wishes. Unconsciously, he also wished to keep me as a noncompetitor who would benignly limit his passion, but not from a competitive, oppositional perspective, rather in the role of a benevolent protector. Meyerson (1981) pointed out how repressed material always occurs in an interpersonal context. I would add that previously repressed material, as it emerges, requires a new interpersonal context, at least a wished-for, newly configured context that the analyst can attempt to explore. At the same time, the analyst may also be interested in how the repressed returns in surprising and disguised ways.

I think that in analytic work we are often insufficiently attentive to how the repetition in the transference relates simultaneously to old and new object experiences. This repetition was illustrated briefly in the case of Sarah (chapter 3). To put it as simply as possible, the transference is often characterized by how a patient selectively perceives and experiences the analyst. Often this takes the form of the transference to the analyst resembling an important person from the patient's life, most often a mother or father. Given the power of transference—that is, these tendencies to organize images that repeat experiences with important others—we as analysts can also sometimes minimize ways in which patients are experiencing and describing different experiences with us at the same time as they are repeating old ones.

One of the reasons we may minimize these simultaneously held experiences of us as old and new objects is that, understandably, we do not want to minimize or divert the patient from his transference experience. We do not want to avoid a negative transference or divert the patient's attention from important affects. But I begin with the notion emphasized much more in interpersonal theory, particularly most recently by Bromberg (1979, 1995, 1998), that individuals simultaneously try to insure stability and to grow, or as he put it, "trying to change while trying to stay the same" (1998, p. 209). A painting by

Robert Frank entitled *Hold Still—Keep Going* seems to capture this idea beautifully through a representation. This position overlaps with but is also different from Kohut's assumption that people use defenses to secure object relations more empathic than the ones they met up with in childhood. I think that Bromberg's formulation is less teleological in characterizing forces of repetition and growth.

I often find that it takes me quite a while to see how, in interpreting aspects of negative and positive transference from old object experience, I might be minimizing qualities of transferential newness.

MOLLY: TRANSFERENCE-COUNTERTRANSFERENCE DESIRE AND DREAD AND THE PROBLEM OF REGRESSION AND ANTIREGRESSION

In doing analysis, I am comforted to some extent by the knowledge (or faith) that, for all the limitations of analysts and patients working together in the realms of desire, hostility, love, and hate and beset by their anxiety, avoidance, and reluctance, patients do their best with what they have—their analysts. If this sounds like less than resounding self-praise for my clinical technique in the following case description, you are correct. It is, however, a not uncommon story of relational compromise—two people working with each other's limitations and aspects of our inner worlds that influence and interact with each other in the crucible of transference and countertransference.

The more we make use of our subjectivity as analysts, the more it is necessary for us to be aware of our tendencies to understand, work with, or avoid various affects or conflicts. Partly this awareness helps us to understand unfolding regression, countertransference enactment, and the like. Particularly with regard to love and hate, we get to know our strengths and vulnerabilities. We also need to be aware of what might be called our usual characteristics as a stimulus value—our personality features, sense of humor, intellect, and physical appearance. This is not to say that all patients will resonate or respond to these quotidian characteristics in similar ways. If anything, our awareness of transference suggests just the opposite. But it is still an important feature to throw into the mix of understanding what is happening in our interactions with patients.

While I have found it pleasing, gratifying, and, of course, sometimes exciting to have female patients feel that they were attracted to me, their responses to me have sometimes made me anxious about being too seductive. In turn, I have sometimes consciously or unconsciously erred on the side of avoiding being overly seductive by minimizing aspects of the erotic transference when it is present. I am, though, more comfortable now feeling and tolerating my attractiveness to patients than I was when I began doing psychotherapy. As I age, I see it as less seductively depriving and more an inroad into the exploration of desire, although this particular story is one about Molly's discomfort with her desire and some of my discomfort in working with her around these issues. I believe that the analyst has to try to steer a middle course between unmitigated curiosity and enjoyment at being the object of the patient's desire and phobic reluctance to explore the resistance against the full expression of the sexual transference.

When Molly, a divorced, 30-year-old woman, mother of a one-year-old son, began analysis a number of years ago, I anticipated that her treatment would be extraordinarily challenging with regard to multidimensional aspects of love, desire, and anger. I say this because, at the conclusion of the first analytic hour, Molly said to me, with a warm, inviting smile and dreamy eyes as she walked past me at the door, "Has anyone ever told you that you look like Rex Harrison?" In fact, no one had. It seemed to me that this was a particularly striking expression of her psychic reality. My first and lasting association to this way of ending the first hour was to *My Fair Lady*, the adaptation of Pygmalion in which a stodgy male teacher tries to make a "proper" lady of Eliza, and, as they drive each other crazy, they fall in love. Like Eliza, in some ways Molly seemed like a little girl who needed a mother to tell her how to get dressed. She cultivated a kind of disheveled, cute, playful style in her clothing and manner of presentation, which I privately labeled "nouveau waif." Now this sounds like a rousing beginning for an analysis, full of the potentially playful vicissitudes of eroticism and fear, doesn't it? Yet what ensued in large part in this analysis had much more to do with her finding and refinding desire with regard to me and various men in her life.

Molly began analysis feeling profoundly ambivalent about her previous and any future relationships and career. She experienced many wishes to be closer to men she met, yet she pushed them away and felt cramped when they were available. She viewed her previous husband and herself as lost babes in the woods. Their mutual dependency on each other and inability to set limits with their young son was a source of sadness and at times rage. Molly had entered analysis to explore why she felt unable to set limits on her child and her close female friends. She could never say no, and she insisted that, when she did, no one would listen. She also was beset by various ongoing phobic concerns, what she knew were intellectualizing defenses and the demands and exigencies of everyday life in the context of being a new single mother.

Molly was an artist reliant on her imagination as a satisfying and pleasurable resource in the face of uncertainty and disappointment. Molly felt, in her words, adored by her father, but she felt as though she never really knew him, nor he her. He worked long hours and was exhausted when he was home. A joke in their family was that when he was in his late 30s and early 40s he had slept through his own analysis. Molly's mother had been a devoted, intelligent housewife who returned to school and was coming into her own as a scholar during Molly's adolescence but who died quickly of an illness when Molly, then 17, was preparing to attend college. Attempting to grieve the loss of her mother, Molly had since had much psychotherapy exclusively with women. She began analysis with me, a man, in order to "work out the man thing." I made her nervous because I seemed like a smart, "nice guy," and she found me attractive, which seemed to fit the calculus of her selection formula.

Early in the treatment Molly seemed to me to be afraid to feel strongly for or about me; she shut off a level of vulnerability early in her analysis. She seemed quite drawn to me emotionally, chemically, and intellectually. For myself, I was drawn to Molly. I liked her and felt engaged in the work, but I did not feel an extraordinary charge of physical attraction or erotic countertransference. She was pretty, very, very smart, ironic yet naive in some ways, sometimes playful, and often quite controlling. She became frightened at the beginning of the analysis because of an immediate feeling of having a crush on me, and she tried very hard not to feel this way since she said it would get in the way of accomplishing the work she wished to accomplish. She did not see how working with these feelings might in fact be part of our work.

For example, as Molly tried to explore fantasies about what might happen in this analysis, she wondered, as I did, if her association of Rex

Harrison to me might relate to her wanting me to make a new woman of her. We both associated to a Pygmalion fantasy. Molly was intrigued by this idea but then quickly gave expression to feelings that she carried through during a great deal of the early stages of her analysis. She was afraid to have what she called a crush on me. She felt a vulnerability around this crush and was afraid that it would mirror some of her past relationships with men prior to her marriage. She agreed with my wondering if she might feel crushed by a crush, but she insisted that the exploration of these feelings would only make her anxious and interfere with the work of her analysis. She wished to keep me out of the realm of desire and tried repeatedly to make me a puzzle-solver about her conflicts. She abhorred the idea of having "messy feelings" toward me with no place to take them.

Her fear of messiness—and I guess I would call it an attitude or position—began to ossify. We both thought of this in connection with her feelings of having felt abandoned by her husband, but Molly also connected it in some ways to her feelings about her father and numerous other men whom she had known throughout her life. I tried to consider how Molly's resistance might also relate to fears of a maternal transference (such as fears of becoming dependent on her mother and losing her again) but these never felt very affectively salient to me nor I thought, to her.

I began trying to explore Molly's attitude as a kind of avoidance of the wishes to have me be engaged with her or to "make a new woman out of her" (magically and otherwise). She said at the time that she was frightened by those feelings and that she did not want once again to have feelings toward a phantom object—a professor, a married man, or an analyst who was unavailable to her. She said, "I can't have those kinds of feelings because there is no place to go with them." I felt frustrated by Molly's relentless rationality and saw it as largely defensive. She seemed unable to experience the paradoxical aspects of the real and unreal nature of transference. Molly was convinced somehow that she would not be able to bear the play and exploration that we might do together. Yet she also viewed this stance as an aspect of growth for her. This pattern of not wanting to explore the transference or utilize fantasy was replicated in a number of aspects of Molly's style of exploration and conflict resolution. She would approach dreams as puzzles to be figured out. Feelings of all kinds were approached practically—if they did not function in some important way, they were ignored or explained away. Her style was highly phobic regarding the environment, food, and, as I suggested to her more than once, feelings. She was a kind of new-age junkie, fascinated by many new therapies as well as ritual, which I tried to understand with her as both a place for her imagination and her sexuality to go as well as a kind of defensive retreat or diffusion of her experience of her body, her wants, fears, desires, and conflict. There were maternal longings expressed in this affective reservoir and these pursuits as well as oedipal desires.

Molly seemed afraid of the symbolic register on which all analysis is played out. She was concretely treating me as a "real" object for whom she wished to avoid dependency and longing. In many ways, Molly was like those patients for whom resistance and the fight against regression are intertwined. Molly had always been extremely dependent on intellectualizing defenses and had relied on her intellect in order to provide a solipsistic, enveloping bubble that insulated her from the outside world. Sandler and Sandler (1994b) have discussed how the relation between resistance and "antiregression" are typically seen in patients who fear a loss of control and cannot let go of their defensive need to intellectualize. Such patients typically cannot allow themselves to express irrational fantasies in analysis, "to create an analytic space in which they can allow themselves freedom for fantasy and play" (p. 436).

As the analysis began to develop, however, I understood the ways in which Molly's anxiety about regression and analytic play might also involve new forms of play. What I regarded as a form of resistance in the transference during the first few years of analysis turned out to have aspects of new object experience that were made clearer to me only as the analysis progressed. I felt that Molly was trying not to repeat what she experienced as a form of erotic masochism related to her long-standing crush on her father and other unavailable men. This attempt to avoid erotic masochism was also a pattern related to her resolve to try to set limits on her son and female friends. She was in fact trying to do something different with me, and I began to see why she might be motivated to do this, rather than only feel resentful about her fear of letting herself experience more confusing, affect-laden material related to desire.

In some ways, my seeing something new in her stance could also be seen as an interpretive position that prevented regression because it failed to take up the defensive component—the way in which she fended off desire and longing. Alternatively, it could be viewed as Molly's expression of defense as what Schafer (1968) referred to as a double agent, operating simultaneously to fend off and express something. By telling me her demands, she was creating conditions in which her desire could be explored, conditions that I unwittingly overlooked during too long a period of her analysis because of a preoccupation with her "antiregressive" tendencies. In other words, Molly was showing how she wished to change while staying the same.

My increased ability to see how Molly was doing something new also defensively served something of my own countertransference resistance to exploring her anxiety about experiencing and expressing desire. In response to Molly's feelings that she did not want to "fall for me" and subject herself to yet another experience of being with an unavailable man, I became exceedingly uncomfortable being in the position (or fearing the position) of trying to get her to feel desire that she said she did not want to feel or explore. I felt as if I were going after her, seducing her, and inevitably frustrating her, despite the fact that her expressions of interest and desire seemed quite visible in the material and in her long, seductive looks at me as she entered and left my office. I wondered if she would experience me as trying to get her to feel desire because of my own needs. I was also struck that I had been losing a sense of Molly's emotional and physical appeal. I was much better able to experience her as being angry without knowing it, yet not seeing her as someone wanting and not knowing what to do with her desire. By not allowing myself to have sexual thoughts and feelings about Molly, I was engaging in the same kind of constriction, the same kind of antiregressive activity, that I had observed in her. Alternatively, I *was* enacting my own kind of regressive activity, which is to restrain myself from pursuing for fear of being overly seductive and dealing with it by withdrawal. By equating my interpretation of emotional closeness, erotic interest, and other feelings of affection with seduction, I was similarly not working within the symbolic register. It is also true that there was an unconscious aggressive aspect to my restraint or withdrawal.

Thus, I began losing a sense of the tensions between the real and unreal in the analysis. I felt as though I *really* would be seducing her if I noted the desire that I could see in her associations and in her highly flirtatious looks and smiles when she left and entered my office. I began to feel myself withdrawing from her. I seemed to be working with her in a compromised way, giving up on interpreting the stops and starts and vicissitudes of her hostility and desire. Instead I accepted her prescribed role for me as a puzzle-solver. As the analysis deepened, a series of dreams ensued in which Molly was trying to awaken a man who she said seemed like a slumbering giant (I am at least a foot taller than Molly). She could not rouse him and felt herself to be small and ineffectual. She associated to being a Lilliputian trying to wake up Gulliver, the giant (that would be me). She was not sure whether she would be able to wake me up.

As the slumbering giant image emerged, Molly revisited a number of memories of her father being asleep during the evening hours, often falling asleep while reading in the midst of family activities—the children playing, doing their homework, and the like. He needed to get up very early for work. Although I had never felt literally sleepy with Molly, I had been feeling withdrawn in the compromised way I have described and at times even felt a bit dull or bovine—if I really tell her what I think is going on, she can't join me. Her little-girl qualities had begun to make me feel like sort of a grumpy old man. For example, while I shared an interest in her frequent references to her enjoyment of writers like Calvino (writers who combined an interest in the real and the fantastic and whom I enjoy), I felt some opposition to this style in her. I wanted her to become less a fantasist and more a real person—to have a body, to have desire, and to try to put into words what she showed me in her gazes. I felt the same about her interest in many kinds of alternative therapies and self-help too. I think that she chose me because of a certain level of open-mindedness that she experienced in me or had heard about; but, in fact, listening to Molly sometimes made me feel a kind of countertransference harshness. At times I had fantasies of saying to her something like, "Would you stop this Peter Pan thing. You're an attractive woman and you dress like a waif. Homeopathic remedies may be good when you're sick, but I'd like to tell you about this stuff called Tylenol. I don't think that your computer screen or a microwave oven will kill you. You don't have to check your son for deer ticks quite as often as you do," etc. Trying to explore some of these countertransference feelings as reflective of her wishes for me to be a mother who would take care of her seemed important early in the analysis, but by now seemed to be related to my own frustration about her anxieties about being a woman.

She was phobic about a number of things, but mostly about talking directly with me about her body, desire, and anger. As the slumbering giant image emerged, I realized that I was angry and did not know what to do with my anger. I tried to translate my countertransference wishes to say, "You're afraid to talk about your body with me," as a bridge to taking up her wish that I would, as I did state to her, "wake up and smell the Molly." I wondered aloud if her dreams suggested how much she wanted to be able to rouse me or for me to want to wake up and not need to be roused because I wanted to be with her. I often interpreted her fears of being angry with me and her father to the extent that she felt I was holding back something from her. Thus I tried to translate some of my withdrawal into interpretations about how she might wish for me to be different from the sleeping giant and show some desire for her. To these she often responded by saying that she might want this at some abstract level but that she could not really sense it in any heartfelt way.

In some ways we remained stuck within this impasse. Molly improved dramatically in her ability to set limits on her son, developed a good relationship with a man, and her already good capacity for creative and productive work improved. Yet I felt that I would often unwittingly resort to being a sleeping giant when she seemed to find little affective resonance with my attempt to interpret her fear or anger about my distance, her desire, or her wishes that I desire her. She agreed intellectually with the interpretations of these dreams, but a full-blown experience of desire never developed, nor did anything related to anger about my slumbering-giant status. Terminating analysis at her request, Molly insisted that she had accomplished what she wanted from the analysis in terms of feeling stronger with her son and was quite pleased with her relationship with her boyfriend. I felt both pleased with the gains that she had made but unsatisfied that a deeper experience was out of our reach. I think we both felt that we might be seeing each other again. I hoped so.

About six months after termination, Molly returned for analysis saying that she had a series of dreams that got her thinking about some things that she termed "unfinished business." In her first return session, she reported the following dream: "I was with you and you take off your clothes. You are wearing jeans, and you have a ponytail the way I imagine you looked in your 20s. You want me to see you, and you're trying to make a point of wanting me to see you. There's a judgelike figure there who thinks this isn't right." Molly's first association to the dream was to say, "I was thinking about how much I judged myself about desiring you and wanting you to want me. I wanted my father to tell my stepmother on our last visit that he wanted his kids [Molly] to be able to stay an extra day even though his wife, my stepmother, wanted us to go because she hates the disorder caused by the grandchildren. Yet she has a different attitude toward her own grandchildren and children."

The entire hour and the subsequent hours were striking in the way Molly spoke about her father and me. I had never felt as close to her. She called her father a pussy for not standing up to his wife and laughed with delight at the words that were coming out of her mouth (or, I wondered, from other orifices as well). I felt excited by the language because it was familiar—but not really familiar, more like the language I had thought that we would be able to get to, a shared potential that had not been realized. I could feel close to her as I had never felt. In a sense, I could understand her as I had never been able to before. I spoke to her about how she might have felt that I was a pussy too for letting her go from the analysis and never revealing my desire for her more directly. She agreed. I was no longer asleep. I was struck that the judge in the dream not only was her own prohibition about revealing her desire, but also resonated with my own self-judgments about taking risks and allowing myself to show desire to her. I do not mean that I regretted not having actively disclosed this feeling. In fact, I had not really felt such desire, but I did wonder if, had I been more willing to risk pushing her, as it were, might I have been more helpful to her than I was. I had, like her father, been a pussy. Nonetheless, she had used my inhibitions and incorporated them into her own readiness to have a transference based on her father's inhibitions and withdrawal—the sleeping giant. Our subsequent analytic work was characterized by considerably more freedom than before to express both desire and hostility in more open ways as well as to observe more freely her resistance to this exploration. We spoke about her hostility, expressed in leaving analysis, and how she had been uncomfortable and inhibited about expressing it more directly.

Case Discussion

This case fascinates me because it brings up so many interesting issues about what is useful regression, what are defenses against regression, and what is neither. Davies (1998) in an extremely interesting discussion of this case, stated, and I agree, that Molly's experience in analysis is usefully understood as related to a postoedipal need to work with love and desire outside the transference and outside the parental configuration. In various ways I understood, or at least tolerated this need, although I constantly struggled with feeling that we were both avoiding discussion of a more desire-based transference in our relationship. Davies's point about the postoedipal phase is that psychoanalysts often minimize the need of late adolescents and young adults to express their love and desire anywhere but in the transference. The transference is symbolically the parent for whom it is no longer acceptable to love and desire in the way it was during a successful oedipal period. Formulations that revolve strictly around the unavailable oedipal object might sometimes minimize the patient's interest in postoedipal objects, not only as a defense against oedipal desire but as an expression of something that she cannot in a real way obtain from the oedipal object or from an analyst. There is little doubt that Molly felt a great deal of conflict toward me as an unavailable oedipal parent while she wished to do something different in her relationship to me and others.

It is also true, however, that in my own experience it is not only common but inevitable (regardless of postoedipal or oedipal configurations) for analyst and patient mutually and reciprocally to interact in ways that express avoidance of desire as relational compromise and bargain. It is through this process that the dyad finds ways to discuss and explore these issues as much as possible in the intimate and restrained atmosphere of the analytic setting. Through complicated twists and turns, Molly experienced a charged transference with aspects of oedipal and preoedipal need and desire as I became for her what she referred to in her dreams and thoughts as a "slumbering giant." This image was configured by her in ways that related powerfully to a historically held image of her father as well as to aspects of my own defensive retreat from her. It is my sense that previous authors (e.g., Davies, 1994) are quite correct to understand that these configurations are consistent with the complicated ways in which children read both the desires and the restraint (or lack of it) of their parents and other adults.

To a large extent, analytic patients and analysts bring to the analytic situation their habitual modes of loving, hating, and relating in general. These habitual modes include their predilection for avoiding regressive experiences. Gill, however, was quite accurate when, in discussing Freud's paper on transference love he reckoned, "To say that the same falling in love will occur in some other kind of treatment or in real life is to minimize the specific realities of the particular two-person analytic situation. Transference love is specific to this particular situation" (p. 204). Furthermore as Gabbard (1996), Davies (1994), and Tansey (1994) have pointed out, transference love may or may not be reciprocated by the analyst. Analyst and patient are in a constant process of reciprocal relating, influencing, and interacting, bringing to these processes their individual habitual modes of relating.

Molly and I communicated to each other the desire, dread of desire, and relational compromises that were particularly difficult to analyze during the first part of the analysis. Davies (1994) has noted the analyst's need to think constantly about his own erotic desires and the reactivating of his conflicts about desire within the clinical situation: "Any exploration of the analyst's sexual feelings for his patient, in the analytic setting, will reveal the repressive derivatives of this defensive shift, the parent/analyst as an active participant in his child/patient's erotic oedipal experience" (p. 167). In the clinical material described here is a story about my own struggle, moving back and forth between experiencing desire, hostility, and anxiety, on one hand, and, on the other, retreat at times to work with the patient's desires and hostility, both oedipally and preoedipally based. In this work, retreat sometimes took the form of my trying to conceptualize the patient's struggles in isolation, separate from our interactive matrix. In this retreated position, I became more dispassionate, which influenced Molly's use of me in her working through (to whatever extent she could in the context of my limitations) aspects of her conflicts about desire and hostility.

To varying degrees, the analyst's wishes to be loved are also stirred up, as my work with Molly showed quite clearly. In some analyses, antagonism and fighting remain safer than loving for the analytic couple. While our "fighting" never reached overt forms of sadomasochistic provocation, there was a way in which our withdrawal from wishes and from each other offered each of us the illusion of control over the other and over one's needs for the other, in contrast to loving and wanting to be loved. We each settled for the unanalyzed and, I think often unknown, excitement of being able to provoke the other, albeit in less than florid ways, rather than risk the vicissitudes of caring and loving as has been discussed by both Davies (1994) and Coen (1994). My work was to try to be able to disengage from the enacted sadomasochism and confront my own hatred and desire and avoidance of loving feelings.

Coen (1994) has argued that the analyst needs to analyze consistently the patient's protections against feeling and expressing intense loving and hating feelings toward the analyst for those feelings to flower in the analytic setting. This is interesting because some analysts who stimulate erotic transference have to do otherwise. Knowledge or familiarity with the variability of our stimulus value means that the task of holding the paradox that Modell (1991) described about the real and unreal aspects of the analytic situation is always based on our sense of the quotidian aspects of our personality and appearance as well as how a particular patient and analyst feel about each other. Molly and I struggled throughout the analysis with the tendency to treat feelings in overly concrete or real ways even as we progressed to suspend our disbelief in the context of the transference—the playful and dangerous amalgam of the real and unreal.

CONCLUSION

One of the most complicated issues in any discussion of the value and power of therapeutic regression is our tendency to see these matters in polarized terms. We see regression either as iatrogenic or as inevitable rather than as both. We see regression either as useful or as an obstruction; either as inherent to the asymmetry of the analytic situation or as strictly in the eye of the beholder, a result of the analyst's expectations and constructions; either isomorphic with the child's development or as something totally unrelated to the child's development. We see the analyst's regression as either strictly related to countertransference difficulty or as strictly reflective of the patient's psychic reality.

Many analysts are able to embrace the complexity of working in the vast middle ground between these simply stated and schematic polarities. Yet, for me, it is most often the case that in the best of circumstances I am actively struggling with the pitfalls of thinking in one way or another about the complexity of regression as useful, defensive, inherent to the process, a part of my expectations and constructions.

6

IN LOEWALD'S SHADOW

Interpretation and the Psychic Future

AN UNDEREMPHASIZED ASPECT of the analyst's subjectivity and participation in the analytic process is his consciously and unconsciously held views of what will be helpful to the patient, or, put another way, his view of the patient's psychic future. Loewald (1960) described how the analyst's interpretations anticipate the patient's future psychic growth. Yet Loewald's formulations were embedded in epistemological assumptions based on the analyst's superior objectivity and emotional maturity relative to the patient's. Delinking this feature of interpretive process from some of his epistemological assumptions, I am trying to extend Loewald's emphasis on what I call the push of interpretation,

A few brief, relatively routine clinical vignettes illustrate how awareness of the analyst's view of the patient's psychic future can be usefully constructed and deconstructed in clinical analysis. (In the next chapter I discuss some of the ways that the analyst consciously and explicitly places his or her own view of psychic possibility into focus.) In the two clinical examples in this chapter, there are opportunities to examine how American ego psychology and American relational theory interrelate. In the first vignette is a kind of enactment that is elucidated by contemporary relational theory, particularly the analyst's unconscious expressive countertransference and the patient's perception and utilization of this countertransference within her transference experience. The second vignette uses a standard defense interpretation conceptualized through the lens of the analyst's anticipation of the patient's psychic future. Specifically, the interpretation of important observable or "surface" aspects of defense that have been highlighted by Gray (1994) and Busch (1995), writing from a contemporary ego psychology perspective may at times enact the analyst's unconscious hopes and wishes, which, in turn, lead to important interactional patterns within the analysis. It is my sense that ego psychology, despite its contributions to helping patients observe their defensive vicissitudes, pays less attention both to patients' complex experiences of their analysts' subjectivity (Aron, 1991) implicit in interpretation and to the ways in which interpretation seeks to illuminate enactments between analyst and patient.

NEUTRALITY, AUTHORITY, AND THE PSYCHIC FUTURE

My use of the term psychic future refers to the analyst's aggregate consciously and unconsciously held hopes for psychic growth through interpretation that may result from analysis. The term psychic future is not meant necessarily to imply the patient's specific choices or behavioral pathways that may result from interpretation. Often I learn about my view of the patient's psychic future by deconstructing the meaning of my established or ongoing interpretive stance. This process of deconstructed meaning on the part of the analyst can become important both to the analyst's internal dialogue and to the dialogue between patient and analyst, just as is the dialogue about how the past affects the present. If this dialogue and self-analysis on the part of the analyst does not take place, then something essential is not happening.

The analyst's view of the patient's psychic future constitutes one of several organizing features of debate in contemporary clinical psychoanalysis, namely, the degree to which the differing subjectivities of analyst and patient are used in the context of psychoanalytic work. This issue is in many ways at the root of the evolving reformulation of such concepts as psychic reality, analytic neutrality, enactment, and the analyst as new object.

Indeed, the various aspects of a continuum ranging from the analyst's accommodation to the patient's experiential and organizational world to his working with differences between the patient's and the analyst's views of psychic and experiential realities constitute much of the debate about technique among various schools of contemporary psychoanalytic theory. For example, self psychology and Schwaber's (1983, 1992, 1995) neoclassical perspective both place emphasis on the analyst's elaboration of the patient's psychic reality. Within these perspectives, the analyst's experience, which differs from the patient's, is seen largely as an obstruction to elaborating the patient's psychic reality (Schwaber, 1995). Bollas's (1987, 1989) "dialectics of difference" focuses on the generative aspects of the ways in which the analyst's view of psychic reality differs from that of the patient. Analysts from a number of different traditions, including classical, contemporary ego psychology, Kleinian, Middle School relational, and American relational, all make use of the differences between the analyst's views and those of the patient. The meaning and technical use of the analyst's differing views of psychic reality vary along the lines of how actively these experiences are used to formulate interpretation as well as how they are expressed. In particular, the American relational model tries to place into focus not only how we at times make explicit reference to countertransference experience, but, even more significant, how our interpretive stance intrinsically communicates aspects of our subjectivity, including our hopes and wishes for the patient.

Put another way, the conceptualization of the patient's psychic future may provide one more window onto the recent and rich elaboration of such concepts such as analytic neutrality (Greenberg, 1986), enactment (Renik, 1995; Gerson, 1996), and the analyst as new object (Greenberg, 1986; Cooper and Levit, 1998). Renik (1995) and O'Connell (1996, and in press) have emphasized as central to the workings of therapeutic action various aspects of the analyst's view of how a patient might change (a focus in the chapter that follows). In contrast to these papers, my focus in this chapter is on how the analyst deconstructs and thus learns about his own wishes for the patient's change by examining some of the *routine* formulations and the interpretive stance that he has already assumed. This deconstruction involves integrating the patient's experience of these interpretations as it is folded into various transferential meanings of repetition and, at times, enactment between analyst and patient.

A major obstacle in articulating a view of the psychic future lies in the fact that traditional notions of neutrality suggest that the analyst should not have expectations about how the patient is to develop, grow, or change. Bion's (1963) working maxim—that the analyst should be "without memory and desire"—epitomized this working stance. At the level of clinical analysis, however, it is not uncommon for analysts to have such expectations, regardless of whether or not we make them known to our patients. There is nothing inherently incompatible about having such expectations and trying to understand the meaning of choice and direction that the patient is in the process of making. It is also likely that the patient's view of the analyst's perspective of the patient's psychic future is a part of most analyses, perhaps related to what Aron (1991) has called the patient's experience of the analyst's subjectivity.

It is not surprising that psychoanalysts have had much less to say about the future than about the past. The repetition compulsion, by definition, suggests that the idea of a future separate from the past is not easily accomplished. Chodorow (1996) has raised the possibility that our theory and technique have given undue "authority to the past." In recent years, the present, or the here-and-now, has been increasingly emphasized across various approaches to technique and interpretation (Kernberg, 1993). From a technical point of view, Gill (1982; Gill and Hoffman, 1982) observed that we have been employing a model of transference interpretation that is too skewed toward making transference interpretations that reconstruct past relationships rather than examine the patient's current experience of the analyst based on unique perceptual experiences in the here-and-now. Schwaber (1983) has also made this argument, although her technical use of these data is at odds with the position of Gill and Hoffman, particularly in her different use of the countertransference. So, while technique has brought more balance to the importance of the here-and-now in comparison with the influence of the past, the future continues to lag behind.

Freud considered the dangers of the analyst's investment in the patient's future in his discussion of the analyst's need to cure. He regarded that need as an abandonment of analytic modesty. Specifically, he viewed the analyst's need to cure as a defense against sadistic impulses. In his postscript to "The Question of Lay Analysis," Freud (1927b) wrote:

"I have never been a doctor in the proper sense; I have no knowledge of having had any craving in my early childhood to help suffering humanity. My innate sadistic disposition was not a very strong one, so that I had no need to develop this one of its derivatives. . . . in my youth I felt an overwhelming need to understand something of the riddles of the world . . . and perhaps even to contribute something to their solution" [p. 23].

In these remarks, Freud addressed the problems inherent in an overriding need to help and effect change. I agree with his admonitions, although his comments did not speak to the analyst's natural wish to influence, which is a part of any therapeutic work. It seems to me to be well within the limits of clinical modesty to assume that the analyst be invested in the patient's change and that this dimension of the analyst's subjectivity needs to be understood as a part of the unfolding analytic process.

Loewald, more than any analyst before him, addressed the question of how the analyst relates to and represents aspects of the patient's growth and future resulting from the analytic process. Loewald took this discussion out of the realm of pathological countertransference and into the routine aspects of analytic work. He did not, however, explore the experience of the analyst and the variety of ways of thinking about the analyst's subjective experience regarding wishes for the patient to change. Instead, Loewald's view of the analyst was steeped in an epistemological position in which the analyst should be objective and stand for the possibility of an objective appraisal of psychic reality.

Regarding the patient's future, Loewald (1960) wrote:

In analysis, a mature object-relationship is maintained with a given patient if the analyst relates to the patient in tune with the shifting levels of development manifested by the patient at different times, but always from the viewpoint of potential growth, that is, from the viewpoint of the future. It seems to be the fear of molding the patient in one's own image that has prevented analysts from coming to grips with the dimension of the future in analytic theory and practice, a strange omission considering the fact that growth and development are at the center of all psychoanalytic concern [p. 230].

While Loewald's emphasis on the mature analyst's facilitating the patient's growth has been seriously questioned or even abandoned in the context of the analyst's diminished authority, Loewald's concern with the relationship between the analyst's conceptualization of the future and his interpretation and formulation is still not accorded its proper value in many current discussions of psychoanalytic formulation. Loewald was also beginning to address the analyst's symbolic function in therapeutic action—i.e., that the analyst and the analytic process itself can represent growth and aspects of the patient's psychic future.

We are now in a better position than ever to think about the analyst's view of the patient's future in ways that are disentangled from the authoritarianism that was associated with a technical position in which the analyst was the arbiter of reality. The notion of the analyst as relatively more mature and objective than the patient (Loewald, 1960) has been usefully questioned on many fronts, particularly from a constructivist position (D. B. Stern, 1985; Hoffman, 1991, 1992; Mitchell, 1993, 1997). It seems to me that these authors have sought to reconcile the actual and the symbolic functions of the analyst's efforts to know and understand something new for the patient, albeit that the analyst is not necessarily in a position to know more than the patient does about the truth of the matter.

In particular, Hoffman's (1992, 1994a) discussions of psychoanalytic authority, mutuality, and authenticity can help us integrate and reconcile Loewald's interest in the analyst's standing for growth and development with the notion that the analyst is in a position neither epistemologically nor psychologically superior to that of the patient. For Loewald, the analyst's standing for growth and development was predicated on the idea that the analyst could be more objective and neutral, correcting, in benevolent fashion, the patient's transference-based distortions. In contrast, Hoffman (1994) has illustrated how the ritualized asymmetry of the analytic setup, invested by the patient and society with a kind of power and authority, can serve to interpret our authority through the analysis of transference (p. 198).

Like Loewald, Hoffman observes that the power that is invested in analysts by both society and patients is continuous with the power that children attribute to parents in shaping development. This power, and its magical attributes, are augmented by the relative anonymity of the analyst. Equally important to the therapeutic action, in Hoffman's view, is that the analyst is likely to be affirming, generous, and insightful because of the relatively protected position he occupies over the course of an analysis. Hoffman argues that, because the patient knows little about the analyst, it is easier to regard him highly. In fact, according to Hoffman, the analyst's authority will help the patient to identify with him and use his understandings for change. Hoffman's position also includes the patient's experience of the analyst, whose power and parental authority need to be analyzed, although Hoffman leaves open a place for elements of this idealization that may never, nor should they be, fully "analyzable."

Hoffman's elucidation of the analyst's authority, which is based partly on contributions from Aron (1991), Modell (1991), Burke (1992), and himself (Hoffman, 1991), is profoundly different from Loewald's. For Hoffman, there is an ongoing dialectic between the patient's perception of the analyst as superior to him or her in judgment and wisdom and the patient's perception of the analyst as a person like himself or herself. Naturally, one of these ways of seeing the analyst is always more overtly prominent than the other and may or may not be held for various defensive reasons; this dialectical tension was not something that Loewald ever made explicit in his argument.

In my view, the analyst's fantasies, thoughts, and wishes about the patient's psychic future do not imply that the analyst is in a position of relative maturity or cognitive superiority, although he is certainly not, in relation to the patient, equidistant to the patient's conflicts. It is interesting that our role or position of symbolizing growth and new psychic possibility constitutes an important aspect of asymmetry in the analytic situation—not that we know more, but instead, that we represent something that the patient hopes to attain. This psychoanalytic arrangement is a part of what I regard as an extension of Hoffman's (1991) ritualized asymmetry of the analytic situation as it might apply to the representation of the patient's psychic future within the psychoanalytic dyad. In this sense, the authority of the analyst is imbued by the patient as representing psychic possibility. Naturally this investment may be riddled with defensive idealization or disavowed hopes that the patient is unable to claim for himself.

Renik (1995) has also addressed some of the ways in which the analyst considers how the patient might change. In Renik's view, the analyst's determination of resistance is intrinsic to how the patient might change; in turn, the analyst's view of how the patient might change is itself always undergoing change and revision and necessitates complicated negotiations between patient and analyst. Renik argues that something is amiss when the analyst and the patient are not making their respective appraisals of the purpose of the analysis a part of the dialogue.

O'Connell (1996 and in press) has made an argument similar to Renik's, although O'Connell characterizes the analyst's investment in the patient's change as a form of aggression or assertion on the part of the analyst. This aggression, which is to be distinguished from anger or animosity, is described as a part of what directs the analyst's interpretive process and allows the analyst to pose alternative ways of examining the observational field that the analyst and patient are examining.

I am very much in agreement with Renik and O'Connell about these matters. Sandler and Sandler (1994) have remarked that some analyses go on for too long because the analyst cannot deal with the limitations of the method for a particular individual. In the light of the discussion of limits in chapter 9 and that which follows, this elongation of analysis would be an example of the analyst's (and often the analyst's and patient's) not really coming to grips with the future, denying its specificity by saying that the future holds infinite or undefined possibilities for growth. In a sense, interpretation of all kinds confronts something about the patient's psychic reality that is an attempt to foreclose opportunities for a modified psychic future (another form of resistance)—one that the patient no doubt comes by honestly, but that nevertheless bears exploration.

I am suggesting, then, that the analyst's views of the patient's psychic future and his investment in the patient's future are a ubiquitous feature of routine analytic work. The demands of neutrality, usefully redefined by Greenberg (1986), argue against our having an *overriding* need to cure. Greenberg describes a set of dialectical tensions between the patient's experience of the analyst as an old and new object, as well as various affective experiences of danger and safety. There is also a tension between the analyst's functions as a recipient of the historical transference (Cooper, 1987) and as an object helping or influencing the patient to work toward the capability for new experience.

I would add to Greenberg's notion of neutrality another axis along which interpretation embodies and expresses hope. This aspect of neutrality, difficult as it is to define as a concept in psychoanalysis, refers to the way that analysts maintain a tension between psychic possibility and limitation.

Interpretation to some extent embodies and expresses hope. There is an interaction between the analyst's role as embodying hope and social authority, and our role as transference object.

Caper (1992) has pointed to the frequency with which patients project their own omnipotence into the analyst, so that the analyst becomes a magical healer. Caper discusses the analyst's susceptibility to accepting this role and the problems that may accompany his doing so. In such an instance, the analyst loses a sense of conscious balance in maintaining tensions between possibility and limitation. At any given moment, naturally, the analyst is on one side of this issue or another, and the sense of balance I am suggesting is an ideal to strive for as one examines process, stance, interpretive direction, transference and countertransference experience.

In contrast to the dramatic susceptibility of the analyst to accepting the patient's wishes for him to be an omnipotent healer, the following case examples are of more or less routine enactments that the analyst can use in elaborating both the patient's resistance to change and aspects of his own resistance in the countertransference to working with the patient's resistance. These inevitable aspects of the analyst's participation accord with the dimensions of neutrality that Greenberg (1986) has elucidated. In Greenberg's definition of neutrality and Kris's (1990) notion of functional neutrality, the concept of neutrality has been conceptualized not as a static stance, but as one that incorporates aspects of the analyst's and patient's shifting views of psychic reality.

The following examples illustrate the analyst's process of learning about his implicit predilection for particular formulations of the patient's psychic future that is contained in the analyst's interpretive stance. They illustrate what Hoffman (1994a) stated so clearly:

> The fact that analysts cannot know exactly how they should position themselves with respect to the dialectic of overtly expressive participation and relatively standard, authority-enhancing technique is precisely the wellspring for an overarchingly authentic way of being with the patient, one that is marked by a sense of struggle with uncertainty, by a willingness to "play it both ways," and by an openness to consideration of the unconscious meanings, for the analyst and patient, of whatever course has been taken [p. 200].

Interestingly, the analyst often discovers his view of the future in retrospect as he deconstructs the meaning of his understandings and interpretations and continues to listen and understand his patient's reactions and experience of the interpretations. We are always discovering how we attempt to influence, particularly in pursuing the routine rather than heroic or pathological ways we think about how to intervene. Within this general activity of formulating reside fantasy elements on the part of both analyst and patient about what will occur as a result of this effort. These elements are often at the heart of resistances on both sides.

CLINICAL VIGNETTE 1: SARAH

Sarah is the patient I described in chapter 3. She was a 25-year-old, recently divorced woman who had been frequently depressed when she began analysis several years earlier. In the phase of analysis from which this brief vignette is selected, we were examining Sarah's tendency to get involved with married or otherwise unavailable men and to avoid men who might be more readily available for a relationship. We agreed that, despite her frustration with the unavailable men, she remained attached to men who represented to some extent her unavailable and somewhat critical father.

Sarah tended selectively to perceive and experience my remarks as not affirming or supportive, and at times she minimized my acknowledgments of her achievements and strengths. She agreed with my observation that at times her selective perceiving represented a repetition of her relationship with her father, to which she painfully held on. There were also times such as the one I highlight here when I would enact something of a critical father role because of a certain insensitivity to her need to feel affirmed, even as we took up something about her selective perception. This example illustrates this pattern of interpretation and discussion in the wake of the intervention.

In this particular hour, Sarah was speaking of her involvement with a couple of men who she knew were not available to her for a romantic relationship. She found herself becoming more and more preoccupied with trying to win them over. At the same time, a man who was available to her had asked her to go out. She was proud of this development and said that she felt anxious about going on what we jokingly referred to as "a real date" with him. She wasn't sure what her anxiety was about. First I acknowledged that this "real date" was something new and exciting as we began to discuss her anxiety. I asked if she could elaborate on her anxiety. From an ego-psychological perspective, her anxiety was an affect immediately accessible as she began to contemplate using her avoidant compromises less prominently—the relaxation of a defense immediately yields to a fended-off affect of anxiety. She was not able to elaborate on it much and, we agreed that, whatever it was, it seemed to be something that she wished, in part, to avoid. Her thoughts then turned to how she immediately had begun to feel that I might be criticizing her for "taking so long" to get to the possibility of avoiding less. I became aware that, by making a fairly standard interpretation of her avoidance, really a kind of acknowledgement of her possible movement into a less avoidant direction, an aspect of transference (toward her critical father) came to the fore.

A little later in the hour, as she was saying that she felt that she might be becoming more interested in available men, unfortunately I clumsily made matters worse. I suggested that, if "real dates" became something she explored, we might be able to look further at what this anxiety was about and that maybe it might explain why "real dates" were so difficult for her to pursue. Her mood of warmth and friendliness immediately changed. She became angry and said that, by putting it this way—"if"—I was minimizing what she had been able to do. "Why do you have to say it that way?" I agreed that I had misspoken, and began to take her question seriously: "Why had I said it that way?"

When I made my comment, I was feeling increasingly pleased with her growing ability to take in this new experience. I was conscious of a kind of anticipation that her openness to men was becoming a more available opportunity for her, and I felt hopeful. At a more experience-distant level, I was thinking about how Sarah used outside "surreal relationships" (a term that characterizes many patients who use impossible relationships partly as a way to perpetuate unconscious, oedipally frustrating fantasies) to avoid dealing with her conflicts with available men. I was also thinking about her defensive use of the erotic transference and how she wished at times to use her relationship with me in a substitutive manner to avoid conflicts with available men. What I was not aware of at the moment I spoke was how I might be once again enacting the role of her father, who was experienced as conditionally supportive. Then, voicing these thoughts to Sarah, I told her that I had been more hopeful as I spoke, but that I could see quite clearly how she had experienced my remarks. She told me that she believed that I had felt pleased with her and hopeful but that she still resented my speaking to her in the way that I had. I then said that, while I had participated in the familiar (to her) role of a conditionally supportive father, I wondered if she perhaps was less likely to experience the way I was speaking with anticipation and hope about where she might be going, than with disappointment about who she was now. She readily agreed with this observation. Sarah said that our interaction had felt very like how we had been looking at her attachment to painful feelings toward her father and unavailable men. She also said that she felt attached to, and in some sense liked the opportunity she experienced in talking to, her father and me about our failings. We spent a considerable amount of time trying to analyze these pleasurable feelings, which involved shifting self- and object aspects of a sadomasochistic relationship with me and her father.

This vignette emphasizes the tension between my consciously experienced hopes for the patient—an opportunity for her growth and capacity to form a relationship that would be more satisfying to her—and a kind of enactment of the old object, coconstituted by the two of us. I hesitate to say that my enactment (i.e., saying what I said the way I said it) could be explained solely by a kind of role responsiveness, because I am not at all certain that I was responding to something in Sarah. What was of note was her readiness to experience me as a familiar object and my tendency to act in ways that would elicit this feeling in her. At one level, this example reaffirms what we already know—that analysts participate in aspects of repetition and that patients cling to attachments even in the face of something new that the analyst might be doing. At another level, however, I think that this clinical moment illustrates something more specific about how the ways in which the analyst's interpretive anticipation of where the patient might go may sometimes enact something that is an amalgam of the old and the new object, coconstituted by the patient and the analyst.

CLINICAL VIGNETTE 2: SAM

Another interpretive moment involving a shift in my stance illustrates a more subtle process of deconstruction of my formulations and interpretive stance. I hope in this example to capture a sense of the unfolding understanding of my implicit view of the patient's psychic future.

Sam is a single, 28-year-old scientist who came into analysis struggling with difficulty integrating some feelings of sexual inhibition toward his girlfriends, on one hand, with his consciously experienced desire. He used the term inhibition to indicate that he greatly enjoyed his sexual relationship with his current girlfriend of several months but sometimes felt reluctant to initiate sexual activity. At times, he experienced himself as an adolescent, uncomfortable with his sexuality. Despite his youth, Sam was seen by many of his senior colleagues at his company and even his older sisters as overridingly rational, reasonable, and benevolent in his pursuit of conflict resolution. Sam wished to be less reasonable and more expressive.

Sam was the youngest of four children and the only boy. His three sisters were close and caring toward him, but he also experienced them as jealous of the attention he received from his mother. Sam had known in high school, college, and graduate school that many girls and women were attracted to him despite his own affective sense that he was not as attractive as he wished. Furthermore, his older sisters had confirmed that they knew many girls who wanted to get to know him. Sam grew up in an academically oriented family in which science was the most obvious and allowable expression of passion. Sam felt that his mother was frustrated sexually and viewed Sam, her only son, as sexually exciting. His father, also a scientist, was somewhat contemptuous about athletics and overt expression of sexuality. Sam felt that his father was more generally supportive of his sisters' activities and achievements than of his.

In the several hours I am summarizing here, Sam was doing something with me that was usual for him during the first year of his analysis. As the hour developed, he would often tell me, after a moment of silence or a break in his associations, that he was having a silent conversation with his good friend, Abe, a college friend who is a businessman and now lives in another city. Abe is intense and hostile and, loving to provoke a good fight, sometimes gravitates toward politically incorrect or controversial encounters with his elders. Sam recoils at the way Abe used to elicit irritation in others within their social circles. Sam knows that unconsciously or even consciously he always partly delighted in Abe's passion about his beliefs, despite the fact that Sam sometimes felt that Abe was misguided and oversimplified complex issues. Sam's other friends found Abe abrasive and hypercritical. Only Sam's current girlfriend seemed to enjoy Abe; she indulged his acerbic humor and sometimes even flirted with him. Sam and Abe are quite good friends and engage in many interesting talks, especially during Sam's analytic hours. But usually the conversation with Abe during the hour consisted of Abe's harangues about how the analytic process is a self-indulgent, bourgeois activity. Abe, who is less wealthy than Sam, criticized Sam for needing me and spending the money to come and see me.

I generally took up these harangues on Abe's part and Sam's conversations with Abe as an indication that perhaps Abe was speaking for Sam in a way that Sam could not speak for himself. I wondered if Abe could be expressive, hostile or affectionate, toward me in a way that Sam could not. I also wondered if it was easier to have three of us in the room rather than just the two of us. Each time I took up Abe's words as a possible expression of something Sam might feel, he would respond with apparent agreement. He was bemused, comforted, and pleased that he might have the opportunity to experience and express these feelings—indeed, that he already was indirectly expressing some of these feelings. But Sam did not seem to get into this material any more expressively than before, and even became at times less intelligible. I began wondering what would happen if I asked—if you will, joked with—Sam about whether I could speak with Abe more directly at the point that Abe began speaking to him. When I decided to do this, Sam laughed with delight and said that he thought maybe this would be a good idea, though he never commented in more detail directly about his feelings regarding my shift in stance. The material gradually began to change in several directions. In fact, Sam never spoke to me directly as Abe. But he spoke to me as himself in a more affectively present and vivid manner. He began a deeper exploration of his feelings about his sense of himself as a boy anticipating sexual experience rather than someone who should be experienced and talented in this regard. Sam also became more observant about how Abe shut off his expressiveness. Abe was critical of Sam needing me and the analysis in general. Abe was also resentful of women being attractive and alluring to men. As Sam became more aware of what he was feeling about his own desires and his anxiety, the interpretation of Abe as an expression of unacceptable anger and desire and as both a defensive presence to mitigate these feelings and a kind of facilitator of expression of these feelings became more real and accessible to him.

From a standard way of conceptualizing this clinical moment (which I have condensed in a way that I hope captures something meaningful about the working of my mind during the clinical process), I would say that I began with a familiar and usually productive technical stance focused on helping my patient to integrate hostile and desirous feelings that he defended against by externalization. He was intrigued and amused by this interpretation, but nothing seemed to change in his expressiveness. When I changed direction to talk directly to his friend, he became even more amused, and the material seemed to deepen. I considered whether my change in approach was an enactment, moving from analysis to play therapy—was I soon going to be offering him an Abe puppet to play with? Thus I wondered if I was enacting the role of the permissive parent who encourages him to do whatever he wished or if I was in some way providing a father able to acknowledge my body and his whom he did not feel he had during development. Was I a lover, offering a different level of play within our dialogue? I believe that, in part, all these levels were in operation. But I also began to realize that what I had been enacting before (in the way that all interpretations involve some form of enactment) was the role of a parent who expected him to observe feelings in a pseudomature way, without actually engaging in experience. I became more aware of how Sam experienced my interventions or intent within his transference-based perception of me. At one level I invited Sam to elaborate his feeling by asking if I could speak more directly with Abe rather than interpret too quickly the underlying determinant. At another level, I can now see that I also moved into a more playful mode in my interpretive and exploratory activity. I came to believe that unwittingly, in the context of Sam's familiar experience with his family, Sam had experienced my earlier interpretation as a demand to move into a pseudomature rather than exploratory mode.

Abe's presence had really been at quite a distance in the analysis, not unlike the distance Sam kept from his girlfriend and me. In this un-witting role of encouraging pseudomaturity, I may have been communicating something akin to "Know what you're feeling before actually feeling it." I began to understand a commonplace interpretation of externalization in a different way. This was one of the very interesting clinical moments that bring together aspects of American ego psychology and American relational theory. For example, from the point of view of ego psychology, I observed an accessible "surface" phenomenon involving Sam's conversation with Abe, viewed as a form of defensive externalization or displacement in which Abe spoke feelings for Sam. But there are times when the analyst's interpretation of defense enacts some aspects of transference-countertransference attention that need be examined in conjunction with the interpretation of defense. Sam had felt, once again, a transference-based pressure to be grown-up and reasonable and to take on all the work, a pressure he had experienced with his father but with which he was reluctant to comply. I learned that my consciously and unconsciously held plan for Sam involved his taking ownership of affect before experiencing it. I believe that my shift to a different type of intervention allowed him to bring in his friend, Abe, and himself more vividly.

Over time, my initial interpretive stance was suspended, and I learned that my interpretations. and especially Sam's reactions, revealed an implicit view of his psychic future that was similar to the pseudomature mode he had experienced as a boy within his family. My interpretive stance changed, and consequently I entered into the present with Sam more vividly, just as he could become more expressive of his immediate experience. Thus I believe that, unconsciously, Sam was struggling with whether or not he could invite the sexual, loving, wild, and angry part of himself to our house. This struggle eventually led to a reduction in externalization to his friend, Abe, and to more direct expression of his feelings toward me.

One of the matters I have considered in thinking about my view of Sam's psychic future is how my shift in interpretive stance might have involved a seduction or a kind of suggestion in order to circumvent a piece of resistance. To whatever extent these processes were at work, I believe that in attempting to analyze the process—in this case working with my own fantasies about how I regarded Sam's psychic future as deconstructed from my previous interpretive stance—I was also trying to understand more about the unconscious fantasy elements operating in both of us within the analysis. In one sense, through my initial interpretation, I was unwittingly putting the analysis of transference before the experience and elaboration of transference. In this instance, there was little way to understand this error prior to the unfolding of analytic process in much the same way that has been discussed by Renik (1995) and Cooper (1998a).

CONCLUSION

At the most general of levels, I believe that the many kinds of interventions aimed at providing an auxilliary observing ego often can be usefully understood as involving various kinds of psychic holding. Consider an adult female patient who is becoming more and more able to become separate from her extremely needy and vulnerable mother. She is discussing how she is unable to tell her mother that she and her husband will not be inviting her to join them for their vacation. Even a conservative question regarding the issue, "What is making you anxious about not asking her?" might be understood as holding some of the patient's anxiety to permit exploration. The analyst is often providing a form of containment during this kind of intervention. Some would prefer to conceptualize this intervention as providing an auxilliary ego function while other analysts prefer to put this function in relational terms as a type of holding. To me, one of the most important functions of our interventions involves anticipating the patient's psychic future—that is, if this patient is able to explore what unconscious factors are at play in avoiding more separateness with her mother, perhaps she will be able to move forward. The analyst takes the patient one step into the future with such a question, just as he helps the patient one step back toward the regressive longings and fears that maintain her psychic status quo. This conceptualization of interpretation was at the heart of Loewald's (1960) seminal formulation about the therapeutic action of psychoanalysis. I find it useful to think of the analyst as often "holding the patient's psychic future" during most interventions. This means that if the analyst is intervening, he imagines that something new might be learned, often in a way that the patient cannot.

When the analyst takes a look at what his underlying view of the future holds for the patient within a particular interpretive line, he may *sometimes* find that there is an implicit correspondence between this interpretive position and what the patient experienced from parental demands about how to deal with affect, impulses, and fantasies. This observation parallels some of the processes that Sandler (1976) outlined regarding role responsiveness. The focus I have suggested here, however, allows for an examination of not only how the present repeats the past, but also how the analyst's wishes for the patient's future partly repeat the past. Furthermore, I do not believe with any certainty that my stance with the two patients I described here is comprehensively explained by the idea of role responsiveness. I think that another way to understand what happened is that I may have acted in ways best described as a kind of "role induction"—that is, that my interpretive stance partly directed or induced the patient's behavior and associations as well. Thus how the analyst comes to understand a view of the patient's psychic future is reciprocally determined and often enacted before it can become understood by the analytic pair.

Naturally, the experience of the patient is usually codetermined by what the patient brings to the analytic situation and what the analyst unwittingly or consciously enacts. As stated earlier, the analyst is sometimes best able to ponder this process while it is occurring rather than prior to the interpretation. Sarah and I were able to talk quite explicitly about these processes in each of us. I felt as though my stance regarding her future contained an anticipation—I hope, in the Loewaldian sense, that interpretation can sometimes anticipate—of where she might be able to go. She experienced my position, in part, as the repetition of her father's expecting more of her rather than being pleased with who she was. In the clinical circumstance with Sam, I became reflective about the process when his seeming compliance signaled to me the possibility that my interpretive line might not be addressing important elements of resistance or wishes to do something new. My new awareness of how I was unconsciously maintaining expectations of Sam that mirrored those we had previously reconstructed from his earlier experience, allowed me to understand my interpretive stance as I had not understood previously. This observation is in keeping with Bion's (1977a) and Britton and Steiner's (1994) discussions of the overvalued idea or selective fact. These phenomena can lead to indoctrination (Balint, 1968) or repetition or impasse within an analysis.

In a sense, beginning to explore the blind spot in the moment described with Sam involved addressing more explicitly Sam's wishes to play and express, rather than observing how he avoided play. Obviously, an analyst might come to the same awareness of this blind spot without considering whether or not he technically holds a view of the patient's psychic future. My point, however, is that our consideration of this dimension, namely, the ways in which our interpretive directions fit into various transference patterns, may signal blind spots in the analyst.

Generally speaking, I believe that an analyst's conscious and unconscious participation in a patient's psychic future has important implications for understanding how he decides about whether to focus on proximal or on more distal events regarding what to interpret, defense or transference. It is also a factor in why an analyst might move into areas of overt play or humor. In a sense, the moment I have described with Sam reveals both his unconsciously determined, overly constrained view of his present and his future psychic life, a view that was unwittingly shared by me in my initial interpretive stance. My initial stance was constrained, at least partially, because it addressed exclusively an avoidant aspect of Sam's expressiveness. Perhaps my shift in stance to an explicit willingness to play also addressed Sam's unconsciously held wish for a psychic future in which he could play as related by him through his friend, Abe. My shift also expressed a wish to be able to play with him in a more vibrant way. This aspect of play, as revealed in my comment to Sam, might have been addressed in any one of a number of ways. For example, rather than invite Abe to express himself, I might have asked if he was reluctant to speak with me more directly. I might have joked about whether Abe was waiting for an invitation or whether he liked to assault the analysis and then hide.

In a way, it could be said that I am trying to draw attention to some aspects of dynamic tension between the intrapsychic and interpersonal aims and meaning of interpretation. For example, when we shift from following a patient's affect or perceptual elaboration of a situation or experience into a mode of addressing underlying unconscious contributions to why they might experience something the way that they do, we probably have a thought or fantasy that such a shift will allow for the development of greater observing capacity or a richer internal or external dialogue about how one feels or behaves. When we shift in the opposite direction, as I did with Sam, from an explanatory level regarding the patient's unconscious contribution to a more specific focus on a proximal event such as the experience of affect, we often have a sense that it is a goal of the work to augment the patient's capacity to stay with or bear a particular experience. These decisions are usually easily justified by our particular explicitly or implicitly held theory of technique (e.g., making the unconscious conscious, deepening interpersonal and relational understanding). But I am suggesting, as Mitchell (1997) has, that every direction we take in facilitating awareness of something inside the patient may reveal or conceal something that is important to examine interpersonally between the patient and analyst. The opposite is also true.

For example, in the work of Gray (1990) there is an emphasis on the general value of pointing out to the patient observable and conscious determinants of associations. But there may be circumstances in which the interpretive line suggested by Gray may enact an aspect of transference that the analyst discovers over time. This observation does not necessarily mean that the interpretive stance is incorrect. Rather, it suggests the next level of interpretation. Thus I am suggesting that the decision about whether to interpret an observable affect or an aspect of unconscious influence or determinant needs be considered from both an intrapsychic and an interpersonal vantage point. For example, in reversing figure and ground at times, by placing our (the analyst's) fantasy of what the patient should do in the foreground as we examine and deconstruct from time to time why we decide to do what we do, we may be able to understand better our constant struggle with functional neutrality (Kris, 1990) and the notion of neutrality as a process (Greenberg, 1986), not a static position. This way of thinking about how the analyst works is generally an anathema to the often-stated analytic ideal of trying to keep our wanting to influence out of the analytic situation. But if we assume, as I do, that neutrality is a process and never a fully achievable goal, we may understand better how much our ideas about how to influence represent a constant dynamic force on both parties in the analytic dyad to understand both transference and resistance.

In the best of circumstances, part of the analyst's attention is directed to trying to observe (not plan) in concert with the unfolding associative material, what his wishes are about how to influence and what he wishes the patient to accomplish in the future. But these wishes are most decidedly a moving target. Indeed, this observing is usually done on the analytic run. In addition to the analyst's conscious and unconsciously held views of the patient's future, the patient often experiences (or does not experience) and draws conclusions about what he believes are the analyst's hopes for him. This experience of interpretation is often an important part of the transference and may relate to the patient's general reservoir of feeling about parental objects about what he should do or feel that he is expected to do.

The question of integrating what the analyst intends to be his interpretive thrust and the patient's experience of the interpretation is a complex and difficult issue to examine. Any attempt to categorize the nature of our interpretations seems necessarily to appear overly schematic, because each intervention intrudes upon the unique psychic world of a particular patient. Support for one patient is experienced as a deep kind of interpretation or intervention by another. From a contemporary perspective, Strachey's (1934) differentiation between interpretation and suggestion seems to be quite schematic and dichotomous rather than embracing this complexity. Strachey did not seem to consider that support or suggestion could, at times, contain elements of interpretation or an invitation for exploration. Conversely, an intended interpretation by the analyst can be experienced as highly supportive or suggestive. So any attempt to characterize the analyst's view of the patient's psychic future as deconstructed simply from his interpretive stance without listening to the patient's associations or experience is necessarily simplistic and one-sided. At the same time, the patient's experience of the interpretation is to be considered as only one of several determinants of this deconstructive process.

7

COUNTERTRANSFERENCE EXPRESSIVENESS
AND AMERICAN EGO PSYCHOLOGY
A Clinical Comparative Perspective

HERE IS A GREAT DEAL of variability among contemporary analysts regarding the use of countertransference expressiveness in general and, in particular, countertransference disclosure. The analyst's use of disclosure is embedded within a complex set of theoretical and technical assumptions about the therapeutic action of analysis. Further muddying the waters are our varying levels of comfort for exposing our subjective involvement with our patients—not only what we directly or explicitly reveal, but also, and perhaps more pervasively, how vigorously we attempt to understand how our patients allude to their experiences of us. I venture to guess that not all analysts would agree that the interventions that I describe in this chapter are best understood as disclosures of countertransference. However, our common ground surrounding the use of countertransference (Gabbard, 1995) across various theoretical and technical approaches to analytic work has opened up new vistas for conceptualizing and using countertransference in our clinical work.

In this chapter I map a very small portion of the countertransference terrain, namely, a particular use of countertransference disclosure in which the analyst's experience is at odds with the patient's experience and the analyst decides to disclose this difference. In this context, at best, the analyst puts forward this observation, not as gospel, but as something for the patient and the analyst to work on together and understand. Among analysts who decide to disclose this kind of countertransference, there is also a great deal of variability about the extent to which the analyst has thought through the disclosure before making it versus using it as part of a process of discovery with the patient (Burke, 1992), which, to some degree, involves the analyst's comfort with or belief in the value of sharing some aspects of relatively less formulated experience or "unformulated experience" (Stern, 1983) with the aim of better understanding.

Most discussions of countertransference disclosure refer quite usefully to points of impasse and stalemate, or what I would term heroic uses of disclosure. The interpretation of projective identification almost always involves a disclosure of the analyst's countertransference experience at a particular moment, usually one of intense affect that seems warded off by the patient. At its best, this kind of disclosure helps the patient and the analyst observe and understand a piece of resistance that might not otherwise have been available to the patient. At its worst, with this form of disclosure the analyst may be unable to contain and process affects evoked in the patient that are overwhelming for the analysand. Such disclosure can also be a gross example of what Gray (1990) has referred to as the analyst's using authority to overcome resistance while losing a possible opportunity for a closer examination of the details and nuances of analytic process.

Ehrenberg (1992, 1995) and Maroda (1991), in particular, have contributed to the understanding of a broad variety of circumstances in which countertransference disclosure may be useful. In this chapter and the next, which deals with the analyst's use of disclosure to convey psychic possibility, I use the term *countertransference disclosure* to refer narrowly to *the analyst's attempt to make explicit to the patient an experience or set of thoughts within the immediacy of the analytic engagement which may differ from the way the patient experienced or perceived the same moment.* Thus it is best defined as a form of "totalist" countertransference (Kernberg, 1965; Tansey and Burke, 1989). The notion of totalist countertransference assumes that the analyst will experience a wide variety of feelings in analytic work, some of which may relate to the patient's conflicts and some of which may not. The kind of countertransference experience I am describing might be called by others simply the analyst's differing impression or even interpretation of what the patient is describing. I prefer to think of it, however, as a form of countertransference because it tends to capture the routine subjective

reactions that are implied but not made explicit in many of our interpretive efforts. (In a clinical example, I try to suggest a way of com-
paring types or uses of countertransference disclosure that partially
relate to other approaches to analytic technique, particularly defense
analysis from an ego-psychological perspective. The example I have
helped me, partly because of my mistakes, to learn more about what I
regard as a useful approach.)

Because the analyst's disclosure inevitably evokes questions about the
balance and importance of asymmetry and anonymity in analytic
process, I will first briefly elaborate these dimensions of analytic process
as a background against which to discuss the use of countertransference
disclosure.

ANALYST DISCLOSURE, ASYMMETRY, AND MUTUALITY IN THE ANALYTIC PROCESS

I suggested in chapter 2 and in earlier papers (Cooper, 1996a, 1998a,b)
that the technique of self-disclosure is better termed and conceptualized as analyst disclosure because, at its best, the process involves the
use of the analyst as a participant observer in ways that are more common to other interpretive techniques than we sometimes imagine.
What is unique about the expression of the analyst's subjectivity in analyst-disclosure is *the attempt to put forward explicitly a construction of
the analyst's experience or some information about herself or himself to en-
hance exploration or understanding.*

The attempt to put forward something about the analyst's experience
can potentially become concretized or reified as something that is
"true," or reflective of "self" in much the same way as any interpretation by either the patient or the analyst. Gill (1983) has cogently elucidated how the analyst is treading on thin ice if he or she believes that
what is being disclosed is any more true or less defensively tinged than
anything else that the analyst has to say. Thinking of our decisions to
disclose as analyst-based rather than "self"-based respects this aspect of
psychoanalytic life. I am not trying to return us to the notion that as
analysts we are objective or that we are not personally participating.

It is the authority of the analyst within the asymmetrical arrangement of the analytic setup that can make either the patient or the

analyst lose a sense of the constructivist aspects of the analyst's disclosure, though obviously this can be a response to any intervention. So too, the analyst is constantly in the position of needing to maintain a curiosity about his or her own motivations and aims regarding all types of interventions. That disclosure is generally far less frequently used than other kinds of interpretation may also make it stand out and seem more important or more "real." Renik's (1995) attempt to underscore the value of the analyst's interpretive efforts, including at times disclosure, in helping the analyst to make his position less ambiguous to the patient is useful and valid as long as the analyst maintains a hearty skepticism about the constructivist nature of these disclosures; the analyst needs to be aware that what seems at a particular moment to be an unambiguous statement of his or her position may yield in subsequent interactions with the patient to new meanings that cannot necessarily be anticipated.

I view asymmetry within the analytic situation as a precondition to successful analytic work and see nothing inherently incompatible with some aspects of analyst disclosure and the principle of asymmetry. For many analysts, however, the issue of analyst disclosure is particularly threatening to the importance of asymmetry as a necessary part of the therapeutic action of analysis.

Attempts to conceptualize the analyst-as-a-subjective-object (Benjamin, 1988, 1990) do not necessarily refer to the analyst as a direct discloser. Instead, analyst-as-a-subjective-object implies to the many ways in which the analyst can experience herself or himself and use these experiences with the patient, including a thorough attempt to examine the patient's experience of the analyst's subjectivity (Hoffman, 1983; Aron, 1991, 1992, 1996; Renik, 1993, 1995). Some analysts view the analyst's disclosures as axiomatically disruptive to the essential asymmetry of the analytic situation. For example, Etchegoyen (1991) believes that information should come exclusively from the patient. This position minimizes the mutuality (Aron, 1996) inherent to the analytic situation. As Aron explicates the notion of mutuality, the concept refers both to the ways in which mutual regulation (Beebe, Jaffe, and Lachmann, 1992) occurs in the analytic situation and to the ways in which patient and analyst together generate data in the analytic situation. That patient and analyst generate data does not mean that each generates data equally or like the other (Bollas, 1989; Aron, 1996);

asymmetry is retained because the work tasks of each are distinguishable. Within the asymmetrical arrangement of analysis, the patient is the focus of understanding, even though at times the relational field and the analyst's experience or thoughts move to the forefront in the attempt to achieve these understandings. Renik (1995) has detailed how the analyst can become less ambiguous, and at times less anonymous, without necessarily compromising the importance of asymmetry to the therapeutic action of analysis. Jacobs (1995) is also among those analysts who believe that analyst disclosure does not necessarily imply a minimization of the importance of asymmetry.

Aron (1996) has usefully argued that the problem with placing mutuality and asymmetry in opposition to each other is that disclosure becomes seen as something compatible with mutuality and nondisclosure becomes a part of the belief in maintaining the asymmetry of the analytic situation. For example, Burke (1992) argues that ideally the analyst strikes a balance between asymmetry and mutuality. While I agree with the importance of this balance, I do not think that there is an equivalence between the analyst's disclosures and the notion of mutuality. Many analysts (e.g., Aron, 1991, 1996; Hoffman, 1991, 1994a; Renik, 1993, 1995; Cooper, 1998a,b) who believe that data generation comes also from the analyst, do not minimize that the analyst's function lies largely in attempting to listen to and understand the patient's communications, even though the patient and analyst are viewed as having mutually reciprocal influences on each other. Asymmetry is not necessarily lost or minimized by the use of disclosure, unless it is used defensively by the analyst to avoid or minimize essential differences between the patient's and the analyst's roles and motivations within the analytic setting. Paradoxically, some patients experience disclosure as even more a part of the asymmetrical arrangement because they learn only a little bit, "a taste" of something about the analyst's subjectivity. There is nothing inherently asymmetrical or mutual, gratifying or frustrating, about disclosure or anonymity except as they are each construed by the patient and the analyst.

An obvious but sometimes underemphasized dimension of mutuality and asymmetry, as with many other aspects of technique, is that the analyst can go only so far in his or her description of these factors—the other essential part of the equation involves the patient's experience of these aspects of technique and a negotiated balance. The more radical implication of this fact of psychoanalytic life is that there may be instances when one approach to countertransference, such as that illustrated by Schwaber (1992), is more effective than another with a particular patient or during a particular point in the analysis, while the active use of countertransference involving disclosure or interpretations of projective identification is more useful during other points in an analysis or with another patient.

A NOTE ABOUT THE USE OF COUNTERTRANSFERENCE

The analyst's use of countertransference in interpretive process is one of the major points of difference among contemporary analysts: namely, the degree to which the analyst focuses exclusively on the patient's experience versus attempting to integrate his own experience with the patient's perceptions and experience. Schwaber (1992) has referred to countertransference as a retreat from the exploration of the patient's experience. Within her approach, the analyst is encouraged to view the many ways in which he or she may unwittingly shy away from opportunities to elaborate the patient's perceptions. Critics of this approach (e.g. Hoffman, 1991, 1994b; Gill, 1994b) have suggested that this approach may valorize the patient's experience to the exclusion of integrating or negotiating the mutual influences of the patient's and the analyst's perspectives and experience. Contemporary interpersonal, conflict-relational, social-constructivist, Kleinian, and middle school relational theory suggests that the analyst's "totalist" (Kernberg, 1965; Tansey and Burke, 1989) approach to countertransference offers many ways of integrating the analyst's and the patient's experience into understandings of the analytic encounter.

Thus, while some contemporary ego psychology theorists, such as Gray (1990), or neoclassical theorists who integrate aspects of ego psychology and self psychology, such as Schwaber (1992), may differ in the attention paid to different surfaces and thus to technical approaches, there is still general agreement in the approach to countertransference. These theorists would see countertransference in minimalist terms (Tansey and Burke, 1989) as a response to the patient's conflicts versus the kind of use of countertransference that I have described as befitting a totalist approach. Schwaber's (1992) attempt to understand the patient's perceptions and experiences as much as possible is not necessarily at odds with an approach that integrates and utilizes the countertransference. For example, in the approach that I am trying to elaborate here, I find that it is generally quite useful to try to develop and understand the patient's perspective and experience as fully as possible before the analyst offers whatever differing or complementary perspective he or she has in mind. Schwaber, however, seeks to understand her countertransference so as to minimize what she sees as the analyst's impingements on the patient's perceptual and experiential world. In contrast, analysts who use the countertransference more actively, including the judicious use of countertransference disclosure, believe that the patient's experiential and perceptual world may *sometimes* be better understood and elaborated if aspects of the analyst's perceptions and experiences are included. In other words, the patient's psychic reality is viewed as embedded within a relational matrix that requires the silent or sometimes articulated elucidation of the analyst's experience and perception.

In considering the utility of countertransference disclosure, I think it is helpful to decide what are some of the more judicious and conservative approaches to this interpretive direction. In discussing elements of technical procedure and sequence, though, it is important to keep in mind Hoffman's (1994a, 1996) emphasis on the dialectic between expressiveness and restraint. In focusing on particular moments of expressiveness or disclosure, we must consider the ongoing balance between restraint and expressiveness in the overall process of analysis. From a Kleinian perspective, Steiner (1993) has similarly suggested the value in striking a balance between patient-centered and analyst-centered interventions. I would add here that there is a tendency at times for some analysts to equate spontaneity with expressiveness or disclosure, an equivalence I view as problematic. An analyst can be spontaneously silent, interpretive, or revealing. What is crucial is the attempt to strike a balance between disciplined and spontaneous participation.

How do we translate some of Gray's (1973, 1990) useful focus on observables to the active integration of the countertransference within a relational model and matrix? Obviously the surfaces in a topography of consciousness emanating from Gray's approach, on one hand, and a relational matrix, on the other, are aimed at profoundly different levels of inference and theoretical discourse regarding motivation and experience. Yet in exploring the use of countertransference disclosure, I think it is useful to think about how best to protect the patient's autonomy and opportunity for the creation of an analytic space (Ogden, 1986). We want to minimize inference and preserve the uniqueness of the analytic situation as one that can help us to understand the effects of the analyst's influence.

Is relatively more or less inference involved when the analyst tentatively and hypothetically wonders aloud about whether something in her own experience implies a particular feeling in the patient that the patient was less aware of than the analyst is? In Racker's (1968) terms, does a concordant identification in which the analyst might feel similarly to the patient imply a deeper kind of inference than does a complementary identification in which the analyst feels as one of the important objects in the patient's life might feel, at least as construed by the patient? Is a relatively more speculative approach implied when an analyst, listening to the patient's associations, decides to disclose a feeling that is at odds with the patient's experience rather than disclosing one consonant with the patient's stated experience?

The interpretation of projective identification seems to have implications of depth because it implies that the analyst is experiencing a feeling that the patient is not aware of or able to experience more directly. The analyst becomes the container for these feelings, which are presumably too loathsome for the patient to experience directly. Yet, along another axis, of minimalist-totalist uses of countertransference (Tansey and Burke, 1989), the interpretation of projective identification is essentially consistent with Freud's (1912a) minimalist definition of countertransference as the analyst's response to the patient's conflicts. The totalist definition implies that the analyst may experience a wide variety of experiences that are not necessarily derived from the patient's conflicts. Thus, the broader, more inclusive use of countertransference may not necessarily be bound to deep or relatively unconscious experiences of the patient.

In the context of mutually held resistance, how do we understand the question of depth or level of inference when the analyst shares something of his or her experience in order to analyze something that has been difficult for the patient to integrate? By "mutually held resistance" I mean resistance from the patient and the analyst's countertransference response to this resistance that together constitute a mild or even an extreme form of impasse or inertia within the analysis. The analyst may have been unable to analyze the resistance because of affects that he or she is unaware of or is aware of and finds intolerable. Often the judicious use of countertransference disclosure is less speculative and less leading if the analyst first attempts to elaborate as much as possible the patient's view and experience. In other words, there is value in taking seriously Schwaber's (1992) suggestion that countertransference *can* be a retreat from the patient's experience or perception. However, to believe that if the analyst sees things differently from the patient, the countertransference constitutes an obstruction, can become an impediment to the analytic work. There are many times when the analyst sees things in a different way than the patient or is struck by the determinants of the patient's perception that may cause him or her to want to bring these matters to the foreground. If what is being disclosed does not leap into inferences about similarity in the response between patient and analyst or complementarity between the analyst's response and the patient's experience, then the attempt to preserve the potential space of the analytic situation is well served. The analyst's self-analytic experience and technical discipline are essential here (Hoffman, 1992; Renik, 1995). I would argue that there is too much room for the potential space to collapse within the technical recommendations suggested by Schwaber.

Thus a relatively more conservative use of countertransference disclosure involves the analyst's first attempting to elaborate as much as possible the patient's view and experience. If the analyst wishes to introduce a feeling or impression that is at odds with the patient's or attempts in some way to explain the patient's reactions, the analyst can make something available or known to the patient for the patient's consideration and continue the analytic process—continue to explore the interplay between the patient's associative process and the analyst's and patient's attempts to understand this process. Within an interpretive sequence, then, the initial disclosure about what the analyst regards as a mutually held form of resistance may be regarded as less inferential than would be an initial attempt to explain this resistance in terms of its determinants. A later or fuller interpretation using the countertransference is one that integrates what the analyst and the patient have learned about the confluence of factors at play—the patient's affects and conflicts, the understanding of the transference and resistance, and, when applicable, the analyst's experience that has been put forward. It is then that a determination of how both concordance and complementarity in the countertransference (Racker, 1968) may be simultaneously at play, or other meanings of the countertransference may also become accessible and available for interpretation.

In relation to the ideals of the analyst's relative anonymity or the goal of elucidating the patient's experiential and psychic reality, the analyst's disclosure of a particular feeling or impression may, at first glance, be conceptualized as a relatively radical intervention. Yet, when put forward tentatively as a hypothesis attempting to elucidate something that is occurring between patient and analyst, it may be viewed as less inferential than what this disclosure means regarding the patient's experience. Thinking of Renik's (1995) distinctions between anonymity and ambiguity, we might imagine (or recall) instances when the analyst voices reactions that are at odds with the patient's experience, and are relatively closer to the surface, given that the observational field has been implicitly extended more broadly to include a totalist view of the countertransference.

Acknowledging and integrating the implicit forms of subjective participation and expression in all analytic interventions (Hoffman, 1983; Aron, 1991; Cooper, 1993, 1996a; Renik, 1993, 1995) allow us to consider instances when judiciously but explicitly stating our reactions to the patient's associations may provide relatively little speculation as an approach to intervention. This view of the utility of some forms of countertransference disclosure is difficult to reconcile with other surface approaches emanating from ego psychology because the assumptions about what is helpful to the patient or what constitutes the therapeutic action of analysis are strikingly different. For example, Inderbitzen and Levy (1994) would place the use of countertransference disclosure as a form of external reality introduced by the analyst that can serve defensive functions by distracting the patient from the more important purpose of learning about intrapsychic processes. But if the analyst believes that meaning and change occur in relational *and* intrapsychic contexts, then the realm of countertransference experience is credited with more value in the therapeutic action. The direct expression or disclosure of countertransference is not, in my view, deeper, or probably more to the point, wilder, by dint of expressing something of the analyst's experience. What defines the wildness of any kind of countertransference intervention is both the degree to which and how quickly inferences are made exclusively on the basis of the analyst's experience. Intrinsic to this mode of evaluating our interventions is also our ability to view our interpretations as hypotheses or steps toward understanding rather than to state them with premature certainty.

CLINICAL EXAMPLE: ERIC

This example illustrates a way to think about the analyst's choices in integrating his discrepancies in affective experience with those of the patient. The technique that I suggest later as ideal is quite different from what I actually did and what I present here. I was struggling to understand something that was as yet unformulated in my mind. Thus my technical choices were hardly ideal but provide a comparison point for a discussion about the various uses of the countertransference and how they may be used or misused.

Eric was in the process of terminating an analysis, approximately five months hence, when he would be moving to a new city. He talked about a number of issues during the session, most prominently his sense that he would miss some of his colleagues and that his mother and brother seemed to be less enthusiastic than he would have imagined about his return to the city in which they live. During the hour I felt that Eric was deeply experiencing feelings about his friends and family, yet I felt myself to be a bit less engaged than usual and without much inclination to voice what was forming in my mind about what I understood from the material. I had the sense that he probably was alluding to me when he discussed the friends and colleagues that he would miss. I wondered to myself if, in Eric's view, I was a "mother" who was happy to have known him and to have worked with him in analysis. He seem to have felt during the analysis that I was a more enthusiastic and engaged mother than his real mother was. But as the hour proceeded, these thoughts, while available, did not press toward something valuable to say yet. At the time I thought that I would not voice these thoughts because I had been making these kinds of observations about the transference with some regularity during the termination stage of the analysis. He had been working deeply and productively, talking about what he had accomplished in analysis and what I meant to him. During this hour I was struck more with the novelty of my response than with how this material repeated so much of what he had been discussing; specifically, I felt less engaged in this hour and wanted to understand if there was something yet undiscovered about Eric or about our interaction. With about 15 minutes left in the hour, Eric said to me (with a change of affect, including a tone of self-reproach) that he wondered if he had just been riding on the surface today, "getting by" in a way that he felt was familiar to him in some contacts with people. He said that he did not like to engage in this way. He liked to feel that he was in deeper and more sustained contact with others and with me.

I was struck that Eric had seemed quite engaged with the material and that this engagement was peculiarly at odds with my own sense of my being less engaged. I began by asking Eric if there was anything more that he could tell me about his sense of being less engaged. I thought that I would try to keep to myself, for internal processing, my impressions of him that were so different from his and see if I could get a better sense of what he meant. He basically repeated what he had said earlier. Ideally, after deciding to do something other than continue listening and trying to think about this discrepancy, I might have begun a line of inquiry by simply voicing something about the difference between the way he experienced himself and the way that I experienced him. Instead, I rather clumsily wondered with him if there was anything in my behavior today that might have made him feel as though he had just been touching the surface. I was aware of a feeling that, from my point of view, he had done more than just touch the surface. Yet I found myself more quiet than usual during the hour and in some sense less involved. My question to him about whether he noticed something in me was a not uncommon beginning mode of inquiry for me; but usually I inquire in this direction when the patient has directly noted something about me, so, in that sense, my beginning mode of inquiry in this direction was unusual for me. I had the sense that it came from my having noticed, but not yet understood, that I had felt less engaged than usual. Furthermore, I was not convinced of the most obvious potential linking between my countertransference experience of feeling slightly disengaged and the possibility that he was less engaged; on occasion during the analysis, I had been able to make this link between our experiences of disengagement. He responded, first and rather reflexively, by saying that he had not noticed anything about me in the hour that would have made him feel that I was less engaged than usual.

I tried to think about why I might not have been able to sense his disengagement, but I kept running up against an impression of his strong affective presence in the hour. I began to think that maybe his sense of disengagement was an expression of a wish not to have to feel the impact of losing those around him, including me. I had the impression that he was uncomfortable giving credence to his experience of sadness and reluctance to leave and that one way to cope with this feeling was through a withdrawal from these feelings into a position of self-criticism about being disengaged. This formulation seemed plausible but abstract at this point in the hour. Rather than listen and explore more about his sense of disengagement, I decided to say that I had noticed that I was more quiet than usual. This observation seemed really to affect him. He said that, now that I mentioned it, he had felt that I was particularly quiet. After a long pause, he became very sad and said that maybe he had felt disappointed about my not saying more. I wondered aloud that, perhaps had he had noticed this without having really been aware of it until I mentioned it, it might have made him feel as though he had been less engaged with himself or less interesting or engaging for me to listen to. I returned to an interpretation that was familiar throughout the analysis, that he was prone to take observations (often unconsciously experienced) such as this about me or others and conclude, self-critically, that they were failings of his. I also said that I thought that perhaps he wished not to have to feel the impact of losing me or others and that he was anxious or sad about giving credence to these feelings. Eric seemed to resonate deeply with both parts of this interpretation. He even added a familiar observation from our work together—that he would often seize on whatever he could to blame himself for something rather than experience feelings he did not want to feel.

I felt that we had uncovered an important and familiar theme throughout the analysis, generally related to his pervasive sense of self-reproach, that he would criticize himself in the context of an unconscious criticism of me. When I commented further on this pattern, again Eric seemed to agree that there was an accompanying sense of familiarity, that we had covered this territory before. As the hour drew to a close, Eric spoke more about how he was not sure if he would be able to feel "at home" in his new home. He was not sure how much he could bear in really saying good-bye and talking about what I had meant to him. He thought that maybe this uncertainty and sadness had formed in his mind as a sense of being disengaged and that he needed me to help him bear these experiences. He also said that he wanted to know what he meant to me. On that note we ended the hour.

DISCUSSION AND COMPARISON WITH AN EGO-PSYCHOLOGICAL PERSPECTIVE

As a first point of technique regarding countertransference disclosure, I view the way I went about examining the discrepancy between my view of Eric and his view of himself as less than ideal. I think that it probably would have been most useful either to pursue even further Eric's experience of disengagement (which I did as much as seemed fruitful at the time) or to begin my series of interventions by making explicit my different experience of him and see what came up for him in his associations. Instead, I turned his attention to what he had noticed about me prior to my making explicit how I had seen him as more engaged than he had felt himself to be. By asking him so quickly about his perceptions of me I may have foreclosed opportunities for finding out more spontaneously what was on his mind about our different perceptions. It was as if I was so aware of my disengagement and probably uncomfortable or guilty about it that I was leading him to a perception of this or an opportunity to begin to understand it. I may have had an unconscious need to confess to Eric that I felt that I had not been as present as I should have been.

Perhaps the most familiar and, in many ways, sensible approach for most analysts would be to try to ask the patient more about his sense of feeling less engaged and silently monitoring one's own discrepant response. But let us assume for a moment that I had continued this approach rather than eventually moving in other directions, that the discrepancy had continued, and that I had been unable to reconcile my sense that the patient seemed quite involved with his own experience. One sound approach using the countertransference might have begun with the silent registration of my discrepant sense that Eric was engaged and might have ended with my saying something like, "You say that you feel a sense of being less engaged, yet I didn't experience you in that way. Let's try to explore that." This would be a use of the counter-transference that is relatively uninferential because it notes something about the analyst's experience and puts it out on the table before the analyst makes deeper inferences about the meaning of this possible difference in affective reaction between him and the patient. It might be argued that my actual intervention created ambiguity and led the patient in particular directions than would the intervention just suggested.

In a sense, asking Eric about what he noticed about me seemed short of an explicit disclosure about my sense of disengagement but proba-bly borrowed from that experience. I have referred before to these kinds of statements by the analyst as "virtual disclosure." In these instances, the analyst indirectly discloses something about himself or herself but without taking explicit volitional responsibility. My decision to bring up my quietness was ultimately helpful in helping us to understand more about how the patient may have blamed himself for heretofore unconscious perceptions of me as quiet and uninvolved. But I think a more judicious use and expression of the countertransference might have involved beginning by conveying something about our respec-tively different views of him. To do so would have been less ambiguous than asking about his perceptions of me. Then the disclosure or obser-vation about my quietness, if deemed useful, at least is a less ambigu-ous way to begin integrating how the patient may have perceived me.

My technique here, in its raw form, reflected how disclosure, inquiry and interpretation are sometimes at the margin of what analysts do or do not know about their experience. I was beginning to put pieces to-gether—my discrepant sense of his experience, my own experience of not being engaged, my sense of being rather quiet, and my prior knowl-edge that he might be prone to blame himself without consciously reg-istering a sense of disappointment in me. While this reported sequence was hardly ideal, it does capture something about the way an analyst can begin to integrate countertransference experience and at times dis-close it or often not disclose it, toward the goal of understanding the unconscious process between patient and analyst.

As a general rule, to the extent I am predictable in clinical work, whenever I find something immediately affectively incomprehensible about the patient's associations, I find it useful to try to explore the patient's feelings in detail so that I can better understand what he or she is feeling. I do believe, however, that we may not sufficiently integrate some of our discrepancies with the patient's affective experience, at least enough to inquire (not impose our discrepant reactions) further. Renik (1995) has made a cogent argument for the potential value and technical advantages of pursing this line of inquiry. In deconstructing the direction that I took, I would now say that I found something affectively incomprehensible about Eric's reported experience of himself, something that seemed as if it might refer to an unconscious experience.

As I thought later about the hour, I wondered about what had occurred between us that would allow us to look more deeply at his feelings about the ending of analysis and about the process between us. Throughout the hour Eric alluded to stopping, but could he bear to feel it more deeply and directly with me? Could he allow himself once again to look at his disappointments with each of his parents and his analyst without blaming himself? Could he bear to experience his dependency and closeness with me without having to blame himself for these feelings? Could he bear the feelings of dependency on me and his anxiety about leaving without what I considered to be a retreat into self-reproach? Was this shift into blaming himself for "riding the surface" an unconscious request for me to get back to work and be present with him? Obviously, I directed many of these questions to myself as well. Was there something that interfered with my understanding how he might experience himself as disengaged? Could I bear the process of saying good-bye, including his feelings about leaving and my feelings about his leaving? Did I feel an extra need somehow to bring myself into his awareness?

A related angle on this slice of material is that somehow my disengagement and countertransference resistance to my feelings about his leaving may have been affectively resonant with his underlying feelings about leaving (Lipton, 1977). From this perspective, there are several possible meanings. One meaning is that I was affectively responding to the register of his allusions to the transference about missing me and that I wanted to be able to pull away without really saying good-bye or examining his feelings about our ending. Another meaning is that my disengagement was in some sense in resonance with his own sense of not being engaged. While the latter had sometimes been the case, as I stated earlier, I had the sense that the patient was engaged with the material—it was I who was feeling more withdrawn and distant than usual. I take very seriously this distancing on my part and of course would later think about where it might have come from and what it might mean in the context of my life. Yet I am not convinced that in this instance these emotions were necessarily regrettable as impediments to understanding. Instead, I began to think of them as signals that would help me understand the processes occurring between patient and analyst rather than as signals to the need for sanitizing the analytic process. I think that my disengagement had more to do with my own reactions to his leaving than with his and that at this point in the session and work there were no clear reasons for discussing in any detail my reactions to his leaving except to satisfy my own needs and gratification.

In large measure, the patient's view of himself as being disengaged was an iatrogenic response to my having been more quiet and less responsive than usual. While this was partly true and in a sense regrettable, I think that what we had been able to explore at a deeper level was his sense of self-reproach within a different context—an affectively deeper context than usual within which he could trust himself without my being there to support him. Eric's self-reproach was a response that emerged within his analysis in many contexts. He had been able to work on his tendency to withdraw from himself and criticize himself in my presence during the analysis, but now we were examining whether he could do this in the new context of terminating the analysis. We were also learning more about his reactions to being disappointed in me. His experiences of disappointment in me derived both from my being unable to maintain a steady level of engagement, and from my letting him go (the analysis ending). Thus, in the context of this partially iatrogenically derived self-reproach, through my disclosure of my discrepant experience of him, we were able to understand his tendencies toward self-reproach in a new and deeper context.

There are many surfaces available to the analyst who does not wish to disclose a countertransference response that is at odds with the affect that the patient reports. I could have interpreted the patient's allusions to the loss of his colleagues or his anger or disappointment toward his mother as allusions to the transference; to do so would have entailed his sadness about leaving me and even the wish that he could stay with his good mother rather than leave and go to the old object. I could have interpreted his feelings about riding the surface as a wish to see himself as not being involved with the material of the hour, rather than examine how deeply he was in fact experiencing and expressing feelings throughout the hour—a wish that I did, in fact, interpret to him in the sequence that I reported. I could have wondered more generally what Eric had experienced as he turned his attention toward the bad job he was doing as an analysand.

For purposes of comparison, I will briefly examine Gray's (1990) approach, which focuses on the analyst's and patient's sharing observations of the patient's intrapsychic activities of resistance to drive derivatives that the patient briefly has allowed into consciousness. I try to further deconstruct the direction that I did follow in order to elaborate some of the surfaces that the analyst can choose from that integrate an intrapsychic and interpersonal perspective. This process of deconstruction involves examining how the use of countertransference and analyst disclosure relate to the variety of choices (or, in the language of ego psychology, "surfaces") available to the analyst. Differences in surface stem from the variety of ways of using the countertransference, the interaction between analyst and patient, and the gradients of experience between both patient and analyst.

Gray's approach is a model of clarity about his intended technical approach to clinical material. Gray aims to place into focus, "processes of ego maturation set in motion by intellectually gained and experientially exercised insights" (p. 1086). I will try to make a best guess at what Gray would seek to do with this material. Since Gray largely views countertransference, in Tansey and Burke's (1989) minimalist form, as a response (relatively more pathological or nonpathological) to the patient's conflict, I assume and thus speculate that he would focus exclusively on the content of the patient's associations. Were he to experience the set of feelings that I did, he would seek to understand it outside the hour. (I might add that this is also a part of what I see as my task.) Gray's efforts would focus on drawing Eric's attention to his change in affect and content when Eric noted that he felt he was riding the surface. Gray's initial efforts would not be aimed toward uncovering an underlying motive for the patient's shift in affect. Instead, Gray would inquire about this shift in affect and content. Gray (1990) draws the patient's attention to what he considers to be the last defense in a sequence, because it is "the nearest one, the one with which the patient is momentarily coping" (p. 1090). Then, if he has a hypothesis in mind about how this defense relates to familiar solutions to conflicts and why the patient might seek this solution, he might put it forward for the patient to consider and observe. Most important, Gray would not introduce the patient to the analyst's "real" thoughts and feelings but would instead emphasize the patient's imagination of those feelings.

In the example I have outlined, when I noted a shift in the patient's affect and content related to "riding the surface today," I was immediately confronted with a discrepancy between the patient's experience of himself and my experience of him. Were I to imagine leaving out my discrepant experience of the patient at the moment, or at least the importance of this different response, and my additional awareness of being less engaged myself, I might have noted the shift in affect and content and wondered silently about a number of possible motives related to this shift. For example, perhaps there was something about losing me and his colleagues that had led him to feel momentarily that he was riding the surface. Perhaps his experience of riding the surface corresponded to a feeling of having dulled a set of painful feelings about depending on me and having to leave me. What is important here is the notion that, from this perspective, I became distracted by my discrepant response—distracted from learning more about the id and superego pressures reflected in the patient's associations. In contrast, I would say that by integrating my discrepant response, albeit quite clumsily, I learned more about the patient's inner life and intrapsychic processes but within the interactive matrix of the analytic situation. Thus, I regard Gray's approach as, at times, less than all-encompassing because it might minimize the patient's reaction to his perceptions of the analyst.

From a contemporary, ego-psychological perspective (Inderbitzen and Levy, 1994), I diffused and distracted the patient from the more important realm of id and superego pressures reflected in the patient's associations by moving the patient's attention into the realm of perception about me. Thus I too readily brought the patient's attention to something that I had noted in my experience, namely, my quietness; I might have asked the patient to explore more than I did about his sense of what was happening internally for him at the moment that he said he felt disengaged.

When a patient and an analyst see things differently, I think it is usually useful for the analyst to learn as much as possible about how the patient sees and feels about things. It is after this effort that the analyst's expression of a different way of seeing things may be most fruitful and probably least speculative than otherwise in terms of understanding unconscious contributions both to the patient's intrapsychic process and to the interaction between patient and analyst. With regard to my technique with Eric, my question to him about what he had perceived about me did not follow from anything that he had explicitly noticed about me. Furthermore, I did not precede it with an explicit disclosure to him about how I had experienced him as quite involved. As I said earlier, by first making our different perspectives more explicit, I probably would have better set the ground for my decision to mention my quietness and how it may have partly registered unconsciously for him and partly contributed to his experience of only riding the surface.

I find a great deal of value in the perspectives offered by Gray (1990) and Schwaber (1992) as partial technical approaches to psychoanalytic process. It is certainly possible that I provided Eric with a distraction from something internal that we might have mined had I not so readily asked him to think about what he had observed about me. But it is also possible that an approach that never mentioned my discrepant reaction to the patient might not have as easily helped Eric to learn more about how he was unconsciously registering feelings and observations about me that he was too anxious to let into awareness.

My suggestion is that, by making a portion of our impressions, thoughts, and feelings known to our patients when these impressions seem important to our understanding of the clinical process, we create important consequences other than only that of distracting the patient (see Renik, 1993, 1995 for useful discussions of this issue). When the analyst decides at times to make some of his subjective reactions to the material known to the patient, we are prone far more to view the possible deleterious or distracting impact than to consider that there may also be instances when we help the patient to find himself or herself in ways that were less available through exclusive inquiry into affective shifts. It is unfortunate that our literature is so burdened by a kind of technical antagonism between the simultaneous exploration and pursuit of interpersonal and intrapsychic surfaces.

Most important, I view the use of countertransference in which the analyst initially considers how his or her countertransference may be an impediment to understanding the patient's experience as a useful and judicious approach. There are many instances, however, when the analyst's countertransference can help the patient understand unconscious affects and motivations that are made available if the analyst simply notes a discrepant response to that of the patient and continues to listen and make sense of the material. In contrast, I would view an approach that implies immediately a verisimilitude between the analyst's and the patient's reactions as a relatively deeper and more speculative approach to the use of countertransference than one which simply puts the analyst's reaction forward, although at times the former provides understandings which are accurate and helpful to interpret.

The use of countertransference expressiveness at times when the analyst has an experience of the material different from that of the patient has important implications for Renik's (1995) emphasis on the analyst's making his own thoughts known to the patient. For example, Renik has provided a vignette in which a patient had the idea that the analyst was being extremely gentle in a protective way. Renik responded that he was not aware of any particular concern of that sort and that the patient might have some of his own reasons for imagining that the analyst saw him as fragile. Gill might have argued, as did Aron (1996), that Renik's conscious thinking might have been no less defensive or reliable than the patient's. Aron suggested that the plausibility of the patient's thinking might be further explored before the analyst introduces the hypothesis about why the patient might see him this way. While this suggestion is usually helpful, implicit in this position is an assumption that the plausibility of the patient's thinking is necessarily threatened by the analyst's voicing his or her own thoughts or impressions about the matter. We have no way of knowing from Renik's paper, for example, how many times Renik had traversed this ground with the patient before disclosing his experience. I assume that Renik was aware that what he put forward was no more reliable, no less a construction or hypothesis than any other type of intervention is. If the analyst pursues these matters with this caveat in mind, which is probably about the best we can do, then the opportunity for exploring the plausibility of the patient's perception and experience may be preserved, perhaps even at times enhanced.

A crucial and provocative question here is whether or not it is *necessarily* or *always* problematic that the analyst is limited in knowing that his reaction is as defensive as is the patient's attribution to the analyst. Renik has made a cogent case for how the analyst, through self-analytic work, can continue to evaluate his or her own potentially complex reasons for disclosure while simultaneously exploring the plausibility of the patient's attributions. This problem, relates to the often difficult task of evaluating how potential space within the analytic situation has been well served or compromised within any clinical moment.

I am likely to follow the suggestion of Gill (1982; Gill and Hoffman, 1982), Schwaber (1983), and many others (e.g., Aron, 1991) to explore the plausibility of the patient's perception or construction of the analyst before proceeding further. However, I have sometimes done this almost routinely, fully knowing that I had a hypothesis in mind (generated by numerous other clinical moments with a particular patient) about something that might contribute to the patient's selective perceptions. In attempting to redress the relative lack of importance accorded the patient's perceptions of the analyst within classical theory and technique, we need to be aware that, whatever our approach, we are likely to develop routine techniques. In my view, there is no "book" (Hoffman, 1994a) that cautions against directing a patient's attention to underlying determinants that contribute to perception if the analyst believes that he or she has already covered the ground of what the patient has perceived in the analyst. At times the analyst's disclosure, as exemplified by Renik (1995), may help to examine underlying determinants rather than necessarily distract the patient from these determinants.

Hoffman has attempted to expand our horizons for the social construction of reality in the analytic situation. In my view, he is also exquisitely sensitive to the realities, coconstituted by analyst and patient, that comprise unconscious determinants and perceptual experience as interpenetrating domains. In so doing, Hoffman attempts to fill the theoretical vacuum created within classical theory for understanding perception and interpersonal influence as major factors in the construction of conscious and unconscious phenomena. Following Hoffman's (1994a) prophylactic warning to relationally oriented analysts to expect institutionalization of his and others' contributions, I would like to underscore further the utility of the analyst's feeling a degree of free-dom in moving back and forth between the two interpenetrating do-mains of interaction and intrapsychic phenomena and the technical choices available for understanding these domains. Implicit in what I have conveyed in this chapter are some of the ways that countertrans-ference expressiveness or disclosure factors into this view.

There are times when the analyst needs to think aloud with the pa-tient. The more we can think about the variety of ways to employ this aspect of technique, the more thoughtful we can be in its application. While I do not want to "topographize" the countertransference as a sur-face, I do want to think about the most careful and least speculative ways of integrating aspects of countertransference expressiveness when the analyst has decided that doing so would be necessary or useful to the progress of the analysis.

I think of analytic authenticity as the analyst's efforts to direct all available subjective and intellectual capabilities toward understanding. The analyst's need at times to think aloud and to share aspects of asso-ciations (even if the analyst is highly selective here) is a part of what many have referred to as analytic authenticity. which does not mean confession or revelation or a suspension of disciplined reflection and analysis of process. It does imply a willingness to consider how the countertransference experience impedes or elaborates understanding.

There are times when bringing the analyst's differing reactions and experience to the fore can aid in elaborating an understanding of the patient. In discussing aspects of what facilitates understanding, Ehren-berg (1995) has referred to a willingness to risk knowing and being known. I suspect that this is, at some level, always an important part of the therapeutic action because it is one of the ways that the patient experiences psychic possibility. At its heart, the analytic process involves risking saying and feeling new things by both patient and analyst.

8

THE ANALYST'S CONSTRUCTION
OF PSYCHIC POSSIBILITY

J ESSICA BENJAMIN'S (1988) LUCID WORK has helped to explicate
how aspects of reciprocity, activity, and mutual exchange are involved in all interactions and how they generate growth. Developing Winnicott's (1971) description of the importance of the mother as
object ("object mother") in supporting the child's subjective experience
of reality and of others, Benjamin highlights the mother as a subject in
her own right and the value that the child's experience of the mother's
subjectivity has in the child's gradually embracing the external world
and the experience of others. Benjamin refers to the essence of differentiation as "the paradoxical balance between recognition of the other
and assertion of the self" (p. 36).

A related aspect of growth is what I think of as the assertion by the
other, or the push or nudge of interpretation. Interpretation is a nudge;
it is not just a nestle. We are, in Bromberg's (1991) terms, both "empathic and emphatic." Even holding, as elaborated so thoughtfully by
Slochower (1996b), has aspects of the analyst's push, perhaps akin to
what literary critics refer to as "imaginative sympathy." Holding and
imaginative sympathy are active processes of interpretation, inevitably
enjoining the other's personal experience and empathic efforts. Most
psychoanalysts experience a constant tension between acclimating to
the patient's psychic reality and trying to heighten to the patient's capacity for observation and integration of less immediately available aspects of affect and conflict.

In this chapter I present another vignette from the case of Allen, whom I discussed in chapter 4 in connection with mutual aspects of containment. Here I explore a bit further, through some clinical material, how some of our wishes to influence and our views of psychic possibility are conveyed to our patients. One of the most interesting points to consider in this chapter is to think about what I am describing in terms of defense interpretation. I tend to see the analyst's construction of psychic possibility through interpretation or disclosure as essentially a part of defense interpretation. While I have no way of proving it, I believe that, in one form or another, this aspect of analytic work is crucial to many of the processes emphasized in our views of therapeutic action. I think, though, that it is sometimes a more direct, or experience-near, way to describe how people change through analytic work than is the description of defense analysis.

Ego psychology has defined itself largely around interpreting the patient's most observable defenses, or, in ego-psychological terms, surface manifestations of conflict and defense. Both Winnicott and Modell, however, tried to elaborate how, for many patients, defensive organization can revolve less around what Winnicott (1969) termed "ego defense organized against id impulse" (the domain of ego psychology) and more around what Modell (1975) terms "defenses organized against object failure." In these instances, object failure, in the form of impingement, trauma, or aspects of specious parental reality testing or narcissistic vulnerability, communicates to the patient that there is something that needs to be defended against or denied in the experience of some important person, such as the parent. American relational models take this formulation one step further, suggesting that, with enough time and sensitivity, the analyst needs to try to place into focus, affects that are denied and disavowed by the patient but that are located in the analyst's experience.

Every interpretation offers a construction of the analyst's view of where the patient can go, whether it requires another perspective, affect tolerance, curiosity about fantasy or behavior, humor, insight, or recognition. What varies is the way in which the analyst constructs psychic possibility, implicitly or explicitly, consciously or unconsciously, in routine analytic exchanges or in more heroic circumstances. Obviously, the analyst's affects associated with the construction of psychic possibility are crucial in clinical work. Is the analyst actually affectively pushy about the process, guilty about pushing, attempting to minimize the wish to influence, directly acknowledging it, or trying to work in subtle ways with these wishes and fears about influence?

There are many levels on which psychic possibility is represented and explored by patient and analyst. As figures of social authority, we represent the psychic possibility for this change. We become a repository of hope, and this is one of the essential threads that run throughout all dimensions of transference influence and interpretation in the analytic situation. The patient is also a repository of hope and healing for *us* in ways that both overlap with and differ from the patient's hopes for himself. There is, then, a kind of tension between the analyst's functions as a recipient and inducer of the historical transference, or old object, and an object helping or influencing the patient to work toward the capability for new experience (Greenberg, 1986). In other words there is an interaction among our roles as an embodiment of hope, social authority, and a transference object.

I regard our wishes to influence and the way that we symbolize growth and psychic possibility—and in turn communicate this and enact our wishes with our patients, directly and indirectly through everything that we do—as an extension of Hoffman's notion of ritualized asymmetry. Analyst disclosure and especially indirect or "virtual" disclosure (Cooper, 1996a, 1998b)—the analyst's indirect expression of his subjectivity, which is probably a part of most interventions—express and enact these wishes. This is an important portion of what Aron (1991) refers to as the patient's experience of the analyst's subjectivity. Most interventions contain aspects of virtual disclosure to the extent that the analyst's wish for the patient to take in something new, try on a new experience, or consider a new metaphor that is being conveyed, even if the analyst does not express this wish directly.

By "new," I do not mean "unfamiliar." Interpretation often concerns the most familiar events or feelings, but ones that are avoided and, sometimes, whose direct acknowledgment or the experience of which is dreaded. At times, direct analyst disclosure attempts to convey something about the analyst's view of psychic possibility by voicing an affective experience or thought that the analyst holds. However, it is probably often related to the analyst's wish to take something familiar (maybe even too familiar) and make it seem unfamiliar in order to be felt anew or felt at all. If character problems or neuroses are akin to being stuck in a stale metaphor, the analyst is seeking to find a way to probe them and add some new ingredients and perspective. Sometimes such probing occurs through a change in the modality of interpretation, by shifting from a statement that narrowly refers to something observed about the patient to the analyst's explicitly voiced use of her experience to express her observation. Spontaneously emerging exchanges in analysis give us many opportunities for these shifts. Such spontaneity is most natural and, I suppose, easier when a patient becomes cognizant of a pattern and the analyst says something in agreement that reflects how she felt in the transference-countertransference pattern. For example, the patient might say, "I keep making everyone feel trapped, unable to move without hurting my feelings." I might say, "I know what you mean." At other times, a change in modality will occur simply in how we voice a question, take note of something the patient says, or register curiosity as we continue to explore.

DISCLOSURE AND THE CONSTRUCTION
OF PSYCHIC POSSIBILITY

I view disclosure, at its very center, as involving the explication and construction of the analyst as a subjective object in relation to the patient. Thus, disclosure is a mode of explication, construction, and interpretation. Like any change in perspective in analysis or art, it places something (the analyst's thoughts or subjectivity) into the foreground whereas it was previously in the background.

Since analyst disclosure has a wide variety of uses, I am limiting myself to fairly routine instances when I try to make explicit to the patient an experience or set of thoughts within the immediacy of analytic engagement which differs from the way the patient reports experiencing the same moment. (I have in mind particularly those situations in which, from my perspective or experience, I have initiated a shift in how I view a repetitive form of communication or understanding.) For example, Mitchell's (1991) discussion of how a patient's experience is constructed by the analyst and the patient in any of a number of ways as need, wish, or demand can elucidate the complexity of how the analyst tries to create a new experiential and observational field with the patient. I think of the analyst's attempts to shift the patient's experiential framework as an expression of the analyst's hopes for the patient, the push of interpretation.

Disclosure of various kinds often functions, in part, to convey thoughts and feelings about the patient's potential for change. For example, consider those instances when an analyst, after a considerable time working in the transference (i.e., not trying to avoid or dilute it) reveals to a patient that he believes he is already functioning or being experienced as a new object in contrast to the old, historically held transference object. This disclosure is usually made with the possibility of helping a patient to feel that the analyst is not necessarily interested in repeating or hurting him as he felt hurt or pained in the past (Greenberg, 1986). Put another way, it is probably what Freud (1912a) referred to as an interpretation of the defensive use of transference—it is a kind of defense interpretation. The analyst is trying to see if the patient has reasons (e.g., anxiety, guilt, fear of dependence, or hostility) for not being able to experience the analyst as an object different from the historically held object.

There are also instances when the analyst declares himself to be a new object in a way that is dangerous to the patient by dint of threatening an old attachment, as Fairbairn emphasized so dramatically in his theory (cited in Cooper, 1998c). Yet, in both instances, the analyst is presenting himself to the patient in contrast to the patient's usual experience of the analyst. These constructions of ourselves as new objects reflect a kind of paradigm shift within the analysis in the sense that the patient has usually become familiar with particular kinds of feelings and perceptions about us. These new constructs are also a kind of defense interpretation.

In contrast to these kinds of disclosure, virtual disclosure, in the context of communicating about psychic possibility, involves the analyst's indirect and unacknowledged expression of feelings or thoughts about where the patient can go. It seems to me that it is not at all a controversial observation that the analyst conveys psychic possibility in almost everything he interprets, even when highlighting the limits of analysis, as I discuss in chapter 9. For even in these instances something is being conveyed about the possibility of acceptance and bearing experience. A point of debate in doing analytic work is how directly the analyst discloses her view of psychic possibility and how actively she tries to deconstruct her own attitudes and positions about what she may be conveying indirectly to the patient.

At times, the kinds of analyst disclosure I am describing can help the patient to understand better the nature of discrepant realities between analyst and patient and the value of further negotiation and work (Renik, 1995). Analyst disclosure can help to minimize certain kinds of reification or what Bromberg (1995) refers to as linearity in the analyst's thinking that provides a false sense of certainty during shifts in formulation. To be sure, disclosure can also sometimes engender new kinds of problems if it becomes fetishized or is unchallenged. Psychoanalysts can mimic what Churchill described as ideal qualifications to be a politician: to have the ability to foretell what is to happen tomorrow, next week, next month, next year; and to have the ability afterwards to explain why it did not happen. While disclosures used to explain shifts in understanding are no less impervious to unconscious influence than anything else we might think or say, they potentially have the advantage of staying closer to observable affects, albeit affects that partly come from the analyst. In chapter 10 I discuss more directly the relationship between defense analysis, as put forward in American ego psychology, and the use of analyst disclosure. I believe that in particular circumstances the analyst's conveying his experience can be a more conservative or less inferential technique for exploring motivation and creating meaning than are many other kinds of interventions and thus lead to less mystification or reification.

It is my impression that at other times disclosure may temporarily interfere with nascent capacities for perception and recognition of externality and centers of subjectivity outside the self. I have introduced my own explicitly stated feelings or thoughts into the mix in ways that impinge on the potential space; to do so is neither usefully challenging nor constructive. Sometimes these instances have stemmed from exhibitionistic needs more than from anything that I could justify as forwarding the analysis, although, naturally, the patients observed something at those moments that was folded into the mix, toward some good purpose, I hope. Slochower (1996a) addresses how the analyst's explicitly voiced feelings or thoughts can request of some patients an undeveloped or unavailable capability for mutual exchange. I would add that, even for patients who benefit at times from these exchanges, in most instances the analyst can learn more from hearing about the patient's experience of the analyst's subjectivity (Aron, 1991) through the patient's elaboration of feelings, thoughts and fantasies. Perhaps we can apply Bromberg's (1995) useful idea of trying to "engage the patient's capacity for perception" to this determination. If patients are able to work with their experience of the analyst's subjectivity, based on amalgams of perception and fantasy, then reporting our experience of ourselves actually mitigates or concretizes the patient's exploration of the analyst's center of subjectivity. Yet there are times when the only way to understand this kind of impingement is through retrospective learning. In a sense, we are always in a process of discovering how we are disruptive, benignly disruptive, useful, or combinations of these variants in all our choices about how to intervene.

I think that Benjamin's (1988) "paradox of recognition" involves maintaining a tension between acclimation to the patient and introducing and expressing one's subjectivity in analysis. Paradoxically, sometimes disclosure can help to maintain this tension and some of the tensions I discussed earlier in terms of intimacy and solitude. I believe that we are primed to view disclosure as a part of expressiveness and as a part of mutuality in analysis, rather than to see the selectivity of disclosure as inherently maintaining a set of tensions related to self-expression. At least with regard to the kinds of disclosure I am discussing here, most patients feel that what is disclosed is a far cry from their levels of wish and desire to know the analyst.

The analyst as the "other," in Benjamin's terms, plays an active role in the struggle of the analysand to discover creatively and accept reality through *all* kinds of interventions. One might argue that, since I am emphasizing both the push of interpretation in general and more specifically the potential role of disclosure in facilitating a capacity for externality, I am also being concrete. We need to consider how all interpretation, even as it expresses the leading edge of the analyst's understanding, potentially expresses resistive elements as well (Smith, 1996). Most important, the analyst's capacity to bear strong affect, absorb, contain, hold, and witness are just as facilitative of developing a recognition of the other as is the analyst's explicit construction of possibility through disclosure or interpretation.

The ability of the analyst to change, shift, and experientially understand in new ways entails a constant current within the analytic process.

The patient's interaction and identification with this kind of person (as an affective and observing participant and as a representation of psychic possibility) can be an important part of therapeutic change and the negotiation of externality.

CASE EXAMPLE: ALLEN: THE OPERATION WAS A SUCCESS BUT THE ANALYST DIED

Consider a familiar use of countertransference from part of an analysis with Allen, whom I mentioned briefly in chapter 4. Although they might be said to be routine, I think that most of the types of disclosure I am describing hold in common an aim to do something about closure—they attempt to counter foreclosure, impasse, or "stuckness." Again, the notion of defense is very much interwoven into this discussion.

You will recall that Allen is a single man in his mid-30s. While he is able to feel pleasure and excitement prior to intercourse with his current girlfriend of a year, he loses his excitement shortly after penetration. He does not lose his erection and is able to reach orgasm, but without feeling excitement. He is highly accomplished and has been able to establish a more trusting relationship with his girlfriend than in any earlier relationship. He began analysis wanting to experience more pleasure with her and to feel a greater degree of safety, trust, and pleasure with her and others.

Allen, an only child, had felt seduced and controlled by his mother. He described her as highly emotionally volatile, prone to screaming, and crying in unpredictable ways. His father was busy, absent and rather passive toward his wife, pushed around from Allen's perspective. Between Allen's ages two and five years, his father was away traveling for work for long periods of time. In response to his mother's encouragement, Allen often slept in her bed while his father was away. Although there were no recollections of touching or sexual abuse, Allen had always felt generally puzzled, hurt, and angered by his mother's abrupt shifts between seductiveness and aloofness and unavailability throughout his childhood and adult life. He later learned that his father had had a long-standing affair. His parents divorced when he was finishing high school.

As Allen was beginning his second year of analysis, I felt stuck in a particular pattern. Allen seemed to enjoy saying what came to mind, elaborating his experiences and dreams and associating to the dreams with thoughts, feelings, and fantasies as long as I was relatively quiet. However, when I began to speak to him, trying to understand something better or interpret, he would say, pleading like a little boy, "No, let me finish. I really need for you to listen now. Please. Let me finish." I felt a shift in my position from sympathy to much more curiosity about honoring this request. Early in the analysis I had felt quite comfortable listening to this "need," trying to understand what it meant. I felt as if he were asking me to be a good mother, in the particular sense of being able to listen—not to interrupt, or perhaps corrupt him. These words were also Allen's. He often spoke of appreciating how different it was for him to have a space to speak and feel more freely; he did not want me to intrude and demand of him in the way that he said he had felt with his mother. He said that I was the mother he wished to have had. I considered if this need in some way involved a paternal function as well—a father who protected him from his intrusive and exciting mother. While there was a paternal aspect to the transference, it felt to both Allen and me that this was largely expressive of maternal transference in which he wished for me to be able to see him, listen, and create room for him to feel, play, express, and need. Later in his analysis, long after the period that I am alluding to here, we both had access to the experience of a strong paternal transference in which he was furious at his father and felt a desperate wish for more contact with him.

I came to see that Allen felt that unless he "finished" in his associative process he would be misunderstood, interrupted from gratification and expression. I was beginning to associate the words "let me finish" with his using a mode of self-sufficiency or masturbation rather than risk seeing where our interactions would lead. He preempted exchange for fear of being too angry, feeling hurt, feeling intruded on or seduced. I also wondered whether the words "let me finish" could be part of a paternal transference in which he was pleading with me to let him stay with mother, given that he felt angry that he had been so unprotected to begin with. However, the leading edge of this transference again seemed directed to the mother and to express a wish—or from my point of view what was becoming a demand—not to be exploited.

The analyst has a number of choices that I will only selectively and schematically summarize. I wanted to do something to understand this repetitive sequence and see if we could make a shift in our way of interacting. I am aware that Allen sounds somewhat stereotypically like Mr. Z (Kohut, 1979) in that, from Allen's point of view, he had a developmental need that disallowed me from expressing myself more actively. If I spoke about what was happening between us I risked ignoring useful cautionary tales from our developmental arrest and self psychology literature about various kinds of impingement. Should I psychically hold Allen even more than I was, or should I do something different? Even more apparent in my likening the case of Allen to Mr. Z, I was at times debating between formulations of my work with Allen that touched on the two interpretations of Mr. Z's dream. In this dream Mr. Z is with his mother and there is a knock on the door from Mr. Z's father. In the first analysis, the dream is interpreted as Mr. Z's oedipally based wish to exclude his father so that he can have his mother exclusively to himself. In the second analysis, the dream is interpreted more as the boy's wish that the father protect him from his mother's intrusive, critical, and demanding activity toward Mr. Z. As I mentioned, along with his demands for a different kind of maternal presence from me, I also felt that to some extent I was enacting the role of a protective father, a role that disallowed my other analytic self—an interpretive, intrusive maternal presence as experienced by Allen.

These formulations relate to some of the theoretical and technical differences among Kernberg (1975) and Kohut (1979) and Stolorow and Lachmann (1980) in the 1970s and 1980s, which have latter day versions in our contemporary literature (Stern, 1994, versus Tansey and Burke, 1994, or Mitchell, 1994). There are huge technical/theoretical issues at play here involving the degree to which we view the hoped-for empathic object as a natural part of psychic survival expressing, in Kohut's (1984) terms, the innate vigor of the self, or as an omnipotently controlled object. These differences are quite important in discussing the place of hope in analytic work and the transmission of hope between patient and analyst.

I thought of Allen's wishes/needs for me, as he defined them, as for a longed-for mother who would not be too intrusive, seductive, demanding, or prone to define reality unilaterally. I also increasingly felt that the way he expressed this need to me reflected an identification with his mother and our enactment of their roles with each other since the beginning of the analysis. In this enactment I felt a more monotonal expression of his need and gratitude for a different kind of responsiveness and my own natural acclimation to his feelings. I wondered about the extent to which aspects of this gratitude might have held defensive functions and whether my compliance might have involved a repetition of the way Allen had to comply with his mother—but I was entranced by Allen's intense affect. I felt that my work now, however, was to help Allen begin to open up more experiential pathways as I wished to help him increasingly experience and examine his unconscious identifications with his mother. Naturally, I was also seeking to release myself from what I experienced as an analytic straitjacket with Allen so I might more actively express myself about what I saw and was learning.

An analyst could interpret this process without mentioning countertransference but maintaining an exclusively intrapsychic focus. For example, he could assume that anger is what Allen is most immediately frightened of feeling and decide to interpret only what he believes is most immediate to Allen's experience or what is most immediately out of reach. In contrast, here are two other types of interventions that employ elements of countertransference disclosure in the context of conveying psychic possibility. The first involves no explicit mention of the analyst's experience or countertransference and takes us into the territory of what I referred to in chapter 7 as virtual disclosure. Virtual disclosure occurs when the analyst says something indirectly that could easily be construed as something that he or she feels. Often virtual disclosure is used as a problematic kind of compromise between saying and not saying something to the patient about what we feel; it can be useful at times. Obviously, virtual disclosure has all kinds of ambiguities in terms of what the patient will hear or what the analyst, upon reflection, may come to understand about what he or she was thinking, feeling, or intending to say. These ambiguities are a potential problem, as Renik (1995)has noted, but they can at times open the analytic play space for exploration.

Along these lines, consider this intervention: "It's important to you that I be different from your mother, and you fear that I will hurt you. But maybe the way you feel you need to control me at this moment stops you from finding out if something could be different from what you've known." Here the analyst has virtually told the patient that the patient feels controlled but that from the analyst's perspective the most important focus is on how the patient might feel the *need* to control. What is potentially problematic here is that the analyst has interpretively moved the patient's wish, need, or demand (this is always to be decided and negotiated by the dyad) that the analyst listen in a particular way into a sense of the patient's needing to control. It could be the case that the patient's wish, need, or demand to control is unconscious and the analyst is beginning to interpret this unconscious piece without explicitly addressing it. It may also be the case that the analyst is using a part of the countertransference to infer that if the analyst feels controlled, then Allen may feel controlling or controlled. Yet the analyst has not directly acknowledged the data to support this observation. Perhaps the analyst is thinking without saying that Allen is acting like his mother and the analyst is being cast into the role that Allen held as a child. If the sense of being controlling is not accessible to Allen, except as it is experienced by the analyst, it might be clearer to make more explicit this virtual disclosure of feeling controlled. My point is that it may be considerably more inferential to interpret this "need" on the part of the patient than to note something about what the analyst is feeling and see where things go from there. "What should we make of this?" It is interesting that from both Kleinian and American classical perspectives it is often regarded as less inferential or more careful to use a countertransference response to interpret a motive than to place the analyst's affective response out on the table. A fascinating area of discussion lies in how even to consider the notion of surface and depth within a relational framework rather a more topographical one. I raise this question not to "topographize" a relational model but, rather, to think about modulated and reasonable ways to proceed when we do think that direct expressions of our subjectivity can be useful.

There are many possible interventions in which countertransference disclosure could be used more explicitly and less virtually. For example, with Allen I actually said something less formally along the following lines: "We come to these moments now more regularly, moments when you tell me that it's important for me to listen, to let you finish. I find myself wanting to go along with your sense of what is helpful and comforting, and yet I find myself also wanting to try to explore something different." It would probably have been best clinically to stop there. But for these purposes I am going to extend the intervention a bit and project ahead to what I said relatively soon after: "At these moments I feel a bit controlled by you, told not to have my thoughts and feelings or to speak them." Eventually I added another piece: "Is this perhaps like the experience that you had with your mother? Maybe you are afraid of where our interaction will lead if you let me in more, if you let me speak."

In a series of exchanges in this session and over a number of other sessions, Allen wondered why I was changing how I handled this familiar impasse. He felt that he was not saying anything different or feeling in any way different about the content in the hour or his wishes for me to be more silent. I agreed with him that, at least as far as I could tell, my wishes to speak more actively with him were not related to a change that I had noticed in him. I then wondered if he had feelings about the idea that my wish to speak to him more actively did not follow noticeably or directly from something that he said or felt. He did have feelings. He was angry and puzzled, but it was the kind of anger in which he could hear himself saying that he could not allow me to have a sensibility. I suggested to him that he did not want me to want things in our work and that if I did they should not be separate from what he wanted. He agreed and said that he wanted me the way he wanted me. I should not introduce anything of what I thought or felt into the analysis. However, Allen, unlike earlier, did not seem particularly brittle to me during this or any of these exchanges during this period. This is not to say that he was convinced that I was not acting in an egregious way. But I felt reassured by the kind of curiosity he was displaying about this exchange; he appeared to be intrigued by his dawning awareness that, paradoxically, he did not want me to have thoughts and feelings or to act independently of him.

Within this countertransference disclosure there were a number of spoken and unspoken conversations operating between us. First, I had spoken to Allen about an aspect of the maternal transference in which he may have experienced me as a dangerous, old object who could manipulate, seduce, excite, and abandon him. I wondered to myself if I was also safe and familiar as an old object in the Fairbairnian sense of the term—that is, that to the extent that Allen experienced me as this ungratifying and hurtful object he could attempt to control. In contrast, now, as a contemporary and new object, I could be an extraordinarily dangerous object if, to the extent that he had been led to believe that I was trustworthy, he would have to entertain the possibility of risking anew some very old relational experiences that earlier had ended very badly. So I thought to myself that he was seeking to foreclose those relational opportunities with old, cynical, and painful solutions that, from his point of view, minimized further risk and hurt. Note that this use of disclosure of subjectivity characterizes the analyst as a new and dangerous object, in contrast to some disclosures that emphasize the ways that the analyst highlights himself as a new and safe object juxtaposed against the historical, dangerous object.

Early on I found myself easily acclimating to Allen's stated needs or wished-for roles for me to try out. Naturally, it is possible that this acclimation to Allen's needs reflected a concordant experience with him—that is, that I responded in the way Allen had done with his mother when she asked him to sleep in bed with her and was at once enticing, coercive, and unpredictable. As the analysis developed, the statement, "let me finish," and the material leading up to it and following it, led me to associations that differed from those during the early part of the analysis. During the phase I am discussing in this vignette, my associations moved to fantasies of him saying, "Be quiet, just stay still while I fuck you," as well as a set of his wishes, perhaps preoedipal, for the hoped-for, safe, and "needed object" (Stern, 1994).

It could be asked whether my original experience of Allen as a little boy involved an avoidance of him as a complicated, conflict-laden blend of a little boy and big boy. I think that basic countertransference trends, particularly during the early stages of analysis, are often experienced in unidimensional configurations. Later, in the period described here, I felt the wholeness, conflict, and complexity of the patient. For example, I began to wonder if my experience of Allen as more controlling and aggressive was related to Allen's identification with his mother rather than to his feeling exclusively victimized by her or being at her whim.

HOPE IN THE ANALYTIC DYAD

Among the many aspects of conscious and unconscious meaning in this clinical exchange, I want to focus briefly on the various levels, meanings, and dynamics of hope in the analytic situation and how they are communicated. I shifted from one kind of relatedness, coconstructed for a variety of reasons by Allen and me, to another kind of relatedness. In the first kind, I felt danger (manifestly a fear of harming him) in trying to bump up against Allen's stated experienced needs. The second type of relatedness evokes the question of how interpretation aims to anticipate in a general way where the patient might be able to go.

The disclosures (perhaps more accurately described as explanations of the analyst's divergent experience) that I am discussing operate simultaneously on a few different levels. On one level there is a conventional explanation of the analyst's shift in formulation and experience, which elaborates the meaning of differing experiential, perceptual/transferential realities of the patient and analyst. At the same time, this disclosure and explanation, expressing the analyst's agenda or the patient's anticipated psychic future, invariably enact a process related to the analyst's hopes for the patient's growth.

In a sense my wishes to influence represented both my own hopes for how Allen could grow and my own depletion in the current relational pattern of demand and compliance. I know that I wished that he would eventually be more able to feel his penis when he was inside his girlfriend and be able to feel like a man as well as experiencing little-boy feelings with me. It is possible that I also wanted to feel that Allen would let me enter him with what I had to offer. Fortunately, Allen was a patient who could tolerate and benefit from the kind of affective exchanges I have described here. Not all patients can tolerate this level or kind of dialogue (Slochower, 1996a). I was asking myself to be a kind of auxiliary analytic nudge to myself and Allen in facilitating this process—to see psychic possibility in the analytic dyad, hold it, promote it, nudge it.

Pushing or nudging, like many forms of action, is genderized in our culture. The ways that contemporary feminism points us to the "multiplicity of gendered subjectivities" (Chodorow, 1997) apply to men and women alike in our culture. The clinical individuality of both patient and analyst can constantly be overlooked within formulations of maternal and paternal transference, which often push toward stereotype. One could say that my whole experience of wanting to push Allen involved the emergence of a paternal or maternal countertransference. Within our culture, stereotypes of maternal responsiveness accord more with "It's OK to be afraid." In contrast, male stereotyped responses accord more with "Come on, try harder, push. It will be OK if you keep trying;" or even "No pain, no gain." I believe that the pushing or nudging of interpretation is gendered and is always being experienced or reexperienced in a gendered, sexual context, as a mother, father, sibling, lover, grandparent, teacher, or new object who awaits our efforts to construe. Some of us have mothers who push; some, fathers. Some of us have mothers or fathers who have influenced us through their ability to listen and contain, to integrate and solve problems through quiet example. In the context of my own filtered, gendered subjectivity, I think that in the moment I have described with Allen I was probably functioning in part as a new kind of father who was suggesting and imposing a separateness between Allen and his mother.

Obviously, patients experience the push or containment of interpretation in a myriad of ways, influenced constantly by transference and the balance of new- and old-object experiences. We are constantly at play with these forms of push and discovery, as we are with silence, containment, and the act of witnessing. With Allen there were limits to how much I could allow myself to be experienced as the fantasized good mother. I was growing impatient with a conflict between my own wish to be authentically engaged with Allen and being told how best to listen to him—and told to listen in ways that were increasingly incompatible with my impression about what he would be able to integrate. My hopes for Allen to allow us to interact more flexibly seemed to emerge from some blend of my own impatience and my own hopes, expectations, and perceptions of Allen about what he would be able to do in the analysis.

One way to think about the shift that I made is to liken it to how a child moves to a transitional object when he or she experiences the loss of more complete parental attention. Within this view of the therapeutic situation, I became depleted and Allen had to take what he could and adapt to my new formulations, which were organized around whatever compassion and empathy I still had available. I let the bough break and down came Allen, baby and all; now he must adapt. This process probably operates in many analyses.

It is also possible to conceptualize the analysis as an ongoing movement toward embracing and exploring the object world and externality (Winnicott's, 1969, "positive aggression") rather than as a breakdown product of empathic failure or depleted empathic resources. I believe that the analyst's depletion and wish to do something new is some-times met by the patient with a feeling of relief that a limit was set; this wish from the analyst is different from and less tautological than say-ing that the patient wished for this limit or needed it (S. Stern, 1994). Within self psychology or in Stern's interesting attempt at an integrated relational model, the conceptualization of the patient's sense of what is needed usually focuses on what was missing *early* in life. This has the potential to minimize how "needed" relationships undergo a shift in the emergence of transference and the social exigencies and structure of analytic work. The asymmetry of the analytic situation does not en-gender only parent-child interaction. Furthermore, even parent-child interactions change as children grow older (Mitchell, 1988, 1991). By speaking to how the analyst experiences this change over time, there is an opportunity to see how various kinds of constructions of need, wish, and demand can serve multiple functions and evolve within the inter-active matrix for both patient and analyst.

One of the most confusing aspects of this process for the patient is that the data are based largely on the analyst's experience, often cumu-lative experience rather than anything specific that has necessarily shifted observably for the patient. As Allen said, "Nothing has changed—why do we have to do something different?" Kohut's notion of a historically encapsulated template for an empathic object (his view of defense as the attempt to keep alive a hoped for empathic object) seems well suited to Allen's reparative and curative fantasy (Ornstein, 1995). Allen's view of an object of meaning and hope was for me part of the experience of becoming a nihilistic object in the analysis. Thus these negotiations were partly about whether Allen's reparative fantasy could bump up against my reparative fantasy for him. Could Allen in-state my nudge about how he could change? Could Allen work with me around my changes? In short, resistance or the patient's attachment to a state of self-stability (Bromberg, 1995) was being analyzed and I had to try to find a way to make it more observable to the patient. In a very real and important way the analyst's wishes for the patient both to change and to hold on to new affects were also being communicated. Similarly, Bromberg marveled at the patient's capacity to "dismantle his self-stability for the sake of a dangerous image of hope that is held in the mind of the therapist" (p. 187). Allen could do this. Many patients cannot (Slochower, 1996a). Yet I think the interactive process goes beyond the analyst's holding an image of hope in his own mind. The analyst is always communicating to the patient about these images, directly, and indirectly.

Like anything else in analysis, the explanatory function I refer to can become an enactment of the transference—for example, the transmission of the analyst's unrelenting hope, didacticism, or control of a parent recapitulated through explanation or narcissistic indulgence—or it may unwittingly circumvent resistance. But we have paid little attention to how not explaining these shifts through our experience may concretize or reify the content of the interpretation as something that resides inside the patient rather than something that we construct as both inside the patient and between patient and analyst.

Specifically, the contributions of these disclosures and expressive aspects of our interventions to therapeutic movement partly consists of something that the analyst has held on to or is unable to hold on to any longer—something related to the patient's limitations in experiencing the mutual impact of the therapeutic relationship. Perhaps here is the impetus for shifts in our understanding and experience. The patient experiences the analyst's subjectivity in every interpretation (Aron, 1991; Renik, 1995) partly because the analyst wants to express himself, has to express himself. Awareness of this dimension can facilitate judicious and modulated expression and transmission of the analyst's wishes to influence in any kind of intervention. We are, however, left with many interesting and complex questions about how the analyst's explicit and implicit construction of his subjectivity can obstruct or facilitate growth.

While I have emphasized a few aspects of the analyst's role in the push of interpretive process, I want to underscore our need always to examine the extent to which the analyst's wish to influence may reflect, to varying degrees, aspects of unrelenting and malignant hope or responsiveness to the patient's hopes for change. When do our attempts to show aspects of our subjectivity interfere with what Winnicott referred to as the capacity for object usage? For example, a patient who is newly able to engage in fantasy and exploration of his or her experience of the analyst's subjectivity might be derailed by the analyst's needs or wishes to reveal something more directly. Ghent (1992) has come up with a very helpful notion of "object probing" to describe the patient's process toward achieving a capability for object usage. Ghent describes a degree of "penetration and effort to reach and recognize" (p. 150). In my view, the patient's object probing is revealed through such affective exchanges as wishing the object not to exist, making demands on the object, loving the object, and trying to destroy it. But are there circumstances in which the patient's capacity for object probing can be assessed only *after* the analyst has presented something of his own experience, either through interpretation or through direct disclosure? Do we sometimes overlook a patient's potential for object probing by assuming that something more directly expressive will be destructive? In turn, is this assumption based on what Benjamin (1988) calls the pervasive tendency to focus exclusively on the role of the mother as object, minimizing our direct experience as subjects as well as the judicious and powerful ways by which this experience can help us to assess the patient's developing capacities for growth and engagement?

Here I think that the analyst benefits by allowing himself a degree of freedom to explore. Many of our interventions involve playful nuances of construction of certainty and uncertainty that we experience as we listen to our patients. We point to areas we do not understand but want to understand. We say that we have a hunch about something. We suggest areas to pursue further or areas that are curiously ignored or minimized. We point to blank spots and absences of meaning. We pose a construction of ourselves as not knowing, a playful construction, some parts schtick, in that we emphasize what we are genuinely puzzled about, some parts puzzlement and uncertainty, which emerge less consciously. This kind of play is similar to what Winnicott (1969)detailed—an alternation between ambiguity and uncertainty, on one hand, and subjective omnipotence, on the other. We know that we want to find, if not *what* we want to find. We have questions—or sometimes a hunch—and we know how to use it.

I am trying here to move from the *content* of our interventions to the *process* of inquiry, explanation, and even rhetoric and suggestion in the way that we influence in analysis. There is sometimes a paradox of our being pushy about our uncertainty—our "courting of surprise" (Stern, 1983) may sometimes have a shotgun wedding lurking in the background. Behind many questions, there is often a nudge or virtual interpretation along the lines of "Try to speak to me of things you haven't spoken of before." In this way, a form of the analyst's desire or wish to influence is showing, just as some of these wishes are expressed in why and when we look for important triggers or signifiers for interpretation.

Winnicott (1969) discussed authenticity as the recognition of an outside reality that is not one's own projection. Instead it is the experience of what Benjamin calls "contacting other minds." On an immediate level, the experience of contacting other minds is a learn-as-you-go process. When the analyst is changing in some dynamic relation to the patient (Slavin and Kriegman, 1998), trying to convey something about the complexity of or the rationale for a shift, even the internal and interpersonal aspects of the conflict may be helpful and new. Moreover, an important part of the analyst's explanation of cognitive and affective shifts in the way he is formulating psychic possibility is the patient's experience of "discovering another" (Benjamin, 1988). To be sure, explanation is a complex concept to understand in the radical and uniquely unconventional social context of analysis. Explanation within analytic discourse emanates from the ubiquitous fact of analytic life that unconscious factors contribute to any dialogue. Part of the self-analytic process involves monitoring these processes.

PART III

THE CONSPIRATORIAL
TIMELESS UNCONSCIOUS

9

THE CONSPIRATORIAL
TIMELESS UNCONSCIOUS
A Comparative Approach to the Problem
of Limits in the Psychoanalytic Process

I HOPE THAT HANGING ON THE STOREFRONT DOOR of analytic debate is a sign that mirrors the essence of our analytic attitude with our patients. The sign would read: "All unanswerable questions are welcome here." Of course, overwhelmed by the question, we may likely place next to it another sign: "Gone Fishing." This chapter relates to my clinical and theoretical struggle with questions about how to reconcile the nature of psychic possibility with the limits of analytic work. I think that we have a kind of selective, institutionalized incuriosity about some of the tensions between our hopes and the nature of limits in doing psychoanalytic work. We may avoid thinking about the constraints of analytic work, and we may be prone to extending the length of the work, often for the better but, unfortunately, sometimes in ways that may be less than helpful to our patients. Working within limits in the context of an enterprise so profoundly organized around the mobilization of hopes in both participants is complex and challenging. Goethe's words—that constraint is an art—suggest some of what I am exploring here with regard to this particular complexity of analytic work, its possibilities and limitations.

While the increasing duration of analyses in the United States and in some other countries has, in many cases, led to better analytic results than otherwise, it may also be a kind of "symptom" of something not necessarily associated with improved analytic technique. This symptom reflects at least a few identifiable problems. Specifically, I wonder if we have not lost a grip on the essence of the analytic goal of helping people integrate the tensions between new psychic possibility and limitation or repetition. As our theories of psychoanalytic technique have developed and become more sophisticated, and, it is hoped, efficacious, we may also be guilty of having become overly ambitious. In many ways, I believe, we have become less mindful about the blurring of lines between psychoanalysis as a therapy and a way of life, a difficult distinction, to be sure, since good analyses provide patients with a way of seeing and experiencing themselves and others that will accompany the patients for a lifetime. In some ways the issues that I discuss here are made banal by focusing too concretely or exclusively on the length of treatment. I have conducted some lengthy analyses, which, in retrospect, were as beneficial as they were only because the patients and I had a great deal of time together. I am most interested in the question of embracing limits. My aim is to heighten awareness of this factor in several different clinical approaches as it may play out within any specific analysis. An overarching theme in this discussion involves the ways in which various psychoanalytic approaches struggle to help patients to work with loss and mourning.

Our romantic/developmental tradition, most visible in the work of both Winnicott and Kohut, has increased our understanding of early development and the adaptive ways in which we preserve hoped-for objects. In fact, Kohut (1984) redefined defense as the attempt to keep alive hoped-for empathic selfobjects from childhood, an effort requiring a method that explicitly tries to avoid premature interpretation of defense. Ego psychology has turned patients' attention to the vicissitudes of associative and affective shifts, facilitating their capacity to observe how they avoid conflict or feeling. Contemporary American relational theory, which attempts to integrate aspects of British object relations theory, ego psychology, and interpersonal psychoanalysis, has attuned us to the importance of massively dissociated and disavowed affect and conflict and the intersubjective field in which patient and analyst communicate and learn about these processes.

Yet, with all these advances, I wonder at times where and how it will all end, so to speak. I think that the refinement of technique and our increased focus on developmental processes have perhaps taken analyst and patient far into levels of meanings while simultaneously a cocoon or sanctuary is sometimes built, compromising the work of integrating analytic insights into nonanalytic relationships with self and others. Technique may have become valorized, or even fetishized, at the expense of the notion of analysis as a time-limited treatment with specific goals. What is sometimes enacted is a kind of grandiose estimation of the place of analysis in a human life. I say this despite believing strongly that analysis is often what allows a person to have a life.

One of the most paradoxical aspects of this grandiosity is that in many ways analysts across theoretical orientations are unified in a shift away from thinking about the goal of analysis as involving the removal of conflict to a broadened capacity to observe and work with conflict in an ongoing way (e.g., Gill, 1954; Busch, 1993, 1995). Thus despite the fact that our goals are more modest than ever before, our ideas about the amount of time and effort to be directed toward these goals may have increased to such a degree that we enact unconscious fantasies about change through our shifts in technique. I view this problem as common to analysts of various theoretical orientations, although it is manifested in quite distinctive ways. Each of three models I examine here—ego psychology, developmentally based approaches, and American relational theory—has something to teach the others regarding this matter.

To be sure, the goals for any analytic pair are not static. Often the more we get to know about ourselves, the more we want to know and the more we find out, the more we find out that we do not know. Even goals that are guided by a contract with mutually agreed on goals (not something that we can take for granted as a priority by some analysts) will often evolve in accordance with the characters and conscious and unconscious factors of both participants. The horizon is ever-moving in psychoanalytic process.

Critiquing three very different approaches struggling with a common problem, I suggest a very general defense interpretation about analysis as it is practiced by many in the United States. While it may be "too deep" as an interpretation, perhaps it will have some relevance to the conduct of analytic work and theory. In routine analytic circumstances, we are subject to magical and omnipotent fantasies held by both analysand and analyst (Caper, 1992; Cooper, 1997). Sometimes the patient's omnipotent fantasies for change or cure implicate interpretation as magical and substitutive for his need to solve the conflicts and problems he confronts in the analysis. The analyst may unconsciously hold these wishes in a similar fashion. In addition to the ways in which formulation and interpretation broaden the observational field, the analyst, through formulations, can enact these magical fantasies of cure or psychic possibility. I suggest that this magical, fantasy aspect of formulation is a ubiquitous, ongoing part of analysis that needs to be gradually understood in the process of analysis. To some degree, the magical fantasy of the analyst borrows from the original wishes that the child associates with his parents, augmented by the ritualistic aspects of the analytic situation (Hoffman, 1994).

In this chapter we begin to explore the ways in which each of our psychoanalytic models may, to some extent, be enacting these magical, overly ambitious, and even omnipotent fantasies on an institutionalized level. On one level this reflects a kind of enactment of pathological hope or ambition. On another level, we have a kind of institutionalized passivity or avoidance of embracing the nature of limitations about analysis, limitations that, if explored more actively, might be helpful to the outcome of much analytic work. It is ironic that in a book dealing with the subject of hope I explore aspects of problematic or pathological hope. Hope in analytic work always involves a tension between the real and the unreal, between ambition and restraint, regardless of how ethereal and shifting these subjective experiences might be.

In making very general assessments of these three models—American ego psychology, the "developmental tilt" traditions (Mitchell, 1988) of Winnicott and Kohut, and American relational theory—I aspire to what I, along with Schafer (1983), regard as the best we can do in comparative psychoanalysis: to be equally unfair in my caricatures and critiques of each of the three models. Two caveats before I go further. Psychoanalysis is, by the very nature of its scope and ambition, a very long-term treatment, and there are no short cuts that I can see, except to consider as much as we can the ways in which our compromises (both in theory construction and in the execution of analysis) contribute to avoidance. There is little doubt that analysis takes a long time, and, as Kris (1996) put it, learning how to do analysis seems a nearly endless task, hampered by the need to unlearn, selectively, some of what we were taught and appreciatively adopted as our own. When I entered medical school 40 years ago, the Dean addressed us with the cheerful warning: "50% of what we teach you is wrong. We just don't know which 50%." We have a long way to go [p. 9].

Another caveat is that despite my criticisms of the developmental model, I believe that some selective aspects of regression are inevitable and can be helpful, sometimes essential and intrinsic, to the work of many analyses. I do, however, agree with Renik that analysts too often foster regression in ways that are highly unproductive. Often this takes the form of resisting or avoiding points at which the analyst's way of understanding the patient's thoughts and feelings diverge from the patient's, and thus opportunities for learning and change are diluted. Furthermore, the analyst's avoidance of difference with his patient's way of seeing and experiencing may sometimes dilute the efficacy of analysis or contribute to the prolongation of analysis.

THE CONSPIRATORIAL TIMELESS UNCONSCIOUS

One of the most compelling and useful aspects of being in analysis is the vast canvas that it provides, in contrast to some of the exigencies in other parts of life. Part of the breadth of this canvas is created through a very different relationship to time, through experiencing and even cultivating a sense that there really is a kind of timelessness to the unconscious. One of the most powerful analytic experiences in relation to time is the gradual sense of continuity and integration of the past and present and the anticipated future. The chronometer in analysis is always shifting; but, in contrast to a television game show in which the participants hear the clock ticking every moment (an icon or metaphor for time in popular culture), it is possible in analysis to suspend that ticking at least momentarily in an illusory way. I say illusory with both the positive and the negative connotations of the word. The positive aspect has to do with the creation of a feeling of vast space and time. However, as Hoffman (1996, 1998a) has pointed out with his analogy of time passing in a basketball game, in real life there are no timeouts. How do we reconcile the enormous opportunity that is fostered by this kind of expansive climate on one hand and, on the other, the sense that the passage of time and finiteness of life *and of analysis* are essential for the alchemy our work provides. I think that an ignored aspect of technique is the analyst's ability to do some uniquely analytic tick-tocking. By unique I mean that an aspect of interpreting transference and defense is to augment the patient's ability to observe the wasting of time, the resistance to observing conflict, and sometimes even the ways in which analysis can be used to aid in avoiding looking at these matters. In other words, we should expect the analytic enterprise itself to serve defensive functions, particularly when the patient, in an unconscious way, hopes to use analysis to substitute the analytic relationship for relations with others. Paradoxically, the context of free association can constitute one of the least spontaneous, most controlled environments for patients who eschew other kinds of interactions with others.

At its best, analysis allows us to experience aspects of regression in a new and an old, familiar way. This experience requires a patient and an analyst who value and can cultivate the opportunity to revisit old experiences without the patient's being "pushed," through naive hope, fiat, or declaration of the need for change. Analytic nudging, which I believe is an important byproduct of defense and transference interpretation, takes time and, as Loewald (1960) demonstrated so brilliantly, requires the patient's authentic revisiting of old experience while pushing forward into something psychically new in the present relationship with the analyst. The "ghosts of recognition" that Loewald identified in the shadows of our psyche do not come out easily, nor do they disappear quickly. By analytic nudging I mean something akin to the Loewald (1965) characterization of the complex function of interpretation:

> The difference between automatic process and personal activity we convey to the patient when we point out to him that the unconscious he becomes aware of is his unconscious, or that he dreamed the dream he had. Undoubtedly there is suggestion at work here, an appeal is made to the patient; it is similar in nature to the suggestion we make to a child that he is able to take a step by himself. (He may or may not follow the appeal at the time, but is justified by our knowledge that the child has the

wherewithal to walk.) Reliving infantile experiences in the transference starts out as passive, reproductive repetition. Through the analyst's interpretations, revealing and articulating the infantile connections and thus evoking the sense of personal, nonautomatic activity both in the present and in the infantile past, transference repetitions may take on the character of re-creative repetition [p. 93].

Yet where is the boundary between the provision and exploration of this vast analytic or potential space and a level of passivity and inactivity that does not serve our patients or our profession well? In a series of useful papers Renik (1995, 1998) has raised similar questions. I do not have easy answers to these questions because regression and potential space are concepts I hold as important elements of the analytic process and its therapeutic success. What I find most interesting is that I do not recall such issues of limitation being raised during my training. I believe that part of the reason for this omission is that in learning the idiosyncratic language of psychoanalysis—attention to the unconscious, attention to regression, the analyst's restraint in allowing for the emergence of unconscious conflict and defenses employed to mitigate or divert affect—analysts are taught a different way of thinking. Indeed they are learning a new language.

Bromberg (1979, 1998) has addressed the value of learning a new language in relation to restraint. My sense is that analysts who are trained in the interpersonal tradition are much better versed than others in the nature of the analytic tick-tock, but Bromberg's work points to the complexity of paying attention to the inevitability of regression, which he felt at the time was underemphasized within the interpersonal tradition.

The timelessness of the unconscious has for analysts a magnetic pull that can divert us from some important aspects of psychic growth that accompany exploring the limits of time and the limits of the patient and analyst working together. Many analysts from diverse traditions have been aware of this problem, yet I have the sense that it has become minimized with the excitement generated by many recent developments in technique and theory. For example, Ticho (1972) distinguished between "life goals" and "treatment goals." Loewald (1988), discussing how in some instances transference neurosis develops in full force only in the context of termination, suggested that prolonged analysis may prevent the emergence of transference issues related to limit and loss. In her acknowledgments in her recent book, Alvarez (1997) thanked her analyst for helping her to learn that there is life outside psychoanalysis.

While I agree with Hoffman (1996, 1998a) that our denial of time in analytic work relates to what Becker (1973) called the denial of death, I feel that Hoffman's interpretation of our problem is at once only partially true and too deep. I am in strong agreement with Hoffman's attention to our ways of denying time. Conscious and unconscious life also exist in real time. If an analysis is not dealing actively with time from the get-go, then I have questions about whether such an analysis is powered by the kinds of dynamic tensions that are a part of the most exciting and useful interactions in analysis—tensions including intimacy and solitude, expressiveness and containment, and timelessness and "real" time.

But I prefer also to think about the problem of avoiding time and limits as embedded in the particular kinds of compromises that analysts make with their patients and their theories, compromises that express 1) the opened-up and released hopes of both the patient and the analyst; 2) the analyst's conflicts about assertiveness, particularly in the degree to which the analyst avoids negative transference by being an icon of psychic possibility while minimizing his unique role in helping patients to integrate limitation; 3) the analyst's fetishization of technique and loss of sight of the practical realities of his patients' psychic functioning and lives; or 4) a minimizing of transference as a defense against the formation of other outside relationships while favoring a view of outside relationships as allusions to the transference. Interestingly, Freud (1912a) was much more likely to focus on transference as a defense than are many contemporary analysts. Partly owing to the work of Gill (1982; Gill and Hoffman, 1982) we have become much more usefully attuned than ever to patients' allusions to the transference, but we may be minimizing its defensive aspects of transference in the way that we currently practice.

To be sure, an analysis has to be open ended so that we can establish a creative potential space for the patient to "take the risk of not knowing what he will say" (Phillips, 1993, p. 63). One of the most important aspects of our therapeutic modesty is that we often do not know how far someone can go (Russell, 1973). But I think that it is worth thinking about whether analysts have become so oriented toward maintaining potential space that we have lost a disciplined way of thinking about and talking about limits. Along these lines, Sandler and Sandler (1994) suggested that part of the reason some analyses go on for so long is that the patient and analyst have a very difficult time accepting the limits of what we can do. I have a very speculative sense that as a profession we have been moving more and more toward vilifying this kind of analytic activity or attitude—we equate it with the bad parent. We have lost some of the "attitude" in the analytic attitude I believe that Freud held about analysis as a therapy. Much of Freud's analytic attitude was associated with a positivistic thrust. Freud's gigantic intellect sought to explain the breadth of psychic life, the principles of determinism, repetition, sexuality, object choice, and various kinds of psychopathology in a coherent framework. He sought to develop a science of the psychic retrospective. This positivistic thrust has been modified for great benefit as we appreciate the value of shared dialogic meaning, hermeneutic truth, the nature of reciprocal influence, and the mind as an open rather than a monadic system. But I fear that we have thrown out the analytic attitude that holds as dear the notion that we have a therapy.

Another way to put this is that as a field, we have perhaps enacted something about the tension between hope and possibility versus limit and loss. Perhaps we have too quickly adopted the role of apologist for the limitations of analysis rather than actively embracing them (paradoxically a therapeutic enterprise in its own right). Notable exceptions to this overgeneralization include Gill's (1954) humorous remark that we often recognize our friends after analysis. Along similar lines, Busch (1993, 1995) advanced the notion that analytic outcome entails heightened observation of conflict rather than necessarily its removal. From my point of view, these "limitations" of analysis are actually part of what we have to offer—something about helping people both to bear increased psychic possibility (when it is defensively averted) as well as to grieve and mourn limitation. In a sense this involves a kind of optimal disillusionment, one that is borne of authentic rather than compliant or false acceptance of the loss of aspects of omnipotence.

We want to think of ourselves as standing on the exciting and exhilarating side of the possibilities that can emerge through analytic interaction—that one really never knows exactly what's going to happen or what's going to be learned. Yet analysis also means calling a spade a spade. And while I do not want to minimize that we genuinely do not know in advance what is going to happen in analysis, I think that many analysts resist saying when they think that the ultimate benefits of analysis have been reached. I am not talking about foreclosing discussion of what the patient and analyst have done and where they might be able to go. On the contrary, I have in mind facilitating or mobilizing a discussion that examines where things have been and where they might go.

The analyst's authentic participation is vital here. For example, I heard one very experienced analyst say that they would never suggest finishing with a patient unless the patient brought the matter up spontaneously. I would wonder whether this analytic stance (I refer to it as a stance because it seems overly generic and not based on particular aspects of transference-countertransference) would include instances when the analyst no longer genuinely feels that there is something new to be learned. I have questions about this stance if it involves a countertransference experience of feeling a kind of deadness with the patient. Short of suggesting that an analysis should be completed, I wonder why the analyst would not more actively make use of this countertransference experience. More often than not, when analysts avoid making use of the countertransference, it is because they consciously or unconsciously value an unobjectionable positive countertransference and fear or question the value of using a broader range and complexity of countertransference experience. This homogenizing of countertransference was probably a reaction to the authoritarianism prominent during earlier phases of analysis. We can learn a great deal from thinking about countertransference as a retreat from the patient's experience (Schwaber, 1995) just as we can by thinking of our reactions as among the most essential tools at our disposal. Not all our perspectives of psychic reality that diverge from those of our patients constitute retreat, enactment, or countertransference, which interfere with the progress of analysis.

There are many instances in which patients might be anxious about leaving and thus realizing in real and independent terms the gains of analysis. It seems to me that a kind of defense interpretation about this anxiety, as well as some thoughtful and gentle encouragement, might be useful. Some patients cannot ever leave us, and I do not think that the value of work with them should ever be minimized. There are also patients who do not want ever to leave us, and it is in these cases that patient and analyst have to determine together at what cost the relationship continues. Some patients consciously know that they could leave and that the major benefits of analysis have been reaped. Yet they still find value in the work and see no reason to end it. In such circumstances at least there has been an attempt to take a thoughtful look at this assessment and make a measured decision.

To put these remarks another way, we have had difficulty both theoretically and clinically integrating the tension between the romantic and the tragic part of the analytic process. In the romantic part of our endeavor we place emphasis on possibility and change. But I think it is worth asking if there is an anxiety that we will be hurting our patients by wondering about limits and helping them to mourn limitation. After all, the mourning of limitation involves profound change. One very important form of disclosure or self-expression that some analysts avoid is to say something about what we have done and trying to take a look at what we are likely to do in the future. For many patients who are in analysis, this attempt to reexamine goals in the light of past analytic work can catalyze future work. It can leave patients with a good feeling about the work they have accomplished, both those who feel that the rewards of continuing are beginning to wane as well as those who are regrouping for some continuing tough work. Through an unremittingly hopeful attitude (expressed more through the vagaries of possibility than through well-articulated theoretical or technical stances), analysts may partially enact the disavowed and probably dreaded part of their experience—those parts of us that feel less hopeful or that fear the aggression inherent in our unique role of maintaining a tension between psychic possibility and limits.

Naturally, like everything in analysis, this can involve a form of enactment and repetition. The last thing I want to advocate is the foreclosure of something productive that could be done, particularly for those patients who defensively preclude possibility as an expression of character and interactional patterns with others.

AMY AND THE RACE AGAINST TIME

Amy was a married woman in her late 30s who desperately wanted a child yet experienced what Kris (1982) referred to as a divergent conflict. Amy was pulled in two directions, toward the wish to *have* a child and the wish to feel that she could *be* a child with a mother who could love her in a less selfish way than her own mother had. Amy's mother was full of directions, warnings, and criticism throughout Amy's life. Amy had consciously and unconsciously rebelled by sabotaging many situations in which her capabilities were worth sacrificing in order to convey unconsciously to her mother that she had failed Amy. Increasingly, Amy was feeling that her unconscious attempts to punish her mother through her failures were not worth it. Yet she felt compelled to continue failing by not following through on nearly completed scholarly papers in her chosen profession despite the encouragement she received from senior faculty members and friends.

As the analysis began, Amy experienced me as a mother who wanted her to succeed and to feel that she could get some of the things she most wanted—a child and the experience of success and completion in her work. As the analysis progressed, she experienced me as waiting for her either to feel more resolved about her sense of being pulled in two directions (toward being a mother and being a girl) or at least to feel that she could proceed with her wishes (and her husband's wishes) to have a child. Her experience of me in the transference resonated for me with some of the feelings and attitudes that I experienced. I did not feel as though Amy's conflict needed to be resolved "fully" in order for her to have a child, and I wanted her to be able to feel that she could move on with her life while she was able to bear children. I struggled with the concern that I was unwittingly "waiting" for Amy to give me certain kinds of gifts or measures of analytic success through her ability to move toward having a child. I wondered if I wanted Amy to bear a kind of "love child" of ours within the analysis. Yet, at the same time, I felt highly sympathetic to Amy's anger toward her mother, her wishes to retaliate, and her genuine sense of wanting to have a child only if she could determine that the balance fell in the direction of having one.

Quite often as this transference emerged, Amy and I discussed her conflict and the wishes she experienced about wanting to be both a little girl and a mother. She felt her anger toward her mother and wished not to give her mother a grandchild. She felt that her son or daughter would be automatically possessed and owned by her mother. She said that while she felt the same in a much milder way toward me, at some level she feared that her ability to have a child might be regarded by me as a kind of notch in my psychoanalytic belt. At the same time she could sense that I might wish for her to have things, children and more academic success, in an unselfish or nonnarcissistic way.

My comments and interpretations about her being pulled in two directions were both enlightening for her but also were regarded as attempts to influence or coerce her into doing something for my ends, not hers. Amy often brought up the "ticking of the biological clock" and her concerns that she would run out of time. When I affirmed the realities of the passage of time, however, she would often experience a painful recapitulation in the transference of my using the clock to further my goals of getting her to do something that she was not ready to do. Amy held on to a concrete way of thinking about her multiple goals and directions. If she had a child, she would no longer be able to hold her wishes to have a different kind of mother. If she decided to not have a child, she would have to renounce permanently her feelings of wanting to nurture. We discovered that her current stance, while achieving a most uncomfortable kind of homeostasis, did allow her, through compromise, to maintain a twin stance of punishing her mother while not completely letting go of the fantasy of having a child.

As Amy's 40th birthday approached, I began feeling an urgency about time that was markedly different for me. Amy also began to experience time as a heartfelt reality. I began responding to Amy's sense of time as a reality with a more marked kind of affirmation which she, in turn, began to experience as a kind of hopelessness that I had about her ability to resolve and work through her conflicts in analytic work. Her experience of me as giving up on her began a new phase of the analysis. She realized how much she wanted me to hold a hope for her that she could overcome her rage toward her mother. She also felt how much she wanted me to see her as competent and able to publish some of her papers, which a number of colleagues had been urging her to do for a number of years. This was the first time since the earliest phase of analysis that Amy could allow herself to feel less ambivalent (I emphasize less ambivalent rather than without ambivalence) that I would hold hopes for her to successfully resolve these conflicts in a way separate from some need I had to control her or for my own success. In other words, Amy began to experience me as a new object or an object outside this transference. Time was no longer a weapon I used to influence her, as she experienced me in the transference. Time had become a subjectively experienced "objective" reality for Amy, separate from her perception of time as a construct that I used to manipulate her. She began to ponder the possibility that she could have a child and continue to work through her rage toward her mother. Whereas she had always felt guilty about depriving her husband of children, she experienced his wishes to coparent with an increased caring and concern independent of guilt and self-reproach. Amy eventually felt able to get pregnant and continued working on these conflicts quite successfully over two more years of analytic work.

Apart from the negative maternally based transference that I have described, we discovered that her past compromises had also allowed her unconsciously to maintain a fantasy that she would have a virtual love child as a result of her analytic work. This fantasy was modified through her actual ability to have a child and through her struggles to complete our work. This success brought great pleasure and no small sense of loss and mourning in working through her loving feelings toward me as we approached the ending of analysis. I became for Amy a real object rather than a *surreal object*. I was, however, *surreal* to the extent that she had maintained the unconscious hope that if I really loved her we would be able to be together outside the analytic work. At times she was able to laugh at the realization that she had failed to seduce me enough to actualize this fantasy. The more I do analysis, the more I become aware that sometimes what we regard as a transference sometimes involves more—the unconscious fantasy of the analyst as a surreal object, one who will actually provide that which was lost. While these transferences are not psychotic, at times patients lose their usual ability to play with transference as an amalgam of real and unreal.

In working with these kinds of divergent conflicts (often exacerbated in situations in which there are actual implications of waiting for conflict resolution) I have felt a particular kind of countertransference, familiar to most therapists and analysts, that has a great deal of importance to issues of time. When patients feel divergent conflicts, there is simply no getting around the likelihood that they will experience the analyst as being on one side of the conflict. This often makes me want to stay outside the conflict, avoiding taking sides or being construed as taking sides. While there is a great deal of clinical wisdom in respecting that a patient is feeling pulled in two different directions, there are other dangers in trying too hard to stay outside or avoid being experienced in one way or another. A position of "neutrality" in the situation with Amy meant to me that I needed to have a healthy respect for Amy's wishes—her fantasies of having a different kind of mother and retaliating toward her mother by depriving her of something that in fantasy she felt her mother would take away from her if she were able to become a mother; and becoming a mother and a more productive scholar.

An obvious problem in such situations is whether the analyst's "neutrality" is genuine and authentic or a kind of technical position that defies some of his felt experience. Amy was correct about my wanting her to be able to have a child and become more academically productive. She did experience a transference that exaggerated my wishes for her to have these things in order to satisfy my own needs for therapeutic success. No doubt, however, I am highly invested in the idea of doing successful work. In my work with patients, a part of me would evaluate the quality of my work by the patient's ability to make changes and resolve conflict, and my work with Amy was no exception. I was gradually able to try to listen to both sides of her conflict while not trying too hard to be seen as completely "neutral" regarding her decisions. I was not neutral about wishing her to resolve her conflicts, even if I tried to understand and help her elaborate the many-sided conflict she experienced. A part of my authentic involvement related to my awareness of the clock ticking and my wish not to collude in a denial of time's passing. I am bothered by participating in a process in which "the operation is a success but the patient dies." Any kind of action that the analyst takes is a position, a stance that the patient will experience in one way or another within the transference. The shift in my work with Amy occurred when she began to experience her own and my increased awareness of time. Time became more of a reality (felt experience) for Amy, not a coopted device for me to control her or use against her within her maternal transference.

A COMPARATIVE VIEW OF THE PROBLEM:
CONTEMPORARY EGO PSYCHOLOGY, DEVELOPMENTAL TILT
MODELS, AND AMERICAN RELATIONAL THEORY

As is well known, Freud developed the method of psychoanalysis as a relatively brief form of treatment relative to today's standards. For Freud, a major part of therapeutic action lay in discovering the origin of neurotic symptomotology, thereby justifying a focus on interpretations that were "deep" by today's standard. Transference was seen largely as a resistance to remembering (experiencing) earlier anxiety and guilt-provoking events as they were encoded and defensively transformed and symbolized. The lengthening of analysis has occurred for different reasons within several different traditions in psychoanalysis. Although sometimes I may be discussing particular kinds of misuse or misunderstanding of a theoretical model, I do so not to blame the model but rather to help us understand the nature and relation of these clinical misapplications to the particular theoretical model in question.

CONTEMPORARY EGO PSYCHOLOGY:
INTEGRATING "THE NEIGHBORHOOD"

Broadly speaking, ego psychology has provided analysts with a more expansive appreciation of the adaptive aspects of patients' behavior and conflict. If there has been in psychoanalysis any kind of unified working mantra of the last 50 years (which is a highly dubious proposition given our vast diversity as a field), it might be something along the lines of "the patient is doing the best he can." This axiom has also been elaborated much more specifically and uniquely within the traditions of Winnicott and Kohut, which lie outside ego psychology.

Appreciation of the adaptive aspect of patients' functioning has allowed ego psychologically oriented analysts—indeed, all analysts—to get closer to patients' resistance to change, to know it, and learn how to work and play with it in probably less adversarial ways. Now our awareness of what is adaptive about a defense ideally allows us to take it up with a patient, helping the patient to understand why it might be a pattern or mode of experience or behavior that is sought after or held. In particular, the work of Gray (1990, 1994), Kris (1982), and

Busch (1993, 1995) has allowed analysts to develop techniques that include the conscious ego to augment the ability to observe patterns of resistance and avoidance.

It is worth asking whether our increased emphasis on the patient's adaptive functioning has also provided an escape clause for analysts who do not want to, are afraid to, or do not know how to take up aspects of resistance, negative affects, or negative transference. For example, I know that when I am concerned about taking up some particularly difficult aspects of transference or character, I sometimes rationalize my deferral with the empty ring of, "It's too soon. The patient is doing his best. He needs to keep blaming everyone around him. There will be a better time." The notion of doing the best we can can also be a part of an infinite regress for the analytic pair, rationalizing avoidance of difficult issues: The analyst might say to himself, "I'm doing the best I can to take up these issues, even if I know I'm avoiding taking up these issues, so it's OK to hold off. We're both doing the best we can." But it would be glib to ascribe all such deferrals to this escape hatch. Often there is a great deal of clinical wisdom in staying as close as possible to the patient's experience, even if the analyst begins to feel that certain kinds of formulations, interpretations, or even confrontation will bear fruit in the future. I mean to focus on those instances when we rationalize our own deferral and avoidance of trying to take up difficult issues. Obviously the work of Gray, Kris, and Busch has promoted the opposite—to help the analyst with tools that, in turn, will help the patient to understand and observe more about his resistance.

The problem of avoiding resistance, then, is not a problem that ego psychologists alone display but relates to the general use of clinical and theoretical observations of adaptive functioning that grew out of ego psychology. In fact, analysts who are less oriented than ego psychologists toward staying close to defense, such as those who advocate staying close to the patient's experience at all times, may be less likely to take up defense and resistance (e.g., Trop and Stolorow, 1992). (This is of course also a most complex issue. For example, self-psychologically oriented analysts would maintain that by staying close to the patient's experience they are also understanding defense, since defense is redefined as an attempt to keep alive a hoped-for empathic response from another.) My main point here is that our increased appreciation of adaptation has probably sometimes added to or complicated our countertransferential tendencies to take up certain aspects of the patient's defense and resistance whatever our orientation.

Kris (1982), Gray (1990) and Busch (1995) have elaborated specific models of applying defense analysis to the immediate surface of the patient's associations. Despite important differences, they hold in common a sense that, by the analyst's interpreting underlying wishes too soon, defensive intellectualization, compliance, or transference enactment can be fostered. Kris provided a way of augmenting the analyst's attention to the stops and starts of free association as indications of defensive activity. Both Gray and Busch have alerted analysts to the importance of looking for what they refer to as ego resistance, which is more accessible to a patient's attention than the underlying motives that motivate defense.

Presumably increasing focus on defense analysis, particularly increased attention to interpreting "closer to the surface" (Gray, 1973, 1990; Busch, 1993) has led to analytic benefits. In my own work, I spend considerable amounts of time with some patients working with such a method, though seldom as singularly focused on it as I sensed Gray and Busch are. My question, best answered by proponents of the method, is, if time is wasted, and, if so, how can their method be refined? If I were to summarize the nature of my general concern or question, it is whether the focus on process can sometimes become too absorbing in its own right, allowing patient and analyst to lose the forest (goals of analysis) for the trees (process).

Busch (1993) has discussed the importance of being "in the neighborhood," a central part of Gray's (1973, 1990, 1994) work as well. Freud (1910) introduced the phrase, "in the neighborhood": "First, the patient must, through preparation, himself have reached the neighborhood of what he has repressed, and secondly, he must have formed a sufficient attachment (transference) to the physician for his emotional relationship to him to make a fresh flight impossible" (p. 226). Freud's division of repressed content and the nature of the analytic relationship has of course been a matter of broad debate within psychoanalysis for at least the last 30 years within the United States. In this statement, Freud implicitly described the analytic relationship as essentially educational and as either facilitating or obstructing the patient's acceptance of the analyst's observations. In this particular construction, repressed content and relational configurations that might inform the ego processes under scrutiny seem excluded from consideration. But Freud's main intention here was to point out the vast discrepancy between our ability to construct formulations and the patient's ability to make use of these formulations.

Freud, and later Gray and Busch, demonstrated the clinical wisdom of not conflating our ability to formulate about the unconscious with the patient's ability to integrate these formulations. For Busch (1993), in particular, the analyst's attempt to interpret more deeply is viewed as a "bypassing of resistance" through which "the patient's conscious participation is left out of the analysis, except to passively accept the interpretation" (p. 154). There are a number of assumptions in operation here that are worth examining in the light of the discussion about limits and elongation of analysis.

One problem is that we do not know if Busch is referring to a consistent bypassing of resistance or the occasional intervention that aims to uncover underlying wishes, interspersed with attention to engage the patient's conscious awareness of aspects of resistance and available affect and content. For example, one can be quite effective by usually working in one way, such as trying to stay close to the patient's resistance and invite the patient's conscious awareness of how these processes work, and at other times to try to interpret more "deeply" to discover the nature of what we believe is repressed content. Besides, it is my observation from my own work, and that of my colleagues and those whom I supervise, that we tend to use various approaches whether we do so consciously or not. My concern is that to describe a technique such as staying close to the surface as invariable is to risk getting too absorbed in a particular expectation of the process.

Freud (1910) seems to have come to a similar conclusion in observing his own tendency sometimes to bring unconscious wishes to consciousness too quickly: "I have often found that a clumsy procedure like this, even if at first it produced an exacerbation of the patient's condition, led to a recovery in the end" (p. 227). We all are clumsy sometimes whether we like it or not and, while I do not want to promote clumsiness as a technical idea, I think it is probably close to the way we all function as analysts. Furthermore, I agree with Freud that sometimes our clumsiness has what seem to be some beneficial results.

The naturally occurring process by which we interpret aspects of resistance closer to the surface and also, at times, take up an underlying wish is what I refer to, somewhat felicitously, as "integrating the neighborhood." My fear is that as writers of technique, we can sometimes present a perspective in too neat and clean a form, which does an injustice to the variety and humanity in the conduct of clinical work. Each of us who write about technique is subject to this problem. For example, I find it unlikely that an analyst as talented as Schwaber (e.g., 1983) always stays as close to the surface of the patient's psychic reality, just as I find it unlikely that relationally oriented writers who emphasize interpersonal configurations in their interpretations are not paying a great deal of attention to ego-psychological processes. The danger of trying to maintain our work as a therapy with goals and limits is that process can be fetishized too much as an end in itself. All interpretations or interpretive styles enact something, and it is always worth paying attention to how the analytic process constitutes various forms of enactment. Busch (1993) addressed this concern when he stated that his approach is not without goals, but that he is essentially saying to patients, "in your use of the method we can learn such and such from what you are saying" (p. 173).

In fact, I think that Busch would argue that his technical emphasis is aimed at establishing clear goals for analytic work by promoting the patient's conscious participation as much as possible. Yet I see no reason why a patient who is given a deeper interpretation (again, I do not mean as a consistent technical procedure) that might bypass some aspects of resistance is any more likely to accept an interpretation passively than is a patient who is issued an interpretation about his or her resistance. The patient's passivity or compliance is partly a character trait and partly a response to what the analyst is calling forth through his technique. But an analyst who works exclusively in one way, such as repeatedly interpreting the most immediate form of resistance, can also potentially promote particular kinds of compliance. Add to these factors the unfortunate fact of psychoanalytic life that we are chosen as analysts by our patients partly to perpetuate unconscious patterns. A patient who is particularly comfortable with an analyst who points out the most immediate forms of resistance may be so for any of a number of neurotic reasons, and it is possible that the treatment itself can enact aspects of this neurosis. So to say that in bypassing the resistance the patient's conscious participation is left out is, I think, much too simple. No less simplistic is the Lacanian and Kleinian argument, sometimes made in too reductionistic a fashion, that the ego-psychological approach consistently avoids aspects of the patient's unconscious participation.

In relation to the questions I have raised regarding the prolongation of analysis or avoidance of limits, I have sometimes wondered about instances when microanalysis might overlook the larger elements of transference-countertransference phenomena that would be beneficial to analyze. Reading the work of Gray and Busch in particular, given that the surface of the patient's associations is being explored as a kind of modal intervention, raises questions about where the moments are in which transference might be more actively interpreted. Where are the places that the patient's shifts away from specific affects might actually be less important for the analyst to take up than, say, another surface such as transference would be? A question is whether this increased focus on defense analysis interferes at times with the analyst's pointing out important aspects of interaction that express defense, which, in turn, might facilitate observation.

One of my favorite examples illustrating technique is a case in which Gray (1990) thoughtfully showed his young male patient again and again how the patient's associations turned away when he experienced dependency toward women. My sense is that the patient became increasingly able to see this pattern. Less clear was the extent to which the patient and the analyst were looking at this dependency and attachment in the relationship between the two. This model focuses less on the ways that interactional tensions reflect the very conflict and defenses being analyzed; there are times when looking at this surface can allow a patient to observe the defense most readily. In other words, it seems somewhat unclear how attention is paid to the processes of resistance to the analyst's pointing out drive derivatives to the patient. For example, is the analyst's role as educator and guide being enacted in ways that are less addressed by this model than by other models?

Thus, while Busch (1993, 1995) in particular has cogently addressed the potential problems or dangers of not being in the neighborhood, I think that there may be problems as well in being too much in the neighborhood. My guess is that many analysts who find Gray's and Busch's contributions useful already intervene at times in the way that I am discussing. To follow the technique exclusively, particularly with patients who have experienced trauma or deficit and for whom defense is constantly being disavowed and located in the other, seems to me to promote an atmosphere in which the mind is disembodied, leading to an overly intellectualized, hypereducational, and rarefied atmosphere. Then again, such patients would probably gravitate toward analysts who think of the analysis of defense as within both an intrapsychic context and the context of transference and interactional tension. All models have to be careful about valorizing a particular interpretive surface while excluding or minimizing others. My question about Gray's method of interpretation is whether the observation of mind is being overvalued within technique while other surfaces are being minimized or ignored. Kohut (1971) voiced the same concern about ego psychology in general and again in his posthumously published book (Kohut, 1984)—a concern that defense interpretation generated by ego psychology had become overly cognitively or intellectually focused. To their credit, I believe that both Gray and Busch avoided the vagaries of regression by trying to define it within particular kinds of ego phenomena that they observed and without moving to simplistic analogies to childhood development. Furthermore, they attempt to focus on promoting the patient's autonomy by enhancing his or her capacity for self-observation. The problem is (and this is a problem with any technique) that the belief that including the conscious ego within our interventions will necessarily encourage the analysand to take a more active role in treatment (Busch, 1993, p. 170) is questionable. It is my sense that this technical preference will have a variety of meanings for a variety of patients and is no less likely to become a part of passive compliance than any other technical procedure. But this is a fascinating question that cries out for more clinical evidence and discussion. I am suggesting that the patient's complex feelings and fantasies about the analyst as educator seem, at times, to be minimized and delimited in comparison with the notion or internalization and identification with the analyst's observing capacities as the foci of change.

DEVELOPMENTAL STRATEGIES AND PSYCHOANALYTIC HOLDING

The analytic situation borrows from the affective experiences of parent-child interaction in different ways for different patients. The earliest history of psychoanalysis focused more exclusively on oedipal phenomena, just as the last 50 years have perhaps focused too globally on "preoedipal" phenomena.

The vast opportunity for bodily experience at all levels of development is at the heart of analytic work and a developmental focus. It is very difficult to focus on limits of the analytic situation without risking the loss of opportunities that analysis provides through regression and a revisiting of bodily experience. Since analysis revolves around the transformation of felt experience into verbalization, it can easily turn into what Flax (1990, p. 219) termed a more objectified, "semantic project." Analysts bring their own vital bodily experience to analytic work and it is what allows us to become more attuned to our patients (and our own) unconscious states. Yet we are in a very primitive state in terms of how to discuss and use these opportunities.

Analysts such as Wrye (1997) have been helping us develop ways of talking about how to link the mindbody within the analytic dyad. She argues that in many ways analysts have to become far more attuned to their own body than they were trained to in order to understand how to help patients find and relink their mind and body. We have gone from an era of analysis in which the analyst's body was ignored or feared as dangerous to a new era in which we can consider more fully the relationship between the analyst's bodily experience and the patient's bodily experience. Shapiro (1995) says: "The patient may fantasize about our bodily state, but as much as possible our bodily state remains opaque . . . what began as a liberating environment where one could at least talk dirty, has become a straitjacket for analyst and patient alike" (p. 317).

How to understand our patients' bodily states and how to apply our bodily states to the analytic situation are quite difficult. For example, consider what Wrye (1997) says:

> As analysts when we bring our own unnoticed bodily states into our consciousness we enable our patients to bring to life deadened or inaccessible aspects of themselves to life. One image I particularly like in this domain of "inside, outside and somewhere in between" is the idea of holding our patient's beleaguered, oftimes deadened bodies in our mind womb, creating a safe mental and palpably physical space for gestation and psychic rebirth [p. 4].

This description is meaningful to me and evokes memories and experiences of psychic holding in doing analysis. Psychic holding as Wrye describes it is anything but a passive process. It involves the analyst's ability to become aware of his own bodily experience to understand the patient's experience or defensive transformations of experience. But these experiences are only a part of analytic work with the patients who have felt these feelings with me and had this opportunity. I can recall, for example, feeling depleted and sucked dry by some patients whom I have held for long periods of time. I can recall times when patients have wanted to have analyses that stay in the position of my holding and, in so doing, they avoid the important "step" of trying to take their own new steps.

I think psychoanalysis has entered a new phase of getting so focused on maternal metaphors for describing analytic work that we run the risk of oversimplifying extremely complex aspects of psychic growth. Of course, maternal metaphors are anything but simple or unvaried; they include a wide range of sexual and aggressive phenomena. The mother can be holding or intrusive, bloody and milky versus dry, sexy or inhibited, nursing or weaning, married or unmarried. As psychoanalysis has become more and more a profession conducted by women, we have increased opportunities for learning about patients' experiences of their analysts' bodies. Analysts also have considerably more freedom than in earlier phases of psychoanalysis to discuss these experiences with their patients. But with this opportunity we also run the risk of leaving out aspects of growth that male analysts and male patients find important.

Thus the application of developmental concepts to the treatment of adults is essential but poses extremely difficult problems. To me there is no overarching developmental schema with which to understand the analytic situation. For example, Stone's (1961) notion of thinking of the analyst as "the mother of separation" in the analytic situation seems highly relevant to many analyses and less so in others. The only general overlap across analytic context and developmental process that I have been able to determine is that both analyst and parent (good enough) know about how the child/patient has come to be the way he is. This knowing about the evolution of person is a powerful kind of intimacy. It is probably the reason that so many of us look back on our grade school, high school, or college friends and feel such a strong sense of connection. These are friendships forged during a process of becoming, of risking not knowing who we will become. The bonds are sealed with a love about shared risk and uncertainty. These are the kinds of powerful affects often stirred up during the most effective kinds of analytic process and development. Add to this experience of being known, the asymmetry and novelty of saying what is on one's mind in the analytic situation, and there are all kinds of opportunities to feel one's body in new and old ways.

Within what Cooper (1994) has called regrowth strategies and Mitchell (1988, 1997) refers to as the developmental traditions or "developmental tilt" models, there has been a great deal of attention paid to affect attunement and the analyst's acclimation to the patient's psychic reality. I have wondered if the developmental tilt models of Winnicott and Kohut have in some ways fostered a climate or *Zeitgeist* of nonimpingement. Within the developmental models has there perhaps been too much emphasis on a vision of the analyst as merely holding or containing the patient's experience in order to facilitate new growth? This holding can lend itself to a revised version of what Mitchell (1997) calls the myth of the generic analyst and obfuscate the idiosyncratic features of the analyst's participation in the process:

> The major limitation of approaches to interaction that have emerged within developmental traditions results from the overestimation of the extent to which the analyst can remove herself as a subject from the interactional field. The vision of the analyst as merely holding or containing the patient's experience in order to facilitate new growth lends itself to a revised version of the myth of the generic analyst and casts a cloud over the idiosyncratic features of the analyst's participation in the process [p. 266].

Essentially this is but the old wine of the blank-screen analyst in a new developmental bottle. In contrast to the caricature of the ego psychologist as an educator who delimits the complexity of surface, the developmental tilt models stand more exclusively on the side of reviving hoped-for objects and psychic possibility. One of the problems with the developmental tilt model is that it may not help patients who, in part, unconsciously defensively use analysis as a refuge from having to change and be challenged. It seems to me that there are some patients who want to be in analysis specifically so that they are not challenged!

Implicitly, the analyst working within this framework privileges positive or unobjectionable countertransference, as if any form of countertransference could be so neatly, homogeneously described.

I am also very much in agreement with Benjamin (1988), who discusses the developmental model as being a newly disguised version of the analyst's avoidance of being a subjective object. By the analyst's being a subjective object and actively making use of the analyst's experience, including when it differs from the patient's psychic reality, unconscious meaning can be explored and often catalyzed in ways unlike some of the developmental models. (Stern and his colleagues, 1998, are an exception to this generalization since they are moving to a complicated notion of therapeutic relationship and therapeutic action.) But there is an additional and vital problematic implication of the analyst's not utilizing himself as a subjective object and instead being the generic analyst. The strategies of therapeutic action that revolve exclusively around mirroring and holding, albeit extremely important for some patients and probably for all patients for a period of time, can also engender a level of passivity on the part of both analyst and patient as well as a climate of retreat. The analyst's aggression, or, probably better put, her assertiveness of difference, is systematically excluded from the interaction and the conceptualization of therapeutic action and benefit. Even Stern et al.'s (1998) fascinating and sophisticated work, which tries to detail aspects of therapeutic action, may center more on the importance of a homogeneously positive (unobjectionable) countertransference than on the complexity of diverse countertransference that can inform analytic work.

This passivity or lack of assertiveness of difference is also probably fallout from the attention to "preoedipal" interaction as exclusively defined by mother-infant interaction and exclude a number of other interactions (Ceccoli, 1998). Mother-infant interactions often beneficially involve mirroring of affect, which, as D. N. Stern (1985; Stern et al., 1998) has demonstrated, is anything but a simple or passive process. When I discuss the analyst's failure to assert difference, I am not referring to the analyst's self-disclosure, but rather to his interpreting unconscious phenomena that are not in the patient's awareness. If we analysts do not allow ourselves points of divergent perception and experience, the analytic process can become too tame, benign to the point of being banal. My concern is that ideas and applications of such concepts as mirroring cause some analysts to restrict themselves to forms of understanding and expression that do not differ from those of their patients. By the analyst's doing so, the opportunity for exploring different feelings, different sides of the same conflict, and, most conspicuously, unconscious experience are diminished. In particular the opportunity for grieving loss and disappointment can be compromised in analytic experiences in which the analyst is exclusively attuned to the patient's experience.

It is interesting, I think, that most classical and American relational analysts might disagree about the use of countertransference expressiveness but they would agree about these problems of the developmental tradition (Inderbitzen, 1997, personal communication). They are equally critical of the idea of applying aspects of childhood development to adult analysis in an isomorphic way. Not enough developmentally based discussions of therapeutic action explain why and how mother-infant interaction applies to the analysis of adults.

To be sure, the essential and complex functions of psychic holding and mirroring (Slochower, 1996b), are anything but a passive process and require a highly skilled analyst. Many analysts working within the developmental tradition are similarly skilled. Any good analyst provides holding while working, feeling, and thinking within a partly developmental context. It is not uncommon to work for sustained periods of time in which the analyst's attention is on holding and creating safety. But I think there may be a fair amount of analysis that is using the developmental tilt model quite loosely, in such a way that interpretation and at times confrontation are avoided. In other words, the developmental model can be used as a kind of avoidant compromise between hopefulness about the patient and an unconsciously less than hopeful attitude about the potential benefits of interpretation and analytic interaction. While we try to tap into the patient's capacity to grow and recover from certain kinds of loss, trauma, or impingement, this model may, at times, produce a countertransference reaction in which intervention or activity is equated with hurting or retraumatization. The fear of hurting the patient is something we all struggle with, particularly when we are beginning to take up some of the most thorny character issues. But there is a real difference between an analysis that takes a long time because of what is being learned despite real limitations in doing the work of understanding intrapsychic and interpersonal process versus an implicit attempt to create a particular kind of atmosphere in which empathic failure does not occur. I regard the latter as a kind of unanalyzed psychoanalytic nihilism because it is based on very little hope about what can happen through the analytic process and interaction.

Some approaches to analysis (e.g., Schwaber 1992, 1995) have been influenced by the culture of nonimpingement but less directly through a developmental model than from a view of therapeutic action that revolves around the value of elucidating the patient's psychic reality. Schwaber has usefully challenged the notion of the analyst as arbiter of reality. She suggests making a shift in epistemological stance, inviting our patients constantly to illuminate our perspective on what they are seeing and experiencing. Yet this model lacks the kinds of tensions that I am describing between the patient's and the analyst's psychic reality. While the analyst may for long periods of time be attuned exclusively to the patient's psychic reality, I cannot see that the analyst is ever able to leave out of the mix his own views even in the effort to flesh out the patient's experience. Impingement is a multifaceted, complex dimension ranging from the destructive to the inevitable to even the *good-enough impingement and retaliation* (Cooper, in press). The latter concept, which I explored in depth through a clinical example in chapter 4 refers to instances when some unconscious aspect of retaliation is expressed and the analyst and patient are able to make use of it. That there are assertive and aggressive aspects of interpretation cannot be left out of our awareness or discussion just because we are engaged in a therapeutic enterprise. All interpretations involve aggressive and loving components, and we are probably reluctant as a profession to explore the aggressive nature of our analytic interventions.

Schwaber (1992, 1995) has heightened our attention to the ways that countertransference can involve "a retreat from the patient's reality." But countertransference is far too informative and complex to think of in a unidimensional way. The point of a more active and, at times, expressive use of countertransference is not to legislate perspective and authority, but to alloy the divergent psychic realities so that a new psychic metal can emerge. Instead, the developmental model, when it focuses on nonimpingement rather than complex forms of generative interaction, makes use of unobjectionable positive countertransference and sees all the other types of countertransference as a retreat from the patient's psychic reality. This more reductionistic view of countertransference can result in a kind of retreat from the analyst's calling things as he sees them. Again, this is one of the meanings of limit that I think we may be collectively avoiding.

The other, even more profound problem that comes up here is that an analyst who avoids taking up points of affective or cognitive divergence with his patients, even though these differences are justified within the developmental model he employs, may not see character issues that are patently obvious to those in the patient's outside life. In such instances I fear that analysis can create a kind of overly protective bubble and a mutually created illusion of relatedness that lacks conflict and both intrapsychic and interpersonal complexity. Obviously, all analytic work involves the need for safety, and safety is antecedent to exploring anything that feels dangerous. I am suggesting that within the developmental tradition there may sometimes be too much safety and a loss of the kind of optimal tension between danger and safety that Greenberg (1986) described as intrinsic to analytic work.

The particularly interesting and difficult issue of too much safety and the problem that we as analysts have in contending with the limits of the analytic situation have to do with ways in which the analyst can provide a substitutive relationship for a patient for long periods of time that go unanalyzed. Again, the circumstances I am describing do not involve problems with a theoretical model but, rather, the translation of a model in the context of highly problematic countertransference reactions. In these situations, patients sometimes come to the analyst partly as a way to safely express rage, sadness, and disappointment toward a spouse or lover. These patients often seek to be understood, loved, or appreciated, a need they are unable to satisfy in their real relationships for various reasons. These reasons may stem from inhibitions in communicating needs to a spouse or lover or from the actual limitations of the spouse in responding to expressed needs. Analyses can be lengthy in this context for reasons of enactment. In one kind of enactment in these situations, the analyst simply accepts the patient's longings for a more gratifying kind of responsiveness without trying to analyze it. What can result is a long-standing process involving an unanalyzed substitutive relationship in which growth is compromised, and sometimes the relationship outside the analysis deteriorates. (In these situations, the male analyst is likely to be involved in what I felicitously call the Warren Beatty *Shampoo* transference-countertransference paradigm.) I mean to try to confront the fact that it can often be quite gratifying for the analyst to be admired or desired, but such admiration can be problematic. In such instances, the analyst may consciously or unconsciously resist trying to explore the nature of the patient's use of the analyst in a substitutive or, sometimes, surreal relationship.

Another manifestation of this problem occurs when the analyst is anxious about the nature of the patient's erotic feelings and too quickly tries to analyze the possible defensive nature of these feelings without having a clear sense of their meaning. The patient has nowhere to go with these erotic experiences and keeps becoming involved in thwarted attempts to bring them to the fore. What can result are patterns of secondary or iatrogenic resistance that are time-consuming and require massive forms of avoidant compromise or, even worse, compliance into a kind of false self-analysis.

The main problem with developmental models in the context of this discussion of limits is that we are confronted with the knowledge that developmental processes are mobilized within analyses, but we have a very difficult time understanding how best to apply this knowledge to the conduct of analytic work. For example, the very label "preoedipal" phenomena may blur the complexity of developmental processes, which are, in turn, misapplied to the analysis of adults. In general, preoedipal phenomena usually connote a developmental formulation that assigns primary importance to the early mother-child relationship and often undervalues the roles of others, most notably the father as he is experienced in real interaction and internalized representationally (Herzog, in press). For example, in male development, the oedipal father is often conceptualized more exclusively as standing for limitations between boy and mother and later identification with the father. This formulation pays insufficient attention to the vital part fathers and other objects play in early development and their participation in dyadic communication, not simply as the third party in mother-child interactions.

To the extent that our formulations focus on preoedipal development through the narrow lens of the mother-infant dyad, regressions of a particular kind may be fostered in ways that are metaphorically inaccurate and often unproductive. For example, while I believe that there are many aspects of regression intrinsic to the analytic situation, I am uncomfortable with thinking about the analytic process or the analyst as more generally the "mother of separation" (Stone, 1961; Adler and Bachant, 1996). Naturally, often maternal transferences develop that stem from separation conflicts and experience, but the expectation of these phenomena can blind us to complex regressive and progressive phenomena in the conduct of analysis.

American Relational Models and the Problem of Healthy versus Defensive Pluralism

The ego-psychological and developmental tilt models are not the only types of psychoanalysis that struggle with the issues I am addressing. The problem of limit is no less a problem for the American relational model, which has in some ways partially constituted itself from a kind of selective integration of comparative approaches. Those of us interested in psychoanalytic pluralism have to be careful not to move too much among theories as a way to unconsciously avoid calling a spade a spade. There are advantages to taking useful points of focus or surfaces from each theory, but there is also a need to be aware of how we might unconsciously or consciously gravitate toward particular kinds of theories when the going gets rough or we run up against conflicts that are difficult to explore with the patient or stances that are difficult to maintain. I call this problem *defensive pluralism* or *defensive multiplicity.*

I wish that I had a useful way to determine when the analyst's ability to formulate and think in a way that integrates the various views from different models is useful and when it may be an avoidance of particular kinds of therapeutic dilemmas. I can only suggest that many of us are capable of using any theory to rationalize or justify a particular therapeutic decision and that we can try to determine when it feels more like a genuine piece of integrative work rather than an avoidance or rationalization. While I naturally gravitate toward an integration of British object relational theory, ego psychology and interpersonal models, I see no reason to think that the ability to think and work pluralistically is any less subject to defensive avoidance than a stance encompassing only one theoretical approach.

It has always been my sense (or my fantasy) that analysis is prolonged if the transference is kept in the abstract and there is too great an emphasis on reconstruction and extratransference work. Yet, even though there is now a convergence of techniques from various theoretical models centered on the earlier interpretation of transference and focus on the here-and-now (Kernberg, 1993), especially within the American relational model, analyses seem to be getting longer. There may be another issue that prolongs analysis even when there is great attention paid to the immediacy of engagement. Perhaps analysts within the American relational model are prone to creating new dyadic, relational realities between patient and analyst that are compelling and involving (Fishman, 1998). Might it be the case that, while the danger of Gray's (1990, 1994) approach is the analyst's potential to valorize the patient's "mind" or the process of observing resistance to expression, for the American relational analyst the danger is to valorize relational meaning? How would we determine whether this is the case for either model? I remind you that I began this chapter by stating my intent to pose unanswerable questions.

Whereas the American relational model has emphasized collaborative and negotiated meaning and truth, there is no escaping the problem of analysts' influencing their patients to adopt their idiom. A patient in a relationally oriented analysis is no less subject to the kinds of unconscious indoctrination that Balint (1968) summarized so well than is a patient in any other kind of analysis. I take it as almost axiomatic that analyst and patient will together create certain kinds of illusions and myths about the psychic life and experience of the patient. These stories have to be challenged notwithstanding that they are the helpful, informative mythologies that fuel an analysis. The counterargument that needs to be levied by American relationists is that the approach has its basic intent to pursue these meanings and interactive tensions as much as possible.

Bader (1998) has recently posed a useful challenge for those of us who have been engaged in postmodern critiques of Freudian positivism. He asks: what takes us from a useful critique of epistemology in classical theory into a practical clinical theory with teachable aspects of technique and a disciplined focus on therapeutic aims and the validation of interpretation? In other words, is American relational theory unwittingly continuing the traditions of the other psychoanalytic approaches I am elaborating here, which take us inexorably into process?

I think that, while social constructivist methodology need not be at odds with a disciplined empiricism, it has not yet fully articulated modes of influence or therapeutic action. For me, it is not a theory that tries to replace ego psychology or British object relations theory. Instead it is a theory that uses aspects of these theories to incorporate a much different approach to the analyst's and the patient's views of psychic reality, and certainly the concept of mind. There are important differences between ego psychology and American relational theory in terms of the extent to which the mind is conceived as monadic and how interaction is seen as aiding the interpretation of defense. What is the implicit or explicit therapeutic action within the social-constructivist or dialectical constructivist paradigm? I believe it is that the construction of events invites the patient's active participation and, as in ego psychology, his observing capacities in figuring out the truth of the matter, which can be a therapeutic and useful outcome of analysis. To put it another way, the coconstruction of meaning within the dyad, indeed the use of our imaginations and subjective experience provides a therapeutic outcome of analysis. In both ego psychology and relational theory in the United States, a goal is to broaden observational capacity. The domain of what is to be broadened and observed has been more clearly defined and circumscribed within ego psychology. Yet some of the areas addressed by American relational theory have been deemphasized in explications of ego-psychological work, particularly when patients have massively dissociated affective states. In those instances, the kind of defense analysis underscored by ego psychology tends to run up against limitations to broadening the patient's observational field. The way that Modell (1975) and Winnicott (1969) put it years ago was that ego analysis has generally involved ego defenses organized against various kinds of impulses but has addressed fewer circumstances in which the individual's defenses are organized against massive aspects of object failure (Cooper, 1989).

Ego psychology has something to offer the American relational model in describing more modal and less heroic moments in analysis.

The work of elaborating technical dimensions and reconciling them with methods capable of validation is a complicated matter because of the tensions between discipline and spontaneity that Hoffman (1991, 1994a, 1996, 1998a) has so clearly articulated. Yet Bader's (1998) criticisms are valid and worth thinking about in the next phase of cross-fertilization between analytic approaches.

Another reason that current relational models may create analyses that are as lengthy as in any other model is that in fact they are quite ambitious about confronting particular kinds of impasse, especially those related to identification with the aggressor and massively disavowed affect as described earlier. In relational models, the use of the analyst's countertransference expressiveness in the attempt to analyze the patient's disavowed affect usually requires getting to know and be known by a patient pretty well and for a reasonably long period of time. This is quite an ambitious enterprise, a place where some analysts feel that the limits of how analysis can be helpful have been reached. It is always worth considering whether our efforts to engender an analytic process are well founded or overly heroic in aim. As genres, the American relational model and probably the Kleinian model have generally dealt more with points of impasse or even stalemate (e.g., Darwin, 1998) than has the ego-psychological model. The latter has, I think, been more interested in modal moments in analysis. I think that in the next phase of dialogue within psychoanalysis it would be useful to hear more from American relational theorists about less heroic circumstances in clinical work and more from ego psychologists about points of impasse. My suspicion is that in reports of these phenomena we would actually see more points of overlap between the two models.

Davies (1994, 1998) has been exploring the nature of "postoedipal" phenomena in analytic process. She argues that we are much more prone to viewing the analyst as an unavailable oedipal object than we are in considering other complexities of the analytic relationship that are based on the analyst and patient as two adults. It is interesting that while Davies's work on self-disclosure is regarded by some as having created certain kinds of dyadic reality (e.g., Fishman, 1998) it is worth considering whether her recent contributions to the understanding of postoedipal development and transference may help us avoid wasting long periods of time by assuming too often that transference belongs to the unavailable oedipal object rather than being comprised of other, more complex wishes. Naturally, a major consideration here is for the analyst to not jump to the "postoedipal" in order to avoid aspects of oedipal or preoedipal experience. All these labels are problematically schematic, since we experience conflict in complex and overlapping ways derived from a developmental process rather than an invariant developmental sequence. But I think that it is worth considering how much we may avoid aspects of postoedipal analytic phenomena during the analytic process.

For example, in chapter 5 I discussed my analytic work with Molly, who taught me how her apparent resistance to exploring what she hinted at as an aspect of erotic transference also represented a powerful set of wishes to stop engaging in erotically masochistic behavior, which had been her wont through a great deal of her life. Her capacity to work with these feelings eventually allowed her to explore various kinds of sexual and aggressive feelings with me. My initial tendency to see her behavior and associations as exclusively "antiregressive" (Sandler and Sandler, 1994)—that is, in terms of her fear of allowing herself to regress in various ways during the analytic process. She was afraid to let herself play within the transference, to suspend her disbelief, and to revisit earlier held feelings of longing and frustration toward her father. My view of Molly's antiregressive stance was partly accurate, but also impeded my ability to see her progression into a new set of conflicts and feelings. These engaged a different kind of therapeutic regression, one in which she could risk feeling love, anger, excitement, and frustration with me in a way that was less organized around masochism and the unavailable oedipal object and more compatible with her experience as an adult. In previous years, my tendency to focus exclusively on her fear of analytic regression and her fixation on her sense of disappointment with the unavailable father as experienced in the transference could have led to iatrogenic frustration with the unavailable oedipal parent—in a good deal of familiar replay but not enough analytic understanding of the complexity and admixture of old and new play. We have to be able to see the new, progressive forest as we look at the old, regressive trees.

With regard to the problem of limits, I believe that we have tremendous potential as analysts in future years to integrate regressive and progressive phenomena as a part of the analytic process.

CONCLUSION:
THE ANALYTIC TICK-TICK AND THE ANALYTIC NUDGE

I have suggested that all our models tend toward expansion of scope or, perhaps even more important, avoidance of limit. The analyst is always in a modest position regarding what will happen. None of us is plugged into the "Psychic Friends Network," even though we are experts at trying to cultivate an atmosphere of exploring and achieving new psychic possibility.

I have tried to draw attention to those aspects of our theoretical and technical approaches that may contain compromise formation and avoidance of conflict. Obviously, many clinical analyses do not feature these issues. I know that I have only nominally distinguished these issues from many analyses in which it takes a great deal of time for the analytic dyad to create safe passage in circumstances involving trauma and other aspects of enormous psychic danger, not to mention encrusted, refractory neurosis. I am not promoting the hasty and harsh confrontation of traumatized patients' unconscious identifications with their representational world, nor do I want to minimize the importance of psychic holding as an important part of most, if not all, analyses. Furthermore, the lessons of trying to not circumvent resistance have been well worth learning, and I do not want to ignore the valuable therapeutic results derived from patients' learning how to observe and work with their accessible, observable resistances and conflicts. For some patients the analytic work is successful only to the extent that they can experience the relaxation of their defensive use of limits (used to mitigate the experience of wishes, longing, aspiration, or aggression).

Thus, in considering the possibility that we are spending large amounts of time in various kinds of compromise formations in each of our theoretical orientations regarding the issues of integrating limits, I have presented only one side of the complexity of this issue. I have not focused a great deal on what the patient looks for and brings to the analytic process. For most people who partake of and practice analysis (there is a huge overlap since probably over half the patients who currently are in analysis are clinicians) the analytic way of thinking is already a kind of way of life. This circumstance is anything but regrettable. But what is important is that we continue to consider the degree to which we may unconsciously cultivate prolonged treatment or unnecessarily regressive relationships. One of the things that is most complicated about any discussion of the value and power of therapeutic regression is our tendency to see these issues in polarized terms as either natural or iatrogenic. while many analysts embrace the complexity of regression, I believe that in the best of circumstances we are actively struggling to resist thinking about this in schematic or polarized terms. The tendency toward this polarization is, I think, related to the strong affective experiences that we have in relation to our own and our patients' capacities for regression. It is a dangerous area, one that offers great opportunity and great risk. This chapter has dealt with a comparative theoretical approach. A much needed dialogue requires more specific case discussion within various theoretical models about the nature of productive and less than productive types of regression.

It is important to note that there have been important contributions to the analytic tick-tock that come from other theories of psychoanalytic technique as well. One form of creating a sense of time within analysis or the analytic tick-tock involves the analyst's efforts to point out, when appropriate, the patient's attachment to old object experience and why. It would be unfair to ascribe these types of interventions to any particular school of analysis. Fairbairn (1952) wrote a great deal about the need to hold on to the old object as a major form of resistance to change. Within the classical tradition, Valenstein (1973) wrote eloquently about our patients' attachment to painful affects and objects and how this attachment makes our interventions refractory to change. Classical theory of technique, as I described earlier, has underscored the importance of keeping termination in mind from the beginning of analysis in order to catalyze experience and conflict. This is an area of classical theory that does try to place the patient's psychic future in the foreground throughout analytic work even though this aspect of theory has never been made explicit (Cooper, 1997).

So too, Freud's (1912a) early emphasis on the use of transference as a defense is still an important way to help patients learn about new experience and what makes it difficult for them to do so. I think that many analysts are not trained to think about how unfolding transferences serve multiple defensive functions. I also believe that there has been a conscious or unconscious idealization of a particular kind of facilitating environment in analysis that seeks to avoid challenge and, at times, confrontation. It is interesting that this is a point of agreement between classical analysis and American relational models. Affect attunement, while essential to each model in making accurate, empathic and useful interpretations, can be translated too literally. Classical approaches and American relational models alike place more value on the notion of friction and difference between analyst and patient as useful interpretive pivoting points than is true of some developmental tilt models. Naturally, the subjectivity of the analyst is much more a point of focus within the analyst's interpretive position in the relational model. Classical as well as relational models tend to diverge from both self psychology and the neoclassical perspective put forward by Schwaber (1983) that centers on the patient's psychic reality as the main interpretive fulcrum.

It is my sense that despite the criticisms I raised earlier about American relational theory and its problems with limit, the work of Hoffman (1994, 1996, 1998) has already offered a great deal in addressing our potential for denying "real," as opposed to analytic, time. Social constructivism and the American relational model have tried to include a developmental orientation while actively considering the analyst's expectations and constructions as important mediators about how we understand developmental phenomena (e.g., Mitchell, 1991). I believe that the contributions of developmental theory need to be better incorporated into relational models, particularly those contributions which conceptualize development in triadic, not primarily dyadic, terms (e.g., Herzog, in press). The relational model in the United States has made efforts to integrate the understanding of unconscious phenomena while trying not to foster undue regression (e.g., Bromberg, 1979, 1998) as is true for the recent work by such ego psychologists as Busch (1993, 1995) and earlier Gray (1973, 1990). Building on the work of Strachey (1934) and Loewald (1960) about the analyst's functions as new and old object, recent efforts have been made to think about transference as much more than the historical object in effigy (Greenberg, 1986; Cooper and Levit, 1998). Instead, the consideration of the analyst's contributions to the transference within relational-conflict theory, social constructivism, interpersonally influenced analysis, and social perspectivism (Aron, 1996) all place importance on the role of interactional tension as a way to learn about the meaning of transference and defense.

Psychoanalytic theory has been debated and modified as we come to appreciate the value of shared dialogic meaning, hermeneutic truth, the nature of reciprocal influence, and the mind as an open rather than a monadic system. The influence of understanding early development has both enriched our method of practicing analysis and probably led to new unsolved and interesting problems in the conduct of most analyses. Psychoanalysis began with a much more direct and confrontational stance regarding the interpretation of unconscious conflict under the guise of id analysis. In becoming more sophisticated about developmental and defensive processes, we have learned how to work with patients in a much more sensitive and tactful way. But I believe that a new stage of development in our technique involves our trying to be more actively responsible about the limits of analysis in a way that we can convey to the community of patients.

The problem for all analysts is that to do this incredibly arduous and challenging work well, we need the compassion and nerve to take on the refractory nature of encrusted and ossified character traits that we all develop. We also must have the nerve and patience to confront the array of spontaneous affective experiences in which analyst and patient influence one another in fluid, rapid, and unpredictable ways. Yet to do analysis well, the analyst has to be aware of how he conveys and believes in psychic possibility, just as he is bound to work within the limits of his ability and method. The developmental strategies have brought an influx of romantic energy to the process, most important a belief that our strategies of survival help us to preserve hopes and wishes toward empathic objects, even if our initial objects of hope have been woefully lacking. There is little doubt that any decent analysis catalyzes the experience and recognition of these hoped-for objects as well as the massive feelings of disappointment toward them. Yet the analyst uniquely integrates this position as the catalyst of hope and wish with a perspective about the limits of what we provide.

At the risk of sounding glib, I think that we need to find ways to say to our patients, with compassion and complex understanding of their unconscious conflicts and dynamics, "To find, to get, to hold, and recover a life." Analysts are uniquely positioned to say this. To return to my game-show conceit, we need to create ways of giving voice to analytic tick-tocking, and it is this aspect of the analytic attitude that has become attenuated. Analytic tick-tocking involves trying to show patients how much their unconscious activity wastes time and energy, just as it defensively preserves particular hopes. And this is especially visible in analytic work.

My fear is that, with our increased attention to understanding patients' psychic reality, an important corrective on classically based analysis, we have homogenized analytic work, made it too politically correct, and diminished the radical nature of what we are trying to do. We are trying to make something happen but as a psychoanalytic culture we have tended over the last 30 years or so to equate analysts' activity with their anxiety, intolerance, resistance to regression, circumvention of resistance, and the like—all of which are always worth considering. But I think that it is also worth considering whether we have, as a community, unconsciously even vilified activeness, equating it with the bad parent. The Rolling Stones's Keith Richards, who is not well known as a psychoanalytic thinker, was once asked in an interview what he liked about his relationship with Mick Jagger. He smiled at the interviewer and said, "Friction." Friction occurs at the level of all change, growth, and excitement. I think any good treatment has friction—an atmosphere of play and exploration in which bumping up against each other's needs, wishes, and fears can occur, always in the context of trying to make sense of something that will help the patient.

For many people who have experienced trauma, play has been truncated in the service of protection, and it takes a long time for the benefits of friction to be experienced as offering possibility. I do a great deal of very long-term work with such patients, work I feel is usually toward a very good end. The arguments I have put forth here are not primarily directed toward this kind of work. I am suggesting instead that the developmental strategies and cultures of affect attunement, nonimpingement, and reconstructive mythologies are in need of modification in the coming years as we try more realistically to appraise both the contributions and the limitations of this method.

I have suggested that in some of our advances in theory development and the training of analysts, the psychoanalytic attitude is in danger of losing its attitude. To me, the essence of that attitude comprises two seemingly different manifestations that have a common goal. One part of that attitude is a commitment to helping patients experience new psychic possibility through increased awareness of what they feel and think. The other is to keep in mind that we hope to help people to feel that they have far better fish to fry than to be in analysis. I think that it is possible that as analysts we like to think of ourselves as teaching our patients about a way of life. From my point of view, analysis is both a therapy and a way of life, but we have lost something essential about trying to be a therapy. The timeless unconscious is conspiratorial only if we forget that we are trying to understand the unconscious in real time. We have a very good therapy, and I think that in some way it is obfuscated by our unconscious attempts to make it a way of life. Analytic patients who do well with our method take away from it a part of the analytic attitude that is a way of life, a therapeutic goal, and, I hope, in the best of circumstances, a place to end with us and continue with others.

10

CONCLUDING REMARKS ON THE LOGIC OF HOPE
The Analyst's Concealed and Revealed Hopes in Psychoanalytic Theory

S OME OF THE FERVOR with which we become attached to ideas and repulsed by others in debating psychoanalytic theory is tied to the notion that theory holds our hope. I think of our body of theory as our logic of hope. Not only does our theory express how we have hopes for our patients, but we hope that our patients will provide support for our theories! In fact, this may be among the largest problems that psychoanalysts have faced over the course of theory development. It is why many young analysts struggle with the experience of feeling that they are doing good work, but not necessarily work that they see expounded on in the articles they read or the theory they are taught.

As psychoanalysts we develop theories of influence based on what we like—what was helpful to us growing up and in our own analyses and what we have discovered as analysts doing therapeutic work. What appeals to us is intricately tied to what has provided us with hope for ourselves and our patients. What is the relationship between our theory of psychoanalysis and our hopes for patients, at least as expressed in the experientially distant form of theory? What is the relationship of our theory to a patient's hopes for us and our view of the patient's future? These are some of the questions that I address here. I will also try to provide a sense of my particular ways of understanding our theoretical diversity, in general, and our increasing need to find ways of learning from each other with respect to these differences.

While the rationale for exploring this dimension of analytic work lies in expanding the analyst's avenues for understanding transference-countertransference dilemmas, as I tried to illustrate in earlier chapters, the more experience-distant level of theory describes some of the ways that the analyst's theory of influence is always operating in various modes of formulation and interpretation.

Even some of the most cynical theories of human nature and philosophical stances provide hope for their practitioners. For example, stoicism or global skepticism can, for some, become a primary attachment even within a belief system whose content seems barren, nihilistic, or destructive to others. Brunschwig (1988) has humorously noted that skepticism is a therapy for philosophical illnesses. As a philosophical position, skepticism does not try to classify those illnesses because the disease to fight against other positions is always dogmatism. To the skeptic, all nonskeptical schools are dogmatic. A psychoanalytic eclectic like me sees, instead, a way in which psychoanalytic observations converge and differ. From my point of view, even the skeptic holds hope—the skeptic is, in Brunschwig's terms a "metaphilosophical dogmatist" because he admits with fervor that philosophers not only seem to contradict each other, they actually do so. In my view, dogmatism is unfortunately, sometimes, the necessary fallout that accompanies passion. What we have to do is work with our inherent pull toward dogmatism and fear of taking in something new. Of course, the skeptic could argue that I am simply theoretically promiscuous.

Historically, a major epistemological and, even more important, clinical problem for psychoanalysts in defining and articulating our particular focus for clinical work is that we put the cart before the horse. We begin with a particular view of therapeutic action and define our focus or points of observation in order to detect the process we are hoping to achieve or, at least, observe. This is a natural process for clinicians because clearly we form our views of therapeutic action as a result of experience. Yet epistemologically the problem is that this view of clinical observation seems to be tautological in nature. Differences between what analysts observe usually involve disputes over theory (Cooper, 1996b). We may be a bit like Humpty Dumpty in *Through the Looking Glass,* who says, "When *I* use a word, it means just what I choose it to mean." Where is the place for unpleasant observations— things that we observe that do not fit our theory?

In the postmodern era the issue of how to fit observation with theory is no less a problem than it was during the positivistic thrust of psychoanalytic theory that dominated its first 75 years. There is now more general agreement that "facts all come with a point of view" (Byrne and Eno, 1980).[1] But, clinically, the main problem with our view of therapeutic action as dictating so much of what we observe is that it mitigates our ability to "court surprise" (Stern, 1983; Stern et al., 1998). Our minds and hearts move quickly. Our patients are constantly expressing and resisting in a way that we, as theoreticians, can never catch up to. Friedman (1995) puts this state of affairs quite eloquently: "The mind won't stand still for scrutiny" (p. 25). Every theory, every metaphor we develop with our patients and as theorists attempts to freeze-frame the mind and the interaction. Maybe an even better metaphor, if you will, is that our theory is a kind of stun-gun that stops the interaction or an affect or idea as we look at it, knowing that we have artificially imposed temporality on the process. How do we get inside the process, as scientists do when they attempt to get metal recording balls inside the center of a tornado without losing the essence of the process? How do we conduct research with reliable observations of psychotherapy without compromising the validity of the method.

Metaphor building is a part of every psychoanalytic theory and every analysis. Metaphor can be usefully defined as the art of seeing something in terms of something else (Ricoeur, 1977). We are always building metaphors with our patients. Indeed, metaphor is one of the centerpins of any analytic relationship. We are always taking something familiar, so familiar it is part of the everyday woodwork, and seeing if by our making it unfamiliar it will stand out more boldly. We might ask a patient why he invariably smiles when he tells us he has been hurt by someone. We note when we are unable to take something familiar for the patient and make it unfamiliar. In a sense, this is one meaning of the concept of resistance. Defense is often a stalemated, static

---

[1] The full statement in a song called "Crosseyed and Painless" is: "facts all come with a point of view, they don't always do what I want them to."

metaphor. It might result in a patient's saying something like, "That's just the way I am." We make something less familiar in one sense by probing, turning it upside down: an obsessional thought, a hypochondriacal concern, a question about why one compulsively has sex, or turn away, reject someone, become clingy, cry, express contempt. One way to think about neurosis is as a dead metaphor—there is a resistance to something new and letting a feeling or mode of behavior be turned upside down. Lacan might say that, where the symptom is lodged, the signifying element is stuck.

Just as defense is ubiquitous in each of our relationships to others and our own inner life, so theory of all kinds has to contend with the notion of dead or ineffective metaphors. From my perspective, each of our theories has significant limitations. Each theory is also made meaningful in a particular period of time and social context. Modell's (1984) sought to illustrate how the metaphors that were vibrant during the first 80 years of psychoanalysis were no longer as meaningful and required change. This does not mean that classical psychoanalytic theory, music, or painting stops breathing or producing meaning and enjoyment. It means only that, for particular practitioners, patients, observers, or listeners, we can benefit from extending our observational field to include new metaphors. Different generations are interested in different metaphors, different music, different dance, and different theory. It is also true that it is extremely easy for all of us to pour old wine into new bottles, just as some who are frightened of change, yet sense it, try to pour new wine into old bottles.

OUR RELATIONSHIP TO THEORY BUILDING: "COURTING SURPRISE"? OR A SHOTGUN WEDDING?

While I have found myself most at home with the writings of American and British relational theorists, I do not find that there is one model or theory of therapeutic action that fully explains my analytic work. I do not even find that what I think is therapeutic is necessarily or always what my patients find therapeutic. We are often flying by the seat of our theoretical pants, and the air is mighty thin up here. When we come down, we usually find holes and contradictions if we are even able to look. I am reminded of the story about a 95-year-old-man, revered in his community for his lifetime of service. On his 95th birthday he was asked, "What is your theory about how you've lived so long?" He said, "I've never had one sip of whiskey my entire life or one puff of a cigarette." Then there was a loud noise from an equally old man upstairs, drunken, yelling. Smoke was pouring into the stairway. The reporter asked, "What's going on up there?" The man said: "That's my twin brother; every so often he goes on a drunken spree."

It is not quite enough to say that this man had a blind spot. On the basis of his experience of life, he tried to fit the most available data with the best possible conclusion, as any good natural science explanation seeks to do. To be sure, he may not have been looking far beyond the tip of his nose, but he tried to answer the question on the basis of what he had consciously observed. He was not able to integrate the experience of his brother or explain the contradiction in his own theory. It might be said that his brother's example remained unconscious—obvious but unseen (Bion, 1963). Much of our current debate in psychoanalytic theory follows some of the outlines of this joke.

One of my favorite writers in the analytic literature, Donnel Stern (1990), has underscored the value of, in his words, "courting surprise." Yet how do we court surprise? Does courting not involve a level of self-consciousness and seduction? Are we not selectively presenting ourselves and selectively looking at the other during courtship? We do not see the flaws that show up in the light of day following the inevitable disillusionment of courtship. Courtship is often a state of revelation and honest connection but also has its share of oblivion and blindness, fluctuating with supreme self-consciousness and seductiveness. Are the two concepts, courting and surprise, not embedded in two diametrically opposed affective fields? Obviously these issues are, in turn, set deeply within the thicket of postmodern philosophical questions regarding construction of fact and the impossible nature of observation without participation. Yet the idea of courting surprise reaches to the very difficult tensions that we, as clinicians, face in the process of immersion and trying to make sense of things. Perhaps we should think of our attachment to a way of listening as involving more of a kind of tension between courting surprise and a shotgun wedding. We are deeply attached to our theories, for they follow us around, for better and worse, like our character, our adaptation. They seduce us and force us to see things through a particular lens.

THEORY AS AN OBJECT OF HOPE FOR THE ANALYST

There is a deeply ambivalent way in which we, as psychoanalysts, relate to our body of theory. We idealize and romanticize the generative aspects of theory, just as we resent it as a containing and foreclosing factor that can potentially interfere with clinical listening.

Psychoanalytic theories are about both psychic possibility and psychic inevitability. I refer to all psychoanalytic theory as our logic of hope because theory comprises both the structure of how we think we influence and our wishes to influence. There is no clean line between interpretation and indoctrination in either the clinical setting or theory. There is no analytic theory, even the classical emphasis on drives and repetition, that does not offer some vision of the change that can occur through analytic process. Most psychoanalytic theories also hold in common that the patient looks to the analyst for change and help— that the analyst in some ways embodies hope and expectation for change. Freud (1905) referred to the patient's trusting expectation of change from the analyst as one of the analyst's best therapeutic aids. The analyst also embodies hope for the patient in real and defensive ways within Lacanian approaches (Nasio, 1997). In the developmental tilt (Mitchell, 1988) models of Winnicott and Kohut, the analyst represents the revival of hoped-for objects who might catalyze the true self that has been submerged. Indeed, in all psychoanalytic models, our patients see us as representatives of psychic possibility.

Most psychoanalytic theories provide a view of therapeutic action emphasizing how the analyst's activities do influence, while often explicitly minimizing the analyst's *wish* to influence. This use of theory, or method of conceptualizing therapeutic action which explains change while avoiding conceptualizing our wishes to influence—seems to me similar to Martin Amos's (1975) claim: "Not only are all characters and scenes in this book entirely fictitious; most of the technical, medical, and psychological data are too. My working maxim here has been as follows: I may not know much about science but I know what I like" (p. 3). Most psychoanalysts know what they like too, and we all develop theories of influence that focus more on the interpretive content of influence than on the affective experience that pushes and motivates interpretations. Hoffman (1994a, 1996) is notably explicit in his discussions of garnering as many sources of influence as possible in doing analytic work. Friedman (1988) and Mitchell (1993) have also addressed the level of elusiveness that theorists display in conceptualizing their wishes to influence.

It may be clear by now that I see our theory as having a large dimension of rhetoric. Yeats, in the poem "Per Amica Sientia Luna," put it that "we make out of the quarrel with others, rhetoric, and with ourselves, poetry." The issues and problems of rhetoric and influence for psychoanalysts are just latter-day versions of the problems Plato and Aristotle discussed. The point of rhetoric is to influence people's opinion. Yet Aristotle thought that morally we ought to lead someone only to the right opinion. Aristotle included within rhetoric both a recitation of the evidence and the logical structure of argument based on the "facts." Psychoanalytic theorists follow the same pattern. Like Aristotle, we want to influence the patient's view of himself, which entails valuing the process of self-observation. Our values include freedom, autonomy, a capacity for intimacy, truthfulness, authenticity, a capacity to bear solitude, responsibility, courage, and the like. Facts really do come with a point of view (Cooper, 1996b).

One aspect of rhetoric, or an indication of how our theorizing involves rhetoric, relates to how easy it is to see our own resistance to learning from new experience in revising theory. So much of what we see is determined or guided by what has already been theorized. Half the time it is a significant accomplishment in itself to just be able to deconstruct the theories unconsciously embedded in our work. Further complicating these matters, as Caper (1988) has pointed out, is that we are not dealing with material facts in psychoanalysis, but with immaterial facts in the form of psychological states in us, in the patient, and in the interaction. Whenever we hear a clinician speak of how she developed her theory, by necessity it sounds like a rigged experiment. To the observer, the rabbit is going to be pulled out of the hat—it's just a matter of sleight of hand or in this case sleight of theory. Why is this?

Wittgenstein (1958) suggested that much of the time we are really not registering what is familiar to us. He poses the question:

Do we have a feeling of unfamiliarity whenever we look at familiar objects? Or do we have it usually? When do we actually have it? It helps us to ask: what do we contrast the feeling of familiarity with? One thing we contrast it with is surprise. One could say: "Unfamiliarity is much more of an experience than familiarity" [p. 23].

From this point of view, we are using familiar structures to take in new experience and often assimilating it in accordance with the familiar.

Part of this problem relates to how most theorists do not really feel comfortable revealing the raw experiences, the affects, the frustration, and the futility they feel when theory fails or runs up against resistance and limitation. True uncertainty and doubt always exist because they are personal. We experience something that makes us lose our theoretical anchor, question our theory, feel unhelped by our theory. We get caught in the center of the tornado, and it is there that our theory starts to change or evolve. Another problem in theory development and revision is no fault of the theorist. As soon as the clinician tells us of her clinical experiences, we tend to wed her to her theory. In other words, as listeners or critics of a theorist, we are prone to construct an explanation for her theory by constructing the data around our knowledge of the theorist's theory. This process resembles Piaget's (1932, 1969) description of how we assimilate exceptional or surprising data into familiar genres.

My own bias regarding theory contrasts with a comment by Freud (1915) in a letter to Ferenczi. Freud wrote: "I consider that one should not make theories. They should arrive unexpectedly in your house, like a stranger one hasn't invited" (p. 113). Similarly, Bion and many other psychoanalysts have cautioned us to try to mitigate whatever theoretical constructs and formulations we might impose on our clinical listening.

These priorities clearly borrow from a positivism and ambition for the analyst to be as objective as possible. Freud (1937) wanted the analyst to be an investigator. Yet this was stated as a kind of ideal (Cooper, 1993, 1996b). Rubovits-Seitz (1994) has lucidly argued that Freud struggled throughout his work with a methodological conflict between his positivist preferences for pure observation (and a more objective certainty) versus his clinical need for less certain modes of interpretation. Rather than focus on the analyst's "interpretive fallibility" (Cooper, 1993), Rubovits-Seitz (1994) suggests that, more often than not, Freud suggested that free association would provide a "plentiful store of ideas" that would lead to "plain and numerous hints" (Freud, 1924, pp. 195-196) to aid the analyst in guessing at what is repressed. Similarly, Schimek (1975) suggests that Freud described his interpretations as the inevitable causal inferences of a natural science rather than as the construction of meaning inherent to the human sciences.

While I agree with Freud's admonitions about the attempt to cultivate a theory more dispassionately, I would say that theory is almost always an ambivalently held acquaintance one *has* invited, consciously or unconsciously to one's home. Indeed, it is often difficult to determine who really is the host at the gathering. We do not choose or invite the theory, at least not without harboring an unconscious component. The theory becomes a part of us. Thus "theory" expresses our implicit or explicit technical stance, our views of therapeutic action, our subjectivity. Of course, we should always try to consider when or whether we want to invite him back, or perhaps more pointedly, with whom among his associates (tenets, ideas, technical consequences, and even related theories) we wish to get better acquainted.

Theory is not something that can be suspended or put aside even when we wish to. In attempting to place priority on the psychoanalytic process as knowable by intuition, Bion (1977) quoted Darwin, "It is fatal to reason whilst observing, though so necessary beforehand and so useful afterwards" (p. 12). I presume that Darwin was referring to the function of theory that involves the conscious process of putting together new and old observation, organizing it, mapping it, and eventually communicating such maps to colleagues. While this is again an ideal form of constructing theory, it begs the postmodern question of how much theory guides observation. Ironically enough, Bion was acutely attuned to the problematic way in which this application of theory can potentially limit the taking in of new information during clinical process. Britton and Steiner (1994) cogently address this issue in their discussion of Bion's concept of the overvalued idea. This concept refers to the analyst's predilection to develop a formulation and then hear everything that comes his way through this filter. While formulation is helpful, it can also, inevitably, narrow our observational field.

Each analysis is likely to develop an overvalued idea, a kind of dominant metaphor that serves a defensive function. An analyst may find that a patient has been able to see how a basic sense of reality was usurped when his mother failed to be convinced that when he felt sick, he might actually be sick. "You felt that your mother hurt and even undermined your sense of trusting your experience when she failed to give your complaints much credence." While this statement may have lively affective resonance for a patient and analyst at a particular point in treatment, it may over time become a stale way of understanding the patient's childhood and its relation to his current experience. The patient may have used this painful event as a way to identify with his mother by aggressively legislating reality with those he loves the most. The analyst has to take an overvalued idea (dominant affective experience) and see its multiplicity of meanings and functions. He has to make the familiar unfamiliar. What at one point is an untouchable area of experience in an analysis may later become a point of renegotiation (Russell, 1973; Pizer, 1992, 1998) and new theorizing between patient and analyst.

Part of the reason that overvalued ideas develop so consistently involves the way that strong affect mobilizes and organizes ideas. Strong affect and, even more so, trauma have a way of truncating complex modes of thinking and organization of experience. A good example of how understanding becomes truncated around the emergence of affect could be seen in the dominant response to a 1969 photograph of a Vietnamese soldier holding a gun to the head of a man whom he was executing. The Pulitzer Prize-winning photograph was widely regarded as a visual statement about the injustice of war and execution-style murder. It was also widely interpreted as the execution of an innocent South Vietnamese man by a Viet Cong soldier. The photograph was actually of a South Vietnamese soldier preparing to kill a Viet Cong man who had murdered a number of men, women, and children in a village. The affects that were mobilized around the picture developed into a metaphor for injustice, which, in turn, made it difficult for most people to integrate that the "victim" was not only a victim. It caused the photographer, Eddie Adams, many years later to state: "Photographs lie."

Another use of theory involves our unconscious application of it as a map that leads to perception and observation. As Sandler and Sandler (1994) have noted, our unconscious predilections for a particular kind of fact or theory always determine, in part, what we observe or, if you will, what we wish or hope to observe. Indeed, our very choice of theory expresses all kinds of aspects of our subjectivity in the analytic process. One such area is the relationship between the analyst's theory and formulation and the analyst's aims, encompassing his conception of the patient's future.

The role of the analyst's aims is complicated by the necessary modesty of the analyst captured in Freud's (1912b) analogy to the surgeon: he who "dresses the wound, but does not heal it." Nevertheless, all analysts, even those who conceptualize the analytic process as providing "repair" rather than resuming "growth" (Cooper, 1992), implicitly integrate conceptualizations of influence into their use of formulation and interpretation. Doing so makes a good fact hard to find and raises some interesting questions about whether this "fact" of psychoanalytic life allows us to claim evidential status of clinical data or theoretical propositions or, instead, rich and useful illustrations of our work (Mitchell, 1993).

So, rather than being an unwelcome stranger or guest, I believe that theory is, like Dante's *Virgil,* the guide who leads and determines the analyst's formulations and interpretive activity through shifting foci on past, present, and future threads within the patient's associations and the interaction between patient and analyst. There is often a tension holding theory as friend and foe, self and alien, welcome and unwelcome fellow traveler, and ultimately, constructive and destructive factor in the understanding of clinical process. Theory always expresses our attachment to ideas and important others in our lives. Our body of theory is our metaphorical body—our hearts, minds, limbs, and desires. It expresses our hopes, and herein lies the passion with which we defend our theory, the fervor with which we express it, and often the rigidity and anxiety with which we listen to new ideas and observations.

I would like to advance the kind of simple, but I believe accurate idea for me, that the only times I am very motivated to rethink theory are when I am unhappy with what I know about the theory I have. It is not even that I am always unhappy when I cannot explain something. I am not that conscientious or thoughtful. Rather I tend to seek what Faimberg (1997) terms "the missing concept," in doing clinical work or theorizing, when the ones I have are particularly prone to make me feel disappointed, frustrated and in pain of some kind about the work I am doing. Often I feel the theory as providing a kind of routine way of understanding something, rather than the possibility of something fresh. In my view, theories are like an object attachment or a self-representation that we cling to. They provide safety; they are home. Otherwise, why would so many people, without really knowing what they feel or think, offer, out of hand, blanket rejections of innovations in theory and technique?

For example, nearly every theory has another theory that, by contrast, helps it to define itself. Lacanian analysis has often tried to contrast itself to American ego psychology in order to advance the depth of the Lacanian model. Ego psychology tried to contrast itself with classical analytic models in order to highlight its own focus on the ego's breadth and adaptation. Object relations models, especially in the United States, have developed concepts related to the analyst's subjectivity by contrasting this concept with the notion of the blank screen analyst.

I think that it common for analysts to hold to an abstract theory of technique that they value and yet do not often try to reconcile with their actual clinical conduct and decision making. There have been many such theoretical "bad boys," including classical analysis, self psychology, intersubjectivity, and object relations theory. Alas, just to put matters in historical perspective, at one point, the bad boy to end all bad boys was American ego psychology.

Throughout all our theoretical debate, however, a dominant axis, and one of the largest hot potatoes within theory, has been the difficulty of acknowledging the implicit and explicit ways that analysts wish to influence (Mitchell, 1997).

IMPLICIT STRATEGIES FOR AVOIDING
THINKING ABOUT INFLUENCE

Here I briefly focus on two strategies—though hardly comprehensive—of avoiding or minimizing the analyst's wish to influence in a few theories of therapeutic action, namely, strategies of neutrality and epistemological objectivity and strategies of what Mitchell (1988) refers to as developmental tilt theory. Each strategy has taken many forms and permutations, so I will highlight just a few, relatively recent examples of each pattern (see Mitchell, 1993, for an illuminating discussion of how developmental strategies in particular have avoided this issue). It is interesting that even among recent developments in American rela-tional theory, which focus explicitly on the analyst's wish to influence, there is a revisitation of the problem of trying to avoid influence, which I refer to as *the return of the* repressed *positivistic*. The value of trying to think about how we influence lies in our trying to integrate this aware-ness into clinical work. In particular, I believe that it is much easier to understand, formulate, and interpret aspects of transference and coun-tertransference resistance to the degree that we are aware of our wishes to influence.

The contemporary classical analyst hopes for the patient's capacity for insight and self-observation and identification with the analyst's ca-pacities to observe to be augmented in such a way that the patient in-ternalizes these capacities on his own (Gray, 1990). The contemporary classical neutral stance is antagonistic to the analyst's conscious wishes to influence; that approach emphasizes these wishes monotonally as potential impingements on both the patient's autonomy and his need for an atmosphere promoting free association (Adler and Bachant, 1996). Within this view, the analyst's wish to influence makes him lose a position of neutrality—for instance, the analyst's wish to influence crosses the border of wanting to "dress the wound, not heal it" (Freud, 1927). Bion's admonition to listen without memory or desire speaks again to the importance of the analyst's not being too focused on a psy-chic agenda.

Loewald's (1960) position regarding the analyst's wish to influence reflects his familiar tendency to link between classical and more rela-tional approaches. Loewald stressed that a part of our newness in the analytic situation is in being able to engage the transference with "re-straint and maturity." Yet part of our newness is said to reflect the way in which we anticipate the patient's capacity for growth and matura-tion. The analyst, while epistemologically and emotionally superior to the patient, is, in Loewald's, view not entirely a blank screen. The an-alyst has a psychic agenda for the patient. One of the main contribu-tions of contemporary relational theory and social constructivism in particular (e.g., Hoffman, 1991, 1992, 1994) has been to delink Loe-wald's prescient view of the analyst's psychic agenda from his episte-mological position that the analyst is more objective and mature than the patient (Cooper, 1997).

The Kleinian analyst believes that decolonization and the exorcism of bad objects, along with the detoxification and transformation of persecutory ideas and affects into the depressive position, will lead to and constitute change. To effect this change, the analyst has to maintain a position that allows him to contain affect and process it so that they can be reinternalized and metabolized by the patient. As has been pointed out by Mitchell (1996, 1998), the Kleinian approach does not emphasize the analyst's expressive participation as much as it does these aspects of containing affect.

Lacan (1959) stated that the analyst's agenda is for the patient to be able to dismiss him. He is to fall away in importance "like a piece of shit." For Lacan, the analyst is the one who is supposed to know; he is the missing piece. The analyst is to fall from the pedestal because the patient is able to do for himself what he wished the analyst to do for him.

These theories of how the patient can be influenced by analysis do not say much about how the analyst's wish to influence may come into play in an ongoing way during analytic treatment. An important obstacle to articulating a view of the analyst's wish to influence lies in an understandably cautionary stance regarding our awareness of imposing on to the patient expectations about how the patient will grow, change, or develop. Bion's (1963) working maxim, borrowed from T. S. Eliot's *Four Quartets*, that the analyst should be "without memory and desire," summarizes this working stance. It is important to note that Eliot was referring to botanical imagery—leaves buried beneath snow, not people interacting with other people. Freud (1927b) regarded the analyst's need to cure as an abandonment of one's analytic modesty and a defense against one's own sadistic impulses. The line between our wishes to influence and our need to influence is a fuzzy one, but certainly one that each analyst needs to figure out on his own and with the patient as analysis proceeds. It is clear that these strategies of neutrality and epistemological objectivity stem from the notion that wishes to influence usually lie in the territory of pathological countertransference.

Theories of stunted growth and developmental arrest usually focus on the patient's thwarted points of development related to object failure. For various theorists within this tradition, the rub is in different places. For Winnicott, the problem of impingement engenders a false self-adaptation. For Kohut, parental limitations result in a thwarting rather than a promoting of the child's healthy, evolving narcissistic needs. In turn, the child's "innate vigor" (Kohut, 1982) and development of the self is truncated in various ways. For both Winnicott and Kohut, the analyst's purview and aims are extraordinarily ambitious in that they attempt to catalyze the resumption of growth (Cooper, 1994). Yet, for Kohut, the analyst's subjectivity, in the form of either conscious wishes to influence or a general awareness of countertransference, is put on the back burner in favor of coalescing to the patient's affects and defensive/adaptational configurations. Influence occurs less through conscious wish than by meeting the patient's natural developmental capacities, what Winnicott (1969) referred to as the moment of hope and Kohut (1984) termed, "the innate vigor of the self."

In the abstract sense of goals of psychoanalytic work, Winnicott did refer quite dramatically to the analyst's psychic agenda or wish to influence: "If psychoanalysis could be a way of life, then such a treatment might be said to have done what it was supposed to do. But psychoanalysis is no way of life. We all hope that our patients will finish with us and forget us, and that they will find living itself that becomes the therapy that makes sense" (p. 87). This position is similar to that of Lacan, yet the method for achieving and conceptualizing the ongoing analytic process is different.

Winnicott is quite complex and difficult to understand regarding the analyst's use of subjectivity and the wish to influence, because he straddled the worlds of developmental tilt theorists (Mitchell, 1988) and theorists that promote active and expressive use of the countertransference. On one hand, he articulated that the mother's actions encompass at least two functions. She functions and is experienced as both environment mother and object mother. As environment mother, she needs to provide containment and to coalesce to the infant in order for growth to occur. As object mother, she is recipient of various kinds of needs, including instinctual needs. Her presence as a subjective object (Benjamin, 1988) seems most important when she is depleted—her limits and "hatred" for the object when she is sucked dry and depleted are essential to help the child to learn the limits of others and to help the child move from hallucinatory wish and omnipotent fantasy to reality appraisal. Yet it is primarily only in these catastrophic circumstances of the mother's depletion that Winnicott acknowledged the subjectivity of the mother. The analyst's wish to influence is, for Winnicott, channeled into the attempt to meet the patient where he is.

Meeting the patient in this way does not seem *explicitly* to include anticipating (correctly or incorrectly) where the patient might go, conscious and unconscious aspects of suggestion, disclosing contrasting thoughts and feelings, or psychic collision between patient and analyst.

Like Loewald, Winnicott straddles two worlds of psychoanalytic thought regarding influence. But Winnicott is by far the more elusive of the two theorists. His clinical examples are filled with attempts to interpret more deeply than many other therapists, and, in so doing, he conveyed a willingness to bear and confront patients with these experiences. Winnicott's (1951, 1971) interpretive ideals revolved around making interpretation a matter of play and transitional phenomena between patient and analyst.

The transitional object, however, has a complicated function in influencing development. On one hand, the parent is responsible for making it available and not transforming it in any significant way. Thus, the child's inner, subjective world is honored, and so is a level of omnipotent control. At the same time, however, the transitional object is selected in the context of separation and is, in Winnicott's theory, a part of what has already amounted to an assault on the infant's sense of omnipotent control. The infant is partly backstepping by now, his hopes for omnipotent control thwarted. The whole idea of the transitional object is that it provides a bridge between oral eroticism and the capacity for reality appraisal. So, in a sense, the parent (and later the analyst) influences the other by handling the regressive loss of control, honoring a substitute world to the infant that, in turn, allows the child to embrace reality. The mother is said to bring the world to the infant. Influence is surreptitious. As a reader of Winnicott, we never know if the infant is reeling from the loss of symbiosis (Winnicott, 1951) or partly embracing the object world in what Winnicott termed "positive aggression" (Winnicott, 1971), Winnicott's term for the infant's motive or wish to embrace the object world. Embedded in his model of developmental theory is a tension between a classical emphasis on the preservation of the pleasure principle and a drive toward object relating embodied in motility itself. And, to make things even more complicated, embedded in this tension in developmental theory is a kind of ambivalence about how actively and conspicuously the analyst brings into the play his differences with the patient, his own subjectivity. For Winnicott, the analyst is situated somewhere between offering interpretation as a link to the patient (e.g., Aron, 1996, p. 101) and challenging an area of omnipotent control (Winnicott, 1971).

There are other important examples of the strategy involving re-growth and developmental arrest within psychoanalytic theory including those of Kohut, Stolorow and Lachmann, and Schwaber. My intention is not to explicate their theories of growth and change in psychoanalysis but, instead, to place into focus how the analyst's direct influence is generally associated with impingement. These theories have in common a focus on the experiential world of the patient. Kohut's main strategy for promoting regrowth revolved around his theory of defense, which he defined as the attempt to keep alive a hoped-for self-object from childhood. Kohut (1971, 1977, 1984) warned that the analyst can easily thwart growth by attempting to interpret defense (as conventionally defined) as concealment of wish. Stolorow and Lachmann (1980) seek to redress what they regard as a problem involving analyst's tendencies to view integrative failure in self-representation and experience as a function of defense. Instead, they have reinterpreted certain aspects of splitting and projective identification as basic problems in integration of the self and, in so doing, have made technical suggestions oriented toward elucidating the patient's psychic reality. Schwaber (1983, 1995) has also focused on the patient's psychic reality in an attempt to modify the analyst's epistemological stance within classical analysis. She regards the analyst's tendencies to impose his or her viewpoint as an obstruction to progress in analysis. For Schwaber, the main source of analytic influence lies in elucidating the patient's psychic reality.

In my view, while Schwaber (1995) has usefully shifted classical analysis away from a one-person psychology focused on drives and the epistemological superiority of the analyst, she uses the countertransference in too narrow a way—as an obstruction to understanding the patient's experience. In so doing, she minimizes the ways that the therapist's countertransference can potentially inform the therapist about the patient's patterning of relationship. In a series of articles, she (Schwaber, 1997) and Gabbard (Gabbard, 1997) debated this issue. It is clear from this exchange that one of Schwaber's main concerns in integrating the analyst's countertransference as informing interpretation is the possibility of the analyst's using these experiences to override the patient's psychic reality. Gabbard points out, and I agree, that this possibility is not the necessary consequence of using the analyst's subjectivity actively. The analyst's countertransference reactions need not be used reflexively to equate the analyst's experience with a warded-off self- and object representation, as is sometimes the stereotyped picture of how projective identification is interpreted within a Kleinian perspective. Racker (1968) has repeatedly warned against this potential interpretive tendency.

Schwaber's attempt to preserve the patient's psychic reality as a primary mode of therapeutic action seems to me to be, as I term it, "the return of the repressed positivistic" fantasy—that is, the analyst is able to put aside his feelings and thoughts so as not to have them influence his view of the patient's psychic reality. This return of the repressed positivistic rears its head in other forms too. For instance, another strategy for avoiding the wish to influence is one that fully and openly acknowledges that wish but allows the analyst, by means of various methods, to analyze or abstain from it as much as possible. Gill's (1979, 1982; Gill and Muslin, 1976; Gill and Hoffman, 1982) approach to the analysis of transference embodied a kind of vigilance to the ubiquity of influence and the attempt to analyze it. There may well have been an underlying positivistic fantasy about the capacity of the analyst to analyze all dimensions of influence and suggestion and the belief that this would be most therapeutic, a notion that both Gill (1994) and especially Hoffman (1996) later revised radically. Levenson (1990) has suggested that the analyst's desire to help the patient is problematic and should be renounced. Similarly, Bird (1972) stated that, ironically, one of the greatest impediments for successful analysis is both the analyst's wish to help the patient and the actual help that the patient receives!

Renik's (1993, 1996) recent work has also paid considerable attention to the importance and inevitability of the analyst's influence. Renik (1996), however, in contrast to Hoffman (1994a, 1996) has suggested the importance of trying to analyze as much as possible about influence. Renik's (1996) position regarding this issue is complex and difficult to characterize because he has also been at the forefront of documenting "the perils of neutrality." Renik (1993, 1996) has elucidated the problems with trying to approach influence as something that can be detoxified. He suggests that neutrality is an unachievable ideal and one that can interfere with growth. At the same time, like Gill (1982) and Levenson (1990, 1993), he is ambitious in pointing out to the patient how his influence may be directing the patient in various ways. The purpose behind Renik's and Levinson's proposals about trying to learn about our influence is admirable—after all, influence seems to be a part of our job description. Yet there is something about this ambition that may bring us back to the "return of the repressed positivistic" with regard to understanding our influence. Hoffman (1996) has struck a note of modesty about our ability to analyze influence and suggestion even if we wanted to. He adds, however, that he is not so sure how much he wants to—he seems to be saying that he wants as much as possible of the analyst's ability to elicit powers of suggestion, idealization, and extrainterpretive influence working on the side of change.

I believe that the American relational models offer an enormous opportunity for understanding our wishes to influence through the explication and use of the analyst's construction of psychic possibility. The perspective offered by this body of theory helps analysts of various theoretical persuasions to understand and try to account more fully for our views of therapeutic action. The use of the analyst's subjectivity within the body of relational models, including the wish to influence, is in the foreground both of conceptualizing therapeutic action and of clinical work. This wish to influence is I believe what Renik has in mind when he challenges us to try to understand our influence as much as possible.

There are several strands within this model that relate to the topic of the analyst's wish to influence. One is that mother as subject is essential to affective exchanges between patient and analyst that promote new learning (Benjamin, 1988). The analyst's irreducible subjectivity and the problems inherent to anonymity (Renik, 1993) are highly related to Benjamin's explication of the mother as subject, not simply as object of the patient's affective world. Renik argues that the analyst's ability to make his subjectivity selectively known to the patient is often what can be most helpful and elucidating. Hoffman's (1991, 1992, 1994a) social constructivism highlights the importance of construction and negotiation of two realities (Russell, 1973; Mitchell, 1988; Pizer, 1992) in the analytic situation. Aron's (1996) description of relational perspectivism integrates relational and epistemological axes in ways that relate both to the analyst's influence and the construction of psychic possibility. Aron suggests that what is true, perceived, experienced, and recognized in the analytic situation is always a reflection of interaction. It is in this sense similar to Gill's (1994a) definition of truth as what "patient and analyst come to agree is the truth" (p. 163). Aron's (1991) attention to interpretation as an expression of the analyst's subjectivity certainly includes the expression of the analyst's wish to influence as well as specifics related to the analyst's psychic agenda. As Mitchell (1988, 1993, 1997) has repeatedly described them, within a relational model, growth and autonomy are viewed as an emergent property of interactive processes.

SOME GENERAL CONSIDERATIONS OF FORMULATION AND THE ANALYST'S WISHES TO INFLUENCE: DETECTIVES FRIDAY, COLUMBO, AND MULDER

The analyst's subjectivity, most inclusively captured by his choice of theoretical model, is always involved in his use of formulation. This holds true whether or not the integration of countertransference (narrowly conceived as the analyst's subjectivity) is a major or relatively minor aspect of his actual technical procedure.

The choice of where to begin to formulate and what to interpret, as well as the goals of analysis, is the most obvious expression of the analyst's subjectivity. I like to compare analysts to detectives, not as "symbol decoders" (Bollas, 1987), but in terms of our preferences for inquiry, learning, and synthesis. Here is a highly selective history of television detectives who work, as analysts try to, by discovery and influence. I suggest a trend in psychoanalytic theorizing partly described by a line of development (not necessarily progressive) from Sergeant Friday *(Dragnet),* through Lieutenant Columbo *(Columbo)* to Agent Mulder *(X-Files).*

For Sergeant Friday, the world was a colorless place filled with material reality to be discovered. Sergeant Friday's main mode of inquiry was to assert: "The facts, ma'm, just the facts." A fact for Sergeant Friday and for us psychoanalysts (of all schools) is always contextually bound. The main context for Sergeant Friday had everything to do with discovering "the truth," such as who murdered, who stole, who bribed. Postmodernist conceptualizations of truth and meaning were not a part of the Los Angeles police force in the 1950s or 60s, nor, perhaps more important, of the world of the people creating such television shows. So, for Sergeant Friday, there was a discovery to be made of a rather concrete sort. Sergeant Friday also believed that emotions would only obfuscate or deter this discovery. Sergeant Friday was not the most sentient of detectives or, if you will, analysts. "The facts ma'm, just the facts" often seemed to mean, "Spare me the emotions. don't get soft on me, no tears." Sergeant Friday expected the witnesses to be able to separate wheat from chaff, to distill kernels of meaning, and to discard irrelevant details. Of course, to the extent that they could not do so, he would do it.

All analysts, of all theoretical schools, consciously attempt to take an approach very different from Sergeant Friday's. It is purportedly out of the mass of relatively unfiltered affect and detail that we come to understand something about what our patients feel or believe or how they behave. The context for most analysts, from a methodological point of view, is to advise patients to say as much as possible about what comes to mind: "Everything that comes to mind, ma'm or sir, just everything that comes to mind." But it is also the case that our theories and our subjectivity itself exerts an effect on what patients choose to say. So we have something in common with Sergeant Friday—regardless of our conscious attempts to do the opposite, we exert influence by narrowing the field of observation.

Thus there is a dialectical tension between the inherently constructive and destructive aspects of our theoretical orientations in analytic work. By the term destructive I mean to suggest the ways in which these orientations, by necessity, also foreclose possible meanings. This foreclosure, like that of Sergeant Friday, is required in order to narrow the observational field so that the analyst may place something in particular in focus.

In contrast to Sergeant Friday, Lieutenant Columbo's persona was based on a playful construction of himself as uninformed and rather clueless, disguising his developing theory and accumulating evidence: "Do you think it could be the case?" or, through self-conscious inquiry, "There's something I don't understand." His world view was in some ways similar to Sergeant Friday's, only his methodology was different and filled with irony and illusion. Columbo actively pieced things together. But he felt that sharing his uncertainty with all the potential witnesses or culprits would lead to new information. He was seeking comfort, but, wily guy that he was, he also sought to reconstruct the crime scene, again and again, not only to piece together what happened in the past, but to create new crime scenes in the present that would force the participants into revealing new information. Far from a postmodern emphasis on the complexity of truth and questions of "whose truth," however, Columbo's sense of uncertainty was not always "honest." Through manipulation, Columbo constructed himself as a kind of bumbling fellow and disguised his hypotheses with feigned uncertainty. Models of active countertransference expressiveness and disclosure are not based on deceit, trickery, or manipulation, but they do hold in common with Lieutenant Columbo a belief that putting on the table one's confusion and curiosity can be quite informative.

Agent Mulder *(X-Files)* is a whole different kettle of fish. He plays counterpoint to his colleague, the physician Scully, who believes in material reality. He is wont to say to her: "Scully, no one has jurisdiction over the truth." Agent Mulder doesn't believe that the truth is easily discovered. He is captivated by mystery and by a kind of working assumption that there is an infinite number of mysteries to learn about in life, multiple levels of truth. He actively enjoys playing the devil's advocate to Sergeant Friday or to any proponents of a working theoretical model that, to him, obviously forecloses the process of inquiry.

My point in reviewing these detectives is less related to the rise of postmodern trends in viewing reality among television writers in Los Angeles than to the importance of noting how artful language creates its own logic. So does theory. I take it as a fact of psychoanalytic life that every analyst (and every analyst is a theorist) creates his own logic, one cocreated with his patient. We cannot form a neat separation between the process of the analyst's discovery and the process of indoctrination, an insight that Balint (1968) was particularly prescient in detailing. Here I agree with Hoffman (1996) that this element of influence is often helpful in getting results in therapy and analysis and cannot always be analyzed completely even if we wanted it to be.

The analyst's choice of what to observe and formulate is probably the most visible line of divergence across most theoretical approaches. Cooper (1994) states that analytic fervor is not (any longer) in the service of a single theory or proving an analytic proposition. Rather, he argues, analytic fervor is currently aimed at deepening introspective curiosity. While I am not sure that there is a single type or unique species of analytic fervor today that binds together all theories, I think that his description probably comes the closest to a commonly held goal of formulation and interpretation within varied approaches to the analytic process. I think it unfortunate that as analysts we do not emphasize what is implicit in our valuing of the deepening of introspective curiosity, namely, that we believe that the deepening of curiosity is one of the most important *outcomes* of analysis.

A related question emerges: How do various analysts regard the issue of the domain of introspective curiosity—that is, *introspective curiosity about what?* Is it introspective curiosity about the way we function psychically with regard to observing or integrating conflicts, affects, or interaction? I hope it has been clear throughout this book that, in my personal synthesis of theory, I view these three domains as interpenetrating, as interaction interpenetrated by conflict and affect.

As only one example of the many kinds of diversity with which analysts approach introspective curiosity, I will briefly examine the ways in which some different analysts refer to various entities and aspects of clinical process in describing "defense analysis." In the United States, defense analysis is currently so varied that often analysts disagree about how even to define the concept of defense (Mitchell, 1992; Richards, 1992; Trop and Stolorow, 1992). In their dialogue with each other, these four theorists do not agree about what the patient might attempt to become more curious about regarding defensive functioning. Whereas Trop and Stolorow view defense as the patient's attempt to keep vivid hoped-for empathic selfobjects from childhood as described by Kohut, both Mitchell and Richards agree that the patient's identification with disappointing others might provide a way to explore further the patient's defensive adaptation.

Consider the differences between the ways Brenner (1982), Modell (1975), and Kohut (1984) define defense (Cooper, 1989). Brenner (1982) defines defense as anything in the psychic apparatus that mitigates drives, drive derivatives, or depressive affect. Modell (1975), following Winnicott's (1960) seminal work on defense, defines defense within a "two-person context" in which defenses arise in the context of object failure—defense can operate against an object failure rather than exclusively in the area of internal drive or affect. Kohut (1984) defined defense as an attempt to keep alive the hope for an empathic selfobject. His theory implies that the analyst's major interpretive efforts hinge exclusively on the attempt to elucidate these empathic failures both in the past and in the present process with the analyst.

These varying definitions of defense have a direct impact on how analysts formulate and interpret. In his interpretations of defense, a self psychologist includes the patient's adaptive need to keep alive longed-for satisfying or empathic selfobjects. Brenner might also include adaptive aspects of the patient's defensive stance, but these factors would be more contextually bound to the imperative need to mitigate particular affects that would otherwise cause anxiety or depressive affect.

Even within a particular school, such as ego psychology, individual analysts differ in how they technically approach defense formulation and interpretation. For example, Kris (1982, 1983, 1990) used a methodological approach in which technical stance and formulation were often oriented to what interrupted or impeded free association. Gray (1973, 1990) is most interested in proximal events and believes that many psychoanalysts turn their attention too readily to the deeper levels of meaning, such as underlying wishes that determine associative content. Gray believes that it is useful to address formulation and interpretation to readily available levels of observation for the patient. Thus, he is attuned to breaks in associative content, such as shifts in affect, content, or silence that might suggest the patient's unconsciously determined attempt to mitigate affect or thought. He believes that, by addressing this surface "behavior," the patient will be able to broaden his observational field and more easily notice the ways in which he avoids or attenuates the particular kinds of affect that are presumably embedded within conflict-laden contexts.

The practice of analysis leads to other essential questions related to how we attempt to broaden the observational field relative to introspective curiosity. To what degree does an analyst place relational factors, particularly the analyst's participation in the process, in the foreground both with regard to formulation or technical stance? There are also profound differences in approach which examine the representational world as it is encoded in and contributes to past and current conflict, on one hand, and, on the other, which emphasize current interpersonal phenomena as primary influences on the direction of association in the analytic situation. Naturally, many analysts would see nothing contradictory about working within both frameworks, that is, representational and interpersonal. Another of the major differences in understanding relational factors as they affect formulation involves the traditions of intimacy and solitude (as explored in chapter 2).

A major dividing line among analysts is the degree to which they focus on multiple levels of reality and multiple levels of what influences perceptions of reality. A self-psychological approach is invariably directed toward elucidating the patient's experiential reality, most pointedly, the patient's experience of the analyst, especially the inevitable failures in empathy on the part of the analyst regarding the patient's experience. Ornstein and Ornstein (1994) for example, "define clinical facts as psychoanalytic when the patient's subjective experiences are formulated and organized in the language of one of the psychoanalytic theoretical systems" (p. 978). Consider for a moment the overlap and difference in the way that Sandler and Sandler (1994) define a clinical fact and the formulation of facts. They state that facts "are the particular ways in which we organize the data received by our senses" (p. 995). Sandler and Sandler's view encompasses the analyst's senses, a view that allows for the possibility that the patient's experience is not the exclusive domain of the analyst's formulative activity. Many analysts would agree with the idea of using multiple levels of psychic reality, including countertransference responses, in composing a particular formulation. Yet there is tremendous variety in how analysts employ their countertransference in formulating aspects of reality in the analytic context.

While many analysts differ in their use of projective identification in the process of formulating, there is a general overlap in that Kleinians, other object relations theorists (Modell, 1975, 1984; Ogden, 1989), and contemporary British and American interpersonally influenced analysts (Greenberg, 1986; Bollas, 1987; Mitchell, 1988; Hoffman, 1992) move back and forth between the analyst's and the patient's views of psychic reality. From a self-psychological perspective, in contrast, it is axiomatic that differences between the patient and the analyst regarding psychic reality can be a source of disruption to the selfobject experience in analysis.

In the United States, this disagreement regarding the use of multiple levels of psychic reality in formulation has now moved far beyond the narrowly defined schools of thought embedded within self psychology or in sharp opposition to this school. For example, Schwaber (1983) and McLaughlin (1994) point to the value of a primary commitment to understanding the patient's perceptions of the analytic situation, the patient's psychic reality. As McLaughlin put it, "I will listen to whatever you wish to say, with the intent to understand your meaning and viewpoint, and with the intent to understand your meaning and viewpoint with the least imposition to my own view or meaning as I can manage" (p. 13). In response to this perspective, Gill (1994b) argued that "where Freud valorized an unobjectionable positive transference as the energizer of the search for truth, McLaughlin valorizes an unobjectionable positive countertransference in its place, thereby neglecting the wide range of countertransference meanings that the analyst's participation may represent" (p. 24). Gill (1994b) and Hoffman (1994b) argued that what many analysts minimize in their formulation of the patient's reality is the analyst's focus on the nature of the interaction of the two participants. In this way, Gill argues, an earlier overemphasis in psychoanalysis on the importance of the analyst's perspective has been replaced with an overemphasis on the patient's manifest experience as a guide to the patient's psychic reality. It is along this dimension that classical and relational perspectives alike have a great deal in common.

There are a number of technical dimensions that cut across theoretical approaches to formulation. The degree to which the analyst focuses on transference or extratransference elaboration is one such dimension. Is transference seen as a defense against free association (Freud's, 1914, early model of transference) or is the analyst more focused on defenses against the emergence of transference (Gill and Muslin, 1976)? The degree to which reconstruction is emphasized is another dimension that can appear in various forms in a number of theories of technique. The use of constructivism is a dimension that is not bound to one school of thought but, rather, permeates most theoretical schools of formulation to varying degrees (Cooper, 1993).

CONCLUSION: THE ANALYST'S SUBJECTIVITY AND
IMPLICATIONS FOR UNDERSTANDING FORMULATION
AND OUR WISHES TO INFLUENCE

While most analysts agree that their subjectivity, variously defined, is central to the unfolding analytic process, I have suggested throughout this book that the analyst's choices of how to formulate and conceptualize and the technique that follows from these choices are themselves the most blatant expression of the analyst's subjectivity. The analyst's consciously and unconsciously held beliefs about modes of influence and hoped-for outcomes are also a part of this subjectivity. Gardner (1994) has summarized this position: the facts we construct are inseparable from the theoretical and other subjectivity that go into our assumptions, observations and conclusions" (p. 934).

As Sandler and Sandler (1994) detail, our choices about where to begin and what to interpret are often determined by unconscious influences and affect not only what the analyst selects to interpret (Tuckett, 1993), but also what the analyst perceives in the first place. The previous discussion of the variability of the analyst's views of psychic reality clearly has major technical implications but also relates to the analyst's utilization of his subjectivity. The most obvious point of divergence lies in how the analyst's interpretive approach makes use of his differences with the patient's views. Ornstein and Ornstein (1994) suggest that the analyst's reactions and points of divergence constitute breaches in empathy with the patient's experiential perspective. In contrast, many classically and relationally oriented analysts point to how their differences with patients in viewing patients' associations become a part of an ever-widening observational field that both patient and analyst attempt to integrate.

Among analytic approaches that broadly consider the analyst's differences in relation to the patient to be of value in the process of formulation and interpretation, the analyst nevertheless wishes to promote an atmosphere of increased freedom to feel and associate. For example, Gardner (1994) puts it like this regarding his own interpretive efforts: "I want especially to invite attention to the ways in which the choice of where to begin reflects a never entirely successful effort to promote a relatively spontaneous unfolding of events rather than a forcing into the areas of our preferences" (p. 931). One of the interesting points of confusion in contemporary psychoanalysis is that, while there is probably agreement about Gardner's statement, at a different level of discourse, many analysts would say that it is never possible or desirable to achieve such spontaneity. I think that the chief point of confusion is that all analysts want to minimize compliance by their patients, but relationally oriented analysts see their wishes to influence and inevitably affect the patient as an important factor in understanding the nature of the interaction between patient and analyst. Even more complex is the question of whether our central point of attention is to free association and, in addition, to the multiple points of transference-countertransference interaction and enactment that arise in conjunction with the patient's associations.

Another example of the variety of points of intervention connected to formulation (the analyst's subjective preferences) relates to the shared goal of tracing the analysand's affect in the clinical context. Most theories, with the possible exception of the Lacanian approach, aim to intervene at the most dominant affective point in a particular session (Kernberg, 1993). A picture emerges from a focus on immediate moments (affects, shifts in affect, particular possible allusions to the analyst, etc.). An analogy between the analytic process and a pointillist painting is relevant here. We focus on particular moments or points, which, when we gradually step back, present a far different picture for both analysand and analyst. This distinction was stressed by Strachey (1934) in his discussion of affective urgency and was subsequently emphasized in ego-psychological approaches (Kris, 1982, 1983; Gray, 1990) and more recently in contributions from the independent school (Casement, 1985; Bollas, 1987).

Our thresholds for tolerating stormy weather and our readiness to see some patients' responses as iatrogenically determined are probably quite individually variable, even though specific technical approaches build in certain ways of working with and formulating the analysand's disagreements with our interpretations (Cooper, 1993). Cooper's (1994) approach illustrates his orientation to developing clinical facts and formulations that concern the layers of resistance and unconscious fantasies. He describes interpretations as "trial balloons" that subsequently allow us to examine the patient's responses. Cooper states that he is not discouraged by "stormy weather." In contrast, self-psychological models (e.g., Ornstein and Ornstein, 1994), as well as technical orientations such as that of Schwaber (1986, 1990) and McLaughlin (1994) address the material that produces conscious affective display. While self-psychological models often view the analyst's interpretations as leading iatrogenically to certain disruptions in the analytic experience, this attunement to the analyst's influence on the patient is not unique to self psychology. Many analysts who might agree with the notion of floating interpretations as trial balloons have varying approaches to how they might do this. Some analysts generally make formulations and interpretations of unconscious conflict with accompanying statements about the adaptive reasons that a patient clings to his particular position or stance. This could be seen as a countertransferentially motivated "hedge" on the part of the analyst to avoid stormy weather. It may well be the conscious experience of the analyst that interpretations that address the patient's adaptive tendency to see things the way that he does are more likely to be listened to and integrated.

Analysts also differ in their sensitivity to how patients might experience indoctrinating influences of their interpretive stance or direction. Balint's (1968) paper "The Hazards of Consistent Interpretation," directed against the Kleinian school at the time of its publication, warned against the potentially indoctrinating influence of a particular interpretive direction on the part of the analyst. Despite Balint's agenda, the idea that the analyst needs to listen to the effects of his formulations and interpretive stance on the patient is not unique to one school. From a Kleinian perspective, Britton and Steiner's (1994) admonitions about the analyst's dependence on what Bion referred to as the overvalued idea also elucidate the dimension of how the analyst listens in a complex way to the effects his remarks have on the patient.

A formulation contains not only the analyst's attempt to broaden the patient's observational field regarding inner life and interaction, but also the relatively routine fantasy elements of what will occur as a result of this effort. In many ways, analysis should provide the analysand with the opportunity to work through and help analyze these fantasy elements within the analyst's formulations, as well as the inherent indoctrinating aspects of formulation and interpretation.

At the level of theory development, probably every helpful and innovative theoretical movement also brings with it magical fantasies and hopes. People are always looking for solutions to the difficult task of living—a new diet, body, religion, therapy. Theoreticians usually feel consciously or unconsciously that they have found such a solution. Because we are so attached to our own theories for some of the reasons I explored earlier, it better be a damn good theory if we're going to change. Theory is partly the repository of our experience and the magical fantasies and desires from the analyst—it contains and holds the analyst's hope. Theory is what we have when, in our dark moments, as we are listening to a patient complain that more isn't happening, we say to ourselves: "Well, I went through something like this and came out the other side," or "If he doesn't experience some of the emptiness and barrenness of his inner life, then he isn't going to find something there that's real."

These are personal attachments to theory that hold and sustain us during moments of uncertainty—and there are many such moments. These attachments are an important, overarching thread that binds all psychoanalysts of varying orientations together. In this way, our attachment to a theory or theories is an adaptation, as well as a source of resistance, to new learning and change. This fact of psychoanalytic life is one of the most important aspects of mutual experience between patient and analyst, albeit occurring within the highly asymmetrical arrangements of psychoanalytic work. We are bound together with excitement, reluctance, and trepidation in the task of changing and learning. In psychoanalysis, at its most complex and compelling moment, both analyst and patient are trying to teach and discover a new and often obscure logic of growth and change.

REFERENCES

Adler, E. & Bachant, J. (1996) Free association and analytic neutrality: The basic structure of the psychoanalytic situation. *J. Amer. Psychoanal. Assn.,* 44:1021-1046.

Adler, G. (1989) Transitional phenomena, projective identification, and the essential ambiguity of the analytic situation. *Psychoanal. Quart.,* 58:81-104.

Akhtar, S. (1996) Someday and if only fantasies: Pathological optimism and inordinate nostologic relatedness. *J. Amer. Psychoanal. Assn.,* 44:723-753.

Alvarez, A. (1993) *Intimate Company.* New York: Guilford Press.

Ammons, A. R. (1999) Embedded storms. *The New Yorker,* March.

Amos, M. (1975) *Dead Babies.* New York: Harmony Books.

Aron, L. (1991) The patient's experience of the analyst's subjectivity. *Psychoanal. Dial.,* 1:29-51.

———— (1992) Interpretation as expression of the analyst's subjectivity. *Psychoanal. Dial.,* 2:475-507.

———— (1996) *A Meeting of Minds: Mutuality in Psychoanalysis.* Hillsdale, NJ: The Analytic Press.

———— & Bushra, A. (1998) Mutual regression: Altered states in the psychoanalytic situation. *J. Amer. Psychoanal. Assn.,* 46:389-412.

Bader, M. (1998) Postmodern epistemology: The problem of validation and the retreat from therapeutics in psychoanalysis. *Psychoanal. Dial.,* 8:1-32.

Balint, M. (1968) *The Basic Fault.* London: Tavistock.

Balsam, R. (1997) Regression in the psychoanalytic situation. Paper delivered to the American Psychoanalytic Situation, May.

Becker, E. (1973) *The Denial of Death.* New York: Free Press.

Beebe, B. & Lachmann, G. (1982) The contribution of mother-infant mutual influence to the origins of self and object representations. *Psychoanal. Psychol.,* 5:305-337.

———— Jaffe, J. & Lachmann, F. (1992) A dyadic systems view of communication. In: *Relational Perspectives in Psychoanalysis,* ed. N. Skolnick & S. Warshaw. Hillsdale, NJ: The Analytic Press, pp. 61-82.

Bellah, R. (1972) Religious evolution. In:*Reader in Comparative Religion,* ed. R. Bellah. New York: Harper & Row, pp. 33-51.

Benjamin, J. (1988) *The Bonds of Love.* New York: Pantheon Books.

———— (1990) An outline of intersubjectivity: The development of recognition. *Psychoanal. Psychol.,* 7:33-46.

———— (1994) Commentary on papers by Tansey, Davies, and Hirsch. *Psychoanal. Dial.,* 4:193-201.

Bion, W. (1959) Attacks on linking. *Internat. J. Psycho-Anal.,* 40:308-315.

———— (1962) *Learning from Experience.* London: Heinemann Medical, Maresfield Library, 1984.

———— (1963) *Elements of Psychoanalysis.* London: Heinemann.

———— (1967) *Second Thoughts.* London: Heinemann.

———— (1975) *Memoirs of the Future: Vol. 1, Dreams.* Rio de Janeiro: Imago.

———— (1977) *Two Papers: The Grid and Caesura.* Rio de Janeiro: Imago.

Bird, B. (1972) Notes on transference: Universal phenomenon and hardest part of analysis. *J. Amer. Psychoanal. Assn.,* 20:267-301.

Bollas, C. (1987) *The Shadow of the Object.* New York: Columbia University Press.

———— (1989) *Forces of Destiny: Psychoanalysis and Human Idiom.* London: Free Association Books.

Bowie, M. (1993) Freud in the future. Review of M. Edmunson's *Toward Reading Freud. Raritan,* 13:151-165.

Brenner, C. (1982) *The Mind in Conflict.* New York: International Universities Press.

Britton, R. & Steiner, J. (1994) Interpretation: Selected fact or overvalued idea? *Internat. J. Psycho-Anal.,* 75:1069-1078.

Bromberg, P. (1979) Interpersonal psychoanalysis and regression. *Contemp. Psychoanal.*, 15:647-655.

——— (1991) On knowing one's patient inside and out: The aesthetics of unconscious communication. *Psychoanal. Dial.*, 1:399-422.

——— (1993) Shadow and substance: A relational perspective on clinical process. *Psychoanal. Psychol.*, 10:147-168.

——— (1994) "Speak! that I may see you": Some reflections on dissociation, reality, and psychoanalytic listening. *Psychoanal. Dial.*, 4:517-548.

——— (1995) Resistance, object-usage, and human relatedness. *Contemp. Psychoanal.*, 31:173-191.

——— (1998) *Standing in the Spaces: Essays on Clinical Process, Trauma, and Dissociation.* Hillsdale, NJ: The Analytic Press.

Brunschwig, J. (1988) Sextus Empiricus on the kriterion: The skeptic as conceptual legatee. In: *The Question of Eclecticism: Studies in Later Greek Philosophy*, ed. J. Dillon & A. Long. Berkeley: University of California Press, pp. 73-97.

Buber, M. (1970) *I and Thou.* New York: Simon & Shuster.

Buchner, G. (1972) *Woyzeck.* Chicago: University of Chicago Press.

Burke, W. (1992) Countertransference disclosure and the asymmetry/mutuality dilemma. *Psychoanal. Dial.*, 2:241-271.

Busch, F. (1993) "In the neighborhood": Aspects of a good interpretation and a "developmental lag" in ego psychology. *J. Amer. Psychoanal. Assn.*, 41:151-177.

——— (1995) Resistance analysis and object relations theory: Erroneous conceptions amidst some timely contributions. *Psychoanal. Psychol.*, 12:43-53.

Byrne, D. & Eno, B. (1980) "Crosseyed and painless." Bleu Disque Music Co., Index Music, Inc., & E. G. Music, Ltd.

Caper, R. (1988) *Material and Immaterial Facts: Freud's Discovery of Psychic Reality and Klein's Development of His Work.* Northvale,NJ: Aronson.

——— (1992) Does psychoanalysis heal? *Internat. J. Psycho-Anal.*, 73:283-292.

——— (1994) What is a clinical fact. *Internat. J. Psycho-Anal.*, 75:903-913.

Casement, P. (1985) *On Learning from the Patient*. London: Tavistock.
———— (1990) The meeting of needs in psychoanalysis. *Psychoanal. Inq.*, 10:25-339.
Ceccoli, V. (1999) Beyond milk and the good breast: Reconfiguring the maternal function in the psychoanalytic dyad. *Psychoanal. Dial.*, 9:683-698.
Celenza, A. (1998) Precursors to therapist-patient sexual misconduct: Preliminary findings. *Psychoanal. Psychol.*, 15:378-395.
Chodorow, N. (1996) Reflections on the authority of the past in psychoanalytic thinking. *Psychoanal. Quart.*, 65:32-51.
———— (1997) Theoretical gender and clinical gender: Epistemological reflections on the psychology of women. *J. Amer. Psychoanal. Assn.*, 44:215-240.
Coen, S. (1994) Love between patient and analyst. *J. Amer. Psychoanal. Assn.*, 42:1107-1136.
———— (1997) How to help patients (and analysts) bear the unbearable. *J. Amer. Psychoanal. Assn.*, 45:1183-1207.
———— (in press) The patient's and analyst's regression in the analytic process. *J. Amer. Psychoanal. Assn.*
Cooper, A. (1987) Changes in psychoanalytic ideas: Transference interpretation. *J. Amer. Psychoanal. Assn.*, 35:77-93.
———— (1992) Psychic change: Development in the theory of psychoanalytic technique. *Internat. J. Psycho-Anal.*, 73:245-250.
———— (1994) Formulations to the patient: Explicit and implicit. *Internat. J. Psycho-Anal.*, 75:1107-1120.
Cooper, S. (1989) Recent contributions to the theory of defense: A comparative perspective. *J. Amer. Psychoanal. Assn.*, 37:865-891.
———— (1993) Interpretive fallibility and psychoanalytic dialogue. *J. Amer. Psychoanal. Assn.*, 41:95-126.
———— (1996a) The thin blue line of the intrapsychic/interpersonal dialectic. *Psychoanal. Dial.*, 6:647-669.
———— (1996b) Facts all come with a point of view. *Internat. J. Psycho-Anal.*, 77:255-273.
———— (1996c) Panel report: Modes of influence in psychoanalysis. *J. Amer. Psychoanal. Assn.*, 77:553-561.
———— (1997) Interpretation and the psychic future. *Internat. J. Psycho-Anal.*, 78:667-681.

———— (1998a) Countertransference disclosure and the conceptualization of technique. *Psychoanal. Quart.,* 67:128-154.

———— (1998b) Analyst-subjectivity, analyst-disclosure, and the aims of psychoanalysis. *Psychoanal. Quart.,* 67:379-406.

———— (1998c) Commentary on paper by Jodie Davies. *Psychoanal. Dial.,* 8:767-779.

———— (in press) Elements of mutual containment in the psychoanalytic process. *Psychoanal. Dial.*

———— & Levit, D. (1998) The old and new object in Fairbairnian and American relational theory. *Psychoanal. Dial.,* 8:603-624.

Darwin, J. (1999) Impasse and intersubjectivity. *Smith College Studies in Social Work,* March, pp. 457-473.

Davies, J. (1994) Love in the afternoon: A relational consideration of desire and dread in the countertransference. *Psychoanal. Dial.,* 4:153-170.

———— (1998) Between the disclosure and foreclosure of erotic transference-countertransference. Can psychoanalysis find a place for adult sexuality? *Psychoanal. Dial.,* 8:747-766.

Derrida, J. (1982) *The Ear of the Other.* London: University of Nebraska Press, 1985.

Eagle, M. (1984) *Recent Developments in Psychoanalysis.* New York: McGraw Hill.

Edmunson, M. (1993) *Towards Reading Freud.* Princeton: Princeton University Press.

Ehrenberg, D. (1992) *The Intimate Edge: Extending the Reach of Psychoanalytic Interaction.* New York: Norton.

———— (1995) Self-disclosure: Therapeutic tool or indulgence? *Contemp. Psychoanal.,* 31:213-228.

Einstein, A. (1931) *Ideas and Opinions.* New York: Crown Publishers, 1954.

Ekstein, R. & Holzman, P. (1959) Repetition functions of transitory regressive thinking. *Psychoanal. Quart.,* 28: 228-251.

Eliot, T. S. (1943) *Four Quartets:* Burnt Norton. New York: Harcourt, Brace & World.

Etchegoyen, R. (1991) *The Fundamentals of Psychoanalytic Technique.* London: Karnac Books.

Faimberg, H. (1997) Misunderstanding and psychic truths. *Internat. J. Psycho-Anal.,* 78:439-451.

Fairbairn, R. (1952) *Psychoanalytic Studies of the Personality.* London: Routledge, 1981.

Feldman, M. (1993) Aspects of reality and the focus of interpretation. *Internat. J. Psycho-Anal.,* 74: 274-295.

Fishman, G. (1998) Love in the afternoon revisited: When should a therapist profess her love—or ever? Paper presented to the Div. 39, American Psychological Association Meetings, April, Boston, MA.

Freud, A. (1936) The role of regression in mental development. In: *The Writings of Anna Freud, Vol. 2.* New York: International Universities Press.

———— (1965) *Normality and Pathology in Childhood. Writings, 6.* New York: International Universities Press.

Freud, S. (1900) The interpretation of dreams. *Standard Edition,* 4 & 5. London: Hogarth Press, 1953.

———— (1905a) Three essays on the theory of sexuality. *Standard Edition,* 7:130-243. London: Hogarth Press, 1953.

———— (1905b) On psychotherapy. *Standard Edition,* 7:257-271. London: Hogarth Press, 1953.

———— (1908) Creative writers and day-dreaming. *Standard Edition,* 9:142-153. London: Hogarth Press, 1959.

———— (1909) Letter to Jung, June. In: *The Freud/Jung Letters: The Correspondence Between Sigmund Freud and C. G. Jung,* ed. W. McGuire. Princeton, NJ: Princeton University Press, 1975.

———— (1910) "Wild" psycho-analysis. *Standard Edition,* 11:221-233. London: Hogarth Press, 1957.

———— (1912a) The dynamics of transference. *Standard Edition,* 12:99-108. London: Hogarth Press, 1958.

———— (1912b) Recommendations to physicians practising psychoanalysis. *Standard Edition,* 12:109-120. London: Hogarth Press, 1958.

———— (1914) Remembering, repeating, and working through. *Standard Edition,* 12:145-156. London: Hogarth Press, 1958.

———— (1915) Letter to Ferenczi, August. In: *Metapsychologie et Metabiology,* by I. Grubrich-Simitis. Paris: Gallimard, 1985.

———— (1924) The dissolution of the Oedipus complex. *Standard Edition,* 19:171-179. London: Hogarth Press, 1961.

———— (1927a) The future of an illusion. *Standard Edition,* 21:3-56. London: Hogarth Press, 1961.

———— (1927b) The question of lay analysis. *Standard Edition*, 20:183-199. London: Hogarth Press, 1959.

———— (1937) Analysis terminable and interminable. *Standard Edition*, 23:216-253. London: Hogarth Press, 1964.

Friedman, L. (1988) *The Anatomy of Psychotherapy.* Hillsdale, NJ: The Analytic Press.

———— (1995) Psychic reality in psychoanalytic theory. *Internat. J. Psycho-Anal.,* 76:25-28.

Gabbard, G. (1994) Commentary on papers by Tansey, Davies, and Hirsch. *Psychoanal. Dial.,* 4:203-313.

———— (1995) Countertransference: The emerging common ground. *Internat. J. Psycho-Anal.,* 76:475-486.

———— (1996) On love and lust in erotic transference. *J. Amer. Psychoanal. Assn.,* 42:385-403.

———— (1997) Response to Evelyn Schwaber. *Internat. J. Psycho-Anal.,* 78:1221-1222.

———— (1998) Commentary on paper by Jodie Messler Davies. *Psychoanal. Dial.,* 8:781-790.

Gadamer, H. (1976) *Philosophical Hermeneutics.* Berkeley: University of California Press.

Gardner, R. (1994) Is that a fact? Empiricism revisited, or a psychoanalyst at sea. *Internat. J. Psycho-Anal.,* 75:927-938.

Gerson, S. (1996) Neutrality, resistance, and self-disclosure in an intersubjective psychoanalysis. *Psychoanal. Dial.,* 6:623-645.

Ghent, E. (1992) Paradox and process. *Psychoanal. Dial.,* 2:135-160.

Gill, M. (1954) Psychoanalysis and exploratory psychotherapy. *J. Amer. Psychoanal. Assn.,* 2:771-797.

———— (1979) The analysis of transference. *J. Amer. Psychoanal. Assn.,* 27:263-288.

———— (1982) *The Analysis of Transference, Vol. 1.* New York: International Universities Press.

———— (1983) The distinction between the interpersonal paradigm and the degree of the therapist's involvement. *Contemp. Psychoanal.,* 19:200-237.

———— (1994a) *Psychoanalysis in Transition.* Hillsdale, NJ: The Analytic Press.

———— (1994b) Discussion of paper by T. McLaughlin. Meeting of the American Psychoanalytic Association, New York.

———— & Hoffman, I. (1982) *Analysis of Transference, Vol. 2.* New York: International Universities Press.

———— & Muslin, H. (1976), Early interpretation of transference. *J. Amer. Psychoanal. Assn.,* 24:779-797.

Goethe, J. *Faust,* trans S. Kaufman. New York: Anchor Books, 1954.

Gray, P. (1973) Psychoanalytic technique: The ego's capacity to view intrapsychic activity. *J. Amer. Psychoanal. Assn.,* 21:474-492.

———— (1990) The nature of therapeutic action in psychoanalysis. *J. Amer. Psychoanal. Assn.,* 38:1083-1099.

———— (1994) *The Ego and the Analysis of Defense.* Northvale, NJ: Aronson.

Greenberg, J. (1986) Theoretical models and the analyst's neutrality. *Contemp. Psychoanal.,* 6:87-106.

———— (1995) Psychoanalytic technique and the interactive matrix. *Psychoanal. Quart.,* 64:1-22.

———— & Mitchell, S. (1983) *Object Relations in Psychoanalytic Theory.* Cambridge, MA: Harvard University Press.

Guntrip, H. (1969) *Schizoid Phenomena, Object Relations, and the Self.* New York: International Universities Press.

———— (1971) *Psychoanalytic Theory, Therapy, and the Self.* New York: Basic Books.

Heidegger, M. (1927) *Sein und Zeit (Being and Time),* trans. J. Macquarrie & E. Robinson. New York: Harper & Row, 1962.

Heilbroner, R. (1995) *Visions of the Future: The Distant Past, Yesterday, Today, Tomorrow.* New York: Oxford University Press.

Herzog, J. (in press) *Father Hunger: Developmental and Clinical Perspectives.* Hillsdale, NJ: The Analytic Press.

Hirsch, I. (1994) Countertransference love and theoretical models. *Psychoanal. Dial.,* 4:171-192.

Hoffman, I. (1983) The patient as interpreter of the analyst's experience. *Contemp. Psychoanal.,* 19:389-422.

———— (1991) Discussion: Toward a social-constructivist view of the psychoanalytic situation. *Psychoanal. Dial.,* 1:74-105.

———— (1992) Some practical implications of a social constructivist view of the psychoanalytic situation. *Psychoanal. Dial.,* 2:287-304.

———— (1994a) Dialectical thinking and therapeutic action in the psychoanalytic process. *Psychoanal. Quart.,* 63:187-218.

——— (1994b) Discussion of paper by T. McLaughlin. Meeting of the American Psychoanalytic Association, New York.

——— (1996) The intimate and ironic authority of the analyst's presence. *Psychoanal. Quart.,* 65:102-136.

——— (1998a) *Ritual and Spontaneity in the Psychoanalytic Process: A Dialectical-Constructivist View.* Hillsdale, NJ: The Analytic Press.

——— (1998b) Poetic transformations of erotic experiences. Commentary on paper by Jodie Messler Davies. *Psychoanal. Dial.,* 8:791-804.

Inderbitzen, L. & Levy, S. (1994) On grist for the mill: External reality as defense. *J. Amer. Psychoanal. Assn.,* 42:763-788.

Jacobi, R. (1983) *The Repression of Psychoanalysis.* New York: Basic Books.

Jacobs, T. (1995) Discussion of Jay Greenberg's paper. *Contemp. Psychoanal.,* 31:237-245.

James, H. (1875) *Roderick Hudson.* New York: Penguin Books, 1969.

Kernberg, O. (1965) Notes on countertransference. *J. Amer. Psychoanal. Assn.,* 13:38-56.

——— (1975) *Borderline Conditions and Pathological Narcissism.* New York: Aronson.

——— (1993) Convergences and divergences in contemporary psychoanalytic technique. *Internat. J. Psycho-Anal.,* 74:659-673.

Kierkegaard, S. (1983) *Fear and Trembling: Repetition.* Princeton: Princeton University Press.

Klein, M. (1946) Notes on some schizoid mechanisms. In *Envy and Gratitude and Other Works, 1946-1960.* London: Hogarth Press, 1975, pp. 1-34.

Kohut, H. (1971) *The Analysis of the Self.* New York: International Universities Press.

——— (1977) *The Restoration of the Self.* New York: International Universities Press.

——— (1979) The two analyses of Mr. Z. *Internat. J. Psycho-Anal.,* 60:3-23.

——— (1984) *How Does Analysis Cure?* ed. A. Goldberg & P. Stepansky. Chicago: University of Chicago Press.

Kris, A. (1982) *Free Association.* New Haven, CT: Yale University Press. (Rev. ed.: Hillsdale, NJ: The Analytic Press, 1996.)

——— (1983) Determinants of free association in narcissistic phenomena. *The Psychoanalytic Study of the Child,* 38:439-458. New Haven, CT: Yale University Press.

——— (1990) Helping patients by analyzing self-criticism. *J. Amer. Psychoanal. Assn.,* 38:605-636.

Lacan, J. (1959) *The Ethics of Psychoanalysis: The Seminar of Jacques Lacan,* ed. J.-A. Miller. New York: Norton.

Levenson, E. (1990) Reply to Hoffman. *Contemp. Psychoanal.,* 26:299-304.

——— (1993) Shoot the messenger: Interpersonal aspects of the analyst's interpretations. *Contemp. Psychoanal.,* 29:383-396.

Levi, P. (1995) *Survival in Auschwitz: The Nazi Assault on Humanity,* trans. S. Woolf. New York: Collier.

Lipton, S. (1977) Clinical observations on resistance to the transference. *Internat. J. Psycho-Anal.,* 58:463-472.

Loewald, H. (1960) On the therapeutic action of psychoanalysis. *Internat. J. Psycho-Anal.,* 41:16-33.

——— (1965) Some considerations on repetition and repetition compulsion. In: *Papers on Psycho-Analysis.* New Haven, CT: Yale University Press, 1980.

——— (1971) On motivation and instinct theory. *The Psychoanalytic Study of the Child,* 26:91-128. New Haven, CT: Yale University Press.

——— (1972) Perspectives on memory. In: *Papers on Psycho-Analysis.* New Haven, CT: Yale University Press, 1980.

——— (1978) Primary process, secondary process, and language. In: *Papers on Psycho-Analysis.* New Haven, CT: Yale University Press, 1980.

——— (1988) *Sublimation.* New Haven, CT: Yale University Press.

Mann, T. (1956) Freud and the future. *Internat. J. Psycho-Anal.,* 37: 106-115. Also in E. Jones, *The Life and Work of Sigmund Freud.* New York: Basic Books, 1953.

Maroda, K. (1991) *The Power of Countertransference.* Chichester, NY: Wiley.

McGuire, W. (1975) *The Freud/Jung Letters: The Correspondence Between Sigmund Freud and C. G. Jung.* Princeton: Princeton University Press.

McLaughlin, T. (1994) The dialectic of influence in the analytic dyad.

Panel: Modes of Influence in Psychoanalysis, American Psychoanalytic Association Meetings, New York City.

Merleau-Ponty, M. (1964) *Sense and Nonsense.* Evanston, IL: Northwestern University Press.

Meyerson, P. (1981) The nature of the transactions that occur in other than classical analysis. *Internat. Rev. Psycho-Anal.,* 8:173-190.

Mitchell, S. (1988) *Relational Concepts in Psychoanalysis.* Cambridge, MA: Harvard University Press.

——— (1991) Wishes, needs and interpersonal negotiations. *Psychoanal. Inq.* 11:147-170.

——— (1992) Discussion of Trop and Stolorow. *Psychoanal. Dial.,* 2:448-454.

——— (1993) *Hope and Dread in Psychoanalysis.* New York: Basic Books.

——— (1994) Something old, something new. Response to S. Stern's "Needed relationships and repeated relationships." *Psychoanal. Dial.,* 4:363-370.

——— (1995) Interaction in the Kleinian and Interpersonal traditions. *Contemp. Psychoanal.,* 31:65-91.

——— (1997) *Influence and Autonomy in Psychoanalysis.* Hillsdale, NJ: The Analytic Press.

Modell, A. (1975) The narcissistic defense against affects and the illusion of self-sufficiency. *Internat. J. Psycho-Anal.,* 56:275-289.

——— (1976) The holding environment and the therapeutic action of psychoanalysis. *J. Amer. Psychoanal. Assn.,* 24:285-307.

——— (1984) *Psychoanalysis in a New Context.* New York: International Universities Press.

——— (1991) The therapeutic relationship as a paradoxical experience. *Psychoanal. Dial.,* 1:13-28.

Nasio, J. (1997) *Hysteria: The Splendid Child of Psychoanalysis.* Northvale: NJ: Aronson.

O'Connell, M. (1996) On wanting the patient to change: Countertransference responsivity and developmental help. Insistence in the analyst. Deutsch Prize Paper presented to the Boston Psychoanalytic Society and Institute, March.

_____(in press) Subjective reality, objective reality, modes of relatedness and therapeutic action. *Psychoanal. Quart.*

Ogden, T. (1986) *The Matrix of the Mind.* Northvale NJ: Aronson.

——— (1989) *The Primitive Edge of Experience.* Northvale, NJ: Aronson.

——— (1994) *Subjects of Analysis.* Northvale, NJ: Aronson.

——— (1996) Reconsidering three aspects of psychoanalytic technique. *Internat. J. Psycho-Anal.,* 77:883-899.

——— (1997) Reverie and metaphor. *Internat. J. Psycho-Anal.,* 78: 719-732.

O'Neill, E. (1956) *Long Day's Journey Into Night.* New Haven, CT: Yale University Press.

Ornstein, A. (1995) The fate of the curative fantasy in psychoanalysis. *Contemp. Psychoanal.,* 31:113-123.

——— & Ornstein, P. (1994) On the conceptualization of clinical facts in psychoanalysis. *Internat. J. Psycho-Anal.,* 75:977-994.

Peppiat, G. (1997) Review of Jackson Pollock Show. *New York Review of Books,* March 3.

Phillips, A. (1993) *On Kissing, Tickling and Being Bored.* Cambridge, MA: Harvard University Press.

Piaget, J. (1932) *The Language and Thought of the Child.* New York: Meridian, 1955.

——— (1969) *The Psychology of the Child.* New York: Basic Books.

Pizer, B. (2000) Negotiating analytic holding: Discussion of Patrick Casement's "Learning from the Patient." *Psychoanal. Inq.,* 20:82-107.

Pizer, S. (1992) The negotiation of paradox in the analytic process. *Psychoanal. Dial.,* 2:215-240.

——— (1998) *Building Bridges: The Negotiation of Paradox in Psychoanalysis.* Hillsdale, NJ: The Analytic Press.

Pope, A. (1734) *An Essay on Man and Other Poems.* New York: Dover, 1994.

Quinodoz, J.-M. (1993) *The Taming of Solitude: Separation Anxiety in Psychoanalysis.* New York: Routledge.

——— (1996) The sense of solitude in the psychoanalytic encounter. *Internat. J. Psycho-Anal.,* 77:481-496.

Racker, H. (1968) *Transference and Countertransference.* New York: International Universities Press.

Reik, T. (1928) *Das Schweigen* [*The Silence*]. Almanach, Internationaler Psychoanalystischer Verlag.

Renik, O. (1993) Analytic interaction: Conceptualizing technique in light of the analyst's irreducible subjectivity. *Psychoanal. Quart.,* 62:466-495.

———— (1995) The ideal of the anonymous analyst and the problem of self-disclosure. *Psychoanal. Quart.,* 64:466-495.

———— (1996) The perils of neutrality. *Psychoanal. Quart.,* 65:495-517.

———— (1998) Getting real in psychoanalysis. *Psychoanal. Quart.,* 67:566-593.

Richards, A. (1992) Commentary on Trop and Stolorow's "Defense analysis in self psychology." *Psychoanal. Dial.,* 2:455-465.

Ricoeur, P. (1977) *The Rule of Metaphor.* Toronto: Toronto University Press.

Rilke, R. (1907) The Archaic Torso of Apollo. In: *Ahead of All Parting: The Selected Poetry and Prose of Rainer Maria Rilke,* ed. S. Mitchell. New York: Modern Library, 1995.

———— (1922) Uncollected Poems. In: *Ahead of All Parting: The Selected Poetry and Prose of Rainer Maria Rilke,* ed. S. Mitchell. New York: Modern Library, 1995.

———— (1929) Letters to a Young Poet. In: *Ahead of All Parting: The Selected Poetry and Prose of Rainer Maria Rilke,* ed. S. Mitchell. New York: Modern Library, 1995.

Roth, S. (1987) *Psychotherapy: The Art of Wooing Nature.* New York: Aronson.

Rothstein, A. (1979) Oedipal conflicts in narcissistic personality disorders. *Internat. J. Psycho-Anal.,* 60:189-198.

Rubovits-Seitz, P. (1994) The fallibility of interpretation. Letter to the editor in response to S. Cooper's paper, "Interpretive fallibility and the psychoanalytic dialogue." *J. Amer. Psychoanal. Assn.,* 42:1310-1312.

Russell, P. (1973) Crises of emotional growth (a.k.a. the theory of the crunch). Unpublished manuscript.

———— (1985) The structure and function of paradox in the treatment process. Unpublished.

Sandler, J. (1976) Countertransference and role-responsiveness. *Internat. Rev. Psycho-Anal.,* 3:43-50.

———— (1993) On communication from patient to analyst: Not everything is projective identification. *Internat. J. Psycho-Anal.,* 74:1097-1107.

———— & Sandler, A. (1984) The past unconscious, the present unconscious, and interpretation of the transference. *Psychoanal. Inq.*, 4:367-399.

———— & ———— (1994a) Comments on the conceptualization of clinical facts in psychoanalysis. *Internat. J. Psycho-Anal.*, 75:995-1010.

———— & ———— (1994b) Theoretical and technical comments on regression and anti-regression. *Internat. J. Psycho-Anal.*, 75:431-439.

Schafer, R. (1968) The mechanisms of defense. *Internat. J. Psycho-Anal.*, 49:49-62.

———— (1983) *The Analytic Attitude*. New York: Basic Books.

———— (1992) *Retelling a Life: Narration and Dialogue in Psychoanalysis*. New York: Basic Books.

Schimek, J. (1975) A critical re-examination of Freud's concept of unconscious mental representation. *Internat. Rev. Psycho-Anal.*, 2:171-187.

Schlesinger, H. (1997) The function of regression in the clinical situation: Is regression necessary, and if so, what should we do about it? Panel, American Psychoanalytic Association: "Regression: Necessary or Iatrogenic Phenomenon?"

Schwaber, E. (1983) Psychoanalytic listening and psychic reality. *Internat. Rev. Psycho-Anal.*, 10:379-392.

———— (1990) Interpretation and the therapeutic action of psychoanalysis. *Internat. J. Psycho-Anal.*, 71:229-240.

———— (1992) The analyst's retreat from the patient's vantage point. *Internat. J. Psycho-Anal.*, 73:349-361.

———— (1995) A particular perspective on impasses in the clinical situation: Further reflections on psychoanalytic listening. *Internat. J. Psycho-Anal.*, 76:711-722.

———— (1997) Response to Glen Gabbard. *Internat. J. Psycho-Anal.*, 78:1222.

———— (1998) The non-verbal dimension in psychoanalysis: "State" and its clinical vicissitudes. *Internat. J. Psycho-Anal.*, 79:667-680.

Slavin, M. & Kriegman, D. (1992) *The Adaptive Design of the Human Psyche*. New York: Guilford Press.

———— & ———— (1998) Why the analyst needs to change: Toward a theory of conflict, negotiation, and mutual influence in the therapeutic process. *Psychoanal. Dial.*, 8:247-284.

Slochower, J. (1994) The evolution of object usage and the holding environment. *Contemp. Psychoanal.*, 30:130-151.

——— (1996a) The holding environment and the fate of the analyst's subjectivity. *Psychoanal. Dial.*, 6:323-353.

——— (1996b) *Holding and Psychoanalysis.* Hillsdale, NJ: The Analytic Press.

Spence, D. (1982) *Narrative Truth and Historical Truth: Meaning and Interpretation in Psychoanalysis.* New York: Norton.

Spillius, E. (1999) Conflict between the patient's and analyst's goals. Lecture to the Boston Psychoanalytic Society and Institute, October.

Steiner, J. (1993) *Psychic Retreats.* London: Routledge.

——— (1996) Revenge and resentment in the "Oedipus situation." *Internat. J. Psycho-Anal.*, 77:433-443.

Stern, D. B. (1983) Unformulated experience. *Contemp. Psychoanal.*, 19:71-99.

——— (1985) Some controversies regarding constructivism and psychoanalysis. *Contemp. Psychoanal.*, 21:201-208.

——— (1990) Courting surprise: Unbidden perceptions in clinical practice. *Contemp. Psychoanal.*, 23:484-491.

——— (1997) *Unformulated Experience: From Dissociation to Imagination in Psychoanalysis.* Hillsdale, NJ: The Analytic Press.

Stern, D. N. (1985) *The Interpersonal World of the Infant.* New York: Basic Books.

——— Sander, L., Nahum, J., Harrison, A., Lyons-Ruth, K., Morgan, A., Bruschweiler-Stern, N. & Tronick, E. (1998) Non-interpretive mechanisms in psychoanalytic therapy. *Internat. J. Psycho-Anal.*, 79:903-921.

Stern, S. (1994) Needed relationships and repeated relationships: An integrated relational perspective. *Psychoanal. Dial.*, 4:317-346.

Stevens, W. (1954) *The Collected Poems.* New York: Vintage Books.

Stolorow, R. & Lachmann, F. (1980) *Psychoanalysis of Developmental Arrest: Theory and Treatment.* New York: International Universities Press.

Stone, L. (1961) *The Psychoanalytic Situation: An Examination of Its Development and Essential Nature.* New York: International Universities Press.

——— (1979) Remarks on certain unique conditions of human aggression. *J. Amer. Psychoanal. Assn.*, 27:27-64.

Strachey, J. (1934) The nature of the therapeutic action of psycho-analysis. *Internat. J. Psycho-Anal.,* 50:275-292, 1969.

Strenger, C. (1989) The classic and romantic vision in psychoanalysis. *Internat. J. Psycho-Anal.,* 70:593-602.

Tansey, M. (1994) Sexual attraction and phobic dread in the counter-transference. *Psychoanal. Dial.,* 4:139-152.

———— & Burke, W. (1989) *Understanding Countertransference: From Projective Identification to Empathy.* Hillsdale, NJ: The Analytic Press.

Thoreau, H. *Elevating Ourselves.* Boston: Houghton Mifflin, 1999.

Ticho, G. (1972) Termination of psychoanalysis: Treatment goals and life goals. *Psychoanal. Quart.,* 41:315-333.

Trop, J. & Stolorow, R. (1992) Defense analysis in self psychology. *Psychoanal. Dial.,* 2:427-442.

Tuckett, D. (1993) Some thoughts on the presentation and discussion of the clinical material of psychoanalysis. *Internat. J. Psycho-Anal.,* 74:1175-1189.

Valenstein, A. (1973) On attachment to painful feelings. *The Psychoanalytic Study of the Child,* 28:365-394. New Haven, CT: Yale University Press.

Wallerstein, R. (1986) *Forty-Two Lives in Treatment: Psychoanalysis and Psychotherapy.* New York: Guilford Press.

Wells, H. G. (1933) *The Shape of Things to Come.* New York: Harper & Row.

Winnicott, D. W. (1951) Transitional objects and transitional phenomena. In: *Collected Papers.* New York: Basic Books, 1958, pp. 229-242.

———— (1958) The capacity to be alone. In: *The Maturational Processes and the Facilitating Environment.* New York: International Universities Press, 1965.

———— (1960) Ego distortion in terms of true and false self. In: *The Maturational Processes and the Facilitating Environment.* New York: International Universities Press, 1965.

———— (1963) Communicating and not communicating leading to a study of certain opposites. In: *The Maturational Processes and the Facilitating Environment.* New York: International Universities Press, 1965.

———— (1969) The use of an object and relating through identifications. In: *Playing and Reality.* New York: Basic Books, 1971.

———— (1971) *Playing and Reality.* New York: Basic Books.

Wittgenstein, L. (1958) *The Brown and Blue Books.* London: Basil Blackwell.

Wrye, H. (1989) The maternal erotic transference. *Internat. J. Psycho-Anal.,* 16:673-685.

———— (1997) The embodiment of desire: Relinking the bodymind within the analytic dyad. New York Memorial Lecture, January.

INDEX

A

abstinence, 58
adaptive functioning, emphasis on, 235–236
Adler, E., 44, 46, 51, 53, 55, 70, 249, 273
Adler, G., 29
affective experience, 21
Akhtar, S., 16
Allen, case of, 105–108, 114, 197, 204–213
aloneness, 48–49, 55, 57, 93. *See also* solitude
Alvarez, A., 226
ambiguity. *See also* uncertainty and ambiguity *vs.* anonymity, 182
Amos, M., 266
Amy, case of, 230–233
analyst-as-a-subjective-object, 176
analyst disclosure, 66–69, 175. *See also* countertransference disclosure; countertransference expressiveness; "virtual disclosure"
aims/goals, 199
analyst's subjectivity in, 67, 76–77
asymmetry, mutuality, and, 79, 93, 175–178
and construction of psychic possibility, 200–204
conveying thoughts and feelings about potential for change, 201
as differentiating analyst from old object, 85, 93
and new/old object continuum, 93–94
newness and, 76–77
used to reveal analyst as safe or dangerous object, 94
analyst(s). *See also specific topics*
as detective, 280–282
encouraging patient, 115
expectations about treatment, 1–2
fear of "interfering," 30
feelings of hopelessness, 29
female *vs.* male, 242
holding hopes and wishes different from patient, 43
linearity in thinking of, 202
as magical healer, 159
as "mother of separation," 242, 249
need to cure as defense against sadistic impulses, 154–155
as new object, 21
as the "other," 203
passivity, 30, 244
patient's choice of, 238

personality and limitations of, 100–101, 103
patient's awareness of, 100, 101, 110–111. See also patient's perception, of analyst
patient's coping with, 108
reasons for practicing analysis and becoming an, 26, 155
as repository of hope, 199
role, 26–27, 43
expressiveness vs. containment, 42
seductiveness, 139. See also Molly, case of
subjectivity, 85. See also specific topics
patient's experience of, 199, 202–203, 214
as superior to patient, 156–157
as symbol/icon of possibility, 21, 199, 266
view of patient's future, 26–27
viewing patient's potential for change as "necessary illusion," 23, 25
willingness to risk being known, 195
with vs. without memory and desire, 2, 273, 274
analytic "attitude," 26, 30, 33, 227
vs. transference authority, 27
analytic interventions, analyst's intentions regarding, 79
analytic nudging, 224
analytic tick-tock and, 254–259
analytic process, romantic and tragic parts of, 229
analytic relationship. See also specific topics
egalitarian atmosphere in, 46, 65
analytic stance, 228
Analyze This, 26

anonymity, analytic, 79, 182, 279. See also blank screen
vs. ambiguity, 182
ideal of, 72
"antiregressive" dimensions within transference and countertransference, mutual, 125
antiregressive phenomena, 125, 253
Aron, L., 16, 25, 30, 44, 55, 67, 70, 77, 79, 100, 125, 132, 152, 154, 157, 176–177, 181, 193, 194, 199, 214, 256, 279–280
asymmetrical relationships, 33
asymmetry
of analytic relationship, 33, 65, 66, 213
analyst disclosure, mutuality, and, 79, 93, 175–178
ritual, 199
attachment(s)
to bad and old objects, 79
painful tendency to hold onto, 80
threatening an old, 201
authentic participation, 228
authenticity, analytic, 68–70, 195
authority of analyst, 72, 156, 157, 199
vs. countertransference expressiveness, 69
and self-disclosure, 175–176
used to overcome resistance, 174

B

Bachant, J., 44, 46, 51, 53, 55, 70, 249, 273
bad and old objects, attachment to, 79
Bader, M., 250, 252
Balint, M., ix, 25, 72, 135, 168, 250, 282, 288
Balsam, R., 129
Becker, E., 226
Beebe, B., 48, 176

Bellah, R., 12
Benjamin, J., xix, 18, 59, 71, 79, 116,
   176, 197, 203, 215, 216, 275,
   279
Bion, W. R., viii, 2, 15, 25, 49, 55,
   57, 93, 108, 113, 154, 168, 265,
   269, 274
Bird, B., 113, 131, 278
blank screen, 243. *See also* anonymity
   and "generic analyst," 116
bodily states and experience
   of analyst, 241–242
   of patient, 52–53, 241
Bollas, C., 43, 126, 153, 176, 280,
   285, 288
borderline patients, 60
boundary, 225
boundary violations, 71, 72
Bowie, M., 14, 15–16, 19, 33
Brenner, C., 283
Britton, R., 25, 168, 269, 289
Bromberg, P. M., viii, xxi, 9, 25, 37,
   59, 63, 64, 104, 127, 128,
   135–137, 197, 202, 203, 213,
   225, 256
Brunschwig, J., 262
Bruschweiler-Stern, N., 244, 263
Buber, M., 117
Burke, W., 16, 46, 75, 79, 81, 93,
   102, 157, 174, 177, 178, 180,
   206
Busch, F., xxi, 29, 51, 129, 152, 221,
   227, 235–240, 256
Bushra, A., 55, 125, 132
Byrne, D., 263

C

Caper, R., 29, 55, 57, 108, 159, 221,
   267
Casement, P., 81, 83, 288
Ceccoli, V., 244
Celenza, A., 72

change (in patient), 23. *See also* future; possibility
   analyst's investment in, 158
   analyst's view of how patient might,
      157–158
   recognizing, 17
   wish for possibility of, 16–17
Chasseguet-Smirgel, J., 64
Chodorow, N. J., 154, 211
classic *vs.* romantic/developmental traditions, 41–42, 220
Coen, S., 55, 149
Columbo, Lieutenant (*Columbo*),
   281–282
confrontation, avoiding, 255
constructivism. *See also* social constructivism
   and new/old object continuum, 78,
      80–93
"contacting other minds," 216
containment, 17, 99–100, 102, 117,
   167. *See also* holding
   of affects
      American relational *vs.* British
         stance regarding, 38–39
   mutual, 100, 103–109
   and experience of time in ana-
      lytic process, 113–117
Cooper, A., xvi, 21, 158, 243, 271,
   273, 275, 282, 288
Cooper, S., 15, 18, 24, 33, 66, 71,
   77, 85, 91, 101, 115, 135, 153,
   167, 175, 177, 182, 199, 201,
   221, 246, 251, 255, 262, 267,
   268, 283, 286, 288
corrective experience, 81
counterresistance. *See* resistance, mutually held
countertransference, 174–175. *See also*
   erotic transference-countertransference; identification; transference-countertransference; *specific*
   topics

as retreat from patient's experience, 178, 181
totalist *vs.* minimalist (approach to), 174, 178, 180, 190
unobjectionable positive, 228, 246, 286
use in interpretative process, 178–183
vs. countertransference disclosure, 208
ego-psychological perspective on, 186–195
countertransference disclosure
to convey psychic possibility, 174
defensive functions served by, 182, 192–194
defined, 174
heroic use, 174
vs. using countertransference to inform interpretation, 208
countertransference expressiveness, 38, 44–45, 214
analyst's authority *vs.*, 69
in contemporary Kleinian analysis, 61
fallacy of intimacy in, 66–74
judicious/conservative use of, 179, 181
and patient's disavowed experience, 63–64
purpose, 67
vs. restraint, 179
of self-perceptions, 72
symbolic meaning, 56–57
when analyst's experience is at odds with patient's, 173–174, 187–190
countertransference interventions, "wildness" of, 182–183
"courting (of) surprise," 215, 265
"crunch," therapeutic, 106–108, 114, 117

cure
magical/omnipotent fantasies of, 12, 29, 213, 221–222
overriding need to, 158

D

Darwin, J., 252, 269
Davies, J. M., xx, 34, 71, 102, 112, 147–149, 252
deadness, feeling of, 228
death, denial of, 116, 226
defense analysis, 283
problems with focusing on, 239–240
defense interpretations, 236, 238, 240, 277, 284
avoiding, 235
new constructs as, 201
that interfere with regression, 133–134
defense(s), 138
conceptions of, 263–264, 277, 283, 284
Kohut's, 15, 17, 213, 220, 235, 283–284
ego, 251
organized around id impulse *vs.* object failure, 198
deficits, developmental. *See also* "developmental tilt" models
patients with, 239–240
Derrida, J., 43
despair, 10, 19–20
destruction
analyst's ability to survive patient's, 38, 60–62
and psychic determinism, 11
developmental atmosphere, 132, 134, 135
developmental metaphor, xiv, 127, 134, 135–136, 242, 244, 245, 248

"developmental tilt" models, 78, 95, 127, 131–132, 234, 243–245, 256, 266, 277
"dialectics of difference," 153
Diebenkorn, R., 45–46
disavowed affects, 38
"discovering another," 216
disruptions, 103. *See also* empathic failures
divergent conflict, 104, 230
Donald, case of, 86–88, 92, 96
double agent (defense), 143
dreams, 13

E

Eagle, M. N., 20
Edmundson, M., 13
ego psychological approach. *See also* Gray, approach of
applied to case material, 186–195
ego psychology, 198, 251
contemporary, 234–236
integrating "the neighborhood," 236–238
Ehrenberg, D. B., 29, 174, 195
Einstein, A., ix, xi, 11
Ekstein, R., 128
Elliot, T. S., 27, 274
empathic failures, 15, 94, 95
empathic object, 15
historically encapsulated template for, 213
empathic selfobjects, hoped-for, 220
enactments, 81, 83, 88, 159. *See also* *specific topics*
patient's becoming aware of analyst's personality during, 100–101
Eno, B., 263
Eric, case of, 183–189
erotic transference-countertransfer-ence, 83, 139, 148, 248. *See also* Molly, case of
containment of desire in, 111–113
Etchegoyen, R., 176
"expectant intrusions," 25
experience-near approach, 235
externality, capacity for, 203

F

Faimberg, H., 29, 271
Fairbairn, W. R. D., 10, 11, 37, 38, 47, 59, 78, 80, 82, 84, 88, 92, 95, 97, 255
faith, 12
familiarity *vs.* unfamiliarity, 267–268
Fishman, G., 252
Flax, J., 241
For Hans Carossa (Rilke), 49
free association, 268–269
defensive use of, 37, 59
vs. free emergence of multiple transference-countertransfer-ence scenarios, 122
as technical rule, 32, 50–51, 53
and tensions between intimacy and solitude, 50–54
Freud, A., 127, 128
Freud, S., ix, 7, 10, 11, 13–16, 19–20, 34, 39, 58, 88, 97, 154–155, 180, 201, 226, 236, 237, 255, 266, 268, 271, 273, 274, 286
rationalism, 14
on theory, 268–269
friction in relationships, 258
Friday, Sergeant (*Dragnet*), 280–281
Friedman, L., 23, 25, 73, 263, 267
future object and self, 94–98
future (psychic), 27, 114, 135, 152. *See also* change; interpretative stance of analyst; possibility

analyst's view of, 26–27, 151,
153–157
transformation in, 28
anticipating/forecasting, 13, 76
broadening patient's view of, 28
Freud's view of, 13–16
vs. Heidegger's view of, 16, 19
holding the, 31, 94–98, 122,
167–169
hope and the, 11, 127. See also
hope(s)
idea of the, 11
"memoir of the future," 15
neutrality, authority, and the,
152–160
reconstructing the, 14–20, 31
future-self-representation, 19

G

Gabbard, G., 71, 83, 148, 173, 277
Gardner, R., 287
gendered subjectivities, 211–212
Gerson, S., 153
Ghent, E., 80, 96, 127, 214–215
"ghosts of recognition," 224
Gill, M. M., vii–viii, 67, 79, 85, 131,
133, 136, 148, 154, 175, 178,
194, 221, 226, 227, 278, 280,
286
good-enough retaliation/impinge-
ment, 104–108
Gray, P., xxi, 29, 51, 127, 129, 152,
170, 174, 178, 179, 250, 256,
273, 288
approach of, 190–192, 234–236,
239, 240, 284
Greenberg, J. R., xvi, xix, 11, 21, 76,
85, 89–90, 95, 121, 153, 158,
159, 199, 201, 247, 256, 285
growth
aspects and components of, 197
vs. repair, 271
Guntrip, H. J. S., 11, 20, 37, 48, 59

H

Harrison, A., 244, 263
hatred. See revenge
Heidegger, M., 16, 19
Heilbroner, R., 16, 34
"hell bent," being, 22–25, 33
Herzog, J., xiv, 248, 256
Hirsch, I., 75
historicity, 130
Hoffman, I. Z., xii, xix, 2, 11, 30, 44,
45, 52–53, 55, 56, 67–69, 90,
91, 101, 116, 121, 122, 154,
156–157, 159, 176–179, 181,
194, 222, 223, 226, 252, 266,
273, 278–279, 282, 285, 286
holding, 17, 167. See also containment
developmental strategies of psychoanalytic, 240–249
patients' lack of capacity for, 103
the psychic future, 31, 94–98, 122,
167–169
holding environment, 29
Holzman, P., 128
hoped-for objects, 115, 116, 243
meaning of, 21–22
patient's preservation of, 18–19,
132, 220
hope(s). See also possibility, and limitation
in analytic dyad, 73, 210–216
mutual influence on, 25
concept of, xiii
defensive use of, xiii
"dismantling" of, 43
and the future, 11. See also future
as imagining, 18
location and relocation of dyadic.
See Jeffrey, case of
moment of, 275
mutual containment of, 21
need and value of holding onto notion of, xiii

overlap and collision between analyst and patient's, 43
pathological, 12
preserving, 17–18
patient's attempts at, 115
and psychoanalytic process, 10–14
psychoanalytic theories and, 12
reasons for psychoanalytic examination of, ix
resistance *vs.*, 8
transformation of, 43
"unillusioned," 14
humor, 111

I

idealization of analyst, 57–58, 90,
101, 157, 159
analyzing *vs.* not analyzing, xii, 90
fostering, 90, 92
identification
complementary, 180, 182
concordant, 68, 182
"if only" pattern, 16
illusions in analytic and nonanalytic
relationships, 91
imagination, 20
Freud on, 19
imaginative sympathy, 197
imagining the real, 16, 25, 117
impingement *vs.* nonimpingement,
246, 277
Inderbitzen, L., 51, 71, 87, 182, 191,
245
indoctrination, 72, 168, 250, 266,
289
infantile neurosis, 16
influence between analyst and patient,
mutual, 18
visual images of, 45–46
influencing patient, 266–267,
278–279. *See also* analytic nudging; indoctrination; suggestion
analyst's fear of, 27

analyst's wishes/need for, 18, 22,
25–26, 28, 30, 170–171, 199,
214, 266, 273, 279
analyst's subjectivity and implications for understanding formulation and the, 286–290
general considerations of formulation and the, 280–286
implicit strategies for avoiding
thinking about, 272–280
interpersonalists, 69
interpretation, 198, 208, 289. *See also*
defense interpretations
aggressive elements, 246
content *vs.* relational impact of, 17
effects and functions, 31–32,
224–225
as embodying and expressing hope,
159
holding and containing functions,
99
vs. providing insight, 17
Loewald's view of, 122–123
surface *vs.* deep/premature,
236–237. *See also* "surface"
using countertransference to inform, 208, 277–278
viewed as magical, 29
interpretative stance of analyst, 170,
171
and patient's psychic future,
159–160, 167, 168
case material, 160–168
"interpretive fallibility" of analyst, 268
intimacy, 43
and solitude, 43–44
in the analytic situation, 41–50
tensions between, 46, 50–54
intimate relationship, sense of isolation within, 58
"intimate separation," 54–55
introspective curiosity, 283
irony, used by patients, 8

isolation within an intimate relationship, sense of, 58

J

Jacobi, R., 14
Jacobs, T. J., 177
Jaffe, J., 176
James, H., viii
Jeffrey, case of, 3–9, 23
Josh, case of, 136–137

K

Kernberg, O. F., 102, 104, 154, 174,
178, 206, 250, 288
Kierkegaard, S., 10
Klein, M., 102, 104
Kleinian analysis, 72, 273–274, 289.
See also specific topics
contemporary, 38, 61
Kohut, H., 18, 131, 132
case of Mr. Z, 206, 220, 240, 275,
277, 283
on defensive functioning, 15, 17,
213, 220, 235, 283–284
Kriegman, D., 20, 216
Kris, A., 51–52, 57, 104, 129, 159,
170, 222–223, 230, 234, 236,
284, 288

L

Lacan, J., 274
Lacanian analysis, 266, 272
Lacanian model and perspective, 66,
264, 272
Lachmann, F. M., 48, 176, 206, 277
Letters to a Young Poet (Rilke), 49
Levenson, E. A., 278
Levi, P., 128
Levin, B., 28
Levit, D., 153, 256
Levy, S., 51, 71, 87, 182, 191
liberation, Freudian view of hope and,
13

Lipton, S., 188
Loewald, H. W., xvi, 11, 21, 24, 27,
31, 76, 116, 122, 127, 130, 151,
155–156, 167, 224–225, 256,
273
logic of hope, 30
types in psychoanalysis, 12
Long Day's Journey into Night
(O'Neill), 10
love
in analytic relationship, 147–149
need to express, 147
Lyons-Ruth, K., 244, 263

M

Mann, T., 11
Maroda, K. J., 174
McLaughlin, J. T., 285, 288
Merleau-Ponty, M., 47
metaphor building, 263
Meyerson, P., 137
mirroring, 244–245
"missing concept," 271
Mitchell, S. A., xviii, xix, xxi, xxiv, 7,
11, 15, 19, 30, 42–44, 53,
56–57, 64, 65, 69–70, 73, 75,
76, 78, 81, 95, 99–100,
105–106, 116, 117, 121, 127,
131, 134–135, 156, 170, 200,
206, 213, 222, 243, 256, 266,
272, 274, 275, 279, 283, 285
Modell, A. H., 17, 31, 48, 59, 63, 92,
99, 149, 157, 198, 251, 264,
283, 285
Molly, case of, 125, 138–149, 253
Morgan, A., 244, 263
mother, as subject and object, 197,
215, 275, 279
"mother of separation," 54
analyst as, 242, 249
Mulder, Agent (*X-Files*), 282
multiplicity, defensive, 249
Muslin, H., 278, 286

mutuality. *See also specific topics*
  analyst disclosure, asymmetry, and,
   79, 93, 175–178

N

Nahum, J., 244, 263
Nasio, J., 266
negotiation, 7, 202, 250, 279
neutrality, 29, 153, 158, 170, 233,
  273, 274, 278
  conceptions of, 159
  functional, 159, 170
  and mutual sense of solitude, 51
new experience, 31
new object. *See also specific topics*
  origin of concept, 76
new/old object continuum
  analyst disclosure and, 93–94
  constructivism and, 78, 80–93
newness, 76–77
  analyst's obstacles to seeing, 80–88
  meaning, 199
  patient's inner obstacles to seeing,
   88–93

O

object experience with analyst,
  "needed," 81
object external to the transference,
  108
"object mother," 197
"object probing," 80, 214–215
objects of hope
  meaning of, 21
  power of, x
O'Connell, M., 153, 158
Ogden, T. H., 32, 50, 53, 58, 93,
  108, 180, 285
one- *vs.* two-person model, 18
O'Neill, E., 10
Ornstein, A., 21, 107, 213, 285, 287,
  288
Ornstein, P., 21, 285, 287, 288

overvalued ideas of analyst, 2,
  269–270

P

"paradox of recognition"/"paradoxical
  role of recognition," 18, 116,
  203
paradoxes in psychoanalytic treatment, 73–74, 127
past. *See also* repetition
  broadening patient's view of, 28
  changes in analyst and patient's
   view of, 28
  classical theory's excessive focus on,
   34
patient(s)
  as baby and adult, paradox of, 127
  containment of analyst, 100. *See*
   also containment, mutual
  doubting whether analyst can be as
   good as he seems, 88–90
  motivations, 22–24
  taking care of analyst (parent),
   108–109
  vigilance toward analyst, 104
patient's perception
  of analyst, 87, 92, 100, 101,
   110–111, 194
  engaging the, 203
Peppiatt, G., 132
perverse support, 8–9
Phillips, A., 54, 55, 226
Piaget, J., 268
Pizer, B., 110
Pizer, S. A., xxiv, 7, 19, 76, 270, 279
pluralism, defensive, 249
Pope, A., 20
positivism, 268
  Freudian, 250–251, 268
possibility. *See also* change; future
  analyst as symbol/icon of, 21, 199,
   266
  holding, 24

and limitation, 11. *See also* psychoanalytic treatment, limitations
of
conflict/tension between, 1,
158–159, 220, 227. *See also*
Jeffrey, case of
new object and, 96–97
psychic
analyst disclosure and construction of, 200–204
creation/construction of, 73,
198, 200–204
representation(s) of, 199
postmodern critiques of Freudian positivism, 250–251
postmodern era, 263
postoedipal development, 112, 147,
252
postoedipal transference, 34, 252–253
potential space, 70–73, 108, 190,
226–227
"preoedipal" phenomena, 248
projective identification, 102–104
interpretation of, 174, 180
and patient's regarding reinternalization, 102–103
psychic retreat, 34, 59, 60, 101
psychoanalysis, comparative, xi–xii, 58
psychoanalytic theory building,
264–265
psychoanalytic theory(ies). *See also*
specific theories and *specific topics*
Freud on, 268–269
as a logic of hope, 12
as objects of hope for analyst,
266–272
psychological functions of, 29–30
psychoanalytic treatment
beginning, 1
(excessively) long analyses, 158,
223, 227, 234, 239, 250. *See
also* timeless unconscious
goals, 28, 221, 258–259, 283

grandiose estimation of its place in
patient's life, 221
limitations of, 158
difficulty accepting, 227
mourning of, 229
sense of therapeutic modesty
and, 57–58
See also possibility, and limitation
psychotic patients, 60

Q

Quinodoz, J.-M., 55, 58

R

Racker, H., 68, 180, 278
reality, multiple levels of, 285
reconstruction, 15, 30–31
regression, 133–134, 149–150
and antiregression
transference-countertransference
desire and dread and the
problem of, 138–149
controversies related to, 126–138
defensive, 127
differing views of, 126
iatrogenic, 127, 149
importance, 128, 131, 135
inhibiting, 133–134
promoting, 126, 131, 133, 223
in response to interpretation, 31
role, 116
tension between growth and, 130
types, 133
as universal in analysis, 134
regressive moment, 129
regressive phenomena
functions, 129–130
progressive aspects, 128
regressive transference
discouraging, 129
interpreting conflict around emergence of, 128–129

reluctance to interpret avoidant aspects of, 134–135
regrowth strategies, 243
Reik, T., 50
relational models/theory, 15. *See also* *specific topics*
  American, xiv
  and problem of healthy *vs.* defensive pluralism, 249–253
  vs. Kohut/self psychology, 18–19
relationships, "needed," 81
reliving infantile experiences, 225
Renik, O., x, xii, 15, 30, 69, 72, 90, 153, 157, 158, 167, 176–177, 181, 188, 192–194, 202, 207, 214, 225, 278, 279
repetition, 27, 81, 83, 88, 89, 96, 113, 137. *See also* new/old object continuum
  passive/reproductive *vs.* re-creative, 225
repetition compulsion, 154
representational world, 22
repressed material, emergence of. *See also* "return of the repressed positivistic"
  interpersonal context and, 137
resistance. *See also* defense
  analysis of, 64–65
  avoiding, 235
  bypassing, 237, 238
  ego, 236
  helping patients become aware of their, 234–235
  iatrogenic, 248
  meanings, 263
  mutually held, 180–181
restraint, analytic, 30
  vs. countertransference expressiveness, 179
retaliation, good-enough, 104–108, 246
retaliatory anxiety, 102, 104

"return of the repressed positivistic," xii–xiii, 273, 278, 279
revenge. *See also* destruction
  intimacy of, 62–65
  transformation into experiences of sadness and need, 60–65
reverie, 32, 51
Richards, A., 65
Ricoeur, P., 263
Rilke, R., 16, 42, 49–50, 108, 117
ritual aspects of analytic situation, 222
ritual asymmetry, 199
"role induction," 168
role responsiveness, 168
Roth, S., 24
Rothstein, A., 63
Rubovits-Seitz, P., 268
Russell, P., xxiv, 7, 19, 49, 76, 106, 114, 115, 227, 270, 279

S

sadism directed toward analyst, 84
Sam, case of, 163–169
Sander, L., 244, 263
Sandler, A., xxi, 28, 29, 58, 125, 142, 158, 227, 253, 270, 285, 287
Sandler, J., xxi, 27–29, 58, 125, 142, 158, 227, 253, 270, 285, 287
Sarah, case of, 81–84, 96, 160–162, 168
Schafer, R., xii, 18, 30, 65, 130, 143, 222
Schimek, J., 269
schizoid and schizoidal patients, 34, 37–38, 65
"schizoid citadel," 20, 37–38, 48, 59, 60
schizoid phenomena, 47
schizoidal defenses, 59
  active use of interpreting, 64–65
schizoidal dilemma, 47
schizoidal experience, 59

Schlesinger, H., xxi, 113, 127, 128–129
Schwaber, E. A., 29, 85, 153, 154, 178–179, 181, 192, 194, 228, 238, 246, 256, 277, 285, 288
self, innate vigor of the, 275
self-disclosure. See analyst disclosure; countertransference disclosure
self psychology, 43, 285. *See also* "developmental tilt" models; Kohut *vs.* relational theory, 18–19
self-stability, attachment to state of, 213
self-sufficiency, defensive, 63, 64
challenging, 48
selfobjects, 18
hoped-for empathic, 220
separation. *See also* "mother of separation"
"intimate," 54–55
shared realities, 43
Shengold, L., 64
skepticism, 262
Slavin, M., 20, 216
Slochower, J., xx, xxi, 31, 99, 127, 197, 202, 206, 211, 213, 245
Smith, H., 203
social constructivism, 53, 55, 194, 251, 279. *See also* constructivism
solitude, 43, 44
capacity for, 48, 58
developmental context, limits of psychoanalysis, and, 54–58
intimacy of, 49
mutual sense of, 49, 51, 55, 57, 93
respecting and protecting each other's, 49–50, 108
and schizoid phenomena, 59–65
Spence, D. P., 130
Spillius, E. B., 60, 63
spontaneity, 69, 200
vs. expressiveness, 70

Steiner, J., xvii, 25, 37, 38, 59–61, 78, 101, 168, 179, 269, 289
Stern, D. B., 53, 66, 156, 174, 215, 263, 265
Stern, D. N., 48, 79, 244
Stern, S., 75, 81, 132, 206, 210, 213
Stoller, R. J., 83
Stolorow, R. D., 64–65, 206, 235, 277
Stone, L., 54, 55, 242, 249
Strachey, J., xvi, 11, 21, 76, 79, 94, 99, 171, 256, 288
Strenger, C., xviii, 41
suggestion, 17, 171
"surface," 190, 198, 208, 235–237, 284

T

Tansey, M., 75, 81, 102, 174, 178, 180, 206
technique
analyst's wish to influence and theories of, 30
conflated with interest in the unconscious, xiii
termination, suggesting/recommending, 228–229
therapeutic factors and processes, 197. *See also* specific factors and processes
therapeutic impasse, 122, 168, 252
Thomas, case of, 63–64
Ticho, E., 225
time, 27
denial of passage of, 116, 226
Freud's chronometrical approach to, 19
race against, 230–234
timeless unconscious, conspirational, 223–229
timelessness of unconscious, 2, 19, 116

transference, 85. *See also* erotic transference-countertransference; idealization of analyst; regressive transference; repetition
discouraging emerging, 129
historical, 21, 158, 199
and hope, 24
negative, 80, 83–84, 235
sustaining and surviving, 109
positive, 83
postoedipal, 34, 252–253
regressive aspects, 76
as representation of possibility, 24
as resistance *vs.* aid to treatment, 7–8, 255
transference authority, *vs.* analytic "attitude," 27
transference-countertransference, mutual "antiregressive" dimensions within, 125
transference-countertransference desire and dread, and the problem of regression and antiregression, 138–149
transference interpretation, 154
transference love, 148
transitional object, 212, 276
trauma survivors, 239–240, 258
Tronick, E., 244, 263
Trop, J., 64–65, 235

trust of analyst, 92, 97–98
Tuckett, D., 287

U

uncertainty and ambiguity, 215
containing, 114, 115
unformulated experience, 66, 174
"unthought known," 126

V

Valenstein, A., 255
"virtual disclosure," 187, 199, 201, 207, 208
Volkan, V. D., 64

W

Wallerstein, R. S., ix
Winnicott, D. W., xvii, xix, 11, 17, 31, 38, 48, 60, 79, 81, 85, 99, 112, 131, 197, 198, 212, 216, 251, 275–277, 283
wishing, 19
withdrawal
in analysis, 60. *See also* psychic retreat
schizoid, 38
Wittgenstein, L., 267–268
Wolff-Bernstein, J., 50
Woyzeck (Buchner), ix–x
Wrye, H., 99, 241